Evil Eye, *Jinn* Possessior
Mental Health Issues

Evil Eye, Jinn *Possession, and Mental Health Issues* raises awareness of the cultural considerations, religion and spirituality involved in the assessment of Muslim patients with mental health problems. The belief that *Jinn* spirits can cause mental illness in humans through affliction or possession is widely accepted among Muslims, meaning this belief is a crucial, but frequently overlooked, aspect of mental health problems with Muslim patients in psychiatric care. This book explores the nature of such beliefs, their relationship to mental health and the reasons for their importance in clinical practice.

The book argues that it is vital to consider mental disorders as a multifactorial affair, in which spiritual, social, psychological and physical factors may all play a role. It suggests differential diagnostic skills may have an important part to play in offering help to those who believe their problems are caused by possession, and provides accessible literature on clinical issues and practice, interventions, management and evidence-based practice to help health workers achieve a better understanding of Muslim beliefs about possession and how to work with patients that hold such beliefs.

Evil Eye, Jinn *Possession, and Mental Health Issues* is an essential manual for mental health professionals, social workers and psychologists. It should also be of interest to academics and students in the healthcare sciences.

G. Hussein Rassool is currently Professor of Islamic Psychology, Dean for the Faculty of Liberal Arts and Sciences, Director of Research & Publications and Head of the Psychology Department at the International Open University (Islamic Online University).

Explorations in Mental Health

The Comprehensive Resource Model
Effective therapeutic techniques for the healing of complex trauma
Lisa Schwarz, Frank Corrigan, Alastair Hull and Rajiv Raju

Respect-Focused Therapy
Honoring clients through the therapeutic relationship and process
Susanne Slay-Westbrook

Depressive Realism
Interdisciplinary perspectives
Colin Feltham

Families Bereaved by Alcohol or Drugs
Coping and support
Edited by Christine Valentine

Trans and Sexuality
An existentially-informed enquiry with implications for counselling psychology
Christina Richards

Narratives of Loneliness
Multidisciplinary perspectives from the 21st century
Edited by Olivia Sagan and Eric D. Miller

Evil Eye, *Jinn* Possession, and Mental Health Issues
An Islamic perspective
G. Hussein Rassool

For more information about this series, please visit www.routledge.com.

Evil Eye, *Jinn* Possession, and Mental Health Issues

An Islamic Perspective

G. Hussein Rassool

Routledge
Taylor & Francis Group

LONDON AND NEW YORK

First published 2019
by Routledge

2 Park Square, Milton Park, Abingdon, Oxfordshire OX14 4RN
52 Vanderbilt Avenue, New York, NY 10017

Routledge is an imprint of the Taylor & Francis Group, an informa business

First issued in paperback 2020

British Library Cataloguing-in-Publication Data
A catalogue record for this book is available from the British
Library

Library of Congress Cataloging-in-Publication Data
Names: Rassool, G. Hussein, author.
Title: Evil eye, Jinn possession, and mental health issues : an
    Islamic perspective/G. Hussein Rassool.
Description: Milton Park, Abingdon, Oxon ; New York, NY :
    Routledge, 2019.
Identifiers: LCCN 2018019021 (print) | LCCN 2018021830 (ebook) |
    ISBN 9781315623764 (E-book) | ISBN 9781138653214 (hbk) |
    ISBN 9781315623764 (ebk)
Subjects: LCSH: Psychotherapy—Religious aspects. | Mental health
    counseling—Religious aspects.
Classification: LCC RC489.S676 (ebook) | LCC RC489.S676 R37
    2019 (print) | DDC 616.89/14—dc23
LC record available at https://lccn.loc.gov/2018019021

ISBN: 978-1-138-65321-4 (hbk)
ISBN: 978-0-367-48927-4 (pbk)

Typeset in Bembo
by Apex CoVantage, LLC

Dedicated to Isra Oya bint Adam Ali Hussein Ibn Hussein Ibn Hassim Ibn Sahaduth Ibn Rosool Ibn Olee Al Mauritiusy, Asiyah Maryam, Idrees Khattab, Adam Ali Hussein, Reshad Hassan, Yasmin Soraya, Bee Bee Mariam, Bibi Safian and Hassim.

Prophet Muhammad (ﷺ) said:

> No Muslim is touched by any worry, or sadness, and says: O Allah, I am Your slave, son of Your slave, son of Your female slave, my forelock is in Your hand, Your command over me is forever executed and Your decree over me is just. I ask You by every Name belonging to You which You named Yourself with, or revealed in Your Book, or You taught to any of Your creation, or You have preserved in the knowledge of the unseen with You, that You make the Qur'an the life of my heart and the light of my breast, and a departure for my sorrow and a release for my anxiety.
>
> (Musnad Ahmad # 1/391 and Al-Albani declared it Sahih)

Contents

Illustrations

Preface

Evil Eye, Jinn *Possession, and Mental Health Issues: An Islamic Perspective* aims to raise awareness of the cultural considerations, religion and spirituality involved in the assessment and treatment interventions of Muslim patients with mental health problems.

In recent years, there has been much publicity about *Jinn* possession, the evil eye and black magic in many parts of the Muslim world. The belief that *Jinn* can cause mental disorder in humans through affliction or possession is widely accepted among Muslims. This means that belief in evil eye, *Jinn* and witchcraft possession is a crucial, but frequently overlooked, aspect of psycho-spiritual and supernatural problems with Muslim patients in psychiatric care. This book explores the nature of such beliefs, their relationship to mental health and the reasons for their importance in clinical practice.

Muslims have a different worldview of mental health and illness and their explanatory models of illness causation in relation to mental disorders may not always be medically oriented. A Muslim patient may believe that their illness is caused by possession and it is tempting to dismiss this as a spiritual problem. Evil eye, *Jinn* possession and black magic are essentially a spiritual problem, but mental disorders are a multifactorial affair, in which spiritual, social, psychological and physical factors may all play an aetiological role. The relationships between these concepts are therefore complex. It would seem reasonable to argue that *Jinn* and witchcraft possession may be an aetiological factor in some cases of mental health problems or psychiatric disorders, but it may also be an aetiological factor in some non-psychiatric conditions. In other cases, it may be encountered in the absence of psychiatric or medical disorders.

Differential diagnostic skills may have a part to play in offering help to those whose problems could be of Possession Syndrome, culture-bound syndrome or medical/psychiatric origin. Even though *Jinn* possession, witchcraft and effects of evil eye are common and cause great suffering in every part of the world amongst Muslim patients, many health workers have a limited understanding about the issues of the Possession Syndrome: spirit possession, *Jinn* possession, black magic and the evil eye and their relationships with mental health problems and psychiatric disorders. In addition, health and social care workers are less comfortable in dealing with both mental health problems and supernatural possessions. However, if one listens to the symptoms for those affected by the issues above, one may notice that many of them are the same as those symptoms of certain mental disorders mentioned in the latest edition of the Diagnostic and Statistical Manual of Mental Disorders (DSM-V).

This book provides accessible literature on the context, clinical issues and practice, interventions, management and evidence-based practice to help health workers achieve a better understanding of Muslim beliefs about possession and how to work with patients that hold such beliefs. This makes it an essential manual for mental health professionals, social workers and psychologists. It should also be of interest to academics and students in the healthcare sciences.

The essence of this book is based on the following notions:

- The fundamental of Islam as a religion is based on the Oneness of God.
- The source of knowledge is based on the Noble Qur'an and Hadith (*Ahl as-Sunnah wa'l-Jamā'ah*).
- Muslims believe that cures come solely from Allah (God) but seeking treatment for psychological and spiritual health does not conflict with seeking help from Allah.
- Islam takes a holistic approach to health. Physical, psychological, social, emotional and spiritual health cannot be separated.
- There is wide consensus amongst Muslim scholars that psychiatric or psychological disorders are legitimate medical conditions that is distinct from illnesses of a supernatural nature.
- Evil eye, *Jinn* possession and witchcraft are a crucial, but sometimes overlooked aspect of mental health problems with Muslim patients in psychiatric care.
- Evil eye, *Jinn* possession and black magic are essentially a psycho-spiritual problem.
- Muslims have a different worldview or perception of mental health and illness. There is a strong belief that evil eye, *Jinn* possession and witchcraft could cause physical and mental health problems.
- Counselling, in the Islamic context, is an act of shared spirituality between Islamic counsellor, where the nature of the shared spirituality is fluid, depending on the client's psychological and spiritual needs.
- Emerging cultural competence in mental health services is aiming to make the services more responsive to the needs of the Muslim communities.

It is a sign of respect that Muslims would utter or repeat the words 'Peace and Blessing Be Upon Him' (PBUH) after hearing (or writing) the name of Prophet Muhammad (ﷺ).

Acknowledgements

Bismillah Ar Rahman Ar Raheem

All Praise is due to Allah, and may the peace and blessings of Allah be upon our Prophet Muhammad (ﷺ) his family and his companions.

I would like to thank the staff at Routledge for their valuable and constructive suggestions during the development of the proposal and during the process of writing and publishing. It is with immense gratitude that I acknowledge the support and help from colleagues and students from the Islamic Online University, I would like to acknowledge the contributions of my teachers who enabled me, through my own reflective practices, to understand Islam and their guidance to follow the right path. I am thankful to my beloved parents, Bibi Safian and Hassim who taught me the value of education. I am forever grateful to Mariam for her unconditional support and encouragement to pursue my interests and for her tolerance for my periodic quest for seclusion to make this book a reality. I owe my gratitude to my family, including: Asiyah Maryam bint Adam Ali Hussein Ibn Hussein Ibn Hassim Ibn Sahaduth Ibn Rosool Al Mauritiusy, Adam Ali Hussein, Reshad Hasan, Yasmin Soraya, Isra Oya and Idrees Khattab for their unconditional love and for being here.

I would also like to show my gratitude to my patients and students for teaching me about mental health and Possession Syndrome, and those individuals who contributed to the case reports. Thanks also go to all my brothers at *Al Mufarideen* for their friendships.

Finally, whatever benefits and correctness you find within this book are out of the Grace of Allah, Alone and whatever mistakes you find are mine alone. I pray to Allah to forgive me for any unintentional shortcomings regarding the contents of this book and to make this humble effort helpful and fruitful to any interested parties.

> *Whatever of good befalls you, it is from Allah; and whatever of ill befalls you, it is from yourself.*

> (An-Nisā' [The Women] 4:79)

Part I

Context and background

Chapter 1

Fundamentals of Islamic faith

Introduction

Islam is a monotheistic, world religion whose constituents include a vast range of races, nationalities and cultures across the globe united by their common Islamic faith. Islam that includes beliefs, values and core practices. It is considered one of the Abrahamic, monotheistic faiths, along with Judaism and Christianity. Islam is an Arabic term, which translated literally means 'surrender' or 'submission' and the term reflects the essence and the central core of Islam, which is the submission to the will of God. The same Arabic root word gives us "*Salaam alaykum*" ("Peace be with you"), the universal Muslim greeting. Islam is both a religion and a complete way of life based on the guidance of God from the Noble Qur'an and teachings and practices of the Prophet Muhammad (☪) (Peace and blessing be upon him). Hence, a Muslim is a person who submits to the will of God, or a follower of Islam. However, in the West, there is an orientalist misperception or negative perception about Islam and this is associated with overt or covert hostility, fear, hatred, prejudice toward Islam and Muslims which have given rise to microaggressions and Islamophobia. This chapter will enable the reader to have a basic understanding of the principles of the Islamic faith, Islamic culture, beliefs and practices.

Global Islam and diversity

There is great diversity in the ethnic composition of Muslims migrants in Western and Northern Europe, North America and Australasia. The increasingly visible presence of different ethnic groups in specific countries is the result of different politico-social and economic factors including forced migration, post-decolonisation migration patterns, labour needs, asylum seekers, refugee flows from war-torn countries (Amnesty International, 2012); and regional conflicts and fleeing 'ethnic cleansing'." The wide diversity of social, socioeconomic, ethnic and religious backgrounds among the Muslim population influences explanatory models of illness, coping mechanisms and help-seeking behaviour. It is important that health and social care professionals have an awareness of this heterogeneous group in order to provide culturally congruent and appropriate care and management.

Nearly one-fourth of the world's population today is Muslim and the total Muslim population is over 1.62 billion followers worldwide, reaching 2.2 billion in 2030 (Pew Forum on Religion & Public Life, 2011). The largest number of Muslims live in the Asia-Pacific region (about 60%), 43.3% live in Africa and fewer than 20% of Muslims live in the Middle East and North Africa. Countries with a significant majority of Muslim populations (about 99.5% or more of the native populations) include Bahrain, Comoros, Kuwait, Maldives, Mauritania, Mayotte, Morocco, Oman, Qatar, Somalia, Saudi Arabia, Tunisia, United Arab Emirates, Western Sahara, and Yemen (Adherents.com). Muslims will remain relatively small but significant minorities in Europe and the Americas, but they are expected to constitute a growing share of the total population in these regions. The United Kingdom (UK) has a long history of contact with Muslims, with links forged from the Middle Ages onward (The Muslim Council of Britain, 2002).

A considerable share of Muslims living in Switzerland is from former Yugoslavia, whereas the biggest groups of Muslims in Catalonia (Spain) are originally from Algeria, Mali, Morocco, Pakistan and Senegal. Muslims from Iran and Iraq are relatively numerous in the Scandinavian countries of Sweden, Norway and Denmark, if compared with other European countries (Amnesty International, 2012). The top countries of origin for Muslim immigrants to the United States (US) in 2009 were from Pakistan and Bangladesh. In Canada, Muslims make up about 3.2% of the population and Islam is the fastest growing religion in Canada (National Household Survey (2011). In Australia, 2.2% of the total Australian population were Muslims, making it the third largest religious grouping, after Christianity and Buddhism.

Mental health and service provision

With the growth of Muslims globally and the rise of Muslim migrants in different countries, there has been a corresponding rise in the need for mental health service provision and delivery as a result of the psychosocial effects of migration, prejudice, discrimination, Islamophobia and microaggressions. Muslims, beside dealing with day-to-day life stressors, also have the responsibility of defending basic religious rights and values as being normal and acceptable (Podikunju-Hussain, 2006). In addition, for indigenous Muslims, there are added psychological problems including the lack of family support; the presence of tensions in the family when conflicting core ethnic values between parents and children emerge (for example, relations with the opposite sex, career decisions, and other social values); prejudice or discrimination in the workplace or in the society; and racism (Das and Kemp, 1997).

More health and social practitioners are coming into contact with Muslim patients but due to the lack of cultural competence, find themselves at a loss to intervene effectively with Muslim patients. Despite the extent and nature of mental health problems in the Islamic community, most Western or Eurocentric-oriented practitioners are not fully cognisant of Islamic values and beliefs, or the conceptions of mental health problems from the worldview of the Muslim patients. Moreover, the Muslims' perception of mental health problems is based on traditional beliefs that include spiritual and supernatural origins for mental illness. Haque and Kamil (2012) uphold the view that the "lack of knowledge about the beliefs and values of a religious group that is under continuous scrutiny can be problematic within a clinical setting, especially in light of the potential importance spirituality may have for a client" (p. 3). Many Muslims with psychosocial and psychiatric disorders are reluctant to seek help from mental health professionals. There is evidence to suggest Muslims are reluctant to seek professional help because they consider it debasing or inappropriate to speak of one's troubles to strangers; professionals are perceived as being stereotyped and being culturally insensitive to their needs (Moshtagh and Dezhkam, 2004); they want their concerns addressed from a religious viewpoint (Abdullah, 2007; Podikunju-Hussain, 2006) and express a hesitancy to trust mental health professionals, fearing that their Islamic values may not be respected (Dwairy, 2006; Hedayat-Diba, 2000; Hodge, 2005; Mohamed, 1996). Consequently, it is important for mental health practitioners to be culturally sensitive to the patients' beliefs, values and practices of Islam and to have an awareness of the impact of these on the psychological well-being of Muslims. This would enhance the rapport and therapeutic relationship between the client and the practitioner and lead to the provision of culturally appropriate intervention strategies.

Fundamentals of Islam as a religion

Islam is not a new religion, but is the continuation of the religion of our patriarch Abraham focusing on monotheistic belief. In the traditional sense, Islam connotes the one true divine religion, taught to mankind by a series of Prophets, some of whom brought a revealed book. Such were the Torah, the Psalms and the Gospel, brought by the Prophets Moses (Musa), David (Dawud) and Jesus (Eesa). Prophet Muhammad (☙) was the last and greatest of the Prophets. The Noble book, the Qur'an, completes and supersedes all previous revelations. Christianity and Judaism like Islam believe in the 'oneness' of God, and go back to the Patriarch Abraham; the Prophets are directly descended from his sons (Morgan, 2010). Islam has at its core a simple message that applies to all human beings. Islam tolerates other beliefs as it is one function of Islamic law to protect the privileged status of minorities, and this is why non-Muslim places of worship have flourished all over the Islamic world. History provides many examples of Muslim tolerance towards other faiths. The Constitution of Medina (Ṣaḥīfat al-Madīnah) is the earliest known written constitution in the world. To this effect, it instituted a number of rights and responsibilities of the

Muslim, Jewish and pagan communities of Medina (Saudi Arabia), bringing them within the fold of one community-the 'Ummah'."

The Qur'an, the last revealed Word of God, is the prime source of every Muslim's faith and practice. The Qur'an is a record of the exact words revealed by God through the Angel Gabriel to the Prophet Muhammad, recited by him and immediately memorised and recorded by large numbers of his companions.

There are 114 chapters in the Qur'an, which is written in classical Arabic. All the chapters except one begin with the sentence '*Bismillah ir Rahman ir Raheem,*' 'In the name of Allah, the Entirely Merciful, the Especially Merciful.' The longest chapter of the Qur'an is Surah *Baqarah* (The Cow) with 286 verses and the shortest is Surah *Al-Kawthar* (abundance) which has 3 verses. The Qur'an includes the history of mankind from the creation and addresses rules for everyday social life like marriage issues, divorce, personal rights, inheritance, charity to the poor, importance of brotherhood and community, social justice, proper human conduct, dealing with ecological issues and an equitable economic system. In addition to the Qur'an, there are the Sunnah (the practices and examples of the Prophet) and Hadith. A Hadith is a reliably transmitted report of what the Prophet said, did, or approved. Belief in the Sunnah is part of the Islamic faith.

The five pillars of Islam

The obligations of Muslims are known as the five pillars of Islam that all Muslims around the world will follow in relation to their daily activities, lifestyle and practices. The model framework of Muslims' lifestyle and practices are: *Shahadah*, prayer (*Salah*), self-purification (*Zakat*), Fasting (*Ramadhan*) and pilgrimage (*Hajj*) to Makkah. The most important fundamental teaching of Islam is belief in the Oneness of God – this is termed *Tawheed*.

- **Shahadah**, the first Article of Faith: "I bear witness that there is no god but Allah and I bear witness that Muhammad is his servant and messenger." In fact, there is no one worthy of worship except Allah. This simple yet profound statement expresses a Muslim's complete acceptance of, and total commitment to Islam.
- **Salah**, prayer, is the second pillar. There are obligatory prayers that are performed five times a day at designated times. The Islamic faith is based on the belief that individuals have a direct relationship with God. In addition, Friday congregational service is also required. Although *Salah* can be performed alone, it is meritorious to perform it with another or with a group. It is permissible to pray at home, at work or even outdoors; however it is recommended that Muslims perform *Salah* in a mosque.
- **Zakat** means purification and growth. Our wealth, held by human beings in trust, is purified by setting aside a proportion for those in need. *Zakat*

is calculated individually and involves the payment each year of a fixed proportion of their wealth to the needy and poor. This provides guidelines for the provision of social justice, positive human behaviour and an equitable socioeconomic system. One of the Hadith (saying) of Prophet Muhammad (🕌) relating to charity is that "The wealth of a servant is never decreased by paying charity." (Muslim). The *Zakat* is equal to 2.5 percent of an individual's total net worth, excluding obligations and family expenses.

- **Sawm**, fasting during the Holy month of *Ramadhan*, is the fourth pillar of Islam. Every year during the month of *Ramadhan*, Muslims fast from first daylight until sunset, abstaining from eating, drinking and sexual relations. Although the fast is beneficial for health, it is regarded spiritually as a method of self-purification. The spiritual dimension involves reflective practices, increased prayers and having positive thought towards other people and remembering Allah in all thoughts and actions. *Ramadhan*, the month during which the *Holy Qur'an* was revealed to the Prophet Muhammad, begins with the sighting of the new moon, after which abstention from eating, drinking and other sensual pleasures is obligatory from dawn to sunset. The end of *Ramadhan* is observed by three days of celebration called *Eid Al-Fitr*, the feast of the breaking of the fast. Customarily, it is a time for a family reunion and the favoured holiday for children who receive new clothing and gifts.

- **Hajj**, the pilgrimage to Makkah, is the fifth pillar and the most significant manifestation of Islamic faith and unity in the world. The annual pilgrimage to the Hajj in Makkah, Kingdom of Saudi Arabia, is an obligation for all Muslims once in a lifetime. However, there are conditions such as only those individuals who are physically and financially able are allowed to perform it. The Hajj rituals take place in the 12th month of the Islamic year (based on the Lunar system, Islamic Year 1420 = CE 2000). The pilgrims wear simple garments, which strip away status, distinctions of class, culture and colour, so that all individuals stand equal before Allah.

In a Hadith, the Messenger of Allah (🕌) said:

Islam is to testify that there is no god but Allah and Muhammad is the messenger of Allah, to perform the prayers, to pay the zakat, to fast in Ramadan, and to make the pilgrimage to the House if you are able to do so. He said: "You have spoken rightly," *Jebreel* (Gabriel).

(Muslim cited in Zarabozo, 2008)

The five pillars of Islam define the basic identity of Muslims, their faith, beliefs and practices, and bind together a worldwide community of believers into a fellowship of shared values and concerns.

Islamic culture, beliefs and practices

There is a great diversity of cultures in Muslim communities in different parts of the world even though a significant majority share the same religious values and practices. However, the attitudes and behaviours of some Muslims are often shaped by cultural practices which may or may not be in concordance with basic Islamic religious practices. Philips (2007) suggested that "the Islam being practices in much of the Muslim world today may be referred to as Cultural Islam. The main feature of this version of Islam is the blind following of local traditions" (p. 33). There are Muslims who identify as a Muslim by name and adhering to certain rituals but adopt Western-oriented lifestyles and behaviours (emotional, cognitive and behavioural). However, these Muslims "are perceived in the Western world by Eurocentric and orientalist as being 'acculturated' or 'integrated' Muslims and most welcomed by politicians and non-Muslims, and popularised by the mass media" (Rassool, 2016, p. 10).

The Islamic culture has roots in authentic Islamic traditions based on the Qur'an and Sunnah (traditions). Generally, religious or Islamic practices include all the practices that dominate every aspect of the individual's life and behaviours. There are matters, rulings and decrees in this collectivist society which concern virtually all facets of one's personal, family and the civil society including God-centred or theocentric and strictly *Tawheed* (monotheism); welfare and society; morals and manners; modesty in dress and behaviour; care of children and elderly; racism and prejudice; dietary rules; marriage and family kinship; defending Islamic values and beliefs; social justice; dealing with environmental issues, relations with non-Muslims; seeking knowledge; and facing trials and tribulations. Islam expects its followers at a minimum, to strike a balance by being mindful of their duties to Allah and to others and by fulfilling the obligations of, and enjoying this life. It is narrated that there is a need to "Always adopt a middle, moderate, regular course, whereby you will reach your target (of paradise)" (Bukhari).

Islamic culture, beliefs and practices are based on the following characteristics and issues:

- Islamic culture is theocentric and based on the unicity and oneness of God (*Tawheed*). The fundamental principles include belief in Allah, and His existence, belief in the angels, belief in the Books, belief in the Messengers, belief in the last Day (Judgment), and belief in the destiny (*Qadar*). The 'Five Pillars' of Islam are the foundation of Islamic life.
- Dignity and morality are at the core of Islam. These include truthfulness, honesty, modesty (*Haya'*), and cleanliness or (*Taharah*). There is an emphasis on charity and generosity. It abhors public nudity, adultery, fornication, homosexuality, gambling, or use of intoxicants, bribery, forgery, usury, backbiting, gossiping, slandering, hoarding, destruction of property and environment, and cruelty to animals.

- Modesty in dress and behaviour: Muslims should wear decent and digni-fied dress. Men should cover their body from their navel to their knees, and woman should cover their entire body except for their face and hands.
- Islam promotes egalitarianism, tolerance and brotherhood. Islam empha-sises that all people are equal and reject any ethnic bias or racialism; and is tolerant of people of all faiths. Fraternity in faith is common regardless of the geographic boundaries. The society is responsible for the welfare of an individual-community obligation (*Fard al-kifaya*).
- Islam is family-oriented and is a strong advocate of marriage and is a moral safeguard as well as a social building block. Furthermore, marriage is the only valid or halal way to indulge in intimacy between a man and a woman. Caring for one's children or parents is considered an honour and blessing.
- Islamic promotes healthy eating. Islamic dietary laws provide direction on what is to be considered halal (lawful) and haram (unlawful). Food hygiene is part of the Islamic dietary law.
- Islam promotes learning and encourages the seeking of knowledge. Islamic culture promotes good art, architecture, aesthetics, health, healthy environ-ment and halal entertainment.
- Islamic emphasises promoting good things with wisdom and patience. There is a belief in inviting or calling all people to Islam without coercion.
- The relationship and collaboration with non-Muslims are encouraged and should only be avoided when it becomes harmful for Muslims.

Conclusion

This chapter has considered the fundamentals of Islam as a religion, the global Muslim and diversity, and the five pillars of Islam and Islamic culture, beliefs and practices. The mismatch of values, customs and practices in many social and cultural domains places psychological strains on Muslims over and above those experienced by their host populations. Muslims are exposed to multi-ple discriminations as compared to other minority groups. In addition to the psychosocial issues they faced, Muslims are also subjected to social isolation, discrimination, racism, poor housing conditions, lowered employment status and poor educational opportunities which are related to mental health prob-lems. Specific challenges in migrant mental health include language difficulties, problems with adaptation, acculturation, intergenerational conflict and social exclusion from mainstream society (Kirmayer et al., 2011). With the signifi-cant growth of the Muslim population, both indigenous and migrants, in many Western countries, there exists a corresponding increase in the need for access to mental health services and delivery. Studies have showed that many Muslims are hesitant to seek help from the mental health professionals in Western coun-tries (Hedayat-Diba, 2000; Hodge, 2005) even when mainstream agencies offer a full complement of mental health services (Basit and Hamid, 2010). However, it is important to note that that people have resources and assets that protect against mental health and psychosocial issues (IASC, 2007).

References

Abdullah, S. (2007). Islam and counseling: Models of practice in Muslim communal life. *Journal of Pastoral Counseling*, 42, 42–55.

Adherents.com. *World's Most Muslim Nations.* www.adherents.com/largecom/com_islam. html (accessed 12 March 2016).

Amnesty International (2012) Discrimination against Muslims in Europe. www.amnesty. org/en/library/ . . . /2012/en/ . . . /eur010012012en.pdf (accessed 12 March 2018).

Basit, A., & Hamid, M. (2010). Mental health issues of Muslim Americans. *The Journal of IMA/Islamic Medical Association of North America*, 42, 3, 106–110. doi:10.5915/42-3-5507.

Bukhari. Book of *To make the Heart Tender* (Ar-Riqaq). Sahih al-Bukhari 6463, Book 81, Hadith 52. http://sunnah.com/bukhari/81 (accessed 6 August 2016)

Das, A. K., and Kemp, S. F. (1997) Between two worlds: Counseling South Asian Americans, *Journal of Multicultural Counseling and Development*, 25, 23–34.

Dwairy, M. (2006) *Counseling and Psychotherapy with Arabs and Muslims.* New York: Teachers College Press.

Hedayat-Diba Z. (2000) Psychotherapy with Muslims, in P. S. Richards, A. E. Bergin (Eds.), *Handbook of Psychotherapy and Religious Diversity.* Washington, DC: American Psychological Association, pp. 289–314.

Haque, A., and Kamil, N. (2012) *Islam, Muslims, and Mental Health.* East Sussex: Routledge, p. 3.

Hodge, D. R. (2005) Social work and the house of Islam: Orienting practitioners to the beliefs and values of Muslims in the United States, *Social Work*, 50, 162–173.

Inter-Agency Standing Committee [IASC] [2007] *IASC Guidelines on Mental Health and Psychosocial Support in Emergency Settings.* Geneva: IASC

Kirmayer, L. J., Narasiah, L., Muzoz, M., Rashid, M., Ryder, A., Guzder, J., . . . Rousseau, C. (2011) Common mental health problems in immigrants and refugees: General approach in primary care. *Canadian Medical Association Journal*, 12, E959–E967.

Mohamed, Y. (1996) *Fitrah: Islamic Concept of Human Nature.* London: Ta-ha.

Morgan C. W. (2010) *This Dynamic World.* Bloomington, IN: Author House.

Moshtagh N., and Dezhkam, N. (2004) Women, Gender and Mental Health in Iran, in S. Joseph (2006) *Encyclopedia of Women & Islamic Cultures, Volume 3 Family, Body, Sexuality and Health*, Leiden: Brill, p. 271).

Muslim. Vol. 4, *Hadith* 6264. https://muflihun.com/muslim/32/6264 (accessed 12 March 2018).

National Household Survey (NHS) (2011) *Muslims in Canada, National Household Survey.* www12.statcan.gc.ca/nhs-enm/index-eng.cfm (accessed 12 March 2018).

Pew Forum on Religion and Public Life (2011) *The Future of the Global Muslim Population. Projections for 2010–2030.* http://pewresearch.org/pubs/1872/muslim-population-projections-worldwide-fast-growth (accessed 12 March 2018).

Philips, A.A.B. (2007) *The Clash of Civilizations: An Islamic View.* Birmingham, UK: Al-Hidaayah Publishing and Distibutions.

Podikunju-Hussain, S. (2006) Working with Muslims: Perspectives and suggestions for counseling, in G. R. Walz, J. Bleuer, R. K. Yep, *VISTAS: Compelling Perspectives on Counseling, 2006.* Alexandria, VA: American Counseling Association, pp. 103–106.

Rassool, G. H. (2016) *Islamic Counselling. An introduction to theory and practice*. East Sussex: Routledge.

The Muslim Council of Britain (2002) *The Quest for Sanity*. London: The Muslim Council of Britain.

Zarabozo, J. M. (2008) Hadith number 2, in *Commentary on the Forty Hadiths of al-Nawawi*. Denver, CO: Al-Basheer Company for Publications & Translation.

Chapter 2

Psychosocial issues within Islamic communities

Introduction

The diversity of ethnic composition of indigenous Muslims and Muslims migrants in Western and Northern Europe, North America and Australasia showed that Muslims should not be perceived, as is the case by Western orientalists, as being homogeneous. That diversity of cultures, identities, literatures and historical developments create a myriad of socio-political and cultural resonances in countries with a large majority of Muslims. In addition, Muslim migrants with a tapestry of cultures and values create some dissonance with the host values and cultures. A number of socio-political occurrences both inside countries with large Muslim majorities and externally have generated a multiplicity of political, social, economic and psychological problems. The actual impact of September 11 has dramatically altered the psychosocial issues in Muslim communities and diasporas scattered throughout the world. The Arab Spring in Northern Africa and the Middle East brought the first winds of change and triggered the destabilisation in some countries, military dictatorship, civil unrest and war, displaced people, ethnic cleansing and refugees. In parallel to the major events affecting Muslims and non-Muslims, most "Western scholarship and media have portrayed Islam and Muslims in terms of global terrorism, Islamic jihadism, fanatic Islamism, fundamentalism, fascism, and Islamic authoritarianism" (El-Aswad, 2008). These global depictions of Muslims have generated not only Islamophobia (Esposito and Ibrahim, 2011) but social exclusion, hate rhetoric, microaggressions and violence.

There are several psychosocial issues faced by indigenous and migrant Muslims living in Western-oriented societies. The post–September 11 climate globally, especially in countries in the Northern hemispheres, has made many Muslim highly concerned with issues including discrimination, prejudice, threats, hate messages or harassment, microaggressions, violence and Islamophobia. In addition, there are psychosocial issues and ramifications which are related to intergenerational conflict, refugee status and radicalism. Some of the key psychosocial issues will be examined in relation to mental health.

Impact of post September 11 and mental health of Muslims

The single event of September 11 changed the lives of Muslims globally. In the aftermath of September 11, Muslims experienced more acts of anti-Muslim discrimination, harassment, verbal abuse or physical attack, hate crimes and anti-Muslim hate groups (Anderson, 2002; American-Arab Anti-Discrimination Committee, 2003; Sheridan, 2006; Southern Poverty Law Center) that further increase the risk for mental health problems. However, it has been established that discrimination toward Muslims was ever present before the attacks on September 11, due to media portrayal of Muslims as being intrinsically intolerant and violent (Giger and Davidhizar, 2002). There is evidence to suggest that the level of experience by all types of discrimination was associated with psychological distress (Moradi and Hassan, 2004), depression (Hassouneh and Kulwicki, 2007), post-traumatic stress disorder (Abu-Ras and Abu-Bader, 2009), subclinical paranoia (Rippy and Newman, 2006), anxiety and depression (Amer and Hovey, 2011). The findings from the study by Padela and Heisler (2010) showed that perceived abuse and discrimination after September 11 were associated with psychological distress, level of happiness and health status.

Islamophobia

Islamophobia is not a new phenomenon but has its roots during the European enlightenment in the early nineteenth century with the rise of Orientalism. According to Said (1978), Orientalism is defined "as the acceptance in the West of the basic distinction between East and West as the starting point for elaborate theories, epics, novels, social descriptions, and political accounts concerning the Orient, its people, customs, 'mind,' destiny and so on" (p. 3). In the context of Muslims generally, Orientalism and, more recently, Eurocentrism is part of that culture that depicts Muslims as inferior, fundamentalist or dangerous. Quellien (1910, cited in Lopez, 2011, p. 563) portrays the Muslims as

> the natural and irreconcilable enemy of the Christian and the European; Islam is the negation of civilisation, and barbarism, bad faith and cruelty are the best one can expect from the Mohammedans. . . . This prejudice against Islam would appear to be slightly exaggerated; the Muslim is not the European's natural born enemy but he can become [his enemy] as a result of local circumstances and notably when he resists armed conquest.

It is this orientation that may have had a significant influence of modern day Islamophobia.

Islamophobia has been used as an umbrella term to denote a wide variety of negative thoughts, emotions and behaviours towards Muslims. Islamophobia is described as a term used to "address the discriminations faced by Muslims that could not be explained by their race, class or immigration status" (Cesari, 2015). The term has also been explained as "a social anxiety towards Islam and Muslim cultures" (Gottschalk and Greenberg, 2008) and "capturing different types of religious stigma towards Muslims" (Kunst et al., 2012, p. 2). In addition, the element of the fear factor is inherent in the concept by "focusing on the fear response towards Muslims and their religion" (Kunst et al., 2012, p. 2.). In fact, in 1997, the Runnymede Trust report refers to 'Islamophobia' as "the shorthand way of referring to the dread or hatred of Islam – and, therefore, to fear or dislike all or most Muslims" (Runnymede Trust Commission, 1997).

The effects of Islamophobia on mental health of Muslims are quite significant. There is evidence to suggest that Islamophobia negatively affects the mental health of Muslims worldwide, ranging from increased feelings of anxiety to depression (Kunst et al., 2012).

A study in a sample with a large majority of Muslim-Americans found that perceived religious discrimination was associated with subclinical paranoia (Rippy and Newman, 2006). High levels of depression and post-traumatic stress disorder among Muslims have also been attributed to the post-September 11 anti-Muslim backlash (Abu-Ras and Abu-Bade, 2009). The findings of another study showed that 82% of Muslim-Americans felt "extremely unsafe" post September 11, and that prejudice may have contributed to the post-traumatic stress disorder that some of subjects later developed (Amer and Hovey, 2011). Muslims are at a greater risk of developing mental health problems as a result of workplace discrimination and chronic daily hassles and harassment that they face in their daily lives (Laird, 2007).

Women: Islamophobia and microaggressions

There is evidence to suggest that Muslim women face numerous stressors that threaten their mental health including discrimination, acculturative stress and trauma (Hassouneh and Kulwicki, 2007), "gendered Islamophobia" and microaggressions. Muslim women in *Hijab* are more likely to experience an ever-increasing rise in 'gendered Islamophobia'." This can be understood as "specific forms of ethno-religious and racialized discrimination against Muslim women that leads from the historically contextualized negative stereotypes that inform individual and systematic forms of oppression" (Zine, 2006, p. 240). That is, "visibly" Muslim women wearing *Hijab* and *Nikab* are frequently exposed to discrimination, harassment and attacks. The nature of gendered Islamophobia operates at all levels: socially, politically and economically to debase Muslim women in society.

In addition to overt and covert forms of discrimination and harassment, Muslim women are particularly vulnerable to microaggressions. Nadal and colleagues (2012) define microaggressions as "subtle forms of discrimination (often unintentional and unconscious) that send negative and denigrating messages to members of marginalized racial groups" (p. 15–16). Some examples include using Islamophobic or mocking language to hurt someone's feelings; the "ethnic" individual is assumed to be foreign born; assigning intellectual ability to an individual on their basis of their race or ethnicity; presuming someone to be a terrorist or criminal of on the basis of appearance; and a white Anglo-Saxon individual given preferential treatment in employment over a Muslim. Microaggressions can also be translated as "microassaults" (intentional racism) and "microinsults" (subtle behavioural and verbal communications) (Sue et al., 2007). As a result of microaggressions, women reported feelings of anger, sadness, frustration, belittlement (Nadal et al., 2012), and being considered "weird" by those who do not understand her motivations for "veiling" (Read and Bartkowski, 2000, p. 416). According to Read and Bartkowski (2000), "For women like her, engaging in a dissident cultural practice underscores the cultural distinctiveness in a way that some people find refreshing and others find threatening" (p. 416). In Allen's study (2014), the women were subjected to verbal abuse, "more high-level" harassment, persistently chased or followed by aggressors, who violently attacked the women. The women in this study reported feelings of humiliation, anger, sadness, isolation and disgust. The whole incidents, in some cases, because of their debilitating effects, restricted their movements and changed the Muslim women's way of lifestyle and behaviour.

Refugee

Most Muslim refugees coming to developed Western countries are a result of conflicts, war, persecutions, rise in terrorisms, ethnic cleansing and escaping from torture in their homeland. According to UNHCR (2016), a refugee is

> someone who has been forced to flee his or her country because of persecution, war, or violence. A refugee has a well-founded fear of persecution for reasons of race, religion, nationality, political opinion or membership in a particular social group. Most likely, they cannot return home or are afraid to do so. War and ethnic, tribal and religious violence are leading causes of refugees fleeing their countries.

Due to the distress and trauma experienced in their host country, the perilous journey undertaken to reach their destination associated with refugee camps, and/or detention centres, coupled with the immigration and resettlement process, significantly increases the risk for the refugees to develop mental health problems.

The more common mental health diagnoses associated with refugee populations include "post-traumatic stress disorder, major depression, generalised anxiety, panic attacks, adjustment disorder, and somatization. The incidence of diagnoses varies with different populations and their experiences" (RHTAC, 2011a). It has been reported that refugees and asylum seekers have been shown to be at substantially higher risk of developing post-traumatic stress disorder and comorbid mental health problems (Fazel, Jeremy and Danesh, 2005). In addition, the risk factors for the development of mental health problems include "the number of traumas, delayed asylum application process, detention, and the loss of culture and support systems" (RHTAC, 2011b). However, it has been suggested that "the prevalence of specific types of mental health problems is influenced by the nature of the migration experience, in terms of adversity experienced before, during and after resettlement" (Kirmayer et al., 2011, p. E 959).

The exposure to traumatic violent events pre-migration is associated with a broad range of psychological problems in refugee groups. In relation to refugee women, there may be an additional stress associated with pregnancy.

There may be the added problems of grief separation, acculturation, language difficulties, lack of familial support, changing in the family dynamics, the process of resettlement, and birth 'rites de passage' that may place new mothers and their infants at a higher risk of mental health problems. It is reported that the cause of increased morbidity and mortality during pregnancy and child birth in refugee women is due to protracted stress (Gogol' et al., 2006). Refugee pregnant women also experienced poor mental maternal health resulting in post-natal depression due to their past experiences (NSW Refugee Health Service, 2018).

Acculturation

The exposure to different set of culture, values and beliefs can be a risk factor for chronic disease to mental health. One of the main challenges that have been identified for the Muslim population includes difficulty with acculturation and adjustment to their new life (Abu-Ras and Suarez, 2009). The term acculturation generally relates to the changes that happen to migrant individuals and groups when exposed to the host culture. Kim (1982) explains that

> The acculturation process, therefore, is an interactive and continuous process that evolves in and through the communication of an immigrant with the new sociocultural environment. The acquired communication competence, in turn, reflects the degree of that immigrant's acculturation.
>
> (p. 380)

It is the adoption and assimilation of the cultural behaviours of the host country, leading to changes in diet, physical activity level and environmental exposures which have long-term health consequences for resettled refugees (Palinkas and Pickwell, 1995). Mody (2007) explains acculturation as a learning process of the host's values, language and customs that affect health such as dietary habits, activity levels and substance use.

In addition to the development of physical problems, the process of acculturation can also be associated with psychosocial problems (Berry, 1997). Muslim migrants to Western European countries and the United States tend to develop acculturative stress which may lead to psychological problems or disorders. Acculturative stress is the emotional reaction and "psychological impact of adaptation to a new culture" (Smart and Smart, 1995). Acculturation has also been related with depression, social withdrawal, familial isolation, despair, hostility, anxiety and somatisation (Escobar et al.,1986; Aprahamian et al., 2011; Abu-Bader et al., 2011); a sense of isolation (Khawaja, 2007), adjustment difficulties, and family conflicts (Goforth, et al., 2014); and persecution (Bux, 2007). It has been suggested that "longer-lasting mental health concerns such as anxiety, post-traumatic stress disorder (PTSD), depression, and somatization may also be triggered or exacerbated by the acculturation process" (RHTAC, 2011c). Though some of the studies are not related to the Muslim communities, nevertheless the psychological problems and distress experienced may be similar.

Identity and intergenerational conflict

Migration brings along psychosocial issues such as identity development, cultural identity and role confusion. Muslims living in secular societies have to adhere to individualist value-oriented societies and are faced with identity conflict, especially Muslim adolescents. Many of the psychosocial issues faced by Muslim adolescents and the Muslim community at large are inextricably linked to identity crises. The impact of migration on the subsequent health status of individuals may be more prominent amongst adolescents. The adolescent Muslims are subjected to bullying, harassment, treated with biased attitudes and feel socially excluded. It is stated that the challenges faced by adolescents relate to their own self-identity development, and having to "mediate the new culture for their parents, youth often take on roles far beyond the capacity of their actual age" (Khanlou et al., 2007–2009, cited by Khanlou and Jackson, 2011, p. 10). The overt expression of adolescent Muslims reasserting their identity may be perceived in the host country as being potential 'Jihadis' or indicative of a predisposition for extremism. Rashad (2015) stated that identity "comes up repeatedly" when Muslim students approach her about their mental health. Being different and looking 'Muslim' have implications of being bullied and 'othered' by their non-Muslim contemporaries (Mandviwalwa, 2015). This is especially true for female adolescent Muslims who wear head scarfs. In addition to the psychological trauma faced by Muslim adolescents, they also have to face other issues including dressing modestly, dietary restrictions, dating and relationship (opposite gender interaction), etc. In the new cultural environment, when there is role reversal or shifting of role between family members and the feelings of disempowered, intergenerational conflicts seemed to be intensified. For example, because of language deficiencies and the lack of understanding of the host culture, the adolescents have to mediate the new heterogeneous culture for their parents by being the 'voice' of the family. Rosenthal et al. (1996) stated that parental authority declines when their children carry out the day-to-day activities and dealing with civil authorities.

It is acknowledged that each older generation seemed to have conflicts with the newer generations because of incompatible values, attitudes and goals. Inter-generational conflict is referred to as conflict between older and younger generations at the interpersonal level. This phenomenon is accentuated when the generations are differentially acculturated in a host culture (Hall, 2005). The faster the process of acculturation of the adolescents, the more discrepancies in values between the generations leading to intergenerational family conflict. In a study with Asian American students (non-Muslims), the findings showed that values discrepancies were significantly associated with perceived family conflicts and on respecting elders (Tsai-Chae et al., 2008). The maintenance of traditional values by the parents causes family conflicts. For example, "around children's socialising and choice of friends, or their career choices, or their choice of marriage partners" (Pe-Pua et al., 2010, p.V). However, it is reported that most conflicts seem to occur over daily, mundane issues such as doing chores, appearance and getting along with others (Smetana et al., 1991; Steinberg, 1988). Parents usually complain that their children do not conform to the norms of their 'home country' and they fail to accept the traditional roles ascribed by their parents or significant others. From the adolescents' perspective, there is restricted personal freedom compared to peers, with their parents wanting them to live by their culture and rules and lack of understanding of their 'new' identity. These conflicts are associated with increased psychological problems in family members (Doherty and Campbell, 1988). From home to school, it is reported that intergenerational conflict and school-based racial discrimination increased depression and decreased academic outcomes in early adolescence (Ying and Meekyung, 2007).

Stigma

Mental health problems are often stigmatised in Muslim communities and the individuals usually suffer in silence. Often, the individuals with a mental health problem are faced with a 'double whammy' of multiple layers of discrimination as a result of their mental health problems and their identity of being a 'Muslim'. This value-added discrimination experienced by the individuals amplifies their mental health conditions. In addition, not only the stigma is directed towards the individual with mental health problems, but also to their family. The avoidance of seeking help from orthodox medicine is delayed because of the attributions of mental health problems to evil eye and *Jinn* possession. In addition, there is the fear factor that their family will be shamed by the community (Youssef and Deane, 2006; Aloud and Rathur, 2009). Studies of stigma in the Muslim communities indicate that Muslims endorsed common stereotypes about people with mental health problems (Al-Adawi et al., 2002); would not consider marriage or having a close relationship with a person with mental health problem (Shibre et al., 2001; Tabassum et al., 2000); and the disclosure of mental health problem is considered "shameful" (Amer, 2006; Aloud and Rathur, 2009). Due to the lack of acceptance and the perception that mental health issues exist, the culture of shame remains an issue of concern and causes many Muslims not to seek professional help. As Yunus (2015, cited in Irfan, 2015, p. 1) stated:

> the stigma that exists against mental health is alive and thriving in the Muslim community. . . . People who suffer from mental health issues are unable to find the support that they need due to the stigma . . . Combine the cultural views of not airing out dirty laundry with the religious inclination of just turning to God, and you get a hopeless situation for individuals who are suffering.

Conclusion

Major events and psychosocial issues affecting endogenous and migrant Muslims include the impact of September 11, Islamophobia, stigma, identity and intergenerational crisis, acculturation, refugee and microaggressions. In addition, the emergence of radical extremism among young Muslims has triggered more Islamophobia, microaggressions, anti-Muslim activities and hate crimes, and the resulting media coverage has magnified this problem. There is evidence to suggest that the Western media has been playing a considerable role in the social construction of fundamentalism (Ali, 2008). Other psychosocial issues affecting Muslims include family problems, substance misuse, sexual abuse and violence. The multiplicity of anti-Muslim sentiments and psychosocial factors increases the vulnerability of developing mental health problems. People with serious mental health problems illnesses face a greater risk of developing a range of chronic physical conditions (CIHI, 2008). For example, depression has been shown to "antedate some chronic physical illnesses" (Goldberg, 2010). It is hypothesised that Muslims suffering from mental health problems are at higher risk of experiencing a wide range of chronic physical conditions compared to the general population. The failure to address the problems faced by Muslims would result in creating high demands on the medical and psychological healthcare services. Moreover, some of the socio-political and psychological issues faced by Muslims obviously cannot be resolved by the healthcare system alone. There is a need for political leaders to engage with Muslim faith leaders, key community leaders and significant others in addressing the problems faced by Muslims. Cultural and religious diversity should be encouraged and part of the fabric of society. The focus should be both in prevention and responding to anti-Muslim incidents by implementing concrete political, social and economic measures in every level of civil society. The problems faced by Muslims like Islamophobia are not just a Muslim issue, it is a global issue.

References

Abu-Bader, S. H., Tirmazi, M. T., and Ross-Sheriff, F. (2011) The impact of acculturation on depression among older Muslim immigrants in the United States, *Journal of Gerontological Social Work*, 54, 425–448. Doi:10.1080/01634372.2011.560928

Abu-Ras, W., and Abu-Bader, S. H. (2009) Risk factors for depression and posttraumatic stress disorder (PTSD): The case of Arab and Muslim Americans post-9/11, *Journal of Immigrant & Refugee Studies*, 7, 393–418.

Abu-Ras, W. M., and Suarez, Z. E. (2009) Muslim men and women's perception of discrimination, hate crimes, and PTSD symptoms post 9/1, *Traumatology*, 15, 48–63.

Allen, C. (2014) Exploring the impact of islamophobia on visible Muslim women victims: A British case study. *Journal of Muslims in Europe*, 3, 2, 137–159.

Al-Adawi, S., Dorvlo, A. S., Al-Ismaily, S. S., Al-Ghafry, D. A., Al-Noobi, B. Z., Al-Salmi, A., Burke, D. T.,. Shah, M. K., Ghassany, H., and Chand, S. P. (2002) Perception of and attitude towards mental illness in Oman, *The International Journal of Social Psychiatry*, 48, 305–317.

Ali S. (2008) *Second and Third Generation Muslims in Britain: A Socially Excluded Group.* Oxford: Nuffield College, University of Oxford.

Aloud, N., and Rathur, A. (2009) Factors affecting attitudes towards seeking and using formal mental health and psychological services among Arab Muslim populations, *Journal of Muslim Mental Health*, 4, 79–103.

Amer, M. M. (2006) *When multicultural worlds collide: Breaking down barriers to service use.* Paper presented at the annual meeting of American Psychological Association New Orleans: American Psychological Association.

Amer, M. M., and Hovey, J. D. (2011) Anxiety and depression in a post- September 11 sample of Arabs in the USA, *Social Psychiatry and Psychiatric Epidemiology*, 47, 3, 409–418. Doi 10.1007/s00127-011-0341-4.

American-Arab Anti-Discrimination Committee. (2003) *Report on Hate Crimes and Discrimination Against Arab Americans: The Post-September 11 Backlash, September 11, 2001-October 11, 2002.* Washington, DC: American-Arab Anti-Discrimination Committee Research Institute.

Anderson, C. (2002, November 25) *FBI Reports Jump in Violence Against Muslims.* Associated Press.

Aprahamian, M., Kaplan, D. M., Windham, A. M., Sutter, J. A., and Visser, J. (2011) The relationship between acculturation and mental health of Arab Americans, *Journal of Mental Health Counseling*, 33, 80–92. Doi:10.17744/mehc.33.1.0356488305383630.

Berry J. W. (1997) Immigration, acculturation, and adaptation. *Applied Psychology: An International Review*, 46, 5–43. Doi: 10.1080/026999497378467.

Bux, S. (2007) Muslim youths, Islam and violent radicalisation: Addressing some myths. *Police Journal: Theory, Practice and Principles*, 80, 267–278. Doi:10.1350/pojo.2007.80.3.267.

Cesari, J. (2015) *Cited in What Is Islamophobia? The History And Definition Of Anti-Muslim Discrimination In The US, Elizabeth Whitman.* www.ibtimes.com/what-islamophobia-history-definition-anti-muslim-discrimination-us-2218446 (accessed 13 March 2018).

CIHI (Canadian Institute for Health Information) (2008) *A Framework for Health Outcomes Analysis: Diabetes and Depression Case Studies.* Ottawa: CIHI.

Doherty, W. J., and Campbell, T. L. (1988) *Families and health.* Newbury Park, CA: Sage Publications.

El-Sayed el-Aswad (2008) The New Orientalism: A dialect of cultural dualism between West/East and West/Islam, *Thaqafat*, 21, 3, 204–233.

Esposito, J. L., and Ibrahim, K. (2011) *Islamophobia: The Challenge of Pluralism in the 21st Century.* New York: Oxford University Press.

Escobar, J. I., Burnam, A., Karno, M., Forsythe, A., Landsverk, J., and Golding, J. M. (1986) Use of the Mini-Mental State Examination (MMSE) in a community population of mixed ethnicity: Cultural and linguistic artifacts, *Journal of Nervous and Mental Disease,* 174, 10, 607–614.

Fazel, M., Jeremy, W., and Danesh, J. (2005) Prevalence of serious mental disorder in 7000 refugees resettled in western countries: a systematic review, *Lancet,* 365, 130914.

Giger, J. N., and Davidhizar, R. (2002) Culturally competent care: Emphasis on understanding the people of Afghanistan, Afghanistan Americans, and Islamic culture and religion, *International Nursing Review,* 49, 79–86.

Goforth, A. N., Oka, E. R., Leong, F. T. L., and Denis, D. J. (2014) Acculturation, acculturative stress, religiosity and psychological adjustment among Muslim Arab American adolescents, *Journal of Muslim Mental Health,* 8, 3–19. Doi: http://dx.doi.org/10.3998/jmmh.10381607.0008.202.

Gogol, K. N., Gotsiridze, E. G., Guruli, Z. V., Kintraia, N. P., and Tsaava, F. D. (2006) The expectancy-stress factor in pregnant refugee women, *Georgian Medical News,* 138, 13–16. Doi: https://www.researchgate.net/publication/6739275_The_expectancy-stress_factor_in_pregnant_refugee_women (accessed 30 May 2018)

Goldberg, D. (2010) The detection and treatment of depression in the physically ill, *World Psychiatry,* 9, 16–20.

Gottschalk, P., and Greenberg, G. (2008) *Islamophobia: Making Muslims the enemy.* Lanham, MD: Rowman & Littlefield Publishers.

Hall, L. E. (2005) Intergenerational conflict, *Dictionary of Multicultural Psychology: Issues, Terms, and Concepts.* Doi: http://dx.doi.org/10.4135/9781452204437.n123 (accessed 13 March 2018).

Hassouneh D. M, Kulwicki A. (2007) Mental health, discrimination, and trauma in Arab women living in the US: a pilot study, *Mental Health, Religion & Culture,* 10, 257–262

Khanlou, N., Shakya, Y., and Muntaner, C. (2007–2009) Cited in Khanlou, N., and Jackson, B. (2011) *Immigrant Mental Health,* THE METROPOLIS PROJECT. Bridging Research, Policy and Practice, www.multiculturalmentalhealth.ca/wp-content/uploads/2013/10/Immigrant_mental_health_10aug10.pdf (accessed 13 March 2018).

Khawaja, N. G (2007) An investigation of the psychological distress of Muslim migrants in Australia, *Journal of Muslim Mental Health,* 2, 39–56. Doi: 10.1080/15564900701238526

Kim, Y. Y. (1982) Communication and acculturation, in L. A. Samovar, and R. E. Porter (Eds.), *Intercultural Communication: A Reader* (4th ed.), Belmont, CA: Wadsworth, pp. 379–388.

Kirmayer, L. J., Narasiah, L., Munoz, M., Rashid, M., Ryder, A. G., Guzder, J., Hassan, G., Rousseau, C., and Pottie, K. (2011) Common mental health problems in immigrants and refugees: General approach in primary care. *CMAJ : Canadian Medical Association Journal,* 183, 12, E959–E967. http://doi.org/10.1503/cmaj.090292.

Kunst, J. R., David L. Samb, and Pål, Ulleberga. (2012) Perceived islamophobia: Scale development and validation. *International Journal of Intercultural Relations,* 37, 2, 225–237. http://dx.doi.org/10.1016/j.ijintrel.2012.11.001

Laird, L. D., Amer, M. M., Barnett, E. D., & Barnes, L. L. (2007) Muslim patients and health disparities in the UK and the US. *Archives of Disease in Childhood,* 92, 10, 922–926.

Mandviwalwa, T. (2015) Navigating the "Known: "The socio-cultural development of American muslim adolescent girls, *Psychology & Society,* 7, 1, 83–97.

Mody, R. (2007) Chapter 41, Preventive Healthcare in Children, in Walker Patricia and Elizabeth Barnett (Eds.), *Immigrant Medicine.* Atlanta, GA: Elsevier, pp. 515–535. https://doi.org/10.1016/B978-0-323-03454-8.50045-0.

Moradi, B., Hassan, N. T. (2004) Arab American persons' reported experiences of discrimination and mental health: the mediating role of personal control, *Journal of Counselling Psychology*, 51, 418–428.

Nadal, K. L., Griffin, K. E., Hamit, S., Leon, J., Tobio, M., and Rivera, D. P. (2012) Subtle and overt forms of Islamophobia: Microaggressions toward Muslim Americans, *Journal of Muslim Mental Health*, 6, 2, 15–37.

NSW Refugee Health Service (2018) Fact Sheet 5, Refugee Women, https://www.swslhd. health.nsw.gov.au/refugee/pdf/Resource/FactSheet/FactSheet_05.pdf (accessed 30 May 2018).

Padela, A.I., and Heisler, M. (2010) The association of perceived abuse and discrimination after September 11, 2001, with psychological distress, level of happiness, and health status among Arab Americans, *American Journal of Public Health*, 100, 2, 284–291. Doi: 10.2105/ AJPH.2009.164954.

Palinkas, L. A., and Pickwell, S. M. (1995) Acculturation as a risk factor for chronic disease among Cambodian refugees in the United States, *Social Science & Medicine,* 40, 12, 1643–1653.

Pe-Pua, R., Gendera, S. Katz, I., and O'Connor, A. (2010) *Meeting the Needs of Australian Muslim Families: Exploring Marginalisation, Family Issues and 'Best Practice' in Service Provision.* Report prepared for: The Australian Government Department of Immigration and Citizenship Social Policy Research Centre University of New South Wales.

Quellien, A. (1910) *La Politique Musulmane dans l'Afrique Occidentale Française.* Paris: Émile Larose. Cited in Lopez, F. B. (2011) Towards a Definition of Islamophobia: Approximations of the Earliest Twentieth Century, *Journal of Ethnic and Racial Studies*, 34, 4, 556–573.

Rashad, K. (2015). Cited Blumberg, A. 7 Questions With Muslim Mental Health Professio. https://www.huffingtonpost.com/2015/04/09/muslim-mental-health_n_7018428.html (accessed 30 May 2018).

Read, J. G., and Bartkowski, J. P. (2000) To veil or not to veil? A case study of identity negotiation among Muslim women in Austin, Texas, *Gender & Society*, 14, 395–417. http:// dx.doi.org/10.1177/089124300014003003.

RHTAC (2011a) *Refugee Health Technical Assistance Center (Mental Health).* http://refugee healthta.org/physical-mental-health/mental-health/ (accessed 13 March 2018).

RHTAC (2011b) *JSI Research and Training Institute Addressing the Mental, Health Needs of Refugees in Primary Care Settings.* http://wordpress-test.jsi.com/refugeehealthta/files/2011/07/ slides_Refugee_Mental_Health_Primary_Care_RHTAC_Webinar_Jul.pdf

RHTAC (2011c) *Acculturation and Health.* http://refugeehealthta.org/prevention-and-well ness/acculturation-and-health/ (accessed 13 March 2018).

Rippy A. E., Newman E. (2006) Perceived religious discrimination and its relationship to anxiety and paranoia among Muslim Americans, *Journal of Muslim Mental Health*, 1, 5–20.

Rosenthal, D., Ranier, N., and Klimidis, S. (1996) Vietnamese adolescents in Australia: Relationship between perceptions of self and parental values, intergenerational conflict, and gender dissatisfaction, *International Journal of Psychology*, 31, 2, 81–91.

Runnymede Trust Commission. (1997) *Islamophobia: A challenge for us all.* London: The Runnymede Trust.

Shibre, T., Negash, A., Kullgren, G., Kebede, D., Alem, A., Fekadu, A., and Jacobsson, L. (2001) Perception of stigma among family members of individuals with schizophrenia and major affective disorders in rural Ethiopia, *Social Psychiatry and Psychiatric Epidemiology*, 36, 299–303.

Said, E. (1978) *Orientalism.* New York: Pantheon Books, p. 3.

Sheridan, L. P. (2006) Islamophobia Pre-and Post-September 11th, 200, *Journal of Interpersonal Violence*, 21, 317–336.

Smart, J. F., and Smart, W. D. (1995) Acculturative stress the experience of the Hispanic immigrant, *The Counseling Psychologist,* 23, 25–42. Doi: 10.1177/0011000095231003.

Smetana, J. G., Yau, J., Restrepo, A., and Brasges, J. (1991) Adolescent-parent conflict in married and divorced families, *Developmental Psychology*, 27, 1000–1010.

Steinberg, L. (1988) Reciprocal relation between parent-child distance and pubertal maturation, *Developmental Psychology*, 24, 1, 122–128.

Southern Poverty Law Center (SPLC) Anti-Muslims www.splcenter.org/fighting-hate/extremist-files/ideology/anti-muslim (accessed 13 March 2018).

Sue, D. W., Capodilupo, C. M., Torino, G. C., Bucceri, J. M., Holder, A. M., Nadal, K. L., and Esquilin, M. (2007) Racial microaggressions in everyday life: implications for clinical practice, *The American Psychologist*, 62, 4, 271–286.

Tabassum, R., Macaskill, A., and Ahmad, I. (2000) Attitudes towards mental health in an urban Pakistani community in the United Kingdom, *International Journal of Social Psychiatry*, 46, 170–181.

Tsai-Chae, Amy H., and Nagata, Donna K. (2008) Asian values and perceptions of intergenerational family conflict among Asian American students, *Cultural Diversity & Ethnic Minority Psychology*, 14, 205–214.

UNHCR (2016) *What is a refugee.* www.unrefugees.org/what-is-a-refugee/ (accessed 13 March 2018).

Ying, Yu-Wen, and Meekyung Han, M. (2007) The effect of intergenerational conflict and school-based racial discrimination on depression and academic achievement in Filipino American adolescents, *Journal of Immigrant & Refugee Studies*, 4, 4, 19–35.

Youssef, J., and Deane, F. P. (2006) Factors influencing mental-health help-seeking in Arabic-speaking communities in Sydney, Australia, *Mental Health, Religion & Culture,* 9, 1, 43–66

Yunus. (2015) *Cited in Irfan, M. Muslim Community's Mental Health Stigma Stops Healing.* http://muslimobserver.com/muslim-communitys-mental-health-stigma-stops-healing/ (accessed 13 March 2018).

Zine, J. (2006) Unveiled Sentiments: Gendered Islamophobia and Experiences of Veiling among Muslim Girls in a Canadian Islamic School, *Equity & Excellence in Education*, 39, 3, 239–252. Doi: 10.1080/10665680600788503.

Chapter 3

Culture, religion and mental health

Introduction

Cultural and religious factors are the prime movers in people's conception of mental health and illness. In addition, culture and religion have significant influences on the diagnosis and prevalence of psychological disorders. For many who experience serious psychological distress or mental illness, spirituality and religion can provide solace and a sense of coherence and a purpose in life. There is evidence to suggest that spirituality is a recognised factor that contributes to the maintenance of mental health (Rassool, 2016). Traditionally, psychologists and mental health professionals have under-emphasised cultural and religious issues and their effects on mental health. From a Judeo-Christian and orientalist tradition, religion has often been seen by mental health professionals as irrational, out-dated, and dependency forming and has been viewed to result in emotional instability (Crossley, 1995; Dein, 2010).

In the field of psychiatry, there has always been a dichotomy between religion and mental health. Unexplained religious phenomena such as spiritual experiences and *Jinn* possession have been perceived and labelled as 'psychotic disorders.' Religion, in the context of mental health, has been perceived as being a "universal obsessional neurosis" (Freud, 1907, p. 25). According to Loewenthal and Lewis (2011, p. 256), "Freud argued that guilt is created when rituals are not carried out, and assuaged when they are, so a self-perpetuating 'ritualaholic' cycle is set up." The pioneer of cognitive therapy Abu Zayd al-Balkhi, introduced the concept of mental health and 'mental hygiene' and related it to spiritual health (Badri, 2013). According to the cognitive behavioural psychologist, Albert Ellis (1980), the causal relationship between religion and emotional and mental illness is beyond dispute. It was only in the past two decades that 'religious or spiritual problems' was introduced in the DSM-IV as a new diagnostic category that invited professionals to respect the patient's beliefs and rituals. It is argued that "religiousness remains an important aspect of human life and it usually has a positive association with good mental health" (Behere et al. 2013, p. 194). Recently, there has been a growth in the systematic research into religion, spirituality and mental health. Religion remains a significant influence in the field of mental health and psychiatry including "symptoms, phenomenology, and outcome" (Agarwal, 1989) and as part of the intervention strategies.

Culture, religion and spirituality

Culture has a significant and a determinant influence on mental health, mental illness and mental health services. In a clinical setting, there is interplay between the culture of the patient, the culture of the clinician and the culture of the institution. Our culture, which is dynamic and interactive, shapes our worldview and this has an effect on our interactions and behaviours. Culture refers to behaviour, ideals, values, attitudes and traditions shared by a group of people and transmitted from one generation to the next (Brislin, 1993; Cohen, 2009). This shared set of beliefs, norms and values not only has an impact on the perception and meaning of health and illness, but also on how the individuals present their ill health. It has been suggested that

> the meaning of an illness refers to deep-seated attitudes and beliefs a culture holds about whether an illness is 'real' or 'imagined,' whether it is of the body or the mind (or both), whether it warrants sympathy, how much stigma surrounds it, what might cause it, and what type of person might succumb to it.
>
> (Office of the Surgeon General (US) 2001)

The coping mechanisms used by individuals are also shaped by cultural and religious factors.

The concept of spirituality and religiosity for individuals of different cultures, races and communities often carries many interpretations. From a Judeo-Christian tradition, these concepts are not interchangeable words and have been a perennial source of controversy. According to the Royal College of Psychiatrists (2018), in general, spirituality is something everyone can experience; it helps us to find meaning about life and purpose in the things we value; it can bring hope and healing in times of suffering and loss; and it encourages us to seek the best relationship with ourselves, others and what lies beyond. Koenig et al. (2001) explain the concept of spirituality as a personal search for understanding the meaning and purpose of life with or without the development of religious rituals. It is acknowledged that an individual does not have to be religious in order to attain spiritual enlightenment. In contrast, some definition of spirituality is embedded in religious participation. For example, spirituality is

> expressed in an individual's search for ultimate meaning through participation in religion and/or belief in God, family, naturalism, rationalism, humanism, and the arts. All of these factors can influence how patients and

health care professionals perceive health and illness and how they interact with one another.

(AAMC, 1999, pp. 25–26)

Religion, as a concept, is perceived by many (in the West) as not being interchangeable with spirituality. Religion is characterised by a system of beliefs, practices, rituals and symbols designed to facilitate closeness to a God (Koenig et al. 2001). In this context, religion is thus a more exclusive concept than spirituality and involves the belief in spiritual reality and God.

From an Islamic perspective, there is no distinction between religion and spirituality. The concept of religion is embedded in the umbrella of spirituality. In the Islamic context, there is no spirituality without religious thoughts and practices, and the religion provides the spiritual path for salvation and a way of life (Rassool, 2000). According to Rassool (2016),

> Muslims embrace the acceptance of the Divine, and they seek meaning, purpose and happiness in worldly life and the hereafter. This is achieved through the belief in the 'Oneness of God (*Tawheed*),' without any partner, and the understanding and application of Qur'anic practices and the guidance of the Prophet (☙).

(p. 27)

This unicity of God is

> the very foundation of Islam on which all the other pillars and principles depend. If one's *Tawheed* is not sound, the rest of one's Islam becomes, in effect, a series of pagan rituals. In this model, Allah's unity must be maintained.

(Philips, 1994, p. vii)

Culture and Islam

There are cultural differences and practices of Muslims on a global scale despite the fact that they share the same religious values and practices. The cultural practices may or may not be in concordance with basic religious practices. Some cultural practices (or pre-Islamic practices) performed by Muslims are given an Islamic dimension, although these practices are not considered Islamic practices (Rassool, 2016, p. 7). According to Philips (2007), "the Islam being practices in much of the Muslim world today may be referred to as Cultural Islam. The main feature of this version of Islam is the blind following of local traditions" (p. 33) However, in contrast, Islamic culture is based on the practices that have roots in the Qur'an and Sunnah (traditions).

Since Islam covers political and economic aspects of human life, it possesses and promotes distinctive cultural characteristics of its own (Saidi, 2008). Islamic culture is not monolithic and has varieties and a rich diversity. Islamic culture is based on both individualism and collectivism values. It has been suggested that "individualism and collectivism from Islamic viewpoint are not two opposite concepts but are two intertwined precepts complimenting and enhancing each other" (Musah, 2011, p. 71). In essence,

> both the concept of individualism and collectivism is finely displayed in the five pillars or obligations of Islam – declaration of faith, prayers, fasting, zakat and Haj. By removing social hierarchies and barriers, these five duties show the obligations and duties of Muslims.
>
> (Khan, 2013)

This individual sense of responsibility "consists of salient traits of which self-building is one and accountability before Allah (God) is the other" (Musah, 2011, p. 71). The collectivistic value of Islam is embodied in the concept 'Ummah,' which transcends all ethnicities and sects within the religion (Springer et al. 2009). Muslims are responsible to take care of themselves, immediate families, extended families and community, in this respective order. Kobeisy (2004) describes this collective consciousness:

> Because Islam binds Muslims into one international community, Muslim individuals are more likely to be impacted in the form of stress and anxiety by adversities affecting other Muslims in any part of the world. If the concern stems from an event or a tension that is taking place in the client's country of origin, the suffering could be more direct and personal. An illustration of this could be war, terrorism, mass transportation (for examples, planes and trains) tragedies, and natural disasters such as earthquakes or floods.
>
> (p. 63)

The family is central to the Islamic culture. Aloud (2004) stated that "in Arab-Muslim communities, the family is the central and most prominent social unit and thus loyalty to the family is both religiously and culturally valued" (p. 14) The onus of Muslims towards the family kinship is further highlighted in the responsibilities toward the parents, siblings and the extended family (including grandparents) through bonds of kinship. According to El Sergany (2010) '*Selatur Rahim*' (maintaining the bonds of kinship) means dealing properly with relatives, supporting them with whatever possible and warding off bad things. *Selatur Rahim* means "visiting the relatives, asking about them, checking on them, giving them gifts when possible, helping their poor members, visiting their sick members, accepting their invitations, having them as guests, feeling proud of them and elevating them. *Selatur Rahim* also means joining the relatives in their happy moments, sharing their sadness in their sad moments, in addition to any other practice that may help strengthen and reinforce the relations between members of that small society. Therefore, *Selatur Rahim* is a gate for large good. With *Selatur Rahim*, the unity of the Muslim community gets deeper and stronger and members feel assured and free from worry as isolation and loneliness become nobody's habit because everybody feels they are surrounded with their relatives with much love and care and that their relatives support and help them when necessary" (p. 55). With this expectancy, most Muslims will feel obligated to consult with family members, for a mutually supported decision, with all matters of life including seeking professional mental health services. Allah says in the Qur'an (Interpretation of the meaning):

> *Worship Allah and associate nothing with Him, and to parents do good, and to relatives, orphans, the needy, the near neighbour, the neighbour farther away, the companion at your side, the traveller, and those whom your right hands possess. Indeed, Allah does not like those who are self-deluding and boastful.*
>
> (An-Nisā' (The Women) 4:36)

Evidence of religion and spirituality in mental health and stress

Research is now pointing to the relevance of religiosity and spirituality in the lives of individuals. The evidence suggests, on balance, that religious involvement is generally conducive to better mental health and people who are more religious/spiritual have better mental health and adapt more quickly to health problems compared to those who are less religious/ spiritual (Klocker et al., 2011; Koenig, 2012). In addition, the findings show that the strongest association is the link between religious belief and decreased depression, as well as reduced anxiety and suicide risk, and to a lesser extent, reduced psychotic disorders (Klocker et al. 2011). The findings of other studies have also showed that those persons who were more spiritually or religiously involved had higher rates of overall well-being and life satisfaction; lower rates of depressive symptoms and suicide; lower rates of divorce and higher rates of marital satisfaction; and lower rates of alcohol and abuse and other drug abuse, including cigarette smoking and recreational drug use (Larson et al. 1998, Worthington et al., 1996; Abdel-Khalek, 2007). The findings of studies (Koenig, 2007; Bosworth et al., 2003) have showed the impact of remission with medical and psychiatric disorders that have clinical depression. Furthermore, religious coping is used by patients with psychiatric disorders to cope with their distress (D'Souza, 2002; Tepper et al., 2001).

Nowadays, religiosity is no longer seen as a source of pathology but for some people it seemed that religious considerations are not always beneficial (Loewenthal, 2007). Negative religious beliefs have been linked with poorer mental health outcomes, including higher rates of depression and lower quality of life. Some people have inner spiritual conflicts with their perception and understanding of God and the 'punishing God' and this can be problematic. According to Pargament (2013) "a growing body of research has linked these spiritual struggles to higher levels of psychological distress, declines in physical health and even greater risk of mortality." Negative religious coping also has adverse effects on the individual. For example, "negative religious coping approaches such as reinterpreting the stressor as a punishment given by God, passively depending on God to resolve the stressor, attempting to cope on one's own without relying on God's help, mirror 'underlying spiritual tensions and struggles within oneself, with others, and with the divine" (Pargament et al., 2013, p. 51). Thus, they are more likely to have a harmful impact on mental health. It is reported that some "people recount that they experienced organized religion as a source of pain, guilt or oppression" (Mohr and Huguelet, 2004, p. 374).

There is evidence to suggest that increased anxiety is often found amongst those with a strict religious upbringing and those individuals with dogmatic or underdeveloped spirituality (Trenholm et al., 1998; Genia, 1997). It has also been suggested that "certain religious expressions of spirituality may become part of the problem as well as part of the recovery" (Mental Health Foundation, 2006, p. 15). Some people may be alienated from their faith community for all sorts of reasons and "may be rejected by their faith community, burdened by spiritual activities, disappointed and demoralized by their beliefs" (Mohr and Huguelet, 2004, p. 369; Kehoe, 1999). From an Islamic perspective, it is perhaps those individuals, with an internal locus of control and with negative attributions, who misinterpret their trials and tribulations in a way that influences their cognitive process and behaviour. In fact, those individuals with strong religious beliefs attributed their physical or mental health to the will of God or a punishment from God, thus it is beyond their control (Rassool 2000). In contrast, positive events are perceived as reward for adhering to the beliefs and practices of their particular faith.

In summary, it seems that generally religious beliefs or spirituality are effective in promoting mental health and in the prevention of mental disorders. For some individuals, some aspects of spirituality and religion have a counterproductive effect, leading to obsessive self-blame, hopelessness, guilt, shame, powerlessness, helplessness, anxiety, depression or psychotic episodes. However, it should be pointed out that religion does not nurture mental disorders. The evidence to suggest that, for example, no relationship exists between religiosity and any of the clinical features of obsessional compulsive disorder (OCD), including the presence of religious obsessions, was found in a sample of Turkish Muslim OCD sufferers (Tek and Ulug, 2001). Similar findings were observed with orthodox Jew OCD sufferers (Greenberg and Witztum, 2001). Despite the positive and negative association found between spirituality and mental health generally, there are a number of shortcomings in those research studies. The limitations include both conceptual and methodological shortcomings. Most of the studies are derived from the Judeo-Christian tradition, which does not reflect the diversity of spiritual expression that exists in most countries with multi-ethnic and multi-cultural populations. These need to be addressed in order that the maximum potential benefits of the role of spirituality in health are available to all faith communities.

References

Abdel-Khalek, A. (2007) Religiosity, happiness, health, and psychopathology in a probability sample of Muslim adolescents, *Mental Health, Religion & Culture*, 10, 571–583.

Agarwal, A. K. (1989) Religion and mental health, *Editorial, Indian J Psychiatry*, 31, 185–186.

Aloud, N. (2004) Factors affecting attitudes toward seeking and using formal mental health and psychological services among Arab-Muslims population. *Doctoral dissertation*, Graduate School of Ohio State University. https://etd.ohiolink.edu/rws_etd/document/get/osu1078935499/inline (accessed 13 March 2018).

Association of American Medical Colleges (AAMC). (1999) *Report III: Contemporary Issues in Medicine: Communication in Medicine, Medical School Objectives Project.* Washington, DC: Association of American Medical Colleges.

Badri, M. (2013) *Abu Zayd al-Balkhi's Sustenance of the Soul: The Cognitive Behavior Therapy of A Ninth Century Physician.* Richmond: International Institute of Islamic Thought (IIIT).

Behere, P. B., Das, A., Yadav, R., and Behere, A. P. (2013) Religion and mental health, *Indian Journal of Psychiatry*, 55, Suppl 2, S187–S194. http://doi.org/10.4103/0019-5545.105526.

Bosworth, H. B., Park, K. S., McQuoid, D. R., Hays, J. C., and Steffens, D. C. (2003) The impact of religious practice and religious coping on geriatric depression, *International Journal of Geriatric Psychiatry*, 18, 10, 905–914.

Brislin, R. (1993) *Conceptualizing Culture and its Impact. In Understanding Culture's Influence on Behavior.* Fort Worth, TX: Harcourt Brace.

Cohen, A. B. (2009) Many forms of culture, *American Psychologist*, 64, 194–204.

Crossley, D. (1995) Religious experience within mental illness: Opening the door on research, *British Journal of Psychiatry*, 166, 284–286.

Dein, S. (2010) *Religion, Spirituality, and Mental Health.* Psychiatric Times. www.psychiatrictimes.com/articles/religion-spirituality-and-mental-health/page/0/1#sthash.VVbtR4wM.dpuf (accessed 13 March 2018).

D'Souza, R. (2002) Do patients expect psychiatrists to be interested in spiritual issues? *Australasian Psychiatry*, 10, 44–47.

El Sergany, R. (2010) *The Importance of Ethics and Values in Islamic Civilization. Maintaining the Bonds of Kinship in Islam . . . Its Importance and Rights.* https://d1.islamhouse.com/data/en/ih_books/single2/en_The_importance_of_ethics_and_values_in_Islamic_Civilization.pdf (accessed on 13 March 2018).

Ellis, A. (1980) Psychotherapy and atheistic values: A response to A. E. Bergin's "Psychotherapy and religious values," *Journal of Consulting and Clinical Psychology*, 48, 635–639.

Freud, S. (1907) *Obsessive acts, religious practices.* Reprinted (1953–1974) in the Standard Edition of the Complete Psychological Works of Sigmund Freud (Trans. and Ed. J. Strachey), Vol. 7. London: Hogarth Press.

Genia, V. (1997) The spiritual experience index: Revision and reformulation, *Review of Religious Research*, 38, 344–361.

Greenberg, D., and Witztum, E. (2001) *Sanity and Sanctity: Mental Health Work among the Ultra-Orthodox in Jerusalem.* New Haven, CT: Yale University Press.

Kehoe, N. C. (1999) A therapy group on spiritual issues for patients with chronic mental illness, *Psychiatric Services*, 50, 1081–1083.

Khan, M. B. (2013) *Individualism & Collectivism*. www.dawn.com/news/789494 (accessed 13 March 2018).

Klocker, N., Trenerry, B., and Webster, K. (2011) *How does Freedom of Religion and Belief Affect Health and Wellbeing?* Carlton, Victorian Health Promotion Foundation (VicHealth).

Kobeisy, A. N. (2004) *Counseling American Muslims: Understanding the faith and helping the people*. Westport, CT: Praeger Publishers.

Koenig, H. G., McCullough, M., and Larson, D. B. (2001) *Handbook of Religion and Health: A Century of Research Reviewed*. New York: Oxford University Press.

Koenig, H. G. (2007) Religion and remission of depression in medical inpatients with heart failure/pulmonary disease, *The Journal of Nervous and Mental Disease*, 195, 389–395.

Koenig, H. G. (2012) Religion, spirituality, and health: The research and clinical implications, *International Scholarly Research Notices: Psychiatry*, 2012, Article ID 278730, 33 pages, 2012. Doi:10.5402/2012/278730.

Larson, D. B., Swyers, J. P., and McCullough, M. E. (1998) *Scientific Research on Spirituality and Health: A Report Based on the Scientific Progress in Spirituality Conferences*. Washington, DC: National Institute for Healthcare Research.

Loewenthal, K. M. (2007) *Religion, Culture and Mental Health*. Cambridge: Cambridge University Press.

Loewenthal, K. M., and Lewis, C. A. (2011) Mental health, religion and culture, *The Psychologist*, 24, 4, 256–259

Mental Health Foundation (2006) *The Impact of Spirituality on Mental Health. A Review of the Literature*. London: Mental Health Foundation.

Mohr, S., and Huguelet, P. (2004) The relationship between schizophrenia and religion and its implications for care, *Swiss Medical Weekly*, 134, 25–26, 369–376.

Musah, M. B. (2011) The culture of individualism and collectivism in balancing accountability and innovation in education: An Islamic perspective. OIDA International, *Journal of Sustainable Development*, 02, 08, 70–76.

Office of the Surgeon General (US), Center for Mental Health Services (US), and National Institute of Mental Health (US) (2001) *Mental Health: Culture, Race, and Ethnicity: A Supplement to Mental Health: A Report of the Surgeon General*. Rockville (MD): Substance Abuse and Mental Health Services Administration (US); 2001 Aug. Chapter 2 Culture Counts: The Influence of Culture and Society on Mental Health. www.ncbi.nlm.nih.gov/books/NBK44249/ (accessed 13 March 2018).

Pargament, K. I. (2013) *What Role Do Religion and Spirituality Play in Mental Health?* www.apa.org/news/press/releases/2013/03/religion-spirituality.aspx (accessed 13 March 2018).

Philips, A. A. B. (1994) *The Fundamentals of Tawheed (Islamic Monotheism)*. Riyadh, Saudi Arabia: International Islamic Publishing House.

Philips, A. A. B. (2007) *The Clash of Civilization: An Islamic View*. Birmingham: Al-Hidaayah Publishing & Distribution.

Rassool, G. H. (2000) The crescent and Islam: Healing, nursing and spiritual dimension: Some considerations towards an understanding of the Islamic perspectives of caring, *Journal of Advanced Nursing*, 32, 6, 1476–1484.

Rassool, G. H. (2016) *Islamic Counselling. An Introduction to Theory and Practice*. Hove, East Sussex: Routledge.

The Royal College of Psychiatrists (2018) *Spirituality and Mental Health*. www.rcpsych.ac.uk/mentalhealthinformation/therapies/spiritualityandmentalhealth.aspx (accessed 15 March 2018).

Saidi, T. (2008) 'Islam and Culture: Don't mix them up'. Inn Post: Community Voices. www.minnpost.com/community-voices/2008/02/islam-and-culture-dont-mix-them.

Springer, R., Abbott, D. A., and Reisbig, A. M. J. (2009) Therapy with Muslim couples and families: Basic guidelines for effective practice, *The Family Journal: Counseling and Therapy for Couples and Families*, 17, 229–235. Doi:10.1177/1066480709337798

Tek, C., and Ulug, B. (2001) Religiosity and religious obsessions in obsessive compulsive Disorder, *Psychiatry Research*, 104, 99–108.

Tepper, L., Rogers, S. A., Coleman. E. M., and Malony, H. N. (2001) The prevalence of religious coping among persons with persistent mental illness, *Psychiatric Services*, 52, 5, 660–665.

Trenholm, P., Trent, J., and. Compton, W. C.(1998) Negative religious conflict as a predictor of panic disorder, *Journal of Clinical Psychology*, 54, 1, 59–65.

Worthington, E. L., Jr., Kurusu, T. A., McCullough, M. E., and Sandage, S. J. (1996) Empirical research on religion in counseling: A 10-year review and research prospectus, *Psychological Bulletin*, 119, 448–487.

Chapter 4

Perception and somatisation of mental health problems

Culture-bound syndrome

As stated in the previous chapter (3), cultural factors have been shown to influence the perception of illness and health, give meanings and expressions of various physical and psychological elements, determine norms of behaviour (normal and abnormal behaviours), and determine help-seeking behaviour. Culture-bound syndrome is an amalgamation of psychiatric and somatic (bodily) symptoms identified only within a specific society or culture. In theory, culture-bound syndromes are those folk illnesses in which alterations of behaviour and experience figure prominently. In actuality, however, many are not syndromes at all. Instead, they are local ways of explaining any of a wide assortment of misfortunes (Simons, 2001).

The concept culture-bound syndrome was included in the DSM-IV (American Psychiatric Association [APA], 2000). DSM-V updates criteria to reflect cross-cultural variations in presentations, gives more detailed and structured information about cultural concepts of distress, and includes a clinical interview tool to facilitate comprehensive, person-centred assessments (APA 2013). The concept has been replaced by three concepts:

- Cultural syndromes: "clusters of symptoms and attributions that tend to co-occur among individuals in specific cultural groups, communities, or contexts . . . that are recognised locally as coherent patterns of experience" (p. 758);
- Cultural idioms of distress: "ways of expressing distress that may not involve specific symptoms or syndromes, but that provide collective, shared ways of experiencing and talking about personal or social concerns" (p. 758); and
- Cultural explanations of distress or perceived causes: "labels, attributions, or features of an explanatory model that indicate culturally recognised meaning or aetiology for symptoms, illness, or distress" (p. 758).

Simons and Hughes (1986) listed almost 200 folk illnesses that have, at one time or another, been considered culture-bound syndromes. Some of the common culture-bound syndrome include: The evil eye, *Zār or Zaars* (Middle East and African societies); *Dhat* syndrome, Possession Syndrome (Indian subcontinent); *Amok, Koro, Lattah* (Malaysia, Philippines); in Spanish-speaking Latin America: the case of *Nervios, Susto and Ataques de Nervios*; *Khyâl Cap* (Wind Attacks) (Cambodia); *Latah* (Southeast Asia, Japan); Kufungisisa (Thinking Too Much (Zimbabwe); *Maladi Moun* (Humanly Caused Illness) (Haiti); *Ghost Sickness* (Native Americans, Hispanics); *Falling Out* (Southern United States, Caribbean); *Grisi Siknis* (Crazy sickness) (Central and South America); and *Gururumba* (New Guinea). Possession is regarded by some commentators as a culture-bound syndrome, but others argue that, although the manifestations may differ according to culture, the underlying theme is always the same (Pereira et al., 1995).

Muslims' perception of mental health problems

The causation of mental health problems can be classified as either internal attributing factors (genetic, brain disorders, conflicts) or external attributing factors (psychosocial). Two attributional categories for mental health problems across societies and cultures have been identified by Murdock et al. (1980). The first category is natural attribution (stress, trauma, organic problems, internal somatic events) and the second category is psychological and social attributions. Helman (2000) goes further, arguing that apart from causal individual, social and environmental factors in the aetiology of illness, there is the supernatural world where ill health is attributed here to God, ancestor spirits and/ or punishment for wrongdoing or for sin. In addition, attribution of causations to psycho-spiritual and supernatural agents (evil eye, possession, witchcraft and sorcery) appears to be more common in non-Western societies.

Research has identified that religion and religious belief are absolutely central to the way Muslims interpret the cause and development of mental health problems (Nada, 2007). The Islamic perspective of mental health is also dramatically different from the Judeo-Christian nosology of mental health. Muslims have a broad range of beliefs about the cause of mental health problems. For Muslims, by virtue of their religious belief, attribute the ultimate cause of illness to God and their relationship to God. Moreover, Muslims also "attribute mental health problems to different phenomena, including the evil eye (*Hasad or Nathla*), possession by supernatural entities such as demons (*Jinn*) and magic (*Sihr*)" (Rassool, 2016, p. 54), psychosocial and acculturation factors. In a study of the conceptualisations of mental illness among Muslims (Booysen et al. 2016), the findings showed that the main perceived causes of mental illness were evil spirits (66%) and stress (62%). Another finding of a study (Abu-Ras and Abu-Bader, 2008) about perceptions of mental illness indicated that 98% of survey respondents agreed that life stressors are a test of one's faith. Eighty-four percent of respondents believed in devil possession of mentally ill persons (*Jinns*), hallucinations, delusional beliefs and disorganised behaviour. Other purported supernatural causes are black magic, the evil eye and envy (intentional or not) which can invoke negative consequences; charms, markings, jewellery, prayers or rituals are used to distract jealousy and envy. These types of conceptualising of mental health are applicable to Muslims in many countries. For example, in Swedish Somalis (Johnsdotter et al. 2011), Emirati traditional healers and mental health practitioners (Thomas et al., 2014; Petkari, 2015), South African Muslim faith healers and psychiatrists (Ally and Laher, 2008; Bulbulia and Laher, 2013), women Muslim immigrants in the United States (Carter and Rashidi, 2003), Arab-Muslims in the United States (Aloud, 2004), British Muslims (Weatherhead and Daiches, 2010), Omani (Al-Adawi et al,. 2002); Jordanian (Al-Krenawi et al., 2000) and Arab-Muslims (Al-Subaie and Al-Hammed, 2000; Al-Issa, 2000). However, not all mental health problems are associated with spiritual, supernatural or metaphysical causes (Rahman, 1998). In a systematic review of 105 scientific texts on *Jinn* possessions and their relationship with mental disorders (Lim et al., 2014), the findings indicate that Muslims attribute their psychotic symptoms or other symptoms to "*Jinn*." One of the early Muslim scholars in mental healthcare, Ibn Sina, rejected the popular notion that mental health problems originated from evil spirits (Pridmore and Pasha, 2004).

In summary, it seemed that, on a global scale, that the perspective of mental health problems being attributed to demonological or metaphysical causes are dominant among both indigenous Muslims and Muslims living in the West, even if it does not necessarily 'fit' with the normative beliefs of the host countries. However, there is no evidence to suggest this conceptual framework of mental health problems may be changing amongst the heterogeneous Muslim communities on a global scale due to acculturation.

Somatisation of illness

Somatisation disorder (also Briquet's syndrome) is no longer considered a clinical diagnosis as a psychiatric disorder. It is characterised by a recurring, multiple and current history of many physical complaints that occur over a period of several years. The disorder results in significant lifestyle and behavioural impairments. In the International Classification of Diseases 10th edition (WHO, 2010), somatisation is defined as "multiple, recurrent and frequently changing physical symptoms usually present for several years (at least two years) before the patient is referred to a psychiatrist." Currently, a more acceptable terminology is used, 'unexplained somatic complaints,' to describe patients presenting with any physical symptom and frequent medical visits in spite of negative investigations. In the Diagnostic and Statistical Manual of Mental Disorders version V (APA, 2013), the condition has been renamed somatic symptom disorder (SSD).

Somatisation, in the context of this chapter, refers to the expression and presentation of physical symptoms for mental health problems. In Islamic culture, there are no distinctions between physical and psychological health (El-Islam and Ahmed, 1971; El-Islam, 1994). The literature reveals that Arab-Muslim clients do not distinguish emotional or psychological distress from physical illness and that the majority of populations tend to somatise their psychological problems (El-Islam and Abu Dagga, 1992; El-Islam, 1982, Okasha, 1999; Al-Krenawi and Graham, 2000; Al-Krenawi et al., 2000). This type of somatisation is not specific to particular cultures or religious beliefs. Muslim patients express their symptoms of mental health problems in the form of physical symptoms. It has been suggested that this somatisation and inability to express emotions are due to the lack the capacity to label an emotional state (Lipowski, 1990) and to vocabulary inadequacies in the original languages of these communities (Al Busaidi, 2010). However, according to Al-Issa (1995) the rationale behind the tendency towards somatisation in Arab-Muslims patients is not the lack of vocabulary – as the Arabic language, for example, is rich in suitable expressions – but other social and cultural factors. The prevalence of somatic symptoms among Muslims can be attributed to the religio-cultural views regarding the holistic approach in the unity of body, mind and soul.

Muslims and mental health problems

In Western countries, due to the current socio-political climate of Islamaphobia (muscular liberalism), microaggressions, prejudices, hate crimes and social exclusion (social exclusion correlates with mental health problems), the psychological health of Muslim communities is undeniably under threat. The negative portrayal of pious Muslims as potential terrorists by certain media and its considerable role in the social construction of fundamentalism (Ali, 2008) has fuelled this collective consciousness of 'hate a Muslim.' As a consequence of these interrelated factors, there are indicators that Muslims experience both physical and mental health problems (Ali et al., 2005, Sheridan, 2006 Kira et al., 2010). In relation to the prevalence and incidence rates of mental health problems amongst Muslims, there are no large-scale epidemiological reports in the 57 Islamic states who are members of the Organization of the Islamic Conference.

The myriad conflicts in Middle Eastern countries have increased the incidence and prevalence of mental health problems. In Lebanon, there has been an increase in admissions of Syrians over the past few years, with more severe psychopathology (schizophrenia) and suicidality (Lama et al., 2016). Refugees on the Jordanian border and at the northern Syrian/Lebanese border reported anxiety, feeling depressed, lethargy, eating and sleeping problems, anger and fatigue (Quosh et al., 2013). Post-traumatic stress disorder is common, especially from highly-exposed groups in Middle Eastern societies due to civil wars, wars, political violence, natural disasters, occupation and forced displacements (PTSD Research, 2010; Ozer et al., 2013, Abou-Saleh and Mobayad, 2013; Marwa, 2016).

Generally, it is reported that there are high rates of post-traumatic stress disorder (Abu-Ras and Abu-Bader, 2009), depression (Sheridan, 2006; Rehman and Owen, 2013), anxiety (Rehman and Owen, 2013) and stress (Barkdull et al.,

2011) among Muslims. For Muslim American adolescents, Basit and Hamid (2010) reported that adjustment disorder was the highest reported category followed by anxiety disorder, mood disorder, obsessive-compulsive disorder, posttraumatic stress disorder (PTSD), schizophrenia and other psychotic disorders and substance misuse. In Thailand, the findings from Ratanasiripong's study (2012) showed a moderate prevalence of anxiety and high prevalence of depression among Muslim nursing students. Prevalence studies showed that women had a higher rate of depression than men (Ghubash et al., 2001; Mirza and Jenkins, 2004; Douki et al. 2007). Sonuga-Barke and Mistry (2000) found depression and anxiety levels to be more pronounced in Pakistani Muslim women in comparison to Indian Hindu women in England.

Suicide is strictly forbidden in Islam and international studies in Pakistan, Malaysia and Saudi Arabia showed a prevalence of low suicide rates (Al-Khathami, 2001; Murty et al., 2008, Zakiullah et al., 2008). The findings of a review of suicide and overdose in 17 Islamic countries and the UK (Pritchard and Amanullah, 2007) showed that suicide rates were higher for males than females, and higher for 'older' (65+) than a 'younger' age group (15–34). Overdose was considerably higher in 10 Islamic countries than the Western average and eight had overdose rates considerably higher than their suicide rates. The authors suggested that Islamic suicide rates varied widely and the high overdose rates, especially in the Middle East, may be a repository for hiding culturally unacceptable suicides. The prevalence of suicidal ideation has been found to be common among Syrian refugees (Lama et al., 2016). The rate of schizophrenia in Muslims is similar to that of non-Muslims (Al-Issa, 2000). In the UK, the findings from a study (Rehman and Owen, 2013) showed that Pakistanis/Bangladeshis have a relatively low level prevalence of schizophrenia compared to other ethnic groups. Several reports have suggested that consanguinity is more likely among parents of patients with schizophrenia in Middle Eastern countries (Mansour et al., 2010) and that parental consanguinity rates increase the risk for bipolar I disorder in Egypt (Mansour et al., 2009).

In summary, the common mental health problems reported by respondents in England included: anxiety and depression, ADHD (Attention Deficit Hyperactive Disorder) and apparent conduct disorders, substance misuse, alcoholism and gambling, issues regarding identity, relationships and psychosexual problems, domestic violence (both in relation to the perpetration of and the experience of) and religious delusional behaviour (Maynard, 2008). In the US, the reported problems are related to feelings of anxiety and fear of hate crimes, stigmatisation, high rates of post-traumatic stress disorder post-September 11, marital problems, and committing sins like drugs, drinking alcohol and sexual activity (Abu-Ras and Abu-Bader, 2008; Mujahid, 2010).

It is worth pointing out that during the month of fasting for Muslims (Ramadhan), some of the severe psychiatric disorders are more exacerbated. For example, the findings of a study showed that patients with bipolar disorder relapsed into manic episodes during Ramadhan, despite stable lithium levels (Kadri et al., 2000). In contrast, for the significant majority of Muslims, fasting has a positive effect on mental health (Sardarpour Goudarzi and Soltani Zarandi, 2002; Mousavi et al,. 2014). Fasting has shown to be effective on diminishing anxiety and paranoid ideation and augmenting mental health and self-esteem (Kazemi et al., 2006; Javanbakht et al., 2010), and stress is less pronounced in fasting days than ordinary days (Azizi, 2002, 2009).

However, in relation to mental health problems, the epidemiological data reported from most predominantly Muslim countries suffers from lack of adequate reporting facilities and methodology (Al-Issa, 2000). This is more so in the case of suicide as this may not be reported due to fear of self and community stigmatisation. The majority of studies reported are additionally limited by variability in sample types and sizes, and the instruments used. Generally, there is a lack of under-reporting of mental health problems among the diverse communities of Muslims on a global scale.

Stigma of mental health in the Muslim community

The stigma of mental health problems continues to be a major barrier for individuals and families in seeking help. The literature indicates that there is stigma associated with mental health problems in Algeria (Al-Issa, 2000), Dubai (Sulaiman et al., 2001), Jordan (Al-Krenawi et al,. 2000), Oman (Al-Adawi et al., 2002), the UK (Tabassum et al., 2000) and the US (Basit and Hamid, 2010). This discrimination towards mental illness has led to a strong sense of stigmatisation within the Muslim communities (Ciftci et al., 2012). Often, Muslim individuals are stigmatised and families are rejected and isolated for their association with mental health problems, addiction and suicide (Pridmore and Pasha, 2004). In fact, good practice in Islam rejects the notion of stigmatisation of mental health problems. Anas ibn Malik narrates that: A woman, who had a defect in her brain, said: Allah's Messenger (ﷺ) I want to talk to you. He said:

> *Mother of so and so, choose on which side of the road you would like to stand and talk, so that I may fulfil your need. He stood with her on the sidewalk until she spoke to her heart's content.*
>
> (Muslim)

This shows that there is no discrimination or stigma towards those suffering from mental health problems.

The literature distinguishes two types of stigma: label avoidance and public stigma. Label avoidance refers to instances in which individuals choose to not seek help for mental health problems in order to avoid negative labels (Ben-Zeev et al., 2010; Corrigan et al., 2011). Public stigma is the prejudice and discrimination that occurs when members of the community endorse stereotypes about mental health problems. It also is characterised by impeding individuals access to marriage, avenues to employment, educational opportunities, healthcare and housing. Studies have shown that individuals suffering from mental health problems are likely to face discrimination from community members when it comes to issues like marriage proposals, socialisation and business relationships (Ciftci et al., 2012). However, cultural differences also have significant implications with respect to stigma. Families may also keep a member's mental health problems a secret in order to save face, family honour and avoid shame, prejudice and discrimination (Ciftci, 1999; Amer, 2006; Aloud and Rathur, 2009; Marrow and Luhrmann, 2012). In order to avoid psychiatric labels, individuals may choose to not associate themselves with mental health clinics or professionals – avoiding diagnosis by avoiding mental healthcare (Ciftci et al., 2012).

Muslim women may avoid sharing personal distress and seeking help from counsellors due to fear of negative consequences with respect to marital prospects or their current marriages (Ciftci et al., 2012). In a study of Pakistani families in the UK, none of the participants reported that they would consider marriage with a person with mental health problems, only half expressed a willingness to socialise with such a person, and less than a quarter reported they would consider a close relationship (Tabassum et al., 2000). Stigma was the most significant barrier to accessing mental-health services due to the shame of disclosing personal and family issues to outsiders (Youssef and Deane, 2006; Aloud and Rathur, 2009). This kind of public and label avoidance is perhaps the most significant way in which stigma impedes care seeking behaviours.

Conclusion

Muslim religious beliefs have an impact on the mental health of individuals, families and communities, and are considered a way of life for Muslims across different cultures (Eltaiba, 2014). The religious values and beliefs are intricately linked to cultural norms and practices and shape patients' perception of health and illness, health behaviours and utilisation of health services (Rassool, 2016). With the growth of the population of Muslims, both indigenous and settlers, it is incumbent for health and social care institutions to develop a better understanding of the mental health needs and concerns of this community. Misunderstanding the worldview of the patient can lead to communication problems, ethical dilemmas and Eurocentric practices. Stigma remains a perennial problem in the Muslim community and has been unchanging over the past centuries. According to Corrigan (2011), the best practice to erase prejudice and discrimination associated with mental health problems is the need to focus on intervention strategies that are local, with a clear target audience, culturally specific. Islamic institutions and Imams can play a most effective and vital role in the promotion of mental health and the prevention of chronic mental health problems by empowering the Muslim communities to reach out and get professional help. Above all, there is a need to foster communication and trust between Muslim faith leaders and mental health professionals to improve access to culturally appropriate mental health services.

References

Abou-Saleh, M., and Mobayad, M. (2013) Mental Health in Syria, *International Psychiatry*, 10, 3, 58–60.

Abu-Ras, W., and Abu-Bader, S. H. (2008) The impact of the September 11, 2001 Attacks on the well-being of Arab Americans in New York City, *Journal of Muslim Mental Health*, 3, 217–239. http://dx.doi.org/10.1080/15564900802487634.

Abu-Ras, W., and Abu-Bader, S. H. (2009) Risk factors for depression and posttraumatic stress disorder (PTSD): The case of Arab and Muslim Americans post-9/11, *Journal of Immigrant & Refugee Studies*, 7, 4, 393–418.

Ali, S. (2008) *Second and third generation Muslims in Britain: A socially excluded group*. Nuffield College, University of Oxford. www.portmir.org.uk/assets/pdfs/second-and-third-generation-muslims-in-britain-a-socially-excluded-group.pdf (accessed 13 March 2018).

Ally, Y., and Laher S. (2008) South African Muslim faith healers perceptions of mental illness: Understanding, aetiology and treatment, *Journal of Religion and Health*, 47, 1, 45–56. http://dx.doi.org/10.1007/s1094300791332.

Aloud, N., and Rathur, A. (2009) Factors affecting attitudes towards seeking and using formal mental health and psychological services among Arab Muslim populations, *Journal of Muslim Mental Health*, 4, 79–103. http://dx.doi.org/10.1080/15564900802487675.

Al-Adawi, S., Dorvlo, A., Al-Ismaily, S., Al-Ghafry, D., Al-Noobi, B., Al-Salmi, A., Burke, D., Shah, M., Ghassany, H., and Chand, S. (2002) Perception of and attitude toward mental illness in Oman, *International Journal of Social Psychiatry*, 48, 4, 305–317.

Al Busaidi, Z. Q. (2010) The concept of somatisation: A cross-cultural perspective, *Sultan Qaboos University Medical Journal*, 10, 2, 180–186.

Ali, O. M., Milstein, G., and Marzuk, P. M. (2005) The imam's role in meeting the counseling needs of Muslim communities in the United States, *Psychiatric Services*, 56, 2, 202–205.

Al-Khathami, A. (2001) The implementation and evaluation of educational programs for PHC physicians to improve their recognition of mental health problem, in the Eastern Province of Saudi Arabia. *[Dissertation]*, Al Khobar: King Faisal University, Saudi Arabia.

Al-Krenawi, A., Graham, J. R., and Kandah, J. (2000) Gender Utilization of Mental Health Services in Jordan. *Community Mental Health Journal*, 36, 501–511.

Al-Krenawi, A., and Graham J. R. (2000) Culturally sensitive social work practice with Arabs clients in mental health settings, *Health and Social Work*, 25, 9–22.

Al-Issa, I. (1995) The illusion of reality or the reality of illusion. Hallucinations and culture, *British Journal of Psychiatry*, 166, 3, 368–373.

Al-Issa, I. (2000) *Al-Jun ūn: Mental illness in the Islamic World*. Madison, CT: International Universities Press.

Al-Subaie. A., and Alhamad, A. (2000) Psychiatry in Saudi Arabia, in *Al-Jun ūn: Mental Illness in the Islamic World*. Madison, CT: International Universities Press.

Aloud, N. (2004) Factors affecting attitudes toward seeking and using formal mental health and psychological services among Arab-Muslims population. Doctoral dissertation, Graduate School of Ohio State University. https://etd.ohiolink.edu/rws_etd/document/get/osu1078935499/inline (accessed 13 March 2018).

Amer, M. M. (2006) *When multicultural worlds collide: Breaking down barriers to service use*. Paper presented at the annual meeting of American Psychological Association, New Orleans: American Psychological Association.

American Psychiatric Association (2000) *Diagnostic and Statistical Manual of Mental Disorders, Edition IV*. Arlington, VA: American Psychiatric Publication.

American Psychiatric Association. (2013) *Diagnostic and Statistical Manual, Edition V*. Arlington, VA: American Psychiatric Association.

Azizi, F. (2002) Research in Islamic fasting and health, *Annals of Saudi Medicine*, 22, 186–191.

Azizi, F. (2009) Islamic fasting and health, *Annals of Nutrition and Metabolism*, 56, 273–282.

Barkdull, C., Khaja, K., Queiro-Tajalli, I., Swart, A., Cunningham, D., and Dennis, S. (2011) Experiences of Muslims in four Western countries post-9/11, *Journal of Women and Social Work*, 26, 139–153.

Basit, A., and Hamid, M. (2010) Mental health issues of muslim Americans, *The Journal of Islamic Medical Association of North America*, 42, 3, 106–110. http://doi.org/10.5915/42-3-5507.

Ben-Zeev, D., Young, M. A., and Corrigan, P. W. (2010) DSM-V and the stigma of mental illness, *Journal of Mental Health*, 19, 4, 318–327.

Booysen, M., Chikwanha, T. M., Vasco Chikwasha, V., and January, J. (2016) Knowledge and conceptualisation of mental illness among the Muslim population in Harare, Zimbabwe., *Mental Health, Religion & Culture*, 19, 10, 1086–1093. http://dx.doi.org/10.1080/13674676.2017.1318120.

Bulbulia T., and Laher, S. (2013) Perceptions of mental illness among South African Muslim psychiatrist, *South African Journal of Psychiatry*, 19, 2, 52–54.

Carter, D. J., and Rashidi, A. (2003) Theoretical model of psychotherapy: Eastern Asian-Islamic women with mental illness, *Health Care for Women International*, 24, 5, 399–413. http://dx.doi.org/10.1080/07399330390212180.

Ciftci, A. (May, 1999) *Communication in Family*. ARTI Rehabilitation Services Annual Family Conference, Ankara, Turkey.

Ciftci, A., Jones, N., and Corrigan, P. W. (2012) Mental health stigma in the muslim community, *Journal of Muslim Mental Health*, 2, 1. http://hdl.handle.net/2027/spo.10381607.0007.102.

Corrigan, P. W. (2011) Best Practices: Strategic Stigma Change (SSC): Five principles for social marketing campaigns to reduce stigma, *Psychiatric Services*, 62, 8, 824–826.

Corrigan, P. W., Roe, D., and Tsang, H. W. H. (2011) *Challenging the Stigma of Mental Illness. Lessons for Therapists and Advocates*. Chichester: Wiley-Blackwell.

Douki, S., Zineb, S. B., Nacef, F., and Halbreich, U. (2007) Women's mental health in the Muslim world: Cultural, religious, and social issues, *Journal of Affective Disorders*, 102, 177–189.

El-Islam, M. F., and Ahmed, S. A. (1971) Traditional interpretation and treatment of mental illness in an Arabic psychiatric clinics, *Journal of Cross-Cultural Psychology*, 2, 301–307.

El-Islam, M. F. (1982) Arabic cultural psychiatry, *Transcultural Psychiatric Research, Review*, 19, 1, 5–24.

El-Islam, M. F., and Abu Dagga, S. I. (1992) Lay Explanation of symptoms of mental ill health in Kuwait, *International Journal of Social psychiatry*, 38, 150–156.

El-Islam, M. F. (1994) Cultural aspects of morbid fears in Qatari Women, *Social Psychiatry and Psychiatric Epidemiology*, 29, 3, 137–140.

Eltaiba, N. (2014) Counseling with Muslim refugees: Building rapport, *Journal of Social Work Practice*, 28, 397–403. Doi:10.1080/02650533.2013.875523.

Ghubash, R., Daradkeh, T. K., Al-Muzafari, S. M. A., Al-Manssori, M. E., and Abou-Saleh, M. T. (2001) Al-ain community psychiatric survey IV: Socio-cultural changes (traditionality-liberalism) and prevalence of psychiatric disorders, *Social Psychiatry and Psychiatric Epidemiology*, 36, 11, 565–570.

Helman, C (2000) *Culture, Health and Illness: An Introduction for Health Professionals*. London: Hodder Arnold.

Javanbakht, M., Ziaee Seyyed Alireza, H. S., and Rahnama, A. L. (2010) Effect of Ramadan fasting on self-esteem and mental health of students, *Journal of Fundamentals of Mental Health*, 11, 266–273.

Johnsdotter, S., Ingvarsdotter, K., Östman, M., and Carlbom, A. (2011) Koran reading and negotiation with jinn: Strategies to deal with mental ill health among Swedish Somalis, *Mental Health, Religion & Culture*, 14, 8, 741–755.

Kadri, N., Mouchtaq, N., Hakkou, F., and Moussaoui, D. (2000) Relapses in bipolar patients: Changes in social rhythm? *International Journal of Neuropsychopharmacology*, 3, 45–49.

Kazemi, M., Karimi, S., Ansari, A., Negahban, T., Hosseini, S. H., and Vazirinezhad, R. (2006) The effect of Ramadan fasting on psychological health and depression in Sirjan Azad University students, *The Journal of Rafsanjan University of Medical Sciences* (JRUMS), 5, 22–27.

Kira, I. A., Lewandowski, L., Templin, T., Ramaswamy, V., Ozkan, B., and Mohanesh, J. (2010) The effects of perceived discrimination and backlash on Iraqi refugees' mental and physical health, *Journal of Muslim Mental Health*, 5, 59–81.

Lama, S., François, K., Marwan, Z., and Sami, R. (2016) Impact of the Syrian crisis on the hospitalization of Syrians in a psychiatric setting, *Community Mental Health Journal*, 52, 84. Doi:10.1007/s10597-015-9891-3.

Lim, A., Hoek, H. W., and Blom, J. D. (2014) The attribution of psychotic symptoms to jinn in Islamic patients, *Transcultural Psychiatry*, 52, 1, 18–32. Doi10.1177/1363461514543146.

Lipowski, Z. J. (1990) Somatisation and depression, *Psychosomatics*, 31, 13–21.

Mansour, H., Klei, L., Wood, J., Talkowski, M., Chowdari, K., Fathi, W., Eissa, A., Yassin, A,, Salah, H., Tobar, S., El-Boraie, H., Gaafar, H., Elassy, M., Ibrahim, N. E., El-Bahaei, W., Elsayed, M., Shahda, M., El Sheshtawy, E., El-Boraie, O., El-Chennawi, F., Devlin, B., and Nimgaonkar, V. L. (2009) Consanguinity associated with increased risk for bipolar I disorder in Egypt, *American Journal of Medical Genetics Part B: Neuropsychiatric Genetics*, 150B, 6, 879–885.

Mansour, H., Fathi, W., Klei, L., Wood, J., Chowdari, K., Watson, A., . . . Nimgaonkar, V. L. (2010) Consanguinity and increased risk for schizophrenia in Egypt, *Schizophrenia Research*, 120, 1–3, 108–112. http://doi.org/10.1016/j.schres.2010.03.026.

Marrow, J., and Luhrmann, T. M. (2012) The zone of social abandonment in cultural geography: On the street in the United States, inside the family in India, *Culture, Medicine and Psychiatry*, 6, 3, 493–513. Doi: 10.1007/s11013–012–9266-y.

Marwa, K. I. (2016) Psychosocial sequels of Syrian conflict, *Journal of Psychiatry*, 19, 2, 1000355. http://dx.doi.org/ 10.4172/2378–5756.1000355

Maynard, S. (2008) *Muslim Mental Health. A scoping paper on theoretical models, practice and related mental health concerns in Muslim communities.* Stephen Maynard & Associates. www.scribd.com/document/90324305/Muslim-Mental-Health-Stephen-Maynard (accessed 13 March 2018).

Mirza, I., and Jenkins, R. (2004) Risk factors, prevalence and treatment of anxiety and depressive disorders in Pakistan: A systematic review, *British Medical Journal*, 328, 794.

Mousavi, S., Rezaei, M., Amiri Baghni, S., and Seifi, M. (2014) Effect of fasting on mental health in the general population of Kermanshah, Iran, *Journal of Fasting and Health*, 2, 2, 65–70. Doi: 10.22038/jfh.2014.3143

Mujahid, A. M. (2010) *State of Muslim Mental Health.* www.soundvision.com/article/state-of-muslim-mental-health (accessed 13 March 2018)

Murdock, G. P., Wilson, S. F., and Frederick V. (1980) World distribution of theo-ries of illness. *Transcultural Psychiatric Research Review*, 17, 37–64.

Murty, O. P., Cheh, L. B., Bakit, P. A., Hui, F. J., Ibrahim, Z. B., and Jusoh, N. B. (2008) Suicide and ethnicity in Malaysia, *The American Journal of Forensic Medicine and Pathology*, 29, 19–22.

Muslim. Book 030, Number 5751: *The Book Pertaining to the Excellent Qualities of the Holy Prophet (may Peace be upon them) and His Companions (Kitab Al-Fada'il)*, www.iupui.edu/~msaiupui/030.smt.html (accessed 17 March 2018).

Nada, E. (2007) Perceptions of mental health problems in Islam: A textual and experimental analysis. *Thesis (Ph.D.)*, University of Western Australia, http://repository.uwa.edu.au:80/R/-?func=dbin-jump-full&object_id=9033&silo_library=GEN01 (accessed 13 March 2018).

Okasha, A. (1999) Mental Health in the Middle East. An Egyptian Perspective, *Clinical Psychology Review*, 19, 8, 917–933.

Ozer, B., Sirin, S., and Oppedal, B. (2013) *Bahcesehir Study of Syrian Refugee Children in Turkey*. Turkey: Bahcesehir University. www.fhi.no/globalassets/migrering/dokumenter/pdf/bahcesehir-study-report.pdf (accessed 13 March 2018).

Pereira, S., Bhui. K., and Dein, S. (1995) Making sense of possession states: psychopathology and differential diagnosis, *British Journal of Hospital Medicine*, 53, 582–585

Petkari, E. (2015) Explanatory models of mental illness: a qualitative study with Emirati future mental health practitioners, *Mental Health, Religion & Culture*, 18, 9, 738–752.

Pridmore, S., and Pasha, M. I. (2004) Religion and spirituality: Psychiatry and Islam, *Australasian Psychiatry*, 12, 4, 380–385.

Pritchard, C., and Amanullah, S. (2007) An analysis of suicide and undetermined deaths in 17 predominantly Islamic countries contrasted with the UK, *Psychological Medicine*, 37, 3, 421–430. Doi: 10.1017/S0033291706009159.

PTSD Research (2010) *Trauma and PTSD among Civilians in the Middle East*. Vermont: National Center for PTSD. www.ptsd.va.gov/professional/newsletters/research-quarterly/v21n4.pdf (accessed 13 March 2018).

Quosh, C., Liyam Eloul, L., and Ajlani, R. (2013) Mental health of refugees and displaced persons in Syria and surrounding countries: A systematic review. *Intervention*, 11, 3, 276–294.

Rahman, F. (1998) *Health and medicine in the Islamic tradition*. Chicago: ABC International Group, Inc.

Rassool, G. H. (2016) *Islamic Counselling: An Introduction to Theory and Practice*. Hove, East Sussex: Routledge.

Ratanasiripong, P. (2012) Mental health of Muslim nursing students in Thailand, *International Scholarly Research Notices: Nursing*, 2012, 463471, 7. Doi:10.5402/2012/463471.

Rehman, and Owen, D. (2013) *Mental health Survey of Ethnic minorities*. Ethnos Research and Consultancy. www.ethnos.co.uk. www.time-to-change.org.uk/sites/default/files/TTC_Final%20Report_ETHNOS_summary_0.pdf (accessed 13 March 2018).

Sardarpour Goudarzi Sh, Soltani Zarandi, A. (2002) Mental health and fasting in Ramadan, *Journal of Andeesheh va Raftar*, 30, 8, 26–32.

Sheridan, L. P. (2006) Islamophobia pre- and post-September 11th, 2001, *Journal of Interpersonal Violence*, 21, 317–336.

Simons, R. C. (2001) Introduction to Culture-Bound Syndromes. *Psychiatric Times*. www.psychiatrictimes.com/cultural-psychiatry/introduction-culture-bound-syndromes-0 (accessed 13 March 2018).

Simons, R. C., and Hughes, C. C. (1986) *The Culture-Bound Syndromes: Folk Illnesses of Psychiatric and Anthropological Interest*. Boston: D. Reidel Publishing Company.

Sonuga-Barke, E. J. S., and Mistry, M. (2000) The effect of extended family living on the mental health of three generations within two Asian communities, *British Journal of Clinical Psychology*, 39, 129–141.

Sulaiman, S., Bhugra, D., and De Silva, P. (2001) Perceptions of depression in a community sample in Duba, *Transcultural Psychiatry*, 38, 201–218.

Tabassum, R., Macaskill, A., and Ahmad, I. (2000) Attitudes towards mental health in an urban Pakistani community in the United Kingdom, *International Journal of Social Psychiatry*, 46, 3, 170–181.

Thomas, J., Al-Qarni, N., and Furber, S. W. (2014) Conceptualising mental health in the United Arab Emirates: The perspective of traditional healers. *Mental Health, Religion & Culture*, 18, 2, 134–145. http://dx.doi.org/10.1080/13674676.2015.1010196.

Weatherhead, S., and Daiches, A. (2010) Muslim views on mental health and psychotherapy, *Psychology and Psychotherapy: Theory, Research and Practice*, 83, 75–89.

WHO (2010) *International Statistical Classification of Diseases and Related Health Problems 10th Revision.* http://apps.who.int/classifications/icd10/browse/2010/en (accessed 13 March 2018).

Youssef, J. and Deane, F. P. (2006). Factors influencing mental-health help-seeking in Arabic-speaking communities in Sydney, Australia. *Mental Health, Religion and Culture*, 9, 1, 43–66.

Zakiullah, N., Saleem, S., Sadiq, S., Sani, N., Shahpurwala, M., Shamim, A., et al. (2008) Deliberate self-harm: Characteristics of patients presenting to a tertiary care hospital in Karachi, Pakistan, *Crisis: Journal of Crisis Intervention & Suicide*, 29, 32–37.

Chapter 5

Islamic bioethics, law and mental health

Introduction

A branch of philosophy dealing with issues related to morality and moral judgements is known as ethics. Ethics is a broad field and is defined as "the moral principles that govern a person's behaviour or the conducting of an activity" (Oxford Dictionaries). That is, having rules of behaviour based on ideas about what are morally "right" or "wrong" which is similar to many individuals and, in the Islamic context *halal* (acceptable), and *haram* (forbidden). Bioethics, according to the Merriam–Webster dictionary, is a "discipline dealing with the ethical implications of biological research and applications especially in medicine." It is a reflective activity that is concerned with health policy, healthcare and health interventions as solutions to human suffering. The question that arises is whether bioethics should be separable from religious beliefs and values.

According to Ramadan (2008), individuals are free to think about morality or ethical values outside the paradigm of religion. However, in Islam, there is no separation between ethical values and religious constructs. Islamic scholars argue that bioethical deliberation is inseparable from the religion itself, which emphasises the integration of body and mind, metaphysical and spiritual realms and between ethics and jurisprudence (Al-Faruqi, 1982; Daar and Al Khitamy, 2001). Islamic bioethics is intimately linked to the broad ethical teachings of the Qur'an and the tradition of the Prophet Muhammad (ﷺ), and thus to the interpretation of Islamic law (Daar and Al Khitamy, 2001). Ghaly (2013) suggested that Islamic bioethics "is in good health and the twenty-first century witnessed significant break-through in the field of Islamic bioethics" (p. 592). This chapter will explore the Islamic bioethical dimensions and mental health. It will present an introduction to the principles of Islamic bioethics and sources and guiding principles of Islamic law. It will also examine the issues of insanity, confidentiality, therapeutic relationship and suicide. The ethical considerations examined in this chapter will enable healthcare professionals to have a greater awareness and understanding of Islamic ethics related to mental health.

Shari'ah (Islamic law)

In Arabic, Shari'ah means 'the clear, well-trodden path to water' or 'a way.' In the West, the concept of Shari'ah is used interchangeably with Islamic law, but Shari'ah is a much broader term than assumed. Abou El Fadl (2011) argues that

> In the linguistic practices of theologians, ethicists, and jurists, the broad meaning of Shari'ah is the way or path to well-being or goodness, the life source for well-being and thriving existence, and the natural and innate ways and order created by God. Hence, in Islamic literature the term is employed to refer not just to the way-of-life, or what one may call the philosophy and method of life of Muslims alone, but also to any other group of people bonded by a common set of beliefs or conviction.
>
> (p. 315–316)

In its purest form, Islamic law should be referred as *Al-ahkam al-Shari'ah* which refers to "the cumulative body of legal determinations and system of jurisprudential thought of numerous interpretive communities and schools of thought all of which search the Divine Will and its relation to the public good" (Abou El Fadl, 2014, p. xxxii). That is, Islamic laws consist of disciplines, rules and principles concerning human actions for the welfare and public good (the individual, family, neighbours, community, city and nation). In the context of this chapter, *Shari'ah* is referred to the legal system of Islam or Islamic laws. The sources of Shari'ah are from the Qur'an, the Sunnah and fatwas (the rulings of Islamic scholars). For Muslims, all aspects of behaviours and life are governed by the rulings of the Shari'ah. The aims of the Shari'ah are to protect five essentials:

- Protection of religion (*Deen*);
- Maintenance of life (*Nafs*);
- Protection of intellect ('*Aql*);
- Preservation of honour and progeny (*Nasl*);
- Protection of wealth (*Mal*).

According to Al Shatibi (Al-Raysuni, 2005), these five protections are necessities for the establishment of welfare in this world as well as in the world hereafter. In addition, the principle of justice requires that benefits and burdens are fairly distributed, so persons receive that which they deserve and to which they are entitled (Al-Swailem, 2006 2007). Within this framework, Islamic law covers both medicine and medical practices and includes all the aspects of professionalism required to appropriately serve the individual, the family and the community (El-Hazmi, 2002).

Islamic bioethical perspective

Islam is a holistic belief system that takes into account the physical, emotional and spiritual well-being of individuals and societies. The Qur'an and the Sunnah (the aspects of Islamic law based on the Prophet Muhammad's words or acts) offer numerous directives about maintaining health at the community, family and individual levels. Islam has always been in the forefront in dealing with public health issues. Public health, in the Islamic context, is part of bioethics and the focus of Islamic bioethics is not only about the prevention and promotion of health but also guidance, for the believers both lay and professional, in dealing with health and social care issues. Islamic bioethics speaks about the call to virtue, referring to *Ihsan* (striving to perfection) but also to justice, equity and welfare. It is stated that in

> Islamic scholarship, the ethical domain resorts with terms such as virtues (*Akhlaq*), equity (*Istihsan*), the public interest or welfare (*Maslaha*) and the duty to command the right (moral) and forbid the wrong (immoral) (*Al-amr bil ma'ruf wal-naly 'an al munkar*).
>
> (Arda and Rispler-Chaim, 2012, p. 15)

There are a number of principles related to bioethics from an Islamic perspective. One of the principles is man is honoured in the best and most perfect of forms (Qur'an 17:70). To uphold that honour implies the preservation and maintenance of his health, his private affairs and secrets, his right to receive all the information relevant to any medical procedure he will be subjected to, and his right to be the only person entitled to make any decision that concerns his health affairs, so long as that remains within the framework of these values (WHO, 2005).

The second principle is that every human being has the right to live and the maintenance of life. The saving of a life is of paramount importance. Allah says in the Qur'an (Interpretation of the meaning):

> *And whoever saves one – it is as if he had saved mankind entirely.*
>
> (Al-Ma'idah (The Table) 5:32)

This implies that that 'saving a life' goes beyond the physical to include psychological, spiritual and social life-saving (WHO, 2005).

The third principle is based on equity. The Muslims consider justice in its general context to be one of the most obligatory and necessary obligations. Allah commanded it in His saying (Interpretation of the meaning):

> *Indeed, Allah orders justice and good conduct and giving to relatives and forbids immorality and bad conduct and oppression.*
>
> (Ta Ha (Ta Ha) 16:90)

God indicates that equity should be applied in everything and gives a general order to people to practice equity (Qur'an 6:152, 4:58, 49:9 and 4:127).

This means that having justice with Allah

> by worshipping Him Alone without associating any partner; justice in judgements between people: by giving every rightful person his due; justice

between wives and children: by not giving one preference over another; justice in speech: by not testifying falsely, nor saying what is false or a lie; and justice in what is believed: by not believing other than the truth and not lending faith to what is not realistic or what did not occur.

(Al-Jaza'iry, 2001, pp. 311–312)

In relation to healthcare service provision, this means "Equality in the distribution of health resources among society members and in providing them with preventive and therapeutic care, without the slightest discrimination on the basis of gender, race, belief, and political affiliation " (WHO, 2005).

The fourth principle is striving to do well or excel in doing things well (*Ihsan*) in everything. *Ihsan* is one of the most important principles of Islam. It is one of the fundamental values enjoined by God (Qur'an 16:90). The Prophet (﷽), said, "Verily Allah has prescribed perfection (*Ihsan*)) in all things (Muslim)." The concept of *Ihsan* implies "doing everything in an excellent manner and it also means doing the acts of charity and kindness to people in society who are weak, needy and poor" (Rassool, 2016, p. 86)

The fifth principle is "no harm and no causing harm." This principle is the text of a Hadith of the Prophet Muhammad (﷽), "There is not to be any causing of harm nor is there to be any reciprocating of harm" (Ibn Majah). This unambiguous statement means that all forms of harm and of wrongly reciprocating harm are prohibited in Islam. The scholars have broken down 'harm' into two categories. The first category includes acts that only harm others. The second category includes acts that bring some benefit to the individual, but may also cause harm to society in any shape or form. The preceding principles of accountability have been implemented since the early days of Islamic culture. Scholars in Islamic law explain that an individual must be proficient in the particular field in which he is a practitioner. The Prophet (﷽) stated that: "If a person, who practices medicine while he is not known to be medically proficient, causes death or a lesser injury, he is held accountable" (cited in Puteri Nemie et al., 2017, p. 104). However, Islamic principles that apply to bioethical decision-making include: "preservation of life, protection of the species, preservation of mental facilities, preservation of wealth, and the need to maximise the good (beneficence), and minimise harm or evil (non-malfeasance)" (Lovering and Rassool, 2014, p. 43). The resolution of bioethical issues is dealt with by scholars of religious law rather than secular law makers. These scholars of Islamic jurisprudence are called upon to provide rulings on whether a proposed action is acceptable (halal), forbidden (haram), obligatory (fard), discouraged, neutral or recommended.

Insanity

Insanity in the Arabic language is called *Junūn* and the root meaning is 'hidden' or 'invisible.' The meaning infers that insanity is a form of possession from 'invisible' or 'hidden' spirits (*Jinn* or demons). Insanity has been defined by Islamic scholars as "the impairment of the mind, where it prevents action and speech from operating on reason, except rarely" (Majmu'ah min al–Ulama', 1989, cited in Chaleby, 2001 p. 20). In another definition, insanity is described as impairment of the mind that inhibits people from behaving and speaking with reason (Dols, 2007). It is stated in 'al–Mawsoo'ah al–Fiqhiyyah' (Islamqa, 2006) that

> the Islamic jurists are unanimously agreed that insanity is like unconscious-ness and sleep, rather it is more severe in the loss of free will, and it makes whatever he says invalid. For the one who is sleeping, all his verbal state-ments, such as divorce, becoming Muslim, turning apostate, selling, buying, etc., are invalid.

So it is more appropriate that such statements be invalid in the case of insan-ity, because the insane person has no power of reasoning or discernment. They quoted as evidence for this the words of the Prophet (🕌) "The Pen has been raised from three: the sleeper until he awakens, the child until he reaches matu-rity and the insane person until he comes back to his senses."

Islamic law also recognises other mental health problems including sudden perplexity (*dahish*), mental retardation (*atah*) and a lesser mental condition called Safahah (Weiss, 2002; Chaleby, 2004). The *dahish* means "sudden confusion" or "perplexity." It refers to the "Sudden loss of reason as a result of consternation, alarm, or perplexity" (Chaleby, 2004, p. 20). The *atah* is described as "dimin-ished ability of the mind to reason, and is distinguished from insanity or sudden perplexity. The term covers dementia, and mental retardation" (Chaleby, 2004, p. 21). Beside *dahish* and *atah*, Islamic law recognises a mental health condi-tion known as *safahah*. According to Chaleby (2004), a safahah is a person that "behaves in an irresponsible manner, for example squandering his money or spends his money recklessly" (p. 21). This individual my lose his right to have control over his finance and be barred from holding certain kinds of jobs.

Every Muslim is bestowed with legal capacity except those who are minors, those in sleep and the insane. Legal capacity means "the ability of a person to oblige, be obliged and conduct one's affairs by oneself" (Al–Sabouni, 1978). One of the Islamic legal maxims stated that: "Whoever is deprived of legal capacity is exempted from a legal obligation" (Olayiwola, 2016). This is high-lighted in a Hadith of the Prophet (🕌): when he said:

> There are three (persons) whose actions are not recorded: A minor until he reaches puberty, a lunatic until he regains his reason, and a sleeper until he awakes (Ahmad).

That is, three categories of people lacks the capacity to perform religious obli-gations and are exempted from punishment and religious accountability. It is stated that

> like minors, insane persons can only execute acts by themselves only if the acts are entirely beneficial to themselves. For instance, an insane person

may not make a valid Will without supervision of someone. However, they may accept gifts or charity by themselves without the permission of their guardians.

(Mudhakkir, 2016)

Historically, Islamic law protects people who fall within the category legally 'insane.' A guardian is usually appointed in order to protect the wealth and property of such an individual. With regard to the application of criminal law, individuals deemed 'insane' are not held accountable or punishable for a crime but victims of crime are compensated for losses that resulted from the crime. It has been stated that the concept of 'not guilty by reason of insanity' was established at the time of the Prophet (☪).

It was approximately seven centuries later that the first acquittal of an individual based on mental state was recorded in the Western world (Pridmore and Pasha, 2004).

Doctor-patient relationship

The role of the physician within the therapeutic relationship with the patient is that first he operates as a Muslim and then as a doctor. There is an affirmation that "those who claim themselves as Muslim should obey Allah and the Prophet Muhammad (☪) regarding the doctor-patient relationship" (Chamsi-Pasha and Albar, 2016). That is following the dictates of the Qur'an and Sunnah in maintaining essential manners in the development of a positive doctor-patient relationship. It is worth pointing out that the Muslim physician is not the 'healer' but only God is the ultimate healer. Muslim physicians have adopted 'Oath of the Muslim Doctor,' which invokes the name of Allah (The Islamic Code of Medical Ethics, 1982). The Oath of the Muslim Doctor includes an undertaking

> To protect human life in all stages and under all circumstances, doing [one's] utmost to rescue it from death, malady, pain and anxiety. To be, all the way, an instrument of God's mercy, extending medical care to near and far, virtuous and sinner and friend and enemy.
>
> (The Islamic Code of Medical Ethics, 1982)

The development of a therapeutic doctor-patient relationship is significantly influenced by "justice, 'Ihsan' (being good, tolerant, sympathetic, forgiving, polite, cooperative), and, is good treatment of a patient's relatives" (Chamsi-Pasha and Albar, 2016). There are inherent problems with gender issue in the doctor-patient relationship.

Modesty is an important issue for Muslim women, and many female patients may be reluctant to expose their bodies to a nurse or other healthcare professional for a medical examination. Islam requires that Muslims seek treatment from a same gender person whenever it is possible. A summary of the regulations is as follows:

> Priority should be given to the treatment of men by men and women by women. When a sick woman needs to be uncovered (for medical treatment), preference should be given to a qualified female Muslim doctor; if such is not available, the order of preference is then a female non–Muslim doctor, a male Muslim doctor, and lastly, a male non–Muslim doctor. If it is sufficient to be treated by a female doctor, she should not go to a male doctor even if he is a specialist. If a specialist is needed, she should go to a female specialist, but if one is not available, then the female patient may uncover in front of a male specialist. If the female specialist is not qualified to treat the problem and the situation calls for the involvement of a highly skilled, qualified male specialist, then this is permissible. If there is a male specialist who is more highly skilled and more experienced than the female doctor, the female patient should still not go to him unless the situation requires this extra level of experience and skill. Similarly, a man should not be treated by a woman if there is a man who is able to carry out the treatment.
>
> (Sheikh Muhammed Salih Al-Munajjid, n.d.)

In cases of necessity, Islamic scholars agreed that it is permissible for a male doctor to look at the site of illness in a woman when necessary, within the limits set by Islamic laws (*Shari'ah*). This ruling is based on the idea of giving priority to the principle of saving life over the principle of modesty, in cases where there is a conflict between the two (Sheikh Muhammed Salih Al-Munajjid, n.d.). Overall, the patient must be treated in a holistic approach in meeting his physical, psychosocial and spiritual needs.

Confidentiality

Confidentiality in Islam is highly valued. In the Qur'an and Hadith, the maintenance of confidentiality falls within the directive of keeping and guarding a promise. Maintaining confidentiality is honouring a promise between patient and healthcare professional. However, breaking a promise is a big sin and will be asked about on the Day of Judgment. Allah says in the Qur'an (Interpretation of meaning):

> *And fulfill [every] commitment. Indeed, the commitment is ever [that about which one will be] questioned.*
>
> (Al-Isra' (The Night Journey) 17:34)

> *But yes, whoever fulfills his commitment and fears Allah – then indeed, Allah loves those who fear Him.*
>
> (Ali 'Imran (The Family of 'Imran) 3:76)

Breaking a promise, in Islam, is a kind of lying and hypocrisy. The Prophet (ﷺ) said:

> There are four characteristics, whoever has them all is a pure hypocrite, and whoever has one of its characteristics, he has one of the characteristics of hypocrisy, until he gives it up: When he speaks he lies, when he makes a covenant he betrays it, when he makes a promise he breaks it, and when he disputes he resorts to obscene speech.
>
> (Muslim (a))

According to Chaleby (1996 2004), there are a number of rulings in Islamic jurisprudence relating to patient confidentiality. A brief overview is provided and these include:

- According to Shari'ah, human justice cannot force a doctor to reveal information entrusted to him/her by a patient.
- A doctor may not be required to testify against his patient.
- If a doctor testifies that his patient has committed a sin, his testimony will not be accepted as a confession from the patient.
- A doctor cannot be forced by law to disclose confidential matters concerning a patient under any circumstances.
- However, lying into a court in order to preserve the confidentiality of the therapeutic relationship cannot be considered a sin.
- Only the views and the opinions of Muslim psychiatrists are accepted (Pridmore and Pasha, 2004).
- In the case of applying the principle of choosing the lesser of the two evils (one harm should not be avoided by another harm), a doctor must decide whether breaching the confidence will be beneficial to the patient or the community or significant others.

In relation to the last statement, Islamic jurists issued a fatwa allowing a breach of confidentiality in case of the harm of maintaining confidentiality overrides its benefits (International Islamic Fiqh Academy, 1993; Alahmad and Dierickx, 2012). However, there are other circumstances when you intend to keep a promise but cannot because of an emergency, a sin is not deemed to have been committed. It is stated that

> the believer who makes promises to people and breaks his promise may have an excuse or he may not. If he has an excuse then there is no sin on him, but if he does not have an excuse then he is a sinner.
>
> (Islamqa, 2003)

However, the Prophet (ﷺ) has warned us that:

> He who violated the covenant with a Muslim, there is upon him the curse of Allah, of angels and of all people. Neither an obligatory act nor a super-erogatory act would be accepted from him as recompense on the Day of Resurrection.
>
> (Muslim (b))

In certain circumstances the breach of confidentiality to protect other individuals or society as a whole is justifiable in Islam. It has been suggested that the breach of confidentiality is allowed "to ensure a public interest and to prevent a public damage. In all such cases the objectives and priorities are set out by Shari'ah (Islamic law) regarding preserving the faith, human life, reason, descendants, and wealth" (International Islamic Fiqh Academy, 1993). Chamsi-Pasha and Albar (2016) provide examples of the disclose of confidential information which

> include reporting to the assigned authorities probable criminal acts (such as domestic violence or child abuse), serious communicable diseases or circumstances, which pose a threat to others' lives (such as an epileptic patient working as a driver), notification of births and deaths, medical errors, and drug side effects.
>
> (p. 125)

In the case of a patient disclosing his medical condition to his family or guardian, the principles of confidentiality are not applicable.

Informed consent

The principles and components of consent and informed consent that are generally acceptable in Judeo-Christian tradition are also applicable to Muslims. In Islam, informed consent goes beyond the traditional approving or refusing proposed medical interventions and services and includes spousal consent for adult women concerning their reproductive system. Informed consent refers to the exchange of communication between the doctor and the patient and the individual (patient or legal guardian) signing the consent form. For any healthcare medical or surgical interventions, informed consent must be provided by the patient or the legal guardian. In Islam, men are the guardians and providers and their responsibility is to protect, support and maintain their families However, this does not rule out the women's opinion or their wishes. Informed consent is highly supported in Islam. For example, when the patient is mentally not competent to consent, the legal guardian has this responsibility. In fact, effective communication is an essential component of informed consent (Del Pozo and Fins, 2008).

Suicide

Islam places great emphasis on the sanctity of life and the reality of death, and it is categorically opposed to suicide, euthanasia (mercy killing) or rational suicide. About suicide, Allah says (Interpretation of the meaning):

> *And do not kill yourselves [or one another]. Indeed, Allah is to you ever Merciful.*
> (An-Nisā' (The Women) 4:29)

> *Do not throw [yourselves] with your [own] hands into destruction.*
> (Al-Baqarah (The Cow) 2:195)

An Islamic objection to any form of suicide (rational or irrational) is that the motive which prompts individuals to take their own life is contrary to the divine prerogative over human life (Rassool, 2004). According to Siddiqi (2010), "Life is to be protected and promoted as much as possible. It is neither permissible in Islam to kill another human being, nor even to kill one's own self (suicide)." In addition, the Prophetic traditions "explicitly and in unequivocal terms not only proscribe suicide but condemn the perpetrator of such an act to eternal retribution in the form of incessant repetitions of the act and the anguish of the mode of suicide" (Shah and Chandia, 2010). However, a person who commits suicide as a result of a mental health problem like depression or schizophrenia does not have control of his faculties. As for someone who is mentally unstable or insane, Salahi (2004) says:

> We cannot say how God will judge such a person, but we trust to God's justice, because He does not deal unfairly with anyone. We pray for the person concerned, and request God to forgive him. When a man committed suicide during the Prophet's lifetime, the Prophet was distressed. He did not perform the prayer for the deceased (*janazah*), but he ordered his companions to do it. When they did, they prayed for the man and requested God's forgiveness for him. This shows that the Prophet did not exclude the possibility of his being forgiven by God.

From an Islamic perspective, there are sharply delineated rules that inform healthcare professionals what to do in the case of rational suicide or assisted suicide. The principle of beneficence requires positive action in preventing what is bad or harmful, removing what is bad or harmful, and doing or promoting what is good and beneficial (Athar, 1998). From an Islamic perspective, the principle of forbidding what is wrong, in this context suicide and attempted suicide, and enjoining what is good illustrates this.

References

Abou El Fadl, K. (2011) The language of the age: Shari'a and natural justice in the Egyptian revolution, *Harvard International Law Journal*, 52, 311–321.

Abou El Fadl, Khaled (2014) *Reasoning with God: Reclaiming Shari'ah in the Modern Age*. London: Rowman & Littlefield Publishers.

Al Faruqi, I. R. (1982) *Tawhid: Its Implications for Thought and Life*. Kuala Lumpur: International Institute for Islamic Thought.

Ahmad. Narrated by the authors of Sunan and classed as Saheeh by al-Albaani in al-Irwa', No. 297.

Alahmad, G., and Dierickx, K. (2012) What do Islamic institutional fatwas say about medical and research confidentiality and breach of confidentiality? *Developing World Bioethics*, 12, 104–112.

Al-Jaza'iry, Abû Bakr Jâbir (2001) *Minhaj al Muslim: A Book of Creed, Manners, Character, Acts of Worship and Other Deeds, Volume 1*. Riyadh, Saudi Arabia: Darussalam.

Al-Raysuni, A. (2005) *Imam Al Shatibi's Theory of The Higher Objectives And Intents Of Islamic Law*. Herndon, VA: The International Institute of Islamic Thought.

Al-Sabouni, A., Al-Rahman (1978) Mustafaa Al-Siba'ie and Abd Al-Rahman Al-Sabounī (1978) *Al-Madkhal Li-Dirasat Al-Fiqh Al-Islami* 2 at, 24. Al-Maktaba'ah Al-Jadiih, 4th ed.

Al-Swailem, A. (2006) *Bio-ethics from the Islamic point of view*. Bio-ethics and Regulatory Aspects of Bio-medical Workshop, Jeddah, Saudi Arabia.

Al-Swailem, A. (2007) *Nursing and nurses' ethical issues from Islamic perspectives*. Building Bridges to the Future, 2nd International Nursing Conference, Jeddah, Saudi Arabia.

Arda, B., and Rispler–Chaim, V. (2012) *Islam and Bioethics*. Ankara. Proceedings of the 3rd Islamic and Bioethic International Conference, 14–16 2012, Antalya, Turkey. http://kitaplar.ankara.edu.tr/dosyalar/pdf/846.pdf (accessed 17 March 2018).

Athar S. (1998) *Ethical Decision-making in Patient Care: An Islamic Perspective*. Lombard, IL: Islamic Medical Association of North America.

Chaleby K. S. (1996) Issues in forensic psychiatry in Islamic jurisprudence, *The Bulletin of the American Academy of Psychiatry and the Law*, 24, 1, 117–124.

Chaleby, K. S. (2004) *Forensic psychiatry in Islamic Jurisprudence*. 2nd ed. Petaling Jaya: The International Institute of Islamic thought.

Chamsi-Pasha, H., and Albar, M. A. (2016) Doctor-patient relationship: Islamic perspective, *Saudi Medical Journal*, 37, 2, 121–126. http://doi.org/10.15537/smj.2016.2.13602.

Daar, A. S., and Al Khitamy, A. B. (2001) Bioethics for clinicians: 21. Islamic bioethics, *Canadian Medical Association Journal*, 164, 60–63.

Del Pozo, P. R., and Fins, J. J. (2008) Islam and informed consent: Notes from Doha, *Cambridge Quarterly of Healthcare Ethics*, 17, 3, 273–279. http://dx.doi.org/10.1017/S096318010808033X.

Dols, M. W. (2007) Historical perspective: Insanity in Islamic law, *Journal of Muslim Mental Health*, 2, 81–99.

El-Hazmi, M. A. F. (ed) (2002) *Ethics of genetic counseling in Islamic Communities*. Riyadh, KSA: Al-Obeikan Bookstore. (Arabic).

Ghaly, M. (2013) Islamic bioethics in the twenty-first century. *Zygon: Journal of Religion and Science*, 48, 3, 592–599.

Hadith number 32. Cited in Nawawi (Imām Yaḥyá ibn Sharaf al-Nawawī) 40 Hadiths.

Ibn Majah. *Sunan Ibn Majah* Vol. 3, Book of Chapters on Rulings, Hadith 2340.

International Islamic Fiqh Academy (1993) *Resolutions and Recommendations of the Council of the Islamic Fiqh Academy*. International Islamic Fiqh Academy. Decision No. 79 (10/8). www.iifa-aifi.org/?s= (accessed 17 March 2018).

Islamqa (2003) 30861: *What are the situations in which a promise may be broken?* https://islamqa. info/en/30861 (accessed 17 March 2018)

Islamqa (2006) 73412: *Jinn Possession*. https://islamqa.info/en/73412 (accessed 17 March 2018).

Lovering, S. and Rassool, G. H. (2014) Ethical dimensions in caring. In G. Hussein Rassool (Ed.) *Cultural Competence in Caring for Muslim Patients*. Basingstoke, Hampshire: Palgrave Macmillan.

Majmu'ah min al-Ulama', al Mawsu'ah al Fiqhiyyah (1989) Kuwait: Wazarah al – Awqaf wa al-Shu'un al-Islamiyyah, 6, 99–110. Cited in Chaleby, K. S. (2001). *Forensic Psychiatry in Islamic Jurisprudence*. Hemdon: International Institute of Islamic Thought, p. 20.

Mudhakkir, A. (2016) *Legal Capacity (Al-Ahiliyyah) under the Islamic Law (Shari'ah)*. www. linkedin.com/pulse/legal-capacity-al-ahiliyyah-under-islamic-law-shariah-abdul-cife- (accessed 17 March 2018).

Muslim (a) *The Book of Faith. (25)Chapter: The characteristics of the hypocrite*. Sahih Muslim 58: Book 1, Hadith 116. USC-MSA web (English) reference: Book 1, Hadith 111. Kitab al-Iman, Bab 'alamat al-nifaq.

Muslim (b) 15 The Book of Pilgrimage. Sahih Muslim 1370 b.: Book 15, Hadith 532 USC-MSA web (English) reference: Book 7, Hadith 3164.

Olayiwola, S. (2016) Defence mechanism in criminal liability under Islamic law, *International Journal of Innovative Legal & Political Studies*, 4, 4, 19–29.

Pridmore, S. Pasha, M. I. (2004) Religion and spirituality: Psychiatry and Islam, *Australasian Psychiatry*, 12, 380–385.

Puteri Nemie, J. K, Ariff Osman, H. O., and Ramizah, W. M. (2017) Educating future medical professionals with the fundamentals of law and ethics, *International Islamic University of Malaysia (ILUM)*, 16, 2, 101–105. http://iiumedic.net/imjm/v1/download/volume_16_no_2/IMJM-Vol16-No2-101105.pdf (accessed 17 March 2018).

Ramadan, T. (2008) *Radical Reform: Islamic Ethics and Liberation*. Oxford: Oxford University Press.

Rassool, G. H. (2004) Rational suicide: An Islamic perspective, *Journal of Advanced Nursing*, 46, 3281–283.

Rassool, G. H. (2016) *Islamic Counselling: An Introduction to Theory and Practice*. Hove, East Sussex: Routledge.

Salahi, A. (2004) *Committing Suicide Is Strictly Forbidden in Islam*. http://www.arabnews.com/node/251387 (accessed 31 May 2018).

Shah, A., and Chandia, M. (2010) The relationship between suicide and Islam: A cross-national study, Journal *of Injury and Violence Research*, 2, 2, 93–97. http://doi.org/10.5249/jivr.v2i2.60

Sheikh Muhammed Salih Al-Munajjid (n.d.) *Guidelines on the issue of: Looking for the purposes of medical treatment*. http://islamqa.info/en/ref/5693 (accessed 17 March 2018).

Siddiqi, M. (2010) *Is euthanasia allowed in Islam?* www.islamopediaonline.org/fatwa/dr-siddiqi-fiqh-council-north-america-responds-query-euthanasia-allowed-islam (accessed 17 March 2018).

The Islamic code of medical ethics. (1982) *World Medical Journal*, 29, 5, 78–80.

Weiss, B. G. (2002) Studies *in Islamic Legal Theory*. Boston: Brill.

WHO (2005) *Islamic code of medical and health ethics*. EM/RC52/7. Regional Committee for the Eastern Mediterranean, World Health Organization, Egypt. http://applications.emro. who.int/docs/EM_RC52_7_en.pdf (accessed 17 March 2018).

Chapter 6

Islamic perspective on spiritual and mental health

Introduction: perspective of mental health and illness

The nosology of mental health from an Islamic perspective is different from the Judeo-Christian's biomedical psychiatric system. It has been suggested that the Islamic model of mental health "leads to the construction of culture-bound symptoms not found in Western diagnostic schemes and succeeds in providing an explanatory model for abnormal conduct and inexplicable physical sensations" (Studer, 2010:V) and not recognised by the DSM-V. The orientalist perception of mental health in other cultures has influenced the idea of "homogenizing the way the world goes mad" (Watters, 2010, p. 2), not recognising the cultural and religious influences on mental health. It is common for Muslims to believe that mental illness is caused by Allah, either as a punishment for sins, deviation from the religion, as trials and tribulations or as a purification process. In addition, evil eye, black magic and *Jinn* possession are also the perceived source of mental health issues in the Islamic health paradigm. Traditionally, it is important to note that supernatural causes of illnesses are widely acknowledged and are considered very real within Islam, but not all mental health problems are associated with supernatural causes. For Muslims, their concerns are not only about physical and psychological health but also spiritual health. All these dimensions of health are interwoven and the treatment of bio-psychological health cannot be devoid of spiritual medicine.

From an Islamic perspective, there is an interwoven fabric of body, mind and soul. In this holistic paradigm, when the *Nafs* (soul) or spiritual soul is sick, the whole body is physically, psychologically and spiritually sick.

This chapter will examine mental health from an Islamic perspective based on the evidence of the Qur'an and Sunnah, the contributions of early Islamic scholars in the understanding of mental health.

Islamic scholars perspective on mental health

During the golden era of Islamic civilisation, spanning the eighth to the fifteenth centuries, Islamic scholars made many great advances in psychology and medicine. This was the period of the Dark Ages in Europe. Psychological therapy (*Al-ilaj al-nafsy*) in Islamic medicine, is defined as the study of mental illness and is equal to psychotherapy, as it deals with curing/treatment of ideas, soul and vegetative mind (Mohamed, 2008). A psychiatric physician was referred to as *Al-tabib Al-ruhani* or *Tabib Al-qalb* (spiritual physician) (Deuraseh and Abu Talib, 2005), and it was the "early Muslim scholars who originated many psychological theories and practices prevalent today" (Haque, 2004a, p. 360). A brief overview of the contributions of Islamic scholars to mental or psychological theories is presented here.

One of the early Islamic philosophers was Ash'ath Bin Qais Al-Kindi (801–866 CE). Al-Kindi wrote extensively, including books and treatises, and those related to psychology are: On Sleep and Dreams, First Philosophy, and the Eradication of Sorrow. Abu-Zaid Al-Balkhi (850–934 CE), the father of cognitive behavioural therapy, first introduced concepts of mental health and mental hygiene in his book: Sustenance for Body and Soul (*Masalih al-Abdan wa al-anfus*). Al-Balkhi suggested that balanced mental health is attributed between physical self (*Nafs*) and spiritual self (*Ruh*) (Khalili et al., 2002). For example, "if the Nafs (psyche) gets sick, the body may also find no joy in life with development of a physical illness" (Deuraseh and Talib, 2005, p. 76). That is the interaction between body, mind and soul in the development of psychosomatic disorders. Al-Balkhi classified psychological disturbances into four categories: fear and anxiety, anger and aggression, sadness and depression, and obsessions. He also classified depression into reactive and endogenous depression (originated within the body).

Muhammad ibn Zakariya al-Razi (865–925 CE), physician, philosopher and scientist, was the director of the first psychiatric ward in the world which was located in Bagdad, Iraq. Al-Razi was among the first in the world to write on mental illness and psychotherapy (Mohamed, 2008). His works include '*El Mansuri*' dan '*Al Tibb al-Ruhani*' which provided descriptions and treatments for mental health problems (Murad and Gordon, 2002). Ali ibn al-'Abbas al-Majusi (died 982–994) – Al-Majusi – is best known for his Complete Book of the Medical Art (*Kitāb Kāmil aṣ-Ṣinā'a aṭ-Ṭibbiyya*) later called The Complete Art of Medicine, Euroscience and Psychology. Al-Majusi was a pioneer in psychophysiology and psychosomatic medicine. He is the first Islamic scholar to discuss in detail such mental disorders as sleeping sickness, memory loss, coma, meningitis, vertigo, epilepsy and hemiplegia (Mohamed, 2008). He found a correlation between patients who were physically and mentally healthy and those who were physically and mentally unhealthy, and concluded that "joy and contentment can bring a better living status to many who would otherwise be sick and miserable due to unnecessary sadness, fear, worry and anxiety" (Al-Majusi, 1293).

Abu-Ali al-Husayn ibn Abdalah Ibn Sina (980–1030 CE) was a Persian polymath who provided descriptions and treatments for: insomnia, mania, epilepsy, depression and sexual dysfunction in his classical work, the Canon of Medicine

(*Al-Qanun-fi-il-Tabb*). He was a pioneer in the field of psychosomatic medicine, linking changes in mental state to changes in the body (Okasa, 2001). Ibn Sina provided psychological explanations of certain somatic illnesses including: hallucinations, insomnia, mania, nightmare, melancholia, dementia, epilepsy, paralysis, stroke and vertigo (Fidanboylu, 2017, p. 4). He identified melancholia (depression) as a type of mood disorder in which the person may become suspicious and develop certain types of phobias. According to Ibn Sina, it is anger that changes melancholia to mania. Ibn Sina also wrote about symptoms and treatment of love sickness (*Ishq*), nightmare, epilepsy and weak memory (Haque, 2004a). Najab ud-din Muhamed (tenth century) provided characteristics of a number of mental health problems including agitated depression, neurosis, periapism and sexual impotence, psychosis and mania (Sayed, 2002). Ibn Al-Ayn Zarbi (d. 1153) wrote a book on healing art '*Al-Kafi fit-Tibb*'. He describes physical and mental illnesses including mental confusion, amnesia, restlessness, lethargy and epilepsy. It has been suggested that "he never referred to influences of evil spirits in his discussions of mental illness and his approach remained objective and free of cultural influences of the time" (Haque, 2004a p. 369).

Abu Hamid Muhammad Al-Ghazali (1058–1111 CE) was a philosopher, Islamic theologian, jurist, cosmologist, psychologist and Sufi mystic. He divided illness into physical and spiritual. He stated that

> spiritual illnesses are far more dangerous than physical, which results from the ignorance and deviation from the all almighty Allah. He determined some of the spiritual illnesses as; self-centeredness, addiction to wealth, fame and status, ignorance, cowardice, cruelty, lust, doubt (waswas), malevolence, calumny, envy, deceit and avarice.
>
> (Fidanboylu, 2017, p. 5)

Najib ad-Din Abu Hamid Muhammad ibn Ali ibn Umar Samarqandi (thirteenth century) in his book "The Book of Causes and Symptoms" (*Kitab al-asbab wa al-'alamat*) classified mental illnesses into nine categories which included 30 medical cases (Elzamzamy and Patel, 2015).

In modern times, Okasa (2001), in his classical paper on 'Egyptian contribution to the concept of mental health,' suggested that there are three concepts of mental illness from an Islamic perspective. The first concept used in the Qur'an to refer to the mad person (insane or psychotic) is the concept of '*Majnoon*.' That is, the insane individual is possessed by *Jinn*. The second concept is characterised when an individual

> is seen as the one who dares to be innovative, original or creative, or attempts to find alternatives to a static and stagnant mode of living. The writings of various Sufis do indeed reveal the occurrence of psychotic symptoms and much mental suffering in their quest for to self-salvation.
>
> (p. 378)

The third concept of mental illness is that there "is disharmony or constriction of consciousness, which non-believers are susceptible to. This concept holds that there is a denaturing of our basic structure and disruption of our harmonious existence by egotism, detachment or alienation" (p. 378).

Ameen (2006) ascribed three Islamic explanations for mental illness: *Jinn* affliction, witches and witchcraft, and the evil eye. Mental health is linked to having a pure or sound heart (*Qalbin Saleem*) in life means to trust in God, friendship and cooperation with others (Alizadeh, 2012). Raiya and Pargament (2010) have suggested that there are seven factors based on Islamic beliefs and values that influence mental health. These include: "Islamic beliefs, Islamic ethical principles and universality, Islamic religious struggles, Islamic religious duty, obligation and exclusivism, Islamic positive religious coping and identification, Punishing Allah reappraisal and Islamic religious conversion" (p. 184).

Qur'an and Hadith

The essence of human nature, from an Islamic perspective, is regarded as the trustee of God (*Khalifah*) on earth. Rassool (2016) stated that "human beings are believed to be innately good and born with an inclination towards goodness, a natural state that has been implanted in every soul by God" (p. 35). Humans are created with intelligence and free will for the purpose of obeying and serving God. Allah says in the Qur'an (Interpretation of the meaning):

> *And I did not create the jinn and mankind except to worship Me.*
> (Sūrat Adh-Dhāriyāt (The Wind that Scatter) 51:56)

As Badawi (2010) stated; "The secret for the honouring of mankind is that only the human being has to integrate and harmonise the various components of his existence by utilising his physical body, intellect and soul." He went on to suggest that the "reason why human beings are dignified is that they have free choice, and the potential for good and evil." Belief in God begins with belief in His existence and is part of human nature. The innate instinct is termed '*fitrah.*' That is, the inborn belief in the unicity of God and a natural state of submission to Allah. Allah says in the Qur'an (Interpretation of the meaning):

> *So direct your face toward the religion, inclining to truth. [Adhere to] the fitrah of Allah upon which He has created [all] people. No change should there be in the creation of Allah. That is the correct religion, but most of the people do not know.*
> (Sūrat Ar-Rūm (The Romans)30:30)

The Prophet Muhammad (ﷺ) said that

> All human beings are born with *fitrah*, the nature (of Islam). It is their parents who make them a Jew, a Christian or a Zoroastrian.
>
> (Muslim)

That is, circumstantial (for example, parental, familial) and other social influences cause man to change and become alienated from his *fitrah* with deviating beliefs and practices. The theological paradigm for linking human beings with God and each other is the covenant (*mithaq*) and this occupies a fundamental dimension in the Muslims creed (*Aqeedah*). The Qur'an emphatically testifies that all the created souls made a covenant to worship and obey God before the creation of the universe.

In Islam, the spirit, body and soul have been accorded equal importance. Muslims have a strong belief that there is a balanced connection between one's mental health/spiritual state and one's overall health. From an Islamic perspective, the self is represented in several forms: the heart (*Qalb*), the soul or spirit (*Ruh*), and the *Nafs*. In addressing issues of mental health, the Qur'an mentions three components that are directly related with mental health. They are *Nafs* (psyche); *Qalb* (heart) and *'Aql* (mind). The spiritual heart (*Qalb*), mentioned in the Qur'an no less than 137 times, is the most important because it is connected to the soul as an integral component. It is also "the seat of intellectual, cognitive and emotional faculties, volition and intention" (Haque, 2004a, p. 48). The Prophet Muhammad (ﷺ) stated that:

> Truly in the body there is a morsel of flesh, which, if it be whole, all the body is whole, and which, if it is diseased, all of [the body] is diseased. Truly, it is the heart.
>
> (Bukhârî (a))

Allah says in the Qur'an (Interpretation of the meaning): "In their hearts is a disease. . . ("*fi qulubihim maradun*)" (Sūrat Al-Baqarah (The Cow) 2:10). Thus, the heart plays "a significant role in human behaviour and experience and it is not merely a physical organ but has a prominent emotional, cognitive and spiritual role" (Rassool, 2000, p. 42). There are three different types of heart: healthy heart, dead heart and sick heart. For an exposition of the characteristics of the three types of heart, see Imam Ibnul Qayyim Al-Jawziyyah (2006).

The *Nafs* (pl. *Anfus* or *Nufus*) lexically means soul, the psyche, the ego, self, life, person, heart or mind (Afifi al-'Akiti, 1997). It has been suggested that the majority of Muslim scholars maintain that the terms *Nafs* and *Ruh* (spirit, soul or breath of life) are interchangeable. However, according to Utz (2011), the main distinction is that the *Nafs* refers to the soul when inside the body, whereas *Ruh* is used when the soul is separated or apart from the body (p. 66). In Islamic terminology, the Nafs is the essence of an individual and the sum of desires, wishes, experiences, tendencies and temperament. There are three main types of the Nafs in the Qur'an: *Nafs al-Ammara Bissu'* (the *Nafs* that urges evil), *Nafs al-Lawwammah* (the *Nafs* that blames) and *Nafs al-Mutma'innah* (the *Nafs* at peace) (Al-Tabari, 1406/1906). Ibn al-Qayyim maintains that "The Nafs is a single entity, although its state may change: from the Nafs al-Ammara, to the Nafs al-Lawwama, to the Nafs al-Mutma'inna, which is the final aim of perfection" (p. 308). All psychological phenomena, according to Islamic tradition, originate in the *Nafs*. The *Nafs*, according to Karzoon (1997) is

> something internal in the entity of a human whose exact nature is not perceived. It is ready to accept direction towards good or evil. It combines together a number of human attributes and characteristics that have a clear effect on human behaviour.
>
> (p. 16)

'Aql is the Arabic word for intellect or the rational faculty of the soul or mind. The Arabic dictionary *Al-Qamus al-Muhit* (Arabic Language Academy, 1960) defines reason ('Aql) as "knowledge, that is, of the qualities of good and ill, perfection and imperfection, the ability to recognise the best of goods and the most evil of evils, or matters in general." As Nasr (1979) stated:

> It is that faculty which binds man to God, to his Origin. By virtue of being endowed with al-'aql, man becomes man and shares in the attribute of knowledge, al-'ilm, which ultimately belongs to God alone. The possession of *al-'aql* is of such a positive nature that the Holy Quran refers over and over again to the central role of al-'aql and of intellection (*ta'aqqul or tafaqquh*) in man's religious life and in his salvation.
>
> (p. 1)

Many scholars have suggested that a well-functioning mind enables people to distinguish what is right and wrong and not to approach forbidden things. Intellect is thus an ability to constrain the *Nafs* and prevent it from following the lower desires and deviant behaviours.

The Islamic belief, as a fundamental aspect of the religion, is that Allah is the ultimate arbiter of health and illness. Allah says in the Qur'an (Interpretation of the meaning):

> *And if Allah should touch you with adversity, there is no remover of it except Him. And if He touches you with good – then He is over all things competent.*
>
> (Sūrat Al-An 'am (Cattle) 6:17)

One should never despair of the Mercy of Allah because of ill health, trials and tribulations and committing a grave major sin. Allah ordered the believers to never give up hope, nor to ever discontinue trusting in Him. We must not reject the means and the mercy that Allah has afforded us in all manners whether physical, emotional or spiritual. It is only the disbelieving people who despair of Allah's mercy. Allah says in the Qur'an (Interpretation of the meaning):

> *despair not of relief from Allah. Indeed, no one despairs of relief from Allah except the disbelieving people.*
>
> (Sūrat Yusuf (Joseph) 12:87)

The Qur'an is not only a guidance for all humanity but also a spiritual care and healing for all types of conditions, including physical, psychological, social and spiritual. Allah says in the Qur'an (Interpretation of the meaning):

> *And We send down of the Qur'an that which is healing and mercy for the believers, but it does not increase the wrongdoers except in loss.*
>
> (Sūrat Al Isra' (The Night Journey) 17:82)

As for other forms of treatment, Islam does not discourage the use of treatments available to us through pharmacological, medical and spiritual interventions. Narrated by Abu Huraira, The Prophet (ﷺ) said,

> There is no disease that Allah has created, except that He also has created its treatment.
>
> (Bukhârî (b))

However, Allah has given us a means to cure every disease. Narrated by Usamah ibn Sharik: "I came to the Prophet (ﷺ) and his Companions were sitting as if they had birds on their heads. I saluted and sat down. The desert Arabs then came from here and there. They asked: Apostle of Allah, should we make use of medical treatment?" The Prophet (ﷺ) replied:

> Make use of medical treatment, for Allah has not made a disease without appointing a remedy for it, with the exception of one disease, namely old age.
>
> (Abû Dâwûd (a))

Islam also offers its believers the opportunity to treat ailments with Qur'anic treatment and healing through *Ruqyah*. *Ruqyah* refers to Qur'anic verses (and duahs) that are used to treat various ailments. There are no contradictions in using pharmacological and psychosocial and the spiritual interventions with *Ruqyah*. Sheikh Ibn 'Uthaymeen stated that "There is no contradiction between using permissible physical medicines as prescribed by doctors and using spiritual medicines such as ruqyah and seeking refuge with Allah and other *du'ahs'* that are proven in sound reports, the two may be combined, as the *Prophet* (ﷺ) did. It was established that he used both kinds of treatment, and he said,

> Strive to pursue that which will benefit you and seek refuge with Allah, and do not feel helpless.

And he also said:

> Seek treatment, O slaves of Allah, but do not seek treatment with things which are haram (*forbidden*).
>
> (Fataawa Islamiyyah, 4/465, 466)

Allah says in the Qur'an (Interpretation of the meaning):

And when I am ill, it is He who cures me.

(Sūrat Ash Shu'ara (The Poets) 26:82)

Faith and relationship with God

The Qur'an and Sunnah are the sources of guidance for Muslims and non-Muslims and provides the codes of behaviour and lifestyles. The relationship with God helps to provide meaning to life both during good times and trials and tribulations. Research has identified that religion and religious belief are absolutely central to the way Muslims interpret the cause and development of their mental health problems (Eltaiba, 2007). According to El Azayem and Hedayat-Diba (1994), mental health is perceived not as the absence of psychological abnormalities, but the successful blending of the issues of everyday life with the requirements of Islam. Thus developing a strong, good relationship with God is considered to be the goal of human beings on earth. However, it has been suggested that "the relationship and connection to God can be seen as a source of internal and external conflict" (Muhammad, 2012, p. 19). These conflicts or struggles include the belief that God has deserted them and they become angry; questioning religious beliefs and teaching and the conflict; and interpersonal conflicts with family, friends and institutions in relation to mode of behaviour (Muhammad, 2012). In order to maintain the relationship and connection to God, these struggles or conflicts need to be resolved in order to maintain an optimum state of health. Failure to address these conflicts may lead to anger, loneliness, depression and poor coping strategies to handle other life stressors (Raiya and Pargament, 2010). That means that mental health problems stem from straying away from God and Islamic principles. Muslim clerics also endorsed the religious causes for mental illness, such as spiritual poverty, as being more important more so than did Christian clerics (Youssef and Deane, 2013).

Thus, mental illness stems from doubt or uncertainty about the basic teachings of Islam, as well as a direct result of acting in a manner that is in direct opposition to the teachings of Islam (Farooqi, 2006). This is consistent with the findings that depression is caused by spiritual weakness and an inability to believe in God (Al-Mateen and Afzal, 2004), or to have failed to live in harmony with the universality of God (Ali et al. 2004). Thus, mental health problems may be seen as an opportunity to remedy disconnection from Allah or a lack of faith through regular prayer and a sense of self-responsibility (Youssef and Deane, 2006; Padela et al., 2012). A mental health problem is one method of connection with God and should not be considered as alien, but "rather … an event, a mechanism of the body, that is serving to cleanse, purify, and balance us on the physical, emotional, mental, and spiritual planes" (Rassool, 2000, p. 1479).

Good mental health comes from "the unblemished belief in Allah as the Ultimate Maker and Doer, and hence any deviation from the firm acceptance of Allah's ultimate dominance over the lives of his followers leads to disintegration and disruption of inner harmony" (Sayed, 2003, pp. 449–450). Haque (2004b) indicated that the Qur'an explicitly states that certain virtues will preserve good mental health. These virtues include: acts of worship, enjoin what is good, avoid what is forbidden, do good to others and follow Islamic rules of attire, eating, cleanliness, relationships, good intentions, and a desire to seek knowledge of self and knowledge of God. Adhering to the principles and practice of the Islamic faith would result in better psychological adjustment and mental health. In fact, studying the *Qur'an* and performing the five daily prayers can be seen as a medium for contemplation, a prophylactic against stress and a way of promoting psychological and spiritual maturity (El Azayem and Hedayat-Diba, 1994; El-Islam, 2004).

Prick of a thorn: expiation of sins

Mental health problems are part of human suffering and often regarded as a way of atoning for sins or as trials and tests from Allah (Abu-Ras et al., 2008; Rassool, 2000). Muslims believe an illness is not something to be viewed in the negative sense, but rather as a positive event that purifies the body. So, when any disease befalls a Muslim, it can be expiation for his/her sins (Rassool, 2000). There is a narration from the Prophet Muhammad (ﷺ) stating that:

> No affliction befalls a Muslim, but Allah forgives his wrong actions because of it, even if it to be no more than a thorn.
>
> (Bukhârî (c) and Muslim)

In another version, narrated by Abu Sa'id Al-Khudri and Abu Huraira: The Prophet (ﷺ) said,

> No fatigue, nor disease, nor sorrow, nor sadness, nor hurt, nor distress befalls a Muslim, even if it were the prick he receives from a thorn, but that Allah expiates some of his sins for that.
>
> (Bukhârî (d))

Enduring illness, including mental health problems, will earn the individual Allah's forgiveness for his or her sins. Another Hadith narrated by Jabir ibn Abdullah stated that Allah's Messenger (ﷺ) said,

> On the Day of Resurrection, when people who have suffered affliction are given their reward, those who are healthy will wish their skins had been cut to pieces with scissors when they were in the world.
>
> (Tirmidhi)

Those suffering in life are given abundance rewards in the Hereafter. Some of the Hadiths provide explanations that sickness expiates sins. Of these, some are given below (Fiqh-us-Sunnah):

Abu Hurairah narrates that the Prophet (ﷺ) said:

> When Allah wants to be good to someone, He tries him with some hardship.

Ibn Mas'ud said: "I visited the Messenger of Allah (ﷺ)while he had a fever. I exclaimed: 'O Messenger of Allah! You have a high fever!' He said:

> My fever is as much as two among you [might have].

I asked: 'Is it because you have a double reward?' He replied:

> Yes, that is right. No Muslim is afflicted with any hurt, even if it is no more than the pricking of a thorn, but Allah wipes off his sins because of it and his sins fall away from him as leaves fall from a tree."

Abu Hurairah said: "The Prophet (ﷺ) remarked:

> The example of a believer is like a fresh tender plant; from whichever direction the wind blows, it bends the plant. But when the wind dies down, it straightens up again. (Similarly a believer is tested by afflictions to strengthen his faith and heart, and he remains patient and firm). And an evil person is like a pine tree which remains hard and stiff until Allah breaks it whenever He wills.

Trials and tribulations

Muslims believe that Allah tests us with hardship and also prosperity in order to validate the sincerity of our faith. It is normal that we are going to experience stress during the tests and trials that Allah presents to us in this life. Allah says in the Qur'an (Interpretation of the meaning):

> *And We will surely test you with something of fear and hunger and a loss of wealth and lives and fruits, but give good tidings to the patient, Who, when disaster strikes them, say, 'Indeed we belong to Allah, and indeed to Him we will return.' Those are the ones upon whom are blessings from their Lord and mercy. And it is those who are the [rightly] guided.*
>
> (Sūrat Al-Baqarah (The Cow) 2:155–156)

During trials and tribulations, a Muslim must show endurance, resilience and patient as faith will be tested as identified by the following verse of the Qur'an:

> *We have certainly created man into hardship.*
>
> (Sūrat Al-Balad (The City) 90:4)

So, when any disease befalls a Muslim, it can be expiation for his/her sins. For this reason, many Muslims do not seek help, as they believe illness can and will purify the body (Rassool, 2000). El-Islam (1978) argues that considering trials as a causation of mental health problems is clearly identified within other Muslim cultures where misfortune is considered an examination of the person's patience and tolerance (p. 124). Eltaibi (2007) in her analysis of a perception of a cohort of Jordanian Muslims showed that some of the participants considered "the intensity of their problem to be related to the level of their religiosity. The stronger the connection with Allah, the more a person would be subject to trials. Trials in this sense are considered a chance to get rewarded for the level of endurance" (p. 125). Male and female participants in this study considered their mental health problems as being Allah's will and trials and tribulations. The reward may be greater if suffering is endured with patience and prayer. It is a fact that in time of trials and tribulations our spiritual side (whether we believe in God or not) is awakened and we are likely to utter the word 'God' or seek help from God. According to Hamdan (2011), from an Islamic perspective, "tribulations are not meant to oppress us, but instead to assist us in realising the truth of our existence and our potential for spiritual growth" (p. 194).

Trials and tribulations are part of the process in the purification of the soul. The purification of the soul is some kind of 'self-actualisation' of the soul so as to strive to move closer to become as complete and truthful a servant of Allah, depending on potential. Allah explains that purpose in life in the verse (Interpretation of the meaning):

> *I have only created jinn and men that they may worship Me.*
> (Sūrat Al-Ma'idah (The Table Spread) 51:56)

The purification of the soul goes beyond the ritual acts of worship to become a complete servant of Allah. Sheikh Ibn Al Uthaymeen (2010) categories people into four different levels of their reactions to trials and tribulations:

- The First Level: Discontent (Forbidden) with his Lord, showing anger and may even lead to disbelief. Invoking woe, destruction (striking the cheeks, tearing the clothes and pulling out the hair), and the like and this is forbidden.
- The Second Level: Patience (Obligatory). His faith protects him from discontent.
- The Third Level: Acceptance (Highly preferred). That a person accepts misfortune, so that its presence or absence are the same to him.
- The Fourth Level: Gratitude, and this is the highest level. Thanking Allah for the misfortune which has befallen him. His trials and tribulations are expiations of his sins and his reward being increased.

Predestination (*Qadar*)

One of the pillars of faith is predestination (*Qadar*). *Qadar*, coming from the root *qadara* (evaluate), may be defined as "Allah's predestination of everything for His creation in accordance with His prior knowledge" (Philips, 2010), and the dictates of His wisdom. The strong belief in *Qadar* also suggests positive acceptance of Allah's will and higher levels of optimism with respect to healing (Nabolsi and Carson, 2011). Islam calls upon believers to accept the predestined aspects of life and to rely upon God for guidance, healing, provisions, patience and the ability to bear difficulties. Allah said in the Qur'an (Interpretation of the meaning):

> *Indeed, all things We created with predestination.*
> (Sūrat Al-Qamar (The Moon) 54:49)

In Islamic culture, *Qadar* may be cited to explain mental health problems. True or strong faith is expressed when the believers accept the trials and tribulations with patience and hope. However, *Qadar* cannot be used to "justify mistakes or sins of individuals; for those, the sinners should seek forgiveness from Allah" (Hamdan, 2011, p. 91). It is narrated that 'Abd-Allah ibn 'Amr ibn al-'Aas (May Allah be pleased with him) said: I heard the Messenger of Allah (ﷺ) say:

> Allah wrote down the decrees of creation fifty thousand years before He created the heavens and the earth.
> (Muslim)

In another Hadith, the Prophet (ﷺ) said:

> The first thing that Allah created was the Pen, and He said to it, 'Write!' It said, 'O Lord, what should I write?' He said: 'Write down the decrees of all things until the Hour begins.'
> (Abû Dâwûd (b))

Part of that belief is the acceptance that God does not burden a soul beyond its capacity. Allah said in the Qur'an (Interpretation of the meaning):

> *Allah does not charge a soul except [with that within] its capacity. It will have [the consequence of] what [good] it has gained, and it will bear [the consequence of] what [evil] it has earned.*
> (Sūrat Al-Baqarah (The Cow) 2:286)

It is worth noting Muslims will rarely question God's will as this is contrary to the teaching of Islamic beliefs and practices. As supplication is the weapon of the believer, Muslims are encouraged to ask help with their burdens. Allah said in the Qur'an (Interpretation of the meaning):

> *Our Lord, do not impose blame upon us if we have forgotten or erred. Our Lord, and lay not upon us a burden like that which You laid upon those before us. Our Lord, and burden us not with that which we have no ability to bear. And pardon us; and forgive us; and have mercy upon us. You are our protector, so give us victory over the disbelieving people.*
>
> (Sūrat Al-Baqarah (The Cow) 2:286)

The messenger of Allah (ﷺ) asked God for protection against stress, anxiety and sadness (Mubārakfūrī 1996). Ibn 'Abbas reported: The Prophet (ﷺ) at times of sorrow and grief used to supplicate:

> *La ilaha illa Allah Al-'Azim, Al-'Alim, la ilaha illa Allah, Rabbul 'arshil 'Azim, la ilaha illa Allahu, Rabbus-Samawati wa rabbul ardi wa rabbul 'arshi karim*
>
> There is no god but Allah, the Mighty, the Forbearing, there is no god but Allah, the Lord of the mighty throne, there is no god but Allah, the Lord of the heavens and the earth, and the Lord of the throne of honor.
>
> (Bukhârî and Muslim)

Seeking help from Allah is commendable. However, it has been suggested that the "act of seeking help for psychological distress has been construed by some in the Islamic world as weakness in faith or character, and thus contributes to creating stigma for those in need of help and their families" (Saleh, 2013, p. 9).

Is it a punishment?

Some Muslims perceived mental health problems as a result of lack of faith or committing sins, resulting in punishment by God. Believing illness is a punishment from God for some wrongdoing influences some Muslims to take a passive attitude towards dealing with afflictions (Ali et al. 2009). Allah said in the Qur'an (Interpretation of the meaning):

> *And whatever strikes you of disaster — it is for what your hands have earned; but He pardons much.*
>
> (Sūrat Ash-Shura (The Consultation) 42:30)

According to Ibn Kathir, "whatever disasters happen to you, O mankind," are because of sins that you have committed in the past. "And He pardons much" means, of sins; "He does not punish you for them, rather He forgives you." However, Al-Issa (2000) argues that being affected with a mental health problem is not considered a punishment for individuals who have a strong relationship with Allah.

Conclusions

Given the rapidly growing population of Muslims in Western societies, it is imperative to develop a better understanding of the nature of mental health problems from an Islamic perspective. Muslim religious beliefs have an impact on the mental health of individuals, families and communities. In summary, the notions of mental health problems being predestination, Allah's will, trials and tribulations, punishment and the relationship with God are mentioned frequently by Muslims. These concepts are also part of the belief system and pillar of Islam mentioned in both the Qur'an and Hadiths. The analysis of the Qur'an and Hadiths showed that even individuals who have a strong faith might be tested with an affliction including mental health problems. Through faith, dependence upon God, and reliance on family and community, Muslims believe that many problems can be resolved. From an Islamic perspective, calamities, trials and tribulations are part of the way of life and should not be considered a misfortune. They could be a regarded as a blessing from God and serve as a purpose. The lack of understanding of the interplay between religious influences on health or sickness behaviours can have a significant effect upon delivery of healthcare practices. Misunderstanding the worldview of the patient can lead to ethical dilemmas, problems in communication, wrong diagnosis, labelling and practice problems. From an Islamic perspective, when a person has mental stress, a natural reaction would be to turn to God for help.

References

Abû Dâwûd (a) Sunan Abû Dâwûd. *Book of Medicine (Kitab Al-Tibb)* Book 22, Number 3846.

Abû Dâwûd (b) *Meaning of belief in al-Qadar (the divine will and decree)* 4700; classed as Sahih by al-Albani in *Saheeh Abû Dâwûd*. Cited in Islamqa. Meaning of belief in al-Qadar (the divine will and decree). https://islamqa.info/en/34732 (accessed 17 March 2018).

Abu-Ras,W., and Abu-Bader, S. H. (2008) The impact of the September 11, 2001, attacks on the well-being of Arab Americans in New York City, *Journal of Muslim Mental Health*, 3, 217–239.

Afifi al-'Akiti, M. (1997) *The Meaning of Nafs.* [*Mu'jam, Kassis*], www.abc.se/~m9783/Nafs. html (accessed 18 July 2017).

Al-Issa, I. (2000) *Al-Junun:Mental Illness in the Islamic World Location.* Madison, CT: International Universities Press.

Ali, S.R., Liu,W. M., and Humedian, M. (2004) Islam 101: Understanding the Religion and Therapy Implications, *Professional Psychology: Research and Practice*, 35, 6, 635–642.

Ali, O.,Abu-Ras,W., and Hamid, H. (2009) *Muslim Americans.* Statistics and Services Research Division, Nathan Kline Institute for Psychiatric Research. http://ssrdqst.rfmh.org/cecc/index.php?q=node/25 (accessed 18 July 2017).

Alizadeh, H. (2012) Individual psychology and Islam: An exploration of social interest, *The Journal of Individual Psychology*, 68, 216–224.

Al-Majusi (1293) *Kamil al-Sina'ah al-Tibiyyah.* 2 vols. Cairo: Bulaq, 1, 216–7, 263–66, 274.

Al-Mateen, C. S., and Afzal,A. (2004) The Muslim child, adolescent, and family, *Child Adolescent Psychiatric Clinics of North America*, 13, 183–200.

Al-Tabari (1406/1906) Chapter 12 v. 53, in the *Tafsir of al-Tabari: Jami' al-Bayan fi Tafsir al-Qur'an*. 30 vols. Beirut: Daru'l-Ma'rifah reprint of 1323 H. Bulaq edition.

Ameen, Abu'l-Mundhir Khaleel ibn Ibraaheem (2006) *The Jinn & Human Sickness: Remedies in the Light of the Qur'aan & Sunnah*. Riyadh, Saudi Arabia: Darussalam.

Arabic Language Academy (1960) *Al-Mu'jam al-Wasīṭ*. Cairo: Arabic Language Academy.

Badawi, J. (2010) *Moral Teachings of Islam- Human Nature in Islam*. http://jamalbadawi.org/index.php?option=com_content&view=article&id=82:62-moral-teachings-of-islam-human-nature-in-islam&catid=18:volume-6-moral-teachings-of-islam (accessed 18 July 2017).

Bukhârî (a) Sahih al-Bukhari 5678 : Book 76, Hadith 1. USC-MSA web (English) reference: Vol. 7, Book 71, Hadith 582.

Bukhârî (b) Sahih al-Bukhari.b40 Hadith Nawawi 6. English translation: Hadith 6.

Bukhârî (c) Sahih al-Bukhari.Book of Patients, 7 Hadith 544.

Bukhârî (d) Sahih al-Bukhari. Book of Patients, 7 Hadith 545.

Bukhârî and Muslim. Cited in 9 Prophetic *Du'as for Anxiety & Stress*. http://aboutislam.net/reading-islam/about-muhammad/9-prophetic-duas-anxiety-stress/ (accessed 18 July 2017).

Deuraseh, N., and Talib, M. A. (2005) Mental health in Islamic tradition, *The International Medical Journal*, 4, 76–79.

El Azayem, G. A., and Hedayat-Diba, Z. (1994) The psychological aspects of Islam: Basic principles of Islam and their psychological corollary, *International Journal for the Psychology of Religion*, 4, 41–50.

El-Islam, M. F. (1978) Transcultural aspects of psychiatric patients in Qatar. *Comparartive Medicine East and West*, 6, 1, 33–36.

El-Islam, M. F. (2004) Culture in the clinical practice of psychiatry, *Arab Journal of Psychiatry*, 15, 8–16

Eltaiba, N. (2007) *Perceptions of mental health problems in Islam: A textual and experimental analysis*. Thesis (Ph.D.). University of Western Australia. http://research-repository.uwa.edu.au/en/publications/perceptions-of-mental-health-problems-in-islam-a-textual-and-experimental-analysis(f4c538ab-00ef-4df5-8b50-a523991c796a).html?uwaCustom=thesis (accessed 17 March 2018).

Elzamzamy, K., and Patel, S. (2015) *Muslim Historical Contributions to Psychological Theories and Treatment*. Poster session presented at the seventh annual Muslim Mental Health conference, Dearborn, MI. www.academia.edu/11814393/Muslim_Historical_Contributions_to_Psychological_Theories_and_Treatment (accessed 17 March 2018).

Farooqi, Y. N. (2006) Understanding Islamic perspective of mental health and psychotherapy, *Journal of Psychology in Africa*, 1, 101–111.

Fidanboylu, K. H. (2017) *Muslim Contributions to Mental Disorders and Mental Health Ibn-Sina and Al-Ghazali*. Effat University-Humanities & Social Sciences. www.academia.edu/8908081/Muslim_Contributions_to_Mental_Disorders_and_Mental_Health_Ibn-Sina_and_Al-Ghazali (accessed 17 March 2018).

Fiqh-us-Sunnah, Volume 4: *Sickness, Expiation of Sins*. www.islambasics.com/view.php?bkID=20&chapter=59 (accessed 17 March 2018).

Hamdan, Utz (2011) *Psychology from an Islamic Perspective*. Riyadh: International Islamic Publications House.

Haque, A. (2004a) Psychology from Islamic perspective: Contributions of early Muslim scholars and challenges to contemporary Muslim psychologists, *Journal of Religion and Health*, 43, 357–377.

Haque, A. (2004b) Religion and mental health: The case of American Muslims, *Journal of Religion and Health*, 43, 1, 45–58.

Ibn Kathir. Tafsir Sūrat Ash-Shura (The Consultation) 42:30 www.recitequran.com/tafsir/en.ibn-kathir/42:32 (accessed 17 March 2018).

Imam Ibnul Qayyim Al-Jawziyyah (2006) *Spiritual Disease and Its Cure*. London: Al-Firdous Ltd.

Imam Ibnul Qayyim Al-Jawziyyah. *Madarij as-Salikin fi Manazili Iyyaka Na'budu wa Iyyaka Nasta'in*, Vol. 1, p. 308. Cited in Afifi al-'Akiti, M. (1997) *The Meaning of Nafs*. [*Mu'jam, Kassis*], www.abc.se/~m9783/Nafs.html (accessed 15 July 2017).

Karzoon, A. (1997) *Manhaj al-Islaam fi Tazkiyah al-Nafs*. Jeddah: Daar Noor al-Maktabaat.

Khalili, S., Murken, S., Reich, K. H., Shah, A. A., and Vahabzadeh, A. (2002) Religion and mental health in cultural perspective: Observations and reflections after the first international congress on religion and mental health, Tehran, 16–19 April 200, *The International Journal for the Psychology of Religion*, 12, 217–237.

Mohamed, Wael M. Y. (2008) *History of Neuroscience: Arab and Muslim contributions to modern neuroscience*, International Brain Research Organization History of Neuroscience. http://ibro.info/wp-content/uploads/2012/12/Arab-and-Muslim-Contributions-to-Modern-Neuroscience.pdf (accessed 14 July 2017).

Mubārakfūrī, Ṣafī aRaḥmān (1996) *Ar-Raheeq al-Makhtūm = The Sealed Nectar: Biography of the Noble Prophet*. Riyadh, Saudi Arabia: Maktaba Dar-us- Salam.

Muhammad, H. (2012) *Muslim Mental Health: Considerations for Psychotherapy and Counseling -A Literature Review*. In Partial fulfilment of the requirements for the Degree of Master of Arts in Adlerian Counseling and Psychotherapy, The Faculty of the Adler Graduate School. http://alfredadler.edu/sites/default/files/Hadiyah%20Muhammad%20MP%202012.pdf (accessed 17 March 2018).

Murad. I., and Gordon, H. (2002) Psychiatry and the Palestinian population, *Psychiatric Bulletin*, 26, 28–30.

Muslim. *Book of Destiny (Kitab-ul-Qadr)*, Book 33, Number 6416. www.iium.edu.my/deed/hadith/muslim/033_smt.html (accessed 17 March 2018)

Nabolsi, M. M., and Carson, A. M. (2011) Spirituality, illness, and personal responsibility: The experience of Jordanian Muslim men with coronary artery disease, *Scandinavian Journal of Caring Sciences*, 25, 716–724. http://dx.doi.org/10.1111/j.1471-6712.2011.00882.x.

Nasr, S. H. (1979) Intellect and intuition: Their relationship from the Islamic perspective. *Studies in Comparative Religion*, 13, 1–2, 1–9.

Okasa, A. (2001) Egyptian contribution to the concept of mental health, *Egyptian Mediterranean Health Journal*, 7, 3, 377–380.

Padela, A. I., Killawi, A., Forman, J., DeMonner, S., and Heisler, M. (2012) American Muslim perceptions of healing key agents in healing, and their roles, *Qualitative Health Research*, 22, 846–858. http://dx.doi.org/10.1177/1049732312438969.

Philips, B. (2010) *Qadar (Predestination)* https://islamfuture.wordpress.com/2010/07/26/predestination-qadar/ (accessed 18 July 2017)

Raiya, H. A., and Pargament, K. I. (2010) Religiously integrated psychotherapy with Muslim clients: From research to practice. *Journal of Professional Psychology: Research and Practice*, 41, 181–188. Doi: 0735–7028/a0017988.

Rassool, G. H. (2000) The crescent and Islam: healing, nursing and spiritual dimensions. Some considerations towards an understanding of the Islamic perspectives on caring, *Journal of Advanced Nursing*, 32, 2, 1476–1484.

Rassool, G. H. (2016) *Islamic Counselling: An Introduction to Theory and Practice*. Hove, East Sussex: Routledge.

Saleh, M. L. (2013) *Faith in the System: Muslim-American Attitudes toward seeking Mental Health Services*. A Thesis Presented to the Faculty of California State University, Stanislaus. In Partial Fulfilment of the Requirements for the Degree of Master of Science in Psychology. https://scholarworks.csustan.edu/bitstream/handle/011235813/260/SalehM.spring2013thesis.pdf?sequence (accessed 17 March 2018).

Sayed, M. A. (2002) Cited in Mohamed, Wael M. Y. (2008) *History of Neuroscience: Arab and Muslim contributions to modern neuroscience*. International Brain Research Organization History of Neuroscience. http://ibro.info/wp-content/uploads/2012/12/Arab-and-Muslim-Contributions-to-Modern-Neuroscience.pdf (accessed 17 March 2018).

Sayed, M. A. (2003) Psychotherapy of Arab patients in the West: Uniqueness, empathy and "otherness," *American Journal of Psychotherapy*, 57, 4, 445–459.

Sheikh Ibn Al Uthaymeen, M. S. (2010) *In times of calamity, people divide into four levels*. Transcribed from: *Fatawa Arkan-ul-Islam* | Islamic Verdicts on the Pillars of Islam, Volume 1 Creed and Prayer.https://abdurrahman.org/2010/08/29/in-times-of-calamity-people-divide-into-four-levels/ (accessed 17 March 2018).

Sheikh Ibn 'Uthaymeen, *Fataawa Islamiyyah*, 4/465, 466. Cited in Islamqa. 3839: Are physical medicines better, or ruqyah and spiritual medicine? https://islamqa.info/en/3839 (accessed 17 March 2018).

Studer, G. (2010) *Drowning in Enchanted Waters: The Role of Practiced Islam in Mental Health Nosology and Treatment Seeking Behaviors Demonstrated in Urban Bangladesh*. Master thesis, Ruprecht-Karls-Universität Heidelberg, Deutschland. http://crossasia-repository.ub.uni-heidelberg.de/1394/ (accessed 17 March 2018).

Tirmidhi, 2402. See al-Silsilah al-Saheehah, no. 2206.

Utz, A. (2011) *Psychology from the Islamic Perspective*. Riyadh: International Islamic Publishing House.

Watters, E. (2010) *Crazy Like Us. The Globalization of the American Psyche*. New York: Free Press.

Youssef, J. and Deane, F. P. (2006). Factors influencing mental-health help-seeking in Arabic-speaking communities in Sydney, Australia. *Mental Health, Religion and Culture*, 9, 1, 43–66.

Youssef, J., and Deane, F. P. (2013) Arabic-speaking religious leaders' perceptions of the causes of mental illness and the use of medication for treatment, *Australian and New Zealand Journal of Psychiatry*, 47, 11, 1041–1050. Doi: 10.1177/0004867413499076. Epub 2013 Sep 3.

Part II

Evil eye and Possession Syndrome

Chapter 7

Evil eye and envy in Islam

Introduction

One of the cultural syndromes affecting the Muslim communities is the 'Evil Eye.' The 'Evil Eye' is also known as '*Ayn-al-hasad*' in Arabic, or '*Chashm-e-budd*' in Urdu, '*Buri nazar*' in Hindi, '*Nazar*' in Turkish, "*Cheshme Nazar*" in Persian. Every culture has a concept of the evil eye and the belief is strongest in the Mediterranean region, West Asia, Latin America, East and West Africa, Central America, Central Asia, and Europe However modern secular cultures reject the notion of 'Evil Eye' whereas for the Muslim believers and non-Muslims this phenomenon is real. The 'Evil Eye' is a vindictive look which is believed to be able to cause harm upon another person. Ibn Qayyim al-Jawziyyah (2003) stated that "the origin of the evil eye is liking something, then the evil soul follows it, pursues it and seeks to do harm to it, seeking help to apply its poison by looking at the object." The Scholars of the Standing Committee stated that "The Arabic word al-'ayn refers to when a person harms another with his eye. It starts when the person likes a thing, and then his evil feelings affect it, by means of his repeated looking at the object of his jealousy." Allah commanded His prophet, Muhammad (ﷺ), to seek refuge with Him from the envier, as He said (Interpretation of the meaning):

> *And from the evil of the envier when he envies.*
>
> (Sūrah Falaq (Day break) 113:5)

This means to seek refuge from the evil of every envious person. In modern English, envy and jealousy are used almost interchangeably. To be envious of someone is to be jealous of them. The Qur'an narrates the dangers of being envious and jealous on different occasions in the stories of Adam and Satan, Cain (Qabil) and Abel (Habil), Joseph (Yusuf) and his brothers etc. In a Hadith, Prophet Muhammad (ﷺ) said:

> The influence of an evil eye is a fact; if anything would precede the destiny it would be the influence of an evil eye.
>
> (Muslim (a))

This indicates the speed of the evil eye and conveys that if anything was to overtake the decree of Allah, it would have been the evil eye. The reason for the evil eye is mostly because of envy, jealousy or dislike with evil intentions. It is stated that "the reality of envy is the result of hatred and malice, which is the result of anger" (Fath Al-Haq Al-Mubeen, 219, cited in Shamsi, 2016). According to Qamar (2013), "The belief in the evil eye is a belief in the power of envy and jealousy that can mysteriously cause harm and destruction leading despair and hopelessness in Man" (p. 46). This chapter examines evil eye from an Islamic perspective, including evidence from the Qur'an and Sunnah. The effects, signs and symptoms and issues and problems relating to evil eye and envy will also be examined.

Evil eye: sources and types

According to Islamic tradition, the evil eye is a reality and are derived from two sources: the evil eye from mankind and the evil eye from the *Jinn*. It is mainly the envy and jealousy that stimulate the evil eye to cause harm. The Qur'an illustrates envy and jealousy as evils from humans and Satan. Satan, in Arabic Shaitan (شيطان) means "astray," "distant" or sometimes "devil" that lead people astray from the path of God and brings evils and temptations. There are different types of evil eye (Al 'Ayn) according to the scholars;

- *Al 'Ayn* is defined as the envious eye from someone without any evil intentions.
- *Al Hasad* (envy) is defined as the eye from someone who hates you or dislikes you and would like something removed from you.
- *An Nafs* (ego) is referred as the envious or admiring eye you can put on yourself.
- *An Nathara* is the envious/evil eye that comes from the *Jinn*.

For practicing Muslims, the acceptance or rejection of anything is based on the Qur'an and Sunnah. The evidence for the different types of evil eye is found in these two sources.

Concept of envy in Islamic literature

Envy is a psychological state in which a person shows resentment and wishes for the deprivation of a blessing from another person. In other words, to want for oneself what someone else has or possesses. Al-Ghazālī explains "the two dimensions *Hasad* explicitly, *Hasad* involves two emotions, happy (*al-ḥubb*) and hate (*al-karah*). Happy when someone loses favour and hate when someone gets a grace" (cited in Rusdi, 2017). Envy has both positive and negative connotations in Islamic literature. Envy that is free from malice '*Ghibtah*,' is also referred to the positive desire as stated in an authentic Hadith. As narrated by Abdullah Ibn Masud, the Prophet Muhammad (ﷺ) said:

> There is to be no envy except with regard to two: A man whom Allah has given wealth which he strives to spend righteously, and a man to whom Allah has given the Wisdom (i.e. the Qur'an) and he acts according to it and teaches it to others.
>
> (Bukhari (a))

However, envy also is harmful socially, psychologically and spiritually. There are several causes and motives of envy including enmity, pride, supremacy, fear, love of leadership and authority, and evil nature of the soul (*Nafs*). The characteristics of the envier include (Abu'l-Mundhir Khaleel ibn Ibraaheem Ameen, 2005, p. 263):

- Angry at the decrees of Allah.
- Always complain and rarely thanks Allah to show his gratitude.
- Follows up the mistakes of the one whom he envies, tries to seek out his faults, exposes them and exaggerates about them before others.
- Conceals and ignores or belittles the good qualities and distinguishing characteristics of the person whom he envies.
- Feels with hatred and resentment.
- Criticises the one who he envies, with or without evidence.
- Looks for opportunities and makes the most of any chance to harm the one whom he envies in himself or his wealth.
- Having disease of the heart (spiritually and psychologically).

According to Sheikh Muhammad Ibn Saalih al-Uthaymeen (1998), one of the strong signs that a person is inflicted with the disease of *Hasad* is

> that he always tries to conceal the virtues and goodness of others. He does not like it when others talk about the good that a person has done. He remains silent and pretends like he does not know of the good that the other one has done. A true believer who is free of hasad likes it when good things are said about others and when the good deeds of others are appreciated and spoken about . . . He has no envy in his heart for what Allah has bestowed upon the others and, therefore, he spreads that good news to others.
>
> (p. 707)

Islamic scholars also have commented on the concept of envy from a number of perspectives. "Envy is the first sin committed against Allah in heaven; that is Iblis envying Adam. And it is the first sin committed against Allah on earth; that is the son of Adam envying his brother until he murdered him" (Abu al-Hasan Ali Ibn Muhammad Ibn Habib al-Mawardi, 2011). Imam Al-Ghazali, in his book *Al-Hiyā' 'Ulūm ad-Dīn (The Revival of the Religious Sciences)* writes:

> "Be aware that envy is one of the most dangerous diseases of the hearts.... The fact is envy is dangerous for your deen (religion) because with envy, you hated Allah's predestination and hated his blessings that He divided among his servants, and you hated His justice that He established in His world for a wisdom, so you contested that and objected it, and this is against the true oneness and belief....And the fact that envy is dangerous upon your worldly life is that because you suffer from your envy in this life and you are tortured by it, and you will always be in sorrows every time you see the blessing of Allah on the envied person.

With regard to those who love authority, it is reported that Al-Fuḍayl b'Ayyād (May Allah have mercy on him) said: "There is no one who loves authority (leadership) except that he envies, transgresses, chases the faults of others and dislikes anyone being mentioned in a good light." According to Taqī ad-Dīn Ahmad Ibn Taymiyyah, known as Ibn Taymiyyah (1995: 217), "envy is always accompanied by hatred. This is one of the evils of hasad. First the person is envious of the other person. After some time, this envy develops into hatred." Envy is also a deviant characteristic and is regarded as a "kind of opposition or discontent with what Allah has decreed . . . he is putting his religion into a dangerous and precarious position. He is practically declaring himself a better decision maker than Allah" (Sheikh Muhammad Ibn Saalih al-Uthaymeen, 1998, p. 703).

The following statements are the statements from the *Salaf ("al-Salaf al-Sālih")* or the pious predecessors of the first three generations of Muslims, that is the generations of the Prophet Muhammad (ﷺ) and his companions, concerning envy (Al Qaasim, 2012). Mu'âwiyyah (May Allah be pleased with him), said: "Nothing in the evil attitudes is more just than envy for it kills the envier before it reaches the envied." Ibn Sirên (May Allah be pleased with him), said:

> I have never envied anyone for a worldly matter for if he is from the people of Paradise, so how can I envy him for a worldly matter while it is very mean comparing the Paradise? And if he is from the people of the Hellfire, so how can I envy him for a worldly matter while it will be in the Hellfire?

'Abdullâh ibn Al-Mu'tazz, said: "The envier feels a lot of anger towards sinless persons. He is unwilling to spend from what he does not possess, and seeks what he cannot reach." It was narrated that Mu'âwiyyah ibn Abi Sufyân (May Allah be pleased with him), said to his son: "O my son! Beware of Hasad (destructive envy) for it affects you before it affects your enemy." Sufyân ibn Dinâr said:

I have said to Abi Bishr, tell me of the actions of those who were before us (i.e. Salaf). He said: They were doing little but rewarded greatly. I said: Why so? For the purity and soundness of their hearts, he replied.

It was narrated that 'Awn ibn 'Abdullâh entered upon Al-Fadl ibn Al-Muhalab who was the ruler of city named Wâsit at that time and said: "I would like to give you a precious advice. He said: What is this? Beware of arrogance for it is the first sin with which Allâh the Almighty was disobeyed" and then recited the saying of Allah, the Almighty (Interpretation of the meaning):

And (remember) when We said to the angels: "Prostrate yourselves before Adam." And they prostrated except Iblis (Satan).

(Sūrat Al-Baqarah (The Cow) 2:34)

Evil eye and envy

In Arabic, the word *Al 'Ayn* means the one who put the evil eye on another and a person affected by the evil eye is called '*Al-Ma'yoon,*' whereas the word *Hasad* (envier) is more generic in meaning. Envier is mentioned in a verse of the Qur'an:

And from the evil of the envier when he envies.

(Sūrat Falaq (Day break) 113:5)

The envier, accompanied by resentment, wishes that the person who is blessed be deprived of the goodness which caused their envy in the first place.

However, it has been suggested that the *Al 'Ayn* harms others by his eye when he sees them, whereas the envier harms others in both their presence and absence" (Islamweb.net, 2011). It is possible for one to put evil eye on one's own wealth, children or family without having the awareness of doing so. One does not need to be in the presence of the envy person to cast the evil eye and even a blind person can still direct the evil eye to the person afflict that person. Ibn Qayyim al-Jawziyyah (2003) stated that

one who emits the evil eye is not dependent upon seeing the object of his envy; indeed, he might even be blind and the thing (which incites his envy) might be described to him. And many of them have their effect through a description, without having seen the object of their envy.

(p. 459)

Ibn Qayyim al-Jawziyyah (2003) suggested that the evil eye is

> is an arrow which emanates from the soul of the envious one and the one who emits *Al 'Ayn*; if it strikes him when I unprotected, it will affect him, but if he is on his guard and he I armed, it will not affect him and it might even be returned to the one who cast it in like manner. A person might even afflict himself with the evil eye, or he might afflict someone unintentionally, but rather by his (evil) nature and this is the worst kind of evil eye.
>
> (pp. 449–450)

There are differences in opinion between scholars regarding the relationship of evil eye and envy (jealousy). That is, whether or not the evil eye is restricted only to jealousy but not every jealous person casts the evil eye. It has been suggested that every person from whom *Al 'Ayn* is emitted is envious (*Hasad*), but not every envious person causes *Al 'Ayn* (Ibn Al-Qayyim al-Jawziyyah, 2003). Similarly, the Fatwa of the Scholars of The Permanent Committee for Scholarly Research and Ifta' ('Abdullah ibn Qa'ud, 'Abdullah ibn Ghudayyan, 'Abdul-Razzaq 'Afify and 'Abdul-'Aziz ibn 'Abdullah ibn Baz) stated that "Anyone who casts an evil eye on another is an envier, but not every envier is necessarily a caster of the evil eye" (p. 405).

In contrast, another group of scholars maintained that "Not everyone who gives the evil eye is jealous and not every jealous person gives the evil eye." This statement is supported from a Hadith:

> Whoever among you sees something in himself or in his possessions or in his brother that he likes, let him pray for blessings for it because the evil eye is real.
>
> (Ibn al-Sunni, Al-Haakim)

This Hadith explains that "a person may harm himself or his wealth – and no one feels jealous of himself – but he may harm himself with the evil eye by admiring himself, so it is even more possible that he may harm his wife in the same way" (Sheikh Muhammed Salih Al-Munajjid, 2000). Ibn Qayyim al-Jawziyyah (2003) said: "A person might even afflict himself with the evil eye." (p. 450). In cases of casting an evil eye and envy, they both want to harm others and both have the same potential effects. From a practical perspective, there is no difference between evil eye and envy. Sheikh Muhammad Ibn Saalih al-Uthaymeen (2012) stated that "the origin of the evil eye is from envy, that is because the one who causes the evil eye, and we seek refuge in Allah, has in his heart envy for the servants of Allah and he does not love any good for anyone. If therefore he sees something from a person that pleases him and he is envious then this emotion emanates from him and afflicts the individual he envies, and that is why Allah said, "And from the evil of the envier when he envies." According to Ibn Qayyim al-Jawziyyah (2003), the envier may unintentionally envy others because of his personality or temperament and this is one of the worst traits that a human can possess.

Evidence of evil eye from the Qur'an

Allah says in the Qur'an (Interpretation of the meaning):

> And he said: "O my sons! Do not enter by one gate, but enter by different gates, and I cannot avail you against Allah at all. Verily, the decision rests only with Allah. In Him, I put my trust and let all those that trust, put their trust in Him.'
>
> (Sūrat Yusuf (Joseph) 12:67)

In this verse, Jacob, father of Joseph, ordered his children to enter from different gates rather than all of them entering from one gate. Ibn Kathir (2002) reported that the majority of scholars said that Jacob feared the evil eye for his children, because they were handsome and looked beautiful and graceful. He feared that people might direct the evil eye at them, because the evil eye truly harms, by Allah's decree. Other verses of the Qur'an relating to the evil eye include (Interpretation of the meaning):

> And if an evil suggestion comes to you from Satan (Shaitan). Then seek refuge with Allah.
>
> (Sūrat Al-A'raf (The Elevations) 7:200)

> And say, "My Lord, I seek refuge in You from the incitements of the devils."
>
> (Sūrat Al-Mu'minun (The Believers) 23:97)

> And if there comes to you from Satan an evil suggestion, then seek refuge in Allah.
>
> (Sūrat Fussilat (Explained in Details) 41:36)

Another verse of the Qur'an directly addresses to the Prophet Muhammad (🕌) regarding the evil eye. Allah says in the Qur'an (Interpretation of the meaning):

> And indeed, those who disbelieve would almost make you slip with their eyes when they hear the message.
>
> (Sūrat Al-Qualm (The Pen) 68:51)

According to Ibn Kathir (2003), the disbelievers

> will affect you by looking at you with their eyes (i.e., the evil eye). This means, they are jealous of you due to their hatred of you, and were it not for Allah's protection of you, defending you against them (then their evil eye would harm you).

Evidence of evil eye from the Sunnah

The majority of scholars are of the view that people can indeed be afflicted by the evil eye and the following Hadiths from the Prophet (ﷺ) refer to the presence of the evil eye. Some of the Hadiths include: Abu Sa'eed narrated:
A'isha (May Allah have mercy on her) narrates that Prophet (ﷺ) said:

> Seek refuge with Allah, for the evil eye is real.
>
> (Ibn Majah (a))

The Messenger of Allah (ﷺ) would seek refuge from the *Jinn* and the (evil) eye of humans. (Tirmidhi (a))
The Messenger of Allah (ﷺ) said:

> Most of those who will die from my nation (*Ummah*) after what Allah has decreed will be from the evil eye (*Nazar*).
>
> (Fath al-haqq al Mubeen, As-Sahi, p. 747)

Ibn Abbas narrates that Prophet (ﷺ) said:

> The evil eye is true, and if there is anything that would precedes predestiny, it would be the evil eye and when you are asked to take bath (as a cure) from the influence of an evil eye, you should take bath.
>
> (Muslim (a))

Abu Hurairah narrates that Prophet (ﷺ) said:

> The evil eye is true and He (ﷺ) prohibited tattooing.
>
> (Bukhari (b))

Narrated by Jabir Bin Abdullah, the Prophet (ﷺ) said:

> The Evil Eye can take a person into grave (can cause death), & takes the camel into the cooking pot (meaning death).
>
> (Abu Na'eem)

Narrated by Umm Salamah, that the Prophet (ﷺ) saw in her house a slave girl and in her face was "*As-sa-faa'ah*" upon which the Prophet (ﷺ) said:

> Seek Ruqyah for her, for verily she is afflicted with a look (evil eye).
>
> (Bukhari (c))

The scholars have said "*As-sa-faa'ah*" is the evil eye from *Jinn*.

Evidence of envy (*Hasad*) from the Qur'an

Allah says in the Qur'an (Interpretation of the meaning):

> *And from the evil of the envier when he envies.*
>
> (Sūrat Al-Falaq (Day Break) 113:5)

> *Many of the People of the Scripture wish they could turn you back to disbelief after you have believed, out of envy from themselves (even) after the truth has become clear to them.*
>
> (Sūrat Al-Baqarah (The Cow) 2, p. 109)

> *Or do they envy people for what Allah has given them of His bounty? But we had already given the family of Abraham the Scripture and wisdom and conferred upon them a great kingdom.*
>
> (Sūrat An-Nisā' (the Women) 4:54)

Evidence of envy (*Hasad*) from the Sunnah

The Messenger of Allah (ﷺ) said:

> The disease of the nations who came before you has started to spread among you: jealousy and hatred. This is the 'shaver' (destroyer); I do not say that it shaves hair, but that it shaves (destroys) faith. By the One in Whose Hand is my soul, you will not enter Paradise until you believe, and you will not believe until you love one another. Shall I not tell you of that which will strengthen love between you? Spread (the greeting of) Salam amongst yourselves.
>
> (Tirmidhi (b))

It was narrated that Abu Hurayrah said: The Messenger of Allah (ﷺ) said:

> My Ummah will be stricken with the disease of the other nations. "They said: "What is the disease of the other nations?" He (ﷺ) said: "Insolence, arrogance, accumulation (of wealth), competition in worldly gains, mutual hatred and envy, until there will be wrongdoing and then killing."
>
> (Al-Tabaraani)

It is also narrated in *al-Saheehayn* from Abu Hurayrah that the Prophet (ﷺ) said:

> Beware of suspicion, for suspicion is the falsest of speech. Do not eavesdrop; do not spy on one another; do not envy one another; do not forsake one another; do not hate one another. Be, O slaves of Allah, brothers.
>
> (Bukhari (d) and Muslim (b))

Abu Hurayrah stated that the Prophet (ﷺ) said:

Avoid envy, for envy devours good deeds just as fire devours firewood.

(Abu Dâwûd)

Abu Hurayrah reported that the Messenger of Allah (ﷺ) said:

Do not hate one another and do not envy one another. Let the slaves of Allah be brothers.

(Al-Adab Al-Mufrad)

A'mash reported that the Messenger of Allah (ﷺ) said:

Don't sever relations of kinship, don't bear enmity against one another, don't bear aversion against one another and don't feel envy against the other and live as fellow-brothers as Allah has commanded you.

(Muslim (c))

References

Abdullâh ibn Al-Mu'tazz. www.wathakker.info (2012) Flyers (Al-Hasad (Destructive Envy)). www.wathakker.info/flyers/view/100833/?lang=eng (accessed 17 March 2018).

Abu al-Hasan Ali Ibn Muhammad Ibn Habib al-Mawardi (2011) Kitab Adab al-Dunya w'al-Din (The Ethics of Religion and of this World). https://archive.org/details/kitab_adab_dunya_1107_librivox (accessed 17 March 2018).

Abu Dâwûd. Sunan Abî Dâwûd 4903. English reference: Book 16, Hadith 1522. Arabic reference: Book 16, Hadith 1479.

Abu'l-Mundhir Khaleel ibn Ibraaheem Ameen (2005) *The Jinn and Human Sickness: Remedies in the Light of the Qur'aan and Sunnah*. Riyadh: Darussalam Publications.

Abu Na'eem. *Hillyat Al-Awliya'*. Sheikh Al-Albani said it is Hasan Hadith-Al-Silsilah Al-Saheehah, 1250.

Al-Adab Al-Mufrad 408: Book 22, Hadith 12. : Book 22, Hadith 408. Grade: Sahih (Al-Albani).

Al-Fuḍayl. Cited in *Evils of Those who Love Authority*. Ibn 'Abd Al-Barr, Jāmi' Bayān Al-'Ilm article. 971, www.sayingsofthesalaf.net/ (accessed 17 March 2018).

Al-Qaasim, A. M. (2012) Al-Hasad (Destructive Envy) "Rasâ'il At-Tawbah (Treatises of Repentance from)" 26 Dhu al-Hijjah 1433 (11/11/12), http://en.islamway.net/article/11959/al-hasad-destructive-envy (accessed 17 March 2018).

Al-Tabaraani in *Al-Awsat*, Ibn Abii'l Dunya. Cited in Abu'l-Mundhir Khaleel ibn Ibraaheem Ameen (2005) *The Jinn and Human Sickness: Remedies in the Light of the Qur'aan and Sunnah*. Riyadh: Darussalam Publications.

Awn ibn 'Abdullâh. www.wathakker.info (2012) Flyers (Al-Hasad (Destructive Envy), www.wathakker.info/flyers/view/100833/?lang=eng (accessed 17 March 2018).

Bukhari (a) Sahih al-Bukhari 1409. Book 24, Hadith 13. USC-MSA web (English) reference: Vol. 2, Book 24, Hadith 490.

Bukhari (b) Sahih al-Bukhari 5740; Book. 76; English Vol. 7; Book. 71; Hadith. 636.

Bukhari (c) Sahih al-Bukhari 5739; Book 76, Hadith 54;Vol. 7, Book 71, Hadith 635.

Bukhari (d) Sahih al-Bukhari. Eng.Trans. 1/62/no. 73. Fateh-al-Bari page 177 Vol. 1.

Fath Al-Haq Al-Mubeen, 219. Cited in Shamsi, M. S. (2016) *Lesson no. 66. Nazar (evil eye) The Reality of the Evil Eye (Nazar)*, www.tib-e-nabi-for-you.com/nazar.html (accessed 18 March 2018).

Fath al-haqq al Mubeen, As-Sahi: 747. Cited in Shamsi, M. S. (2016) *Lesson no. 66. Nazar (evil eye) The Reality of the Evil Eye (Nazar)*, www.tib-e-nabi-for-you.com/nazar.html (accessed 18 March 2018).

Ibn Kathir, Ismail ibn Umer. (2003) *Tafsir ibn Kathir*. Translated by Safi ur Rehman Al-Mubarakpuri. Riyadh: Darussalam.

Ibn Majah (a) 3636, 3637; Book 31; English Vol. 4; Book. 31, Hadith. 3507, 3508.

Ibn Qayyim al-Jawziyyah (2003) *Provisions for the Hereafter*. Riyadh, Saudi Arabia: Darussalam. Zaad Al-Ma'aad-4/167.

Ibn Sirên. Cited in Al-Qaasim, A.M. (2012) Al-Hasad (Destructive Envy) "Rasâ'il At-Tawbah (Treatises of Repentance from)"26 Dhu al-Hijjah 1433 (11/11/12). http://en.islamway.net/article/11959/al-hasad-destructive-envy (accessed 17 March 2018).

Ibn al-Sunni. *A'mal al-Yawm wal-Layla*h, p. 168, Al-Haakim, 4/216. Classed as Sahih by al-Albani in *Al-Kalim at-Tayyib*, p. 243.

Ibn Taymiyyah (1995) *Majmu Vol. 10, p. 127. Also see al-Duhami, Al-Hath ala Salamah al-Sadr*. Riyadh, Saudi Arabia: Dar al-Watn, 1416 A. H, pp. 38–39.

Imam Al-Ghazali. *Al-Ihya*. www.islamweb.net (2013) The dangers of envy. www.islamweb.net/en/article/88951/the-dangers-of-envy (accessed 17 March 2018). islamweb.net Fatwa No: 21647. Difference between evil eye and envy Fatwa Date: Muharram 11, 1433 / 6–12–2011 www.islamweb.net/emainpage/index.php?page=showfatwa&Option=FatwaId&Id=21647 (accessed 17 March 2018).

Islamweb.net (2011) Fatwa No: 21647. Difference between evil eye and envy https://islamweb.net/emainpage/index.php?page=showfatwa&Option=FatwaId&lang=E&Id=21647, accessed 3 May 2018.

Mu'âwiyyah ibn Abi Sufyân. www.wathakker.info (2012) Flyers (Al-Hasad (Destructive Envy)), www.wathakker.info/flyers/view/100833/?lang=eng (accessed 17 March 2018).

Muslim (a) Sahih Muslim 2188: Book 39, Hadith 56. USC-MSA web (English) reference: Book 26, Hadith 5427.

Muslim (b) Sahih Muslim 2563 a: Book 45, Hadith 35. USC-MSA web (English) reference\: Book 32, Hadith 6214.

Muslim (c) Sahih Muslim 2563 d: Book 45, Hadith 38USC-MSA web (English) reference: Book 32, Hadith 6217.

Qamar, A. H. (2013) The concept of the 'Evil' and the 'Evil Eye' in Islam and Islamic faith-healing traditions, *Journal of Islamic Thought and Civilization*, 3, 2, 44–53.

Rusdi, A. (2017) *Ḥasad (Envy) in Islamic Psychology and Its Measurement* (accessed 17 March 2018).

Sheikh Muhammed Salih Al-Munajjid (2000) 7190: *Can a man harm his beautiful wife with the "evil eye"?* https://islamqa.info/en/7190 (accessed 17 March 2018).

Sheikh Muhammad Ibn Saalih al-Uthaymeen (1998) *Sharh Riyaadus Saaliheen, An Explanation of 'Riyadh al-Saliheen. From the Words of the Master of the Messengers Abee Zakariyyah Muhyyee Al Deen Yahya Al-Nawawee. Explanation and Completion His Eminence Sheikh Ibn Ul-Uthaymeen*. Detroit, MI: The Qur'an and Sunnah Society, Vol. 4, p. 703.

Sheikh Muhammad Ibn Saalih al-Uthaymeen (2012) *The Difference Between Evil Eye and Envy*. Written by Abu Muadh Taqweem Aslam on December 16, 2012. Posted in Aqeedah

(Creed & Belief), Monotheism – Tawheed. www.salaficentre.com/2012/12/the-difference-between-evil-eye-and-envy-shaikh-ibn-ul-uthaymeen/ (accessed 17 March 2018).

The Permanent Committee for Scholarly Research and Iftaa. (Abdullah ibn Qa'ud, 'Abdullah ibn Ghudayyan,' Abdul-Razzaq 'Afify and' Abdul-'Aziz ibn 'Abdullah ibn Baz). *Reality of the evil eye and envy and their treatment*. Permanent Committee, Fatwa no. 6387, www.alifta.net/ (accessed 17 March 2018).

The Scholars of the Standing Committee. Cited in Islamqa20954: *The Evil Eye and Protection Against it*. https://islamqa.info/en/20954 (accessed 17 March 2018).

Tirmidhi (a) *Jami' at-Tirmidhi* Vol. 4, Book of Medicine, 26. Hadith 2058.

Tirmidhi (b) *Jami' at-Tirmidhi*. Number 35 Hadith 2510.www.wathakker.info (2012) Flyers (Al-Hasad (Destructive Envy)), www.wathakker.info/flyers/view/100833/?lang=eng (accessed 17 March 2018).

Chapter 8

Evil eye
Diagnosis, symptoms and protections

Introduction

The aims of this chapter are to examine diagnosis and self-diagnosis of evil eye, recognising the effect of evil eye through signs and symptoms, and the various protections that need to be taken in the prevention of evil eye based on the evidence from the Qur'an and Sunnah. In addition, the non-Islamic methods of protection will be presented.

Diagnosing the evil eye

Evil eye can be recognised in two ways. They are signs and symptoms that the patient will express or show and through incantation (*Ruqyah*) as prescribed in Islam. Those who deal with *Ruqyah* (incantation) have mentioned some of the symptoms from which it may be known whether a person has been affected by the evil eye. They are not definitive symptoms and may vary from individual to individual. They may be sudden and unexpected changes in emotion and behaviour and affect part of the body or the whole body. The Hadith from Sahl ibn Haneef provides an excellent example of how evil eye affected the whole body.

Sahl ibn Haneef narrated that the Prophet (ﷺ), came out and travelled with him towards Makkah, until they were in the mountain pass of al-Kharar in al-Jahfah. There Sahl ibn Haneef did *ghusl* (bathed), and he was a handsome white-skinned man with beautiful skin. 'Amir ibn Rabee'ah, one of Banu 'Adiyy ibn K'ab looked at him whilst he was doing ghusl and said: "I have never seen such beautiful skin as this, not even the skin of a virgin," and Sahl fell to the ground. They went to the Messenger of Allah (ﷺ) and said, "O Messenger of Allah, can you do anything for Sahl, because by Allah he cannot raise his head." He said, "Do you accuse anyone with regard to him?" They said, "'Amir ibn Rabee'ah looked at him." So the Messenger of Allah (ﷺ), called 'Amir and rebuked him strongly. He said, "Why would one of you kill his brother? If you see something that you like, then pray for blessing for him." Then he said to him, "Wash yourself for him." So he washed his face, hands, forearms, knees and the sides of his feet, and inside his izaar (lower garment) in the vessel. Then that water was poured over him, and a man poured it over his head and back from behind. He did that to him, then Sahl got up and joined the people and there was nothing wrong with him" (Ahmad, Malik, Al-Nasai and Ibn Hibban).

Ali (2013) suggested that some symptoms which might appear while reciting this *Ruqyah* are:

- Excruciating pain in the eye.
- Water flowing from the eyes.
- Strange itchiness in the body.
- Heat emitting from the backside or waist.
- Feeling heavy in the head or headache.
- Stomachache or pain in other parts of the body.

If any symptoms occur during the recitation of this *Ruqyah*, or if any disturbance occurs which wasn't there before the start of the *Ruqyah*, then it is ensured that the person is touched by the evil eye.

Recognising the effect of evil eye through symptoms

There are differences in the signs and symptoms expressed by those affected by evil eye. As for the symptoms of being affected by the evil eye, Sheikh 'Abd al-'Azeez al-Sadhan (May Allah preserve him) (2009) said:

> If it is not a real sickness, then the symptoms may take the following forms: Headaches that move from one part of the head to another; yellow pallor in the face; sweating and urinating a great deal; weak appetite; tingling, heat or cold in the limbs; palpitations in the heart; pain in the lower back and shoulders; sadness and anxiety; sleeplessness at night; strong reactions due to abnormal fears; a lot of burping, yawning and sighing; withdrawal and love of solitude; apathy and laziness; a tendency to sleep; health problems with no known medical cause.

These signs or some of them may be present according to the strength of the evil eye or the number of people who put the evil eye on others. Sheikh Abdullah bin Abdulrahman Al-Jibrin (May Allah Protect Him) says under the title "The signs shown by the one affected by an evil eye," that:

> The evil eye affliction has clear signs and ymptoms. They appear if the person or the wealth has distinctive characteristics than others and which was suddenly changed by a disease, affliction, or a traffic accident, for instance. The victim of the evil eye may be afflicted in his sight if it is a strong one, or in his wealth which could be lost or destroyed. The evil eye can also affect his fancy car, huge palace, beautiful wife, his numerous children, and

similar things. Suddenly he faces death, ruin, destruction, and loss. When he becomes ill and goes to hospitals physicians conduct tests and experiments, but fails to find anything wrong with him. He suffers from various pains without being able to tell the cause of it. Then after being treated with incantation (Ruqya) for the reason of evil eye affliction, he is cured from his ailment, Allah Willing. It is often said (He is affected with an evil eye which was gone after being treated by the people who use incantation).

A list of the physical, psychological, social and spiritual signs and symptoms is presented in Table 8.1.

Other symptoms include: constant burping without eating, symptoms increase when reading or listening to the Qur'an, hot and cold flushes for no reason, allergic reactions, hair loss, darkening under the eyes, children crying constantly for no reason. Evil eye can often be combined with other problems like possession or black magic.

According to Sheikh Khalid Al-Hibshi, some of the effects of evil eye are summarised in Table 8.2.

Protection from evil eye

The Muslim has to protect himself against evil eye by having strong faith in Allah and by putting his trust in Him, seeking refuge in Allah and seeking the blessings of Allah. Sheikh Muhammad Ibn Saalih al-Uthaymeen (2003) suggested that

> There is nothing wrong with taking precautions against the evil eye before it happens, and this does not contradict the idea of *tawakkul* (putting one's trust in Allah). In fact this is *tawakkul*, because *tawakkul* means putting one's trust in Allah whilst also implementing the means that have been permitted or enjoined.

Hence, seeking blessings from Allah is an effective approach to protect from evil eye. Prophet Muhammad (ﷺ) has warned us about the reality and influence of the evil eye. Abu Huraira reported Allah's Messenger (ﷺ) as saying:

> The effect of an evil eye is a fact.
>
> (Bukhari and Muslim)

According to Imam Al Quturbi, those who like something must pray for blessing because it will protect against any potential harm. It is even possible to harm yourself, your wealth or a loved one. It is recommended to say:

> *Allahumma baarik feehu, feeha or feehi* (O Allah, bless him, her or it) or the like; or *Allahumma baarik 'alayhi* (O Allah, bless it).

Table 8.1 Signs and symptoms of evil eye

Physical	Psychological	Social	Spiritual
▪ Paleness of the face.	▪ Poor interpersonal relationship.	▪ Loss of one's trade and wealth.	▪ Lack of worship.
▪ Chest congestion.	▪ Hatred of one's family and	▪ Loss of one's job.	▪ Low humility.
▪ Moving headache which increases during incantation.	relatives, wife or husband.	▪ Withdrawal from social contact.	▪ Weak Character.
▪ Feeling of extreme heat.	▪ Inability to concentrate.	▪ Fear of meeting people.	▪ Loss of integrity.
▪ Sweating, especially in the area of the back.	▪ Nervousness.		▪ Weakened faith.
▪ Numbness in arms and legs.	▪ Anxiety.		
▪ Involuntary movements and limbs-shaking.	▪ Depression.		
▪ Heart palpitation.	▪ Dissociative behaviour.		
▪ Tense muscles.	▪ Homicidal impulses.		
▪ General weakness.	▪ Suicidal impulses.		
▪ Cold limbs in general.	▪ Confusion.		
▪ Continuous abnormal yawning, especially during worship and reciting of the Qur'an.	▪ Feelings of futility.		
▪ Crying or tears dropping for no obvious reason.	▪ Hallucinations.		
▪ Constant yawning and dropping of tears as a result of incantation if one is affected with evil eye or envy-common among afflicted women.	▪ Hysterical.		
▪ Bruises.	▪ Feeling of shame.		
	▪ Gut feelings due to having sinned.		
	▪ Feeling of religious unworthiness.		
	▪ Feelings of inadequacy.		
	▪ Obsessive-compulsive symptoms.		
	▪ Hypochondrias.		
	▪ Delusion.		
	▪ Withdrawal.		

Table 8.2 Sheikh Khalid Al-Hibshi's effects of evil eye

Effects on	Potential problems
Religion	Iman (belief), worship, humility, character, integrity etc.
Cognition	Intelligence, memory, concentration, focus etc.
Values	Morality, modesty, truthfulness etc.
Marital and family life	Happiness, pregnancy, childbirth, miscarriages, raising and loving children, marital discord etc.
Physical	Health, hair, face, skin colour, longevity, age relative to appearance etc.
Economic	Livelihood, wealth, income, provisions, livestock, plants, trees and fruits etc.
Inanimate objects	Cars, all kinds of devices, gold, women's cosmetic application or products.

Source: Adapted from Sheikh Khalid Al-Hibshi. Cited in Alruqya Healing Centre, The concept of the evil eye (ayn). http://ruqyainlondon.com/article/evil-eye-and-envy-ayn (accessed 18 March 2018).

MashaAllah is generally used when expressing thanks, gratitude or joy, praising, or looking at anyone or anything with excitement. The word *Ma sha'Allah* means "God has willed it." However, the expression *Ma sha'Allah* combined with *laa quwwata illa Billaah* ("There is no power but with Allah") is used as protection against jealousy, envy and the evil eye. This statement is taken as evidence for the following verse in Surah al-Kahf and a Hadith. Allah says (Interpretation of the meaning):

> *And why did you, when you entered your garden, not say, 'What Allah willed (has occurred); there is no power except in Allah?'*
> (Sūrat Al-Kahf (The Cave 18:39)

However, it is argued that this verse has nothing to do with *Hasad* (envy); in fact, Allah destroyed his garden because of his *kufr* and transgression (Sheikh Muhammed Salih Al-Munajjid, 2000). There is a different opinion about this from The Permanent Committee for Scholarly Research and Ifta' (see Chapter 18, p. 212).

Evidence for using the same expression is also taken from the following Hadith stating that the Messenger of Allah (peace and blessings of Allah be upon him) said, "Whoever sees something that he likes, and says, '*Masha Allaah laa quwwata illa Billaah*,' the evil eye will not affect him." This Hadith has been acknowledged as being very weak (*da'eef jiddan*) and thus rejected.

Sheikh Muhammad Ibn Saalih al-Uthaymeen (a) provides the following recommendations:

If a person sees that which amazes (pleases) him, pertaining to his wealth, then he should say:

Masha Allah Laa Quwwata illa billah,

This is if he sees something amazing (pleasing) with his wealth. If he sees it in other than himself then he should say

Barakallahu Alaihi (May Allah bless it for him)

or a statement similar to it. And if he sees something that amazes (pleases) him from the matters of the Dunya (world) he should say:

Labbaik, Innal Aish, Aishul Aakhirah, as the Prophet (ﷺ) used to say.

So he says *Labbaik* meaning an answer to you then he said verily the (real) life is the life of the hereafter. He makes it firm within himself at the same instance that the world (dunya) and whatever is within it does not remain and there is not any life in it but verily the real life is the life of the hereafter. It is reported that the Prophet (ﷺ) used to seek refuge for al-Hasan and al-Husayn and say:

U'eedhukuma bi kalimat Allah al-tammati min kulli shaytanin wa hammah wa min kulli 'aynin lammah (I seek refuge for you both in the perfect words of Allah, from every devil and every poisonous reptile, and from every evil eye).

And he would say: "'Thus Ibrahim used to seek refuge with Allah for Isma'il and Ishaq,' or he said: 'for Isma'il and Ya'qub'" (Ibn Majah (a)).

There are many supplications that be made for the protection against evil eye. These include (Islamqa (a)):

- I seek refuge in the perfect words of Allah from the evil of that which He has created (*A'oodhu bi kalimat-illah il-tammati min sharri ma khalaqa*).
- I seek refuge in the perfect words of Allah from His wrath and punishment, from the evil of His slaves and from the evil promptings of the devils and from their presence (*A'oodhu bi kalimat-illah il-tammati min ghadabihi wa 'iqabihi, wa min sharri 'ibadihi wa min hamazat al-shayateeni wa an yahduroon*).

And one may recite the words of Allah:

- Allah is sufficient for me. None has the right to be worshipped but He in Him I put my trust and He is the Lord of the Mighty Throne (*Hasbi Allahu la ilaha illa huwa, 'alayhi tawakkaltu wa huwa Rabb ul-'arsh il-'azeem*) (At Tawbah (Repentance) 9:129 – Interpretation of the meaning).

Non-Islamic protection from evil eye

Some misguided Muslims sometimes used non-Islamic ways for the protection of evil eye. This may be due to mistaken cultural beliefs for religious beliefs and acculturations. These include the use of amulets (*Ta'wiz*), talismans, wearing Qur'anic verses, touching wood, beads, using salt, 'Hands of Fatima,' and many other rituals. The use of talismans, amulets or other protective objects is not common in the majority of Muslim world (Pew Research Center, 2012). The use of these so-called 'protective objects' varies with different Muslim communities. The use of talismans is most widespread in Pakistan (41%) and Albania (39%), while in other countries fewer than 3-in-10 Muslims say they wear talismans or precious stones for protection (Pew Research Center, 2012). Furthermore, the findings of the survey showed that although using objects specifically to ward off the evil eye is somewhat more common, only in Azerbaijan (74%) and Kazakhstan (54%) do more than half the Muslims surveyed say they rely on objects for this purpose (Pew Research Center, 2012).

A Ta'wiz (Urdu), Muska (Turkish), Ta'wīdh (Arabic) is an amulet or locket usually containing verses from the Qur'an or other prayers and symbols. Some Muslims also hang amulets all over their houses, shops, bodies, cars and even on animals and trees. People using *Ta'wiz* believe that it has powers to protect and cure against evil, harm and destruction diseases, sufferings and misfortunes. It is reported that there are three kinds of amulets available in the market. The types include "ones with Qur'anic verses written on them, others with numerical charts and those with the names of angels and devils. These amulets are normally written by several unusual substances to make them appear more powerful and authentic, such as *Zamzam* water, saffron, blood, ink, and even urine" (www.masjidma.com, 2011). The use of salt is also common to protect from evil eye. The salt is clenched and then circled around the face/body and then throwing it in the fire or outside the house. Among the Arabs, a type of amulet (*Tamimah*) is used and consists of a string of shells or beads that they used to put around their children's necks, believing that it would protect them from the evil eye.

Peganum harmala, commonly known as 'Esphand' in Persian, 'Spilani' in Pashto or Syrian rue and other names is used to fight against the evil eye. In Turkey, dried capsules from this plant are strung and hung in homes or vehicles to protect against evil eye. In Iran and Afghanistan, and some countries in the Middle East (Syria, Iraq, Saudi Arabia and Jordan), the dried capsules mixed with other ingredients are placed onto red hot charcoal which make a popping sound. The smoke that comes from the burning seeds must be circled around one's head and home. The smoke and the popping sound are said to take away the evil eye. Charm amulets to ward off evil typically take the form of the human eye, and are usually brilliant blue. The Turkish Evil Eye charm (*Nazar Boncugu*) is a ceramic charm to be worn as a necklace or pendants also on the arm, neck or waist, or simply to hang outside homes and as a car keychain. Turkish airlines even painted them on their aeroplanes. Eye-in-hand pendants or the *Hamsa* (Arabic: Khamsah meaning five but also the five fingers of the hand) is also known as the 'Hand of Fatima' after the daughter of the Prophet Muhammad (🕌). It is described as a palm-shaped amulet that is popular in the Maghreb region of North Africa and the Middle East. It is used in wall hangings and jewellery as a defence against the evil eye. Red dried chilies are also used to ward off evil eye. The chilies are circled clockwise and anti-clockwise around the affected person's head seven times and then placed in fire or hung outside the house. The intensity of the smell from the burning shows the seriousness of the evil eye. This process is believed to burn the evil eye. In India, black *Kohl*, *Surmah* or *Kājal*, an ancient eye cosmetic, is used by women to keep from getting affected by the evil eye (known as *Buri Nazar*). Sometimes, a small black *Kohl* dot is also placed on the forehead near the hair of newborn babies to ward off evil eye. Cords strung with blue beads are also used as bracelets on newborn babies. When the cord breaks and the beads are lost, the child is considered to be strong to protect himself or herself from the evil eye.

In Morocco women treat the evil eye in a special ceremony (Islamqa (b)).

> The sick person sits down (e.g. on a chair) while another person holds a glass of water above his head. Another person (this can be the same one as the one holding the glass) lights a match and goes around the face of the sick person with it, meanwhile reciting Surat *al-Fatihah* (The opening Chapter of the Qur'an). Note that the match doesn't touch the face of the sick person. After a few seconds, the match is thrown in the glass of water above the head of the sick person and a second match is lit. This is done seven times. When done, the person who is doing this takes the glass of water and touches all the matches in the glass. If the matches go to the bottom of the glass, it means that the sick person is afflicted by the evil eye. They usually count the matches on the bottom to estimate how sick the person is. The more matches on the bottom, the sicker he is. After this ceremony, people assume that the sick person is cured.

All the above ways and many other rituals to cast off or protect oneself from evil eye are not acceptable as being Islamic by scholars. For example, wearing amulets deviates from the creed of *Tawheed* (unicity of Allah) and ascribing partners with Allah (*Shirk*). Only Allah can protect us from harm, and believing otherwise is a form of *Shirk*. Sheikh Muhammad Ibn Saalih al-Uthaymeen (b) (May Allah have mercy on him) said:

> So long as there is no proof that a thing is a means (to an end) – either according to Islam or natural, physical laws – then it is a kind of minor shirk. That includes, for example, charms and amulets that are said to ward off the evil eye, and the like, because this is deciding that something is a means to an end when Allah has not created it to be such. Thus he is

deciding about something being a means to an end, which is something that is only for Allah to decide. Hence this is like an act of shirk.

Evidence from the Qur'an and Sunnah

Allah says in Surah Yunus (Interpretation of meaning):

> *And if Allah should touch you with adversity, there is no remover of it except Him; and if He intends for you good, then there is no repeller of His bounty. He causes it to reach whom He wills of His servants. And He is the Forgiving, the Merciful.*
> (Sūrat Yunus (Jonas) 10:107)

Uqbah ibn 'Amir narrates that the Messenger of Allah (ﷺ) said:

> If anyone wears an amulet, may Allah not help him in fulfilling his wish. If anyone wears a sea-shell around his neck, may Allah give him no peace.
> (Ahmad and Al-Hakim)

Ibn Mas'oud narrated that:

> Once, when he entered his home, he noticed his wife wearing a knotted object round her neck. He took it away and broke it. Then he remarked: 'The family of 'Abdullah has become so arrogant that they now associate with Allah those for whom He has sent down no authority.'

Then, he added: "I have heard the Messenger of Allah," saying:

> Verily, incantations, amulets, and love charms are acts of shirk (associating false gods with Allah)." The people said: "O Abu Abdullah! We are familiar with incantations and amulets, but what is a love charm (*Al Tawlah*)?" He replied: "It is a sort of magical formula by which women sought to gain their husbands' love."
> (Al-Hakim and Ibn Hibban)

Abdullaah ibn Mas'oud's wife, Zaynab reported that once when Ibn Mas'oud saw a cord necklace around her neck and he asked what it was, she replied, "It is a cord in which a spell has been placed to help me." He snatched it from her neck, broke it up and said "Surely the family of 'Abdullaah has no need for Shirk! I have heard Allah's messenger(ﷺ) say,

> Verily spells, talismans and charms are *Shirk*.

Zaynab replied, "Why are you saying this? My eye used to twitch and when I went to so and so, the Jew, he put a spell on it and it stopped twitching!" Ibn

Masood replied, "Verily it was only a devil prodding it with his hand so when you had it bewitched he left it. It would have been sufficient for you to have said as the Prophet (ﷺ) used to say:

> Remove the suffering, O Lord of mankind and heal it perfectly as You are the true healer. There is no cure except Your cure; a cure which is not followed by sickness!
>
> (Abu Dâwûd (a))

It was narrated from Zaynab the wife of 'Abd-Allah ibn Mas'oud from 'Abd-Allah that he said: "I heard the Messenger of *Allah* (ﷺ) say,

> Spells (*ruqyah*), amulets and love-charms are *shirk*.

I said, "Why do you say this? By Allah, my eye was weeping with a discharge and I kept going to So and so, the Jew, who did a spell for me. When he did the spell, it calmed down." 'Abd–Allah said: "That was just the work of the Shaytan who was picking it with his hand, and when (the Jew) uttered the spell, he stopped. All you needed to do was to say as the Messenger of Allah (ﷺ) used to say:

> Remove the harm, O Lord of mankind, and heal, You are the Healer. There is no healing but Your healing, a healing which leaves no disease behind ('*Adhhib il-ba's Rabb al-naas ishfi anta al-Shaafi laa shifaa'a illa shifaa'uka shifaa'an laa yughaadiru saqaman*)."
>
> (Abu Dâwûd (b) and Ibn Maajah (b))

It was narrated from 'Uqbah ibn 'Aamir al-Juhani that a group came to the Messenger of Allah (ﷺ) (to swear their allegiance [*bay'ah*] to him). He accepted the *bay'ah* of nine of them but not of one of them. They said, "O Messenger of Allah, you accepted the *bay'ah* of nine but not of this one." He said,

> He is wearing an amulet.

The man put his hand (in his shirt) and took it off, then he (the Prophet (ﷺ)) accepted his *bay'ah*. He said,

> Whoever wears an amulet has committed *shirk*.
>
> (Ahmad)

Comments from scholars regarding the use of amulets

These are two opposing groups of scholars regarding the use of various kinds of amulets. One group said it is permissible and the other group not-permissible.

It is beyond the scope of this chapter to examine the arguments for and against the use of amulets. However, according to the Scholars of the Standing Committee (Shaykh 'Abd al-'Azeez ibn Baaz, Shaykh 'Abd-Allaah ibn Ghadyaan, Shaykh 'Abd-Allaah ibn Qa'ood),

> It is haram to wear amulets if they contain anything other than Qur'an, but they differed concerning those which do contain Qur'an. Some of them said that wearing these is permitted, and others said that it is not permitted. The view that it is not permitted is more likely to be correct because of the general meaning of the ahadeeth, and in order to prevent means of *shirk*.

Sheikh Abd al-'Azeez ibn Baaz (May Allah have mercy on him) in a Fatwa pronounced on the 'ruling on wearing amulets by young boys and the sick and hanging Ayahs (verses of the Qur'an) in offices or Masjids,' stated that: "The correct opinion is that amulets which contain the Qur'an are prohibited, based upon the generality of the aforementioned Hadith, to be on the safe side, and to work upon the rule of *Sadd-ul-Dhara'i'* (blocking the means) leading to minor *Shirk*. It could be an act of major *Shirk*, if one who believes that they ward off calamities. With regard to hanging Ayahs (Verses) and Hadiths in offices and schools, there is nothing wrong with this as a means of reminding and admonition. However, it is *Makruh* (disapproved) to hang them in Masjids, for this entails disturbing the people praying. Sheikh al-Albani (May Allah have mercy on him) said:

> This misguidance is still widespread among the Bedouin, *fellahin* (peasants) and some of the city-dwellers. Examples include the pearls which some drivers put in their cars, hanging them from the rear-view mirror. Some of them hang an old shoe on the front or back of the car; some hang a horse-shoe on the front of their house or shop. All of that is to ward off the evil eye, or so they claim. And there are other things which are widespread because of ignorance of *Tawheed* and the things which nullify it such as actions of shirk and idolatry which the Messengers were only sent and the Books were only revealed to put an end to. It is to Allah that we complain of the ignorance of Muslims nowadays, and their being far away from their religion.

Conclusion

For Muslims, the evil eye is real and may affect one's happiness, success or possessions. A person can give himself the evil eye and he can also give it to others. It can also afflict someone without even being seen by the envier. So, it is recommended that we take the necessary precautions and try to prevent being affected by the evil eye. Muslims believe that nothing happens without the permission and knowledge of Allah and this is something that Allah created. Qamar (2013) stated that

> The protective and curative tactics against the evil eye, as advised in Islamic traditions, indicates two fundamental components of the basic Islamic philosophy: first, *Tawheed*, none has the right to be worshipped but He (the One God), the Ever Living, the One Who sustains and protects all that exists and second, *Tawakal* (Allah is sufficient, and when Allah helps, none can overcome).
>
> (p. 51)

Sheikh al-Islam Ibn Taymiyyah affirmed that

> Whoever finds in himself any hasad towards another has to try to neutralise it by means of attaining *taqwa* (piety, consciousness of Allah) and *Sabr* (patience). He should hate that the feeling of *hasad* is in himself.

We make supplications and remembrance upon seeing something amazing and good. We ask Allah to protect us.

References

Abu Dâwûd (a). *Sunan Abī Dâwûd* (English Trans.), Vol. 3, p. 1089, no. 3874), Ahmad Ibn Maajah and Ibn Hibbaan. The du'aa' is also reported by both 'Aa'ishah and Anas and collected by Bukhari.

Abu Dâwûd (b) Cited in 10543: *Ruling on amulets and hanging them up; do amulets ward off the evil eye and hasad (envy)?* https://islamqa.info/en/10543 (accessed 18 March 2018).

Ahmad, 16969. Cited in 10543: *Ruling on amulets and hanging them up; do amulets ward off the evil eye and hasad (envy)?* https://islamqa.info/en/10543 (accessed 18 March 2018). This hadith was classed as Sahih by Sheikh al-Albaani in *al-Silsilah al-Saheehah*, 492.

Ahmad, Malik, al-Nasai and Ibn Hibban. Classed as Sahih (authentic) by Al-Albani in al-Mishkat. Cited in 20954: *The Evil Eye and Protection Against it*. https://islamqa.info/en/20954 (accessed 18 March 2018).

Ali, A. (2013) *Self-diagnosis for evil eye*. http://maithiri.com/en/42984/ (accessed 18 March 2018).

Al-Hakim and Ibn Hibban, and both consider it a Sahih Hadith. www.ummahhelpline.com/qa/368.php (accessed 18 March 2018).

Bukhârî. Sahih al-Bukhârî 5740: Book 76, Hadith 55. USC-MSA web (English) reference: Vol. 7, Book 71, Hadith 636.

Ibn Majah (a) Sunan Ibn Majah " *Chapters on Medicine*. Book 31, Hadith 3654,, English reference: Vol. 4, Book 31, Hadith 3525.

Ibn Maajah (b) 3530. Cited in 10543: *Ruling on amulets and hanging them up; do amulets ward off the evil eye and hasad (envy)?* https://islamqa.info/en/10543 (accessed 18 March 2018).

Imam Al-Qurtubi, Tafsir Al-Qurtubi. *Classical Commentary of the Holy Qur'an*. Author: Aisha Bewley. London: Dar Al Taqwa.

Islamqa (a) 20954: *The Evil Eye and Protection Against it*. https://islamqa.info/en/20954 (accessed 18 March 2018).

Islamqa.(b) 178428: Determining if a Person is Afflicted With Evil Eye. https://islamqa.info/en/178428 (accessed 18 March 2018).

Muslim: *Sahih Muslim* 2187: Book 39, Hadith 55. USC-MSA web (English) reference: Book 26, Hadith 5426.

Pew Research Center (2012) *The World's Muslims: Unity and Diversity. Chapter 4: Other Beliefs and Practices*.www.pewforum.org/2012/08/09/the-worlds-Muslims-unity-and-diversity-4-other-beliefs-and-practices/ (accessed 18 March 2018).

Qamar, A. H. (2013) The Concept of the 'Evil' and the 'Evil Eye' in Islam and Islamic Faith-Healing Traditions. *Journal of Islamic Thought and Civilization*, 3, 2, 44–53.

Scholars of the Standing Committee. Shaykh 'Abd al-'Azeez ibn Baaz, Shaykh 'Abd-Allaah ibn Ghadyaan, Shaykh 'Abd-Allaah ibn Qa'ood. In *Fataawa al-Lajnah al-Daa'imah*, 1/212. Cited in 10543: Ruling on amulets and hanging them up; do amulets ward off the evil eye and hasad (envy)? https://islamqa.info/en/10543 (accessed 18 March 2018).

Sheikh al-Albani. *Silsilat al-Ahaadeeth al-Saheehah*, 1/890, 492. Cited in 10543: Ruling on amulets and hanging them up; do amulets ward off the evil eye and hasad (envy)? https://islamqa.info/en/10543 (accessed 7 July 2017).

Sheikh Abd al-'Azeez ibn Baaz. Grand Mufty of the Kingdom of Saudi Arabia, Chairman of the Council of Senior Scholars and the Departments of Scholarly Research and Ifta'. *Fatwas of Ibn Baz*,Vol. 9, Part No. 9; Page No. 453. www.alifta.net/ (accessed 18 March 2018).

Sheikh 'Abd al-'Azeez al-Sadhan (2009) 125543: *Determining if One is Afflicted by Evil Eye or Possessed*. Al-Ruqyah al-Shar'iyyah. https://islamqa.info/en/125543 (accessed 18 March 2018).

Sheikh Abdullah bin Abdulrahman Al-Jibrin. Cited in Chapter Five (Spiritual Ailments) Types and Signs of the Evil Eye. http://quranichealing.net/spiritual-ailments/types-and-signs-of-the-evil-eye/ (accessed 18 March 2018).

Sheikh al-Islam Ibn Taymiyyah. *Amraad al-Quloob* (Diseases of the heart): Cited in Islamqa (12205: How can he rid himself of jealousy towards his brothers? https://islamqa.info/en/12205 (accessed 18 March 2018).

Sheikh Khalid Al-Hibshi. Alruqya Healing Centre. The concept of the evil eye (ayn). http://ruqyainlondon.com/article/evil-eye-and-envy-ayn (accessed 18 March 2018).

Sheikh Muhammad Ibn Saalih al-Uthaymeen (2003) Cited in Islamqa. 20954: *The Evil Eye and Protection Against it*. https://islamqa.info/en/20954 (accessed 18 March 2018).

Sheikh Muhammad Ibn Saalih al-Uthaymeen (a) – When to say Masha Allah Tabarak Allah: Fatawaa noor 'ala adarb tape no321. www.eaalim.com/download/index.php/blog/entry/when-to-say-mashaallah-in.html (accessed 18 March 2018).

Sheikh Muhammad Ibn Saalih al-Uthaymeen (b). *Majmoo' Fatawa Ibn 'Uthaymeen*. Cited in 178428: Determining if a Person is Afflicted With Evil Eye. https://islamqa.info/en/178428 (accessed 18 March 2018). www.masjidma.com (2011) Islam Strictly Prohibits the Use of Amulets. www.masjidma.com/2011/10/01/islam-strictly-prohibits-the-use-of-amulets/ (accessed 18 March 2018).

Sheikh Muhammed Salih Al-Munajjid (2000) 7190: *Can a man harm his beautiful wife with the "evil eye"?* https://islamqa.info/en/7190 (accessed 24 June 2018).

Chapter 9

The world of *Jinn*

Introduction

Human beings have always been fascinated by the unseen, metaphysical and supernatural. The existence of a world parallel to our own or the spirit world is a realm that is not visible and cannot be subjected to empirical evidence. Amin et al. (2006) argued that

> Though there is expression of criticism by many scientists and psychiatrists about the Jinni related possession but broadly speaking it appears unreasonable to dismiss something so culturally pervasive just because it cannot be proven scientifically. Emphasis on finding scientific evidence appears somewhat unreasonable when a spiritual dimension has already been introduced in the psychiatric literature.
>
> (pp. 477–478)

The beliefs in the spirit world and the spiritual forces coupled with the myths surrounding the supernatural world are evident due to several factors. According to Al-Habeeb (2003), the reasons include:

> the existence of these forces as documented in the Holy Quran; the belief in demons, witchcraft and the evil eye by followers of other major religions; approximately 90% of the world's societies believe in demonic possession; and the support given by transcultural literature for such disorders.
>
> (p. 31)

Jinns (demons or devils) are believed to exist in all major religions, and have the power to possess humans and cause them harm.

Islam provides us an explanation of the unseen world (*al-ghayb*) and it is from this realm that Islam explains to us about the world of the *Jinn*. In the noble Qur'an, Allah informs us that certain types of mental health problems are caused by the influence of the *Jinn*, the spiritual creatures who lived in the unseen world. Some orientalists claims that believing in the existence of *Jinn* is an article of faith which is rather misleading. However, as *Jinn* are mentioned several times in the Qur'an and in the Sunnah, it becomes mandatory upon Muslims to believe in their existence. In addition, the Qur'an not only mentions their existence but also tells that *Satan* was a *Jinn*. Above all, the belief in the unseen world created by Allah is thus a required element of faith in Islam. In fact, *Jinn* is mentioned in more than 40 verses of the Qur'an, which are included in 10 chapters (Sūrat). There is an entire chapter which is named after them (Sūrat Al-*Jinn*), describing their existence and purpose.

Extent of *Jinn* in the Islamic world

The prevalence of *Jinn* possession states in diaspora Islamic communities remains unknown. The limited literature suggests that belief in *Jinn* is substantial across the Muslim world. The Islamic diaspora rate of belief in *Jinn* is above 70% among adherents of Islam in Bangladesh, Pakistan, Malaysia, Afghanistan, Morocco, Tunisia, Lebanon and the UK (Khalifa et al., 2011; Pew Research Center, 2012). In a survey undertaken by the Pew Research Center (2012) in 23 countries with a sample of the Muslim populations, belief in *Jinn* is relatively widespread. In 13 of the 23 countries where the question was asked, more than half of Muslims believe in *Jinn*. Pew Research Center (2012) reported that in the South Asian countries surveyed,

> at least seven-in-ten Muslims affirm that *Jinn* exist, including 84% in Bangladesh. In Southeast Asia, a similar proportion of Malaysian Muslims (77%) believe in *Jinn*, while fewer in Indonesia (53%) and Thailand (47%) share this belief. Across the Middle Eastern and North African nations surveyed, belief in *Jinn* ranges from 86% in Morocco to 55% in Iraq. Overall, Muslims in Central Asia and across Southern and Eastern Europe (Russia and the Balkans) are least likely to say that *Jinn* are real. In Central Asia, Turkey is the only country where a majority (63%) of Muslims believe in *Jinn*. Elsewhere in Central Asia, about a fifth or fewer Muslims accept the existence of *Jinn*. In Southern and Eastern Europe, fewer than four-in-ten in any country surveyed believe in these supernatural beings.

The country with the highest belief in *Jinn* is Morocco (86%) as compared to the Central Asian countries of Azerbaijan, Kazakhstan and Uzbekistan where between 15–16% believe in *Jinn*. These Muslim countries were post-Soviet countries emerging after the collapse of the Soviet Union. Some of the Muslim populations in these countries have recently reasserted their Muslim identity after decades of Soviet religious repression. Perhaps, these findings reflect the influence of decades of institutional religious oppression.

In the UK, *Jinn* possession is most likely to be seen among people from Pakistan, Bangladesh, the Middle East or North Africa. In their study of beliefs about *Jinn*, black magic and evil eye among Muslims in the UK, Khalifa et al.

(2011) found that almost 80% of the participants believed in *Jinn* and almost half of them believed that *Jinn* could cause physical and mental health problems in humans. In a study by Khalifa et al. (2012) on the comparative beliefs among Muslims in Dhaka (Bangladesh) and Leicester (UK), the findings showed that

> Muslims in Leicester (as compared to Muslims in Dhaka) were more likely to believe in *Jinn*; less likely to believe in *Jinn* possession; more likely to believe that *Jinn* could cause mental health difficulties; more likely to cite religious figures as the treating authority; less likely to advocate treatment by doctors; and more likely to advocate joint working between doctors and religious leaders.
>
> (p. 6)

This finding in a Muslim UK population has been endorsed by Dein et al. (2008) in their study of notions of *Jinn* and misfortune among the Bangladeshi community in East London. With regard to gender, there is evidence to suggest that females are more likely than males to believe in the existence of *Jinn* (Khalifa et al., 2011 2012). In summary, the literature indicated that the sample of Muslims believed in the existence of *Jinn* and in *Jinn* possession (Hussein, 1991; Al-Habeeb, 2003; Dein et al., 2008; Irmak, 2014; Lim et al., 2015; Khalifa et al., 2011 2012; Obeid et al., 2012).

There is a need to be cautious about the findings of these studies due to methodological limitations. Those surveys are not representative of the beliefs of Muslims in Islamic countries and the Muslim diaspora as Muslims are not a homogenous group. There is a diversity of cultures which have different perception of the world of the unseen and *Jinn*.

Concept of *Jinn*

The word '*al-Jinn*' (plural: *al-Jaan*) in Arabic refers to something that is covered or concealed. The word *Jinn* in Arabic is derived from the word in Arabic for heaven: *Jannah* which means to hide or conceal. The *Jinn*, it seemed, "are deemed to be closer to heaven than Earth" (Lawrence, 2007, p. 185). Hence, the word '*Jinn*' itself implies the existence of something that cannot be seen. Raslan (2014), showed how similar Arabic words, such as: *janin* (foetus), *mijan* (armour), *Majnoon* (insane or the covering of ones intellect) provide insight into further understanding that *Jinn* refers to that which lives among man but cannot be seen. Asad (2008) explains the meaning of *Jinn* from the Qur'an to be:

> In the usage of the Qur'an, which is certainly different from the usage of primitive folklore, the term *Jinn* have several distinct meanings. The most commonly encountered is that of spiritual forces or beings which, precisely because they have no corporeal existence, are beyond the perception of our corporeal senses: a connotation which includes 'satans' and 'satanic forces'

as well as 'angels' and 'angelic forces,' since all of them are 'concealed from our senses.' In order to make it quite evident that these invisible manifestations are not of corporeal nature, the Qur'an states parabolically that the *Jinn* were created out of 'the fire of scorching winds,' or out of 'a confusing flame of fire,' or simply 'out of fire.'

(p. 113)

The *Jinn* are not fallen angels according to myth. They were created from a smokeless flame of fire. Allah has told us in the Qur'an (Interpretation of the meaning):

And the jinn, We created before from scorching fire.
(Sūrat Ar-Hijr (The Valley of Stone) 15:27)

And He created the jinn from a smokeless flame of fire.
(Sūrat Al-Rahman (The Most Merciful) 55:15)

It is worth briefly examining the use of the concept of Satan (Shaytan). Satan, in the Arabic language, is a general term for any rebel that is arrogant and rebelled against his Lord. It is stated that "the *Shaytan* are from among the *Jinn*; they are the rebellious ones and the most evil among them, just as the devils among mankind are the rebellious ones and the most evil among them. There are among the *Jinn*, as is the case among mankind, devils who are the rebellious ones and the most evil, *Kaafirs* and evildoers. There are also Muslims among them who are righteous and good." Allah says (Interpretation of the meaning):

And thus We have made for every prophet an enemy – devils from mankind and jinn, inspiring to one another decorative speech in delusion. But if your Lord had willed, they would not have done it, so leave them and that which they invent.
(Sūrat Al-'An'am (The Grazing Livestock) 6:112)

(Islamqa, 2001)

The Qur'an teaches that *Jinn* pre-existed before humans; the first recorded *Jinn* to be disobedient is *Iblis*, commonly known as Satan. Allah created the Garden of Eden and made Adam and Eve. Subsequently, Allah commanded that all of the angels and Iblis were to prostrate themselves before Adam. Allah says in the Qur'an (Interpretation of the meaning):

And (mention) when We said to the angels, 'Prostrate before Adam'; so they prostrated, except for Iblis. He refused and was arrogant and became of the disbelievers.
(Sūrat Al-Baqarah (The Cow) 2, p. 34)

All the angels prostrated (as a sign of respect and not worship) except Iblis (He was not an angel but from the *Jinn*). Laughlin (2015) argues that "Because

Jinn were created from fire, this great difference created a boundary between humans and *Jinn*, thus making the *Jinn* feel superior to human. This superiority complex created a great defiance, forever changing the world of Islam" (p. 68). Iblis refused to prostrate due to arrogance and pride and he was removed from heaven. Allah says in the Qur'an (Interpretation of the meaning):

> *(Allah) said, 'What prevented you from prostrating when I commanded you?'*
> *(Satan) said, 'I am better than him. You created me from fire and created him from clay.'*
> *(Allah) said, 'Descend from Paradise, for it is not for you to be arrogant therein. So get out; indeed, you are of the debased.'*
> (Sūrat Al A'raf (The Elevations) 7:12–13)

In the following verse from the Qur'an, Satan went on in defiance and rebellion. According to Ibn Kathir,

> Because (You have put me in error, I will surely sit in wait for them on Your straight path), meaning as You have sent me astray. As You caused my ruin, I will sit in wait for Your servants whom You will create from the offspring of the one you expelled me for." He went on,(Your straight path), the path of truth and the way of safety. I (*Iblis*) will misguide them from this path so that they do not worship You Alone, because You sent me astray. Mujahid said that the "'straight path refers to the truth. (Then I will come to them from before them) Raising doubts in them concerning their Hereafter (and (from) behind them), making them more eager for this life (from their right), causing them confusion in the religion (and from their left) luring them to commit sins.

This is meant to cover all paths of good and evil. Shaytan discourages the people from the path of good and lures them to the path of evil." Allah says in the Qur'an (Interpretation of the meaning):

> *(Satan) said, "Because You have put me in error, I will surely sit in wait for them on Your straight path.*
> *Then I will come to them from before them and from behind them and on their right and on their left, and You will not find most of them grateful (to You)."*
> (Sūrat Al A'raf (The Elevations)7:16–17)

The Prophet (ﷺ) explained how the *Jinn* steal this word and said:

> (These meteors) are shot neither at the death of anyone nor on the birth of anyone. Allah, the Exalted and Glorious, issues Command when He decides to do a thing. Then (the Angels) supporting the Throne sing His glory, then sing the dwellers of heaven who are near to them until this

glory of God reaches them who are in the heaven of this world. Then those who are near the supporters of the Throne ask these supporters of the Throne: What your Lord has said? And they accordingly inform them what He says. Then the dwellers of heaven seek information from them until this information reaches the heaven of the world. In this process of transmission (the *Jinn* snatches) what he manages to overhear and he carries it to his friends. And when the Angels see the *Jinn* they attack them with meteors. If they narrate only which they manage to snatch that is correct but they alloy it with lies and make additions to it.

(Muslim (a)).

It is said that all the *Jinn* living with immortality until the Day of Judgment, whether good or evil, are all descendants of Iblis. They are here to deviate humans from the path of Allah and for worshipping Him.

Similarities and differences between *Jinn* and human

There are similarities and differences between *Jinn* and humans. According to Islamic writings, *Jinn* live alongside other creatures, but form a parallel world other than that of mankind. In Islam, the *Jinn* share a very distinctive characteristic with human beings: free will. Allah says in the Qur'an (Interpretation of the meaning):

We (Allah) have not created the *Jinn* or humans, but to worship Us.
(Sūrat Adh-Dhariyat (The Scattering Winds) 51:56)

Both humans and *Jinn* have the characteristics to think and to reflect. In addition, *Jinn* are accountable for their actions in the same way as humans as they have the freedom to choose between right and wrong and between good and bad. It has been suggested that "*Jinn* are believed to be both less virtuous and less physical than humans, but like humans, endowed with the ability to choose between good and evil" (Esposito, 2003). *Jinn*, like humans, are believers and non-believers and will be judged on the Day of Judgment as promised by Allah. Sūrat Al-*Jinn* (The *Jinn*): 72 reveals that there are broad categories of *Jinn*: believers, disbelievers, misguided and guided (Ibn Kathir). Amongst the *Jinn*, there are those who are obedient to God and others who are not, entirely analogous to humans (Al-*Jinn* (The *Jinn*) 72:14–15).

Like human beings, the *Jinn* must nourish their bodies with food and have the capacity to breed. Procreation is also a characteristic of both humans and *Jinn*. *Jinn* have sexual intercourse in the same manner as humans. It is believed that humans and *Jinn* have even inter-mingled and gotten married; Al-Suyooti and Ibn Tamiyyah mentioned many such reports from the early generations and scholars pointing to the existence of marriages between humans and *Jinn*

(Al-Ashqar, 2003). Both *Jinn* and humans are mortal but it has been suggested that the lifespans of *Jinn* are longer than that of the humans (Al-Ashqar, 2003).

That which clearly distinguishes *Jinn* from humans is their powers and abilities. It has been suggested that "While the world of the *Jinn* is generally believed to be perfectly parallel to the human world, the primary difference is that jinn are able to move between their world and ours, while humans cannot perform this task" (Rothberg, 2004, p. 36). Allah has given the *Jinn* power and ability, including great speed and movement. One of the *Jinn* promised Prophet Suleiman (Solomon) that he would be able to bring the throne of the Queen of Sheba to Jerusalem in a flash of time. That is,

> *I will bring it to you before you can rise from your place* (Interpretation of the meaning).
>
> Sūrat An-Naml (The Ants) 27:39–40

One of the extra powers of the *Jinn* is that they are able to take on any physical form including humans and animals. The ability of the *Jinn* to take on the shapes of humans is stated in the Qur'an (Interpretation of the meaning):

> *And (remember) when Satan made their deeds pleasing to them and said, 'No one can overcome you today from among the people, and indeed, I am your protector.' But when the two armies sighted each other, he turned on his heels and said, 'Indeed, I am disassociated from you. Indeed, I see what you do not see; indeed I fear Allah. And Allah is severe in penalty.'*
>
> (Sūrat Al-Anfal (The Bounties) 8, p. 48)

Abu Hurayrah (May Allah be pleased with him) who said: The Messenger of Allah (ﷺ) put me in charge of guarding the *zakah* (poor-due) of Ramadhan. Someone came to me and started scooping up some of the food, and I said, "By Allah, I will take you to the Messenger of Allah (ﷺ)." He complained of being in need and having dependents, so Abu Hurayrah (May Allah be pleased with him) took pity on him and let him go. This happened three times, and on the third occasion, Abu Hurayrah (May Allah be pleased with him) said: "I will take you to the Messenger of Allah. This is the third time and each time you say that you will not come back, then you come back." He said, "Let me go and I will teach you something by means of which Allah will benefit you." I said: "What is it?" He said: "When you go to bed, recite *Ayat al-Kursi*,"

> *Allah! La ilaha illa Huwa* (None has the right to be worshipped but He), *Al-Hayyul-Qayyum* (the Ever Living, the One Who sustains and protects all that exists).
>
> (Sūrat Al-Baqarah (The Cow) 2:255)

until you complete the verse, then you will always have a protector from Allah, and no devil will come near you until morning comes. So I let him go, and the next morning I told the Messenger of Allah (ﷺ) what had happened. The Messenger of Allah (ﷺ) said:

> 'He told you the truth, although he is a liar. Do you know who you have been speaking to for three nights, O Abu Hurayrah?' He said: 'No.' He said: 'That was a devil (a *shaytan*).'
>
> (Bukhari (a))

In this Hadith it is clear that a devil *Jinn* took the form of a human. This Hadith, according to Al-Hafiz ibn Hajar, "teaches us a number of things . . . that one of the characteristics of the shaytan is lying, and that he may appear in various forms that may be seen, and that the words of Allah (Interpretation of the meaning),

> *Verily, he and Qabiluhu (his soldiers from the Jinn or his tribe) see you from where you cannot see them.*
>
> (Sūrat Al-An'am (The Grazing Livestock) 7:27)

apply to when he is in the form with which he was created." *Jinn* may also take the form of certain animals, for example, camels, snakes, donkeys, cows, dogs or cats, especially black dog and black cats. Sheikh al-Islam Ibn Taymiyah said:

> The *Jinn* may appear in human and animal form, so they may appear as snakes and scorpions etc., or in the form of camels, cattle, sheep, horses, mules and donkeys, or in the form of birds, or in the form of humans, as the *shaytan* came to Quraysh in the form of Suraqah ibn Malik ibn Ju'sham when they wanted to set out for (the battle of) Badr.

In one Hadith, it was narrated that Abu Dharr said: Messenger of Allah (ﷺ) said:

> When anyone of you stands to pray, then he is screened if he has in front of him something as high as the back of a camel saddle. If he does not have something as high as the back of a camel saddle in front of him, then his prayer is nullified by a woman, a donkey or a black dog.

I (one of the narrators) said: What is the difference between a black dog, a yellow one and a red one? He said: I asked the Messenger of Allah (ﷺ)

> just like you and he said: 'The black dog is a *shaytan* (An-Nasa'i).'

In the Qur'an in Sūrat Al-*Jinn* (72), Allah informs about the protection of the Qur'an from the *Jinn* so that they could not steal anything from the Qur'an and tell it to the soothsayers, fortune tellers, or astrologers.

> *And we have sought (to reach) the heaven but found it filled with powerful guards and burning flames.*
> *And we used to sit therein in positions for hearing, but whoever listens now will find a burning flame lying in wait for him.*
> *And we do not know (therefore) whether evil is intended for those on earth or whether their Lord intends for them a right course.*
> (Sūrat Al-*Jinn* (The *Jinn*) 72, pp. 8–10)

Ibn Kathir provides an explanation of the above verses:

> And we have sought to reach the heaven; but found it filled with stern guards and flaming fires. And verily, we used to sit there in stations, to (steal) a hearing, but any who listens now will find a flaming fire watching him in (ambush) meaning, whoever would like to steal some information by listening, he will find a flaming fire waiting in ambush for him. It will not pass him or miss him, but it will wipe him out and destroy him completely.

Another explanation given for the above verses is as follows:

> The *Jinn* are believed to be able to move around the world with incredible speed, compared to light. It is also believed that they congregate and stack themselves up one upon another until they reach the lower levels of heaven where the angels are listening to Allah and discussing His truths with one another. The belief continues that their goal is to gather truths and bring them back to the earth and distort them with lies. If caught, angels throw stars at them in a type of 'star wars.' The point of the *Jinn* establishing at least one truth is that with that one truth, they can influence individuals and corrupt them with a hundred lies.
> (Rogeberg, 2017, p. 105)

Table 9.1 presents a summary of similarities and differences between *Jinn* and humans.

References

Al-Ashqar, U. S. (2003) *The World of the Jinn and Devils in the Light of the Qur'an and Sunnah*. Riyadh: International Islamic Publishing House.
Al-Habeeb, T. A. (2003) A pilot study of faith healers' views on evil eye, Jinn possession, and magic in the Kingdom of Saudi Arabia, *Journal of Family & Community Medicine*, 10, 3, 31–38.
Amin, A., Gadit, M., and Callanan, T. S. (2006) Jinni possession: A clinical enigma in mental health, *The Journal of the Pakistan Medical Association*, 56, 10, 476–478.

Table 9.1 Similarities and differences between humans and Jinn

	Humans	Jinn
Nature.	Created from dried (sounding) clay of altered mud.	Created from a smokeless flame of fire.
Gender.	Male and Female.	Male and Female.
Free will.	Yes	Yes
Believer.	Yes	Yes
Non-believer.	Yes	Yes
Created for the worship of Allah.	Yes	Yes
Wisdom and understanding.	Yes	Yes
Procreate.	Yes	Yes
Eat, drink and sleep.	Yes	Yes
Have children.	Yes	Yes
Accountable for actions and behaviours.	Yes	Yes
Pride and arrogance.	Yes	Yes
Different levels as regards righteousness and God consciousness.	Yes	Yes
Reckoning on the Day of Resurrection.	Yes	Yes
Visible.	Yes	No – invisible to humans.
Dwelling-places.	Human habitat.	Ruins and unclean places like bathrooms, dunghills, garbage dumps and graveyards.
Special powers.	None.	Given the power to take whatever shape or form they wish. Ability to move and travel quickly.

An-Nasa'i. Sunan an-Nasa'i 75: Book 9, Hadith 9. English translation:Vol. 1, Book 9, Hadith 751.

Asad, Muhammad (2008) *The Message of the Qur'an*. Dubai, UAE: Oriental Press.

Bukhari (a) Sahih al-Bukhari 3275. Book 59, Hadith 84USC-MSA web (English) reference: Book 54, Hadith 495.

Dein, S., Alexander, M., and Napier, A. D. (2008) Jinn, psychiatry and contested notions of misfortune among East London Bangladeshis, *Transcultural Psychiatry*, 35, 1, 31–55.

Esposito, J. L. (2003) *Jinn. The Oxford Dictionary of Islam*. Oxford: Oxford University Press

Hussein, F. M. (1991) A study of the role of unorthodox treatments of psychiatric illnesses, *Arabian Journal of Psychiatry*, 2, 170–184.

Ibn Kathir. Tafsir Ibn Kathir www.qtafsir.com/index.php?option=com_content&task=view &id=1467&Itemid=128 (accessed 18 March 2018).

Irmak, K. M. (2014) Schizophrenia or possession? *Journal of Religion and Health*, 53, 773–777. Doi: 10.1007/s10943–012–9673–y.

Islamqa (2001) 8214: *Do the jinn help humans in some ways?* Kitaab Majmoo' Fataawa wa Maqaalaat Mutanawwi'ah li Samaahat al-Shaykh al-'Allaamah 'Abd al-'Azeez ibn 'Abd-Allaah ibn Baaz (May Allah have mercy on him), Vol. 9, p. 373. https://islamqa.info/en/8214 (accessed 18 March 2018).

Khalifa, N., Hardie, T., Latif, S., Jamil, I., and Walker D. M. (2011) Beliefs about Jinn, Black Magic and Evil Eye among Muslims: Age, gender and first language influences, *International Journal of Culture and Mental Health*, 4, 1, 68–77.

Khalifa, N., Hardie, T., and Mullick, M. S. I. (2012) *Jinn and Psychiatry: Comparison of Beliefs Among Muslims in Dhaka and Leicester*. London: Royal College of Psychiatrists, pp. 1–8.

Laughlin, V. A. (2015) A brief overview of al Jinn within Islamic Cosmology and Religiosity, *Journal of Adventist Mission Studies*, 11, 1, 67–78, Art. 9.

Lawrence, B. (2007) *The Qur'an: A Biography*. New York: Grove Press.

Lim, A., Hoek, H. W., and Blom, J. D. (2015) The attribution of psychotic symptoms to Jinn in Islamic patients, *Transcultural Psychiatry*, 52, 1, 18–32. Doi: https://doi.org/10.1177/1363461514543146.

Muslim (a) Sahih Muslim Book of Greetings. Muslim 2229 a Muslim Vol. 5, Book 26, Hadith 5538.

Obeid, T., Abulaban, A., Al-Ghatani, F., Al-Malk, A. R., and Al-Ghamdi, A. (2012) Possession by 'Jinn' as a cause of epilepsy (Saraa): A study from Saudi Arabia, *Seizure*, 21, 4, 245–249.

Pew Research Center (2012) *The World's Muslims: Unity and Diversity. Chapter 4: Other Beliefs and Practices*. www.pewforum.org/2012/08/09/the-worlds-Muslims-unity-and-diversity-4-other-beliefs-and-practices/ (accessed 18 March 2018).

Raslan, M. S. (2014) *Jinn*. Translated by Rasheed ibn Estes Barbee. Durham, NC: MTWS Publishing.

Rogeberg, J. (2017) *Islam in Saudi Arabia: The Homogeneous Portrayal and Heterogeneous Reality*. A Thesis Submitted to The Faculty of the School of Divinity in Fulfilment for the Degree of Master of Arts in Global Studies. Liberty University School of Divinity. http://digitalcommons.liberty.edu/cgi/viewcontent.cgi?article=1444&context=masters (accessed 18 March 2018).

Rothberg, C. E. (2004) *Spirits of Palestine: Gender, Society, and the Stories of the Jinn*. Lanham, MD: Lexington Books.

Sheikh al-Islam Ibn Taymiyah. Cited in Islamqa 40703: *Can We See the Jinn? Do They Have a Real Form?* https://islamqa.info/en/40703 (accessed 18 March 2018).

Chapter 10

Existence and types of *Jinn*

Evidence from the Qur'an, Sunnah and scholars

Introduction

This chapter examines the existence and types of *Jinn* from the Qur'an, Sunnah and statements from scholars.

Types of *Jinn*

Allah, the Almighty, has created different types of *Jinn*. Sūrat Al-*Jinn* 72:14–15 reveals that there are categories of *Jinn*: believers, disbelievers, misguided and guided. There are different categories of *Jinn* according to Ibn Abdul Barr which include:

- *Jinni:* if one is mentioning the *Jinn* purely of themselves.
- *Aamar*: live among mankind.
- *Arwaah:* ones that antagonise the young.
- *Shaytan*: the evil ones that antagonise humans.
- *Maarid:* are the most powerful of all *Jinn* and worse than a demon.
- *Ifreet:* cause even more harm and become strong.

Abu Tha'labah al-Khushani narrated that he Prophet (ﷺ) said:

> The *Jinn* are of three types: a types that has wings, and they fly through the air; a type that looks like snakes and dogs; and a type that stops for a rest then resumes its journey.
>
> (Al-Tahhaawi and Al-Tabaraani)

Every individual has a *Jinn* who has been appointed to be his constant companion (*Qareen*). It is narrated by Ibn Mas'ood, who said: "The Messenger of Allah (ﷺ) said,

> There is none amongst you with whom is not an attaché from amongst the *Jinn* (devil). They (the Companions) said: Allah's Messenger, with you too?

Thereupon he said: Yes, but Allah helps me against him and so I am safe from his hand and he does not command me but for good.

(Muslim (a))

The *Qareen* nudges a person to deviate from of path of Allah and His Prophet, disobeys Allah and pushes him or her to do evil things.

Evidence of the existence of *Jinn* in the Qur'an

There are numerous statements in the Qur'an that affirm the existence of the *Jinn*. Below are a selected verses from the Qur'an. For example, Allah says in the Qur'an (Interpretation of the meaning),

Origin of *Jinn*

And the jinn, We created aforetime from the smokeless flame of fire.
(Sūrat Al-Hijr (The Valley of Stone) 15:26–27)

Listening to the Qur'an

Say (O Muhammad): "It has been revealed to me that a group of Jinns listened (to this Qur'an). They said: 'Indeed, We have heard an amazing Qur'an (i.e., recitation).'"

(Sūrat Al-*Jinn* (The *Jinn*) 72:1)

Satan called Taghut in An-Nisā

Those who believe fight in the cause of Allah, and those who disbelieve fight in the cause of Taghut. So fight against the allies of Satan. Indeed, the plot of Satan has ever been weak.

(Sūrat An-Nisā' (The Women) 4:76)

Iblis (Satan) was one of the *Jinn*

And (mention) when We said to the angels, "Prostrate to Adam," and they prostrated, except for Iblees. He was of the jinn and departed from the command of his Lord.

(Sūrat Al Kahf (The Cave) 18:50)

Satan – human or *Jinn*

And thus We have made for every prophet an enemy – devils from mankind and jinn, inspiring to one another decorative speech in delusion. But if your Lord had willed, they would not have done it, so leave them and that which they invent.

(Sūrat Al-An'am (The Grazing Livestock) 6:112)

Enemy of human

Indeed, Satan is an enemy to you; so take him as an enemy. He only invites his party to be among the companions of the Blaze.

(Sūrat Fatir (The Creator) 35:6)

And never let Satan avert you. Indeed, he is to you a clear enemy.

(Sūrat Az-Zukhruf (Ornament) 43:62)

No power over the Pious worshippers of Allah

Indeed, over My (believing) servants there is for you no authority. And sufficient is your Lord as Disposer of affairs.

(Sūrat Al-Isra' (The Night Journey) 17:65

And he had over them no authority except (it was decreed) that We might make evident who believes in the Hereafter from who is thereof in doubt. And your Lord, over all things, is Guardian.

(Sūrat Sabaa' (The People of Saba') 34:21)

Allah will fill Hell with *Jinn* and Men all together

And they have claimed between Him and the jinn a lineage, but the jinn have already known that they (who made such claims) will be brought to (punishment).

(Sūrat As-Saffaat (Those Lined Up) 37:158)

Except whom your Lord has given mercy, and for that He created them. But the word of your Lord is to be fulfilled that, "I will surely fill Hell with jinn and men all together.

(Sūrat Hud (The Prophet Hud) 11:119)

O company of jinn and mankind, did there not come to you messengers from among you, relating to you My verses and warning you of the meeting of this Day of yours?" They will say, "We bear witness against ourselves"; and the worldly life had deluded them, and they will bear witness against themselves that they were disbelievers.

That is because your Lord would not destroy the cities for wrongdoing while their people were unaware.

(Sūrat Al-An'am (The Grazing Livestock) 6:130–131)

And We have certainly created for Hell many of the jinn and mankind. They have hearts with which they do not understand, they have eyes with which they do not see, and they have ears with which they do not hear. Those are like livestock; rather, they are more astray. It is they who are the heedless.

(Sūrat Al-A'raf (The Elevations) 7:179)

The *Jinn's* power is to Whisper/Deceive

From the evil of the retreating whisperer
Who whispers (evil) into the breasts of mankind,
From among the Jinn and mankind.

(Sūrat An-Nas (People or Mankind) 114:4–6)

And (mention, O Muhammad), the Day when He will gather them together (and say), "O company of jinn, you have (misled) many of mankind."

(Sūrat Al-An'am (The Grazing Livestock) 6:128)

And thus We have made for every prophet an enemy – devils from mankind and jinn, inspiring to one another decorative speech in delusion. But if your Lord had willed, they would not have done it, so leave them and that which they invent.

(Sūrat Al-An'am (The Grazing Livestock) 6:112)

Indeed, there is for him no authority over those who have believed and rely upon their Lord.
His authority is only over those who take him as an ally and those who through him associate others with Allah.

(Sūrat An-Nahl (The Bee) 16:99–100)

And Satan will say when the matter has been concluded, "Indeed, Allah had promised you the promise of truth. And I promised you, but I betrayed you. But I had no authority over you except that I invited you, and you responded to me. So do not blame me; but blame yourselves. I cannot be called to your aid, nor can you be called to my aid. Indeed, I deny your association of me (with Allah) before. Indeed, for the wrongdoers is a painful punishment."

(Sūrat Ibrahim (Abraham) 14:22)

And (mention) when We said to the angles, "Prostrate to Adam," and they prostrated, except for Iblees. He said, "Should I prostrate to one You created from clay?"
(Iblees) said, "Do You see this one whom You have honored above me? If You delay me until the Day of Resurrection, I will surely destroy his descendants, except for a few."
(Allah) said, "Go, for whoever of them follows you, indeed Hell will be the recompense of you – an ample recompense.
And incite (to senselessness) whoever you can among them with your voice and assault them with your horses and foot soldiers and become a partner in their wealth and their children and promise them." But Satan does not promise them except delusion.
Indeed, over My (believing) servants there is for you no authority. And never let Satan avert you. Indeed, he is to you a clear enemy.

(Surah Al-Isra' (The Night Journey) 17:61–65)

Evidence of the existence of *Jinn* from the Sunnah

Aisha narrated that the Prophet (ﷺ) said:

> The angels were created from light, the jinn were created from fire, and Adam was created from that which has been described to you.
>
> (Muslim (b))

Narrated Ibn 'Abbas:

> The Prophet set out with the intention of going to Suq 'Ukaz (market of 'Ukaz) along with some of his companions. At the same time, a barrier was put between the devils and the news of heaven. Fire commenced to be thrown at them. The Devils went to their people, who asked them, "What is wrong with you?" They said, "A barrier has been placed between us and the news of heaven. And fire has been thrown at us." They said, "The thing which has put a barrier between you and the news of heaven must be something which has happened recently. Go eastward and westward and see what has put a barrier between you and the news of heaven." Those who went towards Tuhama came across the Prophet at a place called Nakhla and it was on the way to Suq 'Ukaz and the Prophet was offering the Fajr prayer with his companions. When they heard the Qur'an they listened to it and said, "By Allah, this is the thing which has put a barrier between us and the news of heaven." They went to their people and said, "O our people; verily we have heard a wonderful recital (Qur'an) which shows the true path; we believed in it and would not ascribe partners to our Lord." Allah revealed the following verses to his Prophet (Surah '*Jinn*') (72): "Say: It has been revealed to me." And what was revealed to him was the conversation of the *Jinns*.
>
> (Bukhârî (a))

Narrated 'Abdullah bin 'Abdur-Rahman that Abu Sa'id Al-Khudri said to him,

> "I see that you like sheep and the desert, so when you are looking after your sheep or when you are in the desert and want to pronounce the Adhan, raise your voice, for no *Jinn*, human being or any other things hear the Mu'adh-dhin's voice but will be a witness for him on the Day of Resurrection." Abu Sa'id added, "I heard this from Allah's Apostle."
>
> (Bukhârî (b))

Abu Huraira reported that he heard the Messenger of Allah (ﷺ) said:

> A highly wicked one amongst the *Jinn* escaped yester night to interrupt my prayer, but Allah gave me power over him, so I seized him and intended to

tie him to one of the pillars of the mosque in order that you, all together or all, might look at him, but I remembered the supplication of my brother Suleiman: "My Lord, forgive me, give me such a kingdom as will not be possible for anyone after me" (Qur'an, xxxvii. 35).

(Muslim (c))

Dâwûd reported from 'Amir who said: I asked 'Alqama if Ibn Mas'ud was present with the Messenger of Allah (ﷺ) on the night of the *Jinn* (the night when the Holy Prophet met them). He (Ibn Mas'uad) said: No, but we were in the company of the Messenger of Allah (ﷺ) one night and we missed him. We searched for him in the valleys and the hills and said. He has either been taken away (by *Jinn*) or has been secretly killed. He (the narrator) said. We spent the worst night which people could ever spend. When it was dawn we saw him coming from the side of Hiri. He (the narrator) reported. We said: Messenger of Allah, we missed you and searched for you, but we could not find you and we spent the worst night which people could ever spend. He (the Holy Prophet) said: There came to me an inviter on behalf of the *Jinn* and I went along with him and recited to them the Qur'an. He (the narrator) said: He then went along with us and showed us their traces and traces of their embers. They (the *Jinn*) asked him (the Holy Prophet) about their provision and he said: Every bone on which the name of Allah is recited is your provision. The time it will fall in your hand it would be covered with flesh, and the dung of (the camels) is fodder for your animals. The Messenger of Allah (ﷺ) said:

> Don't perform *istinja* with these (things) for these are the food of your brothers (*Jinn*).

(Muslim (d))

A'isha reported: I said: "Allah's Messenger, the kahins used to tell us about things (unseen) and we found them to be true." Thereupon he said:

> That is a word pertaining to truth which a *Jinn* snatches and throws into the ear of his friend, and makes an addition of one hundred lies to it.

(Muslim (e))

Ibn 'Abbas reported that Allah's Messenger (ﷺ) used to say:

> O Allah, it is unto Thee that I surrender myself. I affirm my faith in Thee and repose my trust in Thee and turn to Thee in repentance and with Thy help fought my adversaries. O Allah, I seek refuge in Thee with Thine Power; there is no god but Thou, lest Thou leadest me astray. Thou art ever-living that dieth not, while the *Jinn* and mankind die.

(Muslim (f)).

Narrated Abdullah ibn Mas'ud: A deputation of the *Jinn* came to the Prophet
(☙) and said:

> Muhammad, forbid your community to cleans themselves with a bone or
> dung or charcoal, for in them Allah has provided sustenance for us. So the
> Prophet (☙) forbade them to do so.
>
> (Abu Dâwûd (a))

Narrated Abdullah ibn Amr:

> When the Messenger of Allah (☙) was travelling and night came on,
> he said: "O earth, my Lord and your Lord is Allah; I seek refuge in Allah
> from your evil, the evil of what you contain, the evil of what has been
> created in you, and the evil of what creeps upon you; I seek refuge in
> Allah from lions, from large black snakes, from other snakes, from scor-
> pions, from the evil of *Jinn* which inhabit a settlement, and from a parent
> and his offspring."
>
> (Abu Dâwûd (b))

Jabir b. Abd Allah reported the Prophet (☙) as saying:

> Gather your children when darkness spreads, or in the evening (according
> to *Musaddad*), for the *Jinn* are abroad and seize them.
>
> (Abu Dâwûd (c))

Abu al-Sa'ib said I went to visit Abu Sa'ld al-Khudri, and while I was sitting
I heard a movement under his couch. When I looked and found a snake there,
I got up. Abu Sa'ld said: what is with you? I said: Here is a snake. He said: what
do you want ? I said: I shall kill it. He then pointed to a room in his house in
front of his room and said: My cousin (son of my uncle) was in this room. He
asked his permission to go to his wife on the occasion of the battle of Troops
(*Ahzab*), as he was recently married. The Messenger of Allah (☙) gave him
permission and ordered him to take his weapon with him. He came to his
house and found his wife standing at the door of the house. When he pointed
to her with the lance, she said; do not make haste till you see what has brought
me out. He entered the house and found an ugly snake there. He pierced in
the lance while it was quivering. He said: I do not know which of them died
first, the man or the snake. His people then came to the Messenger of Allah
(☙) and said: supplicate Allah to restore our companion to life for us. He
said: Ask forgiveness for your Companion. Then he said: In Medina a group of
Jinn have embraced Islam, so when you see one of them, pronounce a warning to it three times and if it appears to you after that, kill it after three days.
(Abu Dâwûd (d))

Anas reported that the Prophet (ﷺ) said,

> The barrier between the eyes of the *Jinn* and the nakedness of the Children of Adam is (created) when a Muslim discards a garment and says, "In the name of Allah besides Whom there is no other god."
>
> (Ibn As-Sinni)

Narrated Jabir bin 'Abdullah: The Prophet (ﷺ) said,

> Cover your utensils and tie your water skins, and close your doors and keep your children close to you at night, as the *Jinns* spread out at such time and snatch things away. When you go to bed, put out your lights, for the mischief-doer (i.e. the rat) may drag away the wick of the candle and burn the dwellers of the house." Ata said, "The devils" (instead of the *Jinns*).
>
> (Bukhârî (c))

Narrated Abu Sa'id al-Khudri: Muhammad ibn Abu Yahya said that his father told him that he and his companion went to Abu Sa'id al-Khudri to pay a sick visit to him. He said: "Then we came out from him and met a companion of ours who wanted to go to him. We went ahead and sat in the mosque. He then came back and told us that he heard Abu Sa'id al-Khudri say: The Apostle of Allah (ﷺ) said:

> Some snakes are *Jinn*; so when anyone sees one of them in his house, he should give it a warning three times. If it return (after that), he should kill it, for it is a devil.
>
> (Abu Dâwûd (e))

Conclusion

Muslims are required to have a firm belief, with no shadow of a doubt, in the existence of the *Jinn*. From the evidence of the Qur'an and Sunnah, it is clear that the world of the *Jinn* exists. Whatever is in accordance with the Qur'an and Sunnah, we should accept it. Ameen (2005) argued that "The *Jinn* exist and are alive; they have powers of understanding and are subject to commands and prohibitions. So the believer who affirms *Tawheed* must believe in the existence of the *Jinn*" (p. 41–42). Nonetheless, the belief in *Jinn* possessing some divine qualities (for example, all-knowing, all-seeing etc.) is categorically in opposition with the Islamic creed (*Aqeedah*) (Philips, 2002). Moreover, scholars agree that supplications to *Jinn* (for example, in the form of prayers, or carrying amulets), or to anything or anybody else but Allah for that matter, is considered *Shirk* (the worship of anything but Allah), the greatest sin in Islam if done intentionally (Younis, 2013). From a theological perspective, why people are afraid of the *Jinn* is one of the greatest misconceptions. The lack of knowledge of *Tawheed*, ignorance, spreading myths and failure to protect oneself from the harm of the *Jinn* have been put forward as the causes of widespread misinformation and misperception (Philips, 2002; Ameen, 2005). In the next chapter we will be examining *Jinn* possession and its effects on mental health.

References

Abu Dâwûd (a) Sunan of Abu Dâwûd Vol. 1, Book 1, Hadith 39.

Abu Dâwûd (b) Sunan of Abu Dâwûd 2603 Vol. 3, Book 15, Hadith 2597.

Abu Dâwûd (c) Sunan of Abu Dâwûd 3733 Vol. 4, Book 27, Hadith 3724.

Abu Dâwûd (d) Sunan of Abu Dâwûd 5257 Vol. 5, Book 43, Hadith 5237.

Abu Dâwûd (e) Sunan of Abu Dâwûd. General Behavior (Kitab Al-Adab) Book 41 : Hadith 5236.

Al-Tahhaawi, and Al-Tabaraani (a) Al-Tahhaawi in *Mushkil al-Athaar*, 4/95, and by al-Tabaraani in *al-Kabeer*, 22/214. Shaykh al-Albaani said in *al-Mishkaat* (2/1206, no. 4148): al-Tahhaawi and Abu'l-Shaykh reported it with a Sahih Isnad.

Ameen, A. M. K. (2005) *The Jinn and Human Sickness: Remedies in the Light of the Qur'aan and Sunnah*. Translated by Nasiruddin Al-Khattab. Riyadh, Saudi Arabia: Darussalam.

Bukhârî (a). Sahih al-Bukhârî 773 al-Bukhârî Vol. 1, Book 12, Hadith 740.

Bukhârî (b). Sahih al-Bukhârî Vol. 9, Book 93, Hadith 638.

Bukhârî (c). Sahih Bukhârî. Book #54, Hadith #533.

Ibn Abdul Barr, cited in Al-Ashqar, U. S. (2003) *The World of the Jinn and Devils in the Light of the Qur'an and Sunnah*. Riyadh, Saudi Arabia: International Islamic Publishing House, p. 7.

Ibn As-Sinni. Cited in Fiqh-us-Sunnah, Volume 4: Supplications Volume 4, Page 124: On Discarding a Piece of Clothing. Fiqh-us-Sunnah Sayyid Saabiq (1987). Maktabat al-Khadamat-e al-Hadithah.

Muslim (a) Sahih Muslim 2814 a: Book 52, Hadith 62 USC-MSA web (English) reference: Book 39, Hadith 6757.

Muslim (b) Sahih Muslim: Book 19, Hadith 39. Arabic/English book reference: Book 19, Hadith 1846.

Muslim (c) Sahih Muslim 541 a. Muslim Vol. 1, Book 4, Hadith 1104.

Muslim (d) Sahih Muslim 450 a. Muslim Vol. 1, Book 4, Hadith 903.

Muslim (e) Sahih Muslim 2228 a. Muslim Vol. 5, Book 26, Hadith 5535.

Muslim (f) Sahih Muslim 2717. Muslim Vol. 6, Book 35, Hadith 6561.

Philips, B. (2002) *The Fundamentals of Tawheed: Islamic Monotheism*. New Delhi: Islamic Book Service.

Younis, T. (2013) *How do Jinn fit in a framework of mental health?* www.muslimpsyche.com/2013/03/how-do-jinn-fit-in-framework-of-mental.html (accessed 18 March 2018).

Chapter 11

Dissociative disorders and *Jinn* possession

Introduction

Dissociative disorders are a group of psycho–spiritual disorders that affect a diversity of people from racial, ethnic and socioeconomic backgrounds. Dissociation has been described as a "disconnection between a person's thoughts, memories, feelings, actions or sense of who he or she is" (Sidran Institute, 2016). Dissociative disorders, according to DSM-V (APA 2013), "involve problems with memory, identity, emotion, perception, behavior and sense of self. Dissociative symptoms can potentially disrupt every area of mental functioning." The main features of dissociative disorders include the escape or dissociation from reality affecting self-identity, thought consciousness and memory. It is common for health professionals to misdiagnose *Jinn* possession for dissociative disorders and *Jinn* possession with psychotic states such as schizophrenia. However, there are both similarities and subtle differences between the different set of conditions. Hussein (n.d.) suggested that

> there is also confusion between schizophrenia and *Jinn* possessions, mainly due to occasional references – though obviously no evidence – of 'supernatural' activity in the experiences of patients with schizophrenia. However, the difference here is clear since with *Jinn* possession, there is often clear physical evidence of this, unlike schizophrenia.

According to Sheikh (2005) "*Jinn* possession is a not uncommon lay 'differential diagnosis' in those with an altered mental state and have a rational basis when viewed from within the Islamic narrative" (p. 339). In this chapter, a brief overview of dissociative disorders is presented, and the causes of humans being possessed by *Jinn* are examined, identifying the *Jinn*-related effects and the signs and symptoms of *Jinn* possession. In addition, *Jinn* possession as an explanatory model in the context of physical and psychological disorders is examined.

Dissociative disorders

The four types of dissociative disorders include Dissociative amnesia, Dissociative identity disorder, Depersonalisation/derealisation disorder and Other dissociative disorder not specified (APA, 2013). The symptoms of dissociative disorders depend on the type of disorder that has been diagnosed. Someone with a dissociative disorder may have problems including: memory loss (amnesia) of orientation to certain time, place, events and personal information; a distorted sense of identity; a sense of detachment and derealisation with self and the emotional dimension; a sense of make-believe; experiences stress-related problems associated with interpersonal relationships and work; and depression, anxiety and suicidal thoughts. In addition, some individuals would present with problems of movement or sensation, convulsions (seizures), paralysis and loss of sensation. Some of the symptoms have no organic or neurological deficit and cannot be explained by Western medicine. An overview of the characteristics and overview of dissociative disorders is presented in Table 11.1.

Concept of possession

Jinn possession is real for Muslims and it is possible for *Jinn* to possess humans. This is confirmed in the Qur'an (2:275). Sheikh al-Islam Ibn Taymiyah (May Allah have mercy on him) said: "The fact that a Jinni may enter the body of a human is proven by the consensus of the Imams of Ahl al-Sunnah wa'l-Jama'ah (the larger body of Muslims who are upon the Prophetic traditions)." Possession is defined by Littlewood (2016) as "possession is the belief that an individual

Table 11.1 Types of dissociative disorders

Types	Characteristics	Key symptoms
Dissociative amnesia.	Inability to remember personal information in a way that cannot be accounted for by forgetfulness.	Sudden amnesic episode. Episode can last minutes, hours, days, or, rarely, months or years.
Depersonalisation disorder.	Feeling that objects in the environment are changing shape or size. People are automated; feeling detached from one's body.	Detachment. Loss of reality (derealisation).
Dissociative identity disorder.	More than one identity present in one person.	Changes in behaviour, memory and thinking. Gaps in memory. Fugue states. Distress. Hallucinations. Behaving out of character. Writing in different handwriting. Violent behaviour (men).
Other dissociative disorder not specified.	Does not fall within the other three types of dissociative disorders.	

has been entered by an alien spirit or other para-human force, which then controls the person or alters that person's actions and identity to a greater or lesser extent" (p. 29). Possession has been articulated as

> a state of unconsciousness . . . in which we are not answerable for our actions, our bodily movements . . . we don't have control of our bodies anymore. It's the total loss of control of the body and the mind. Something else controls – it is the spiritual being.
>
> (Cohen, 2008, p. 9)

It has been emphasised that possession states can be understood only in the combination and context of biological, anthropological, sociological, psycho-pathological and experimental dimensions (Khalifa and Hardie, 2005). Possession can also be referred as a type of "neuro-cultural processes that can be described by means of both cultural and neurological mechanisms and is the response or solution to other underlying problems" (Craffert, 2015, p. 1).

Whitwell and Barker (1980) stated that the word possession is used in two different ways as 'true' possession invoking the supernatural and those with a syndrome consisting of clouding of consciousness, changed demeanour and tone of voice and subsequent amnesia. Bourguignon (2004) distinguishes between Non-Trance Possession and Possession Trance.

Non-Trance Possession develops as a consequence from negative changes in physical health, whilst Possession Trance is characterised by an alteration in the state of consciousness and behaviour (p. 137) In contrast, Lewis (2003) suggests two types of possession: central and peripheral. In the central type, possession is characteristic of religious ceremonies where possession is considered desirable, and the spirits are generally thought to be sympathetic. Peripheral possession indicates being enmeshed with undesirable, immoral and dangerous evil spirits and requires some form of treatment. However, not all orientalists are convinced about the aetiology of 'possession' by *Jinn* or other supernatural beings. Neuner et al. (2012) conclude that in many of the areas of the world where beliefs about spirit possession are widely held, such beliefs are a standard consequence of intense traumatic experiences with dissociative symptoms. It is argued that beliefs about spirit possession can then be used by various local agencies and faith healers to manipulate the behaviour of individuals (Aziz, 2001; Neuner et al., 2012).

Spirit possession in the DSM-IV and DSM-V

In the DSM-IV, spirit possession falls under the category of Dissociative Disorder Not Otherwise Specified [DDNOS] and involves trance and possession (APA, 2000). Dissociative trance disorder is characterised as

> single or episodic disturbances in the state of consciousness, identity, or memory that are indigenous to particular locations and cultures. Dissociative

trance involves narrowing of awareness of immediate surroundings or ste-reotyped behaviors or movements that are experienced as being beyond one's control. Possession trance involves replacement of the customary sense of personal identity by a new identity, attributed to the influence of a spirit, power, deity, or other person, and associated with stereotyped "involuntary" movements or amnesia. Examples include amok (Indonesia), bebainan (Indonesia), latab (Malaysia), pibloktoq (Arctic), ataque de nervios (Latin America), and possession (India). The Dissociative or trance disorder is not a normal part of a broadly accepted collective cultural or religious practice. The DSM-V (APA, 2013) includes possession experiences under the label of dissociative identity disorder (DID).

However, it is stated that the "disturbance is not a normal part of a broadly accepted cultural or religious practice" (APA, 2013). Delmonte et al. (2016) asserted that the possession or dissociative identity disorder is not part of a broadly accepted cultural or religious practice. The authors challenged this notion, asking "How can a clinician living in a culture where possession is partly accepted differentiate pathological from religious possession?" (p. 324). Delmonte et al. (2016) suggested that future revisions of the DSM should address the

> ambiguity of feelings (co-occurrence of positive and negative affect) sur-rounding possession experiences and it should acknowledge the wide-spread report of unusual or anomalous experiences in general populations where they may not be part of accepted cultural practices and move beyond a dualistic account of possession experiences as either religious or pathological.
>
> (p. 332)

Jinn possession and mental health problems

Jinn possession can manifest with a range of bizarre behaviours and unusual movements which could be interpreted as a number of different psychotic and non-psychotic disorders (Al-Habeeb, 2003). Accordingly, "spirit possession is a culturally specific way of displaying symptoms of psychosis, dissociation, social anxiety, etc. and is a fairly global idiom of distress" (Dein and Illaiee, 2013, p. 291). Those with *Jinn*-related possession appear to suffer from intense fear, psychological disorders (for example, depression, anxiety), physical sick-ness, hallucinations, creating animosity between individuals (couples, friends etc.), sexual problems and causing damage to material possessions (with fire, for example), hysteria, mania, Tourette syndrome, epilepsy, schizophrenia or dissociative identity disorder (El-Islam, 1995; Ameen, 2005; Dein and Illaiee, 2013). In addition, those with true *Jinn* possession may make an individual have epileptic-like seizures and 'speak in tongues' or speak in an incomprehensible language (Al-Ashqar, 2003). Many Muslims who suffer from hallucinations or other psychotic symptoms (Lim et al., 2015) and delusions may attribute these experiences to *Jinn* possession.

All these behaviours may be interpreted as symptoms of various mental disorders. As Begum (2016) stated,

> this is where the lines get blurry between mental health and *Jinn*-related issues, particularly with psychosis, schizophrenia and bipolar because the symptoms of these mental health disorders may correlate with some of the characteristics of a *Jinn* possession such as hearing voices, seeing things, being paranoid, doing random out of character things and having irregular mood swings.

For example, there are similarities between the clinical symptoms of schizophrenia and *Jinn* possession. The common symptoms in schizophrenia and *Jinn* possession include hallucinations, delusions and bizarre behaviours. According to Irmak (2014),

> the hallucination in schizophrenia may therefore be an illusion-a false interpretation of a real sensory image formed by demons. This input seems to be construed by the patient as 'bad things,' reflecting the operation of the nervous system on the poorly structured sensory input to form an acceptable percept. On the other hand, auditory hallucinations expressed as voices arguing with one another and talking to the patient in the third person may be a result of the presence of more than one demon in the body.
>
> (p. 776)

Epileptic seizures rather than epilepsy have been linked to *Jinn* possession among Muslims Obeid et al., 2012; Neyaz et al., 2017). Epileptic seizure refers to the sudden attack that happens to a patient, characterised by tension and shaking, accompanied by loss of consciousness. There is a difference of opinion from scholars and some modern Muslim physicians on the cause of epileptic seizures due to *Jinn* possession. This belief is held by a significant majority of Muslims, including Muslim physicians, scientists and scholars, worldwide. According to Obeid et al. (2012), "there is no statement in the Qur'an or Prophet Mohammad's sayings (Hadith) that epilepsy is caused by Jinns" (p. 247). Obeid et al. (2012) claimed that in spite of the fact, Muslim religious scholars such as Ibn Qayyim al-Jawziyya, Umar Al-Ashqar and others have popularised this doctrine. However, Allah says in the Qur'an (Interpretation of the meaning):

> *Those who eat riba (interest) will not stand (on the Day of Resurrection) except like the standing of a person beaten by Shaytan leading him to insanity. That is because they say: 'Trading is only like Riba'.*
>
> (Sūrat Al Baqarah (The Cow) 2:275)

Al-Qurtubi said in his Tafsir (exegesis): "This verse (Ayah) is proof that those people are wrong who deny that epilepsy is caused by the *Jinn* and claim that its causes are only physical, and that the Shaytan does not enter people or cause madness." Ibn Kathir said in his Tafsir, after mentioning the verse quoted previously:

> They will not rise from their graves on the Day of Resurrection except like the way in which the epileptic rises during his seizure, when he is beaten by the Shaytan. This is because they will rise in a very bad state.
>
> (Islamqa.info.(c))

'Abd-Allah ibn al-Imam Ahmad ibn Hanbal said: "I said to my father, 'There are some people who say that the *Jinn* do not enter the body of the epileptic.' He said: 'O my son, they are lying; the *Jinn* could speak through this person.'" Commenting on this, Ibn Qudamah said:

> What he said is well known, because a person may suffer an epileptic seizure and speak in a language that no one understands, and his body may be beaten with blows that would fell a camel, but the epileptic does not feel them at all, and he is also unaware of the words he is saying. The epileptic and others may be dragged about, or the carpet on which he is sitting may be pulled, and utensils may be moved about from place to place, and other things may happen. Anyone who witnesses such a thing will know for sure that the one who is speaking through the person and moving these things is not human.

And he said (May Allah have mercy on him):

> There is no one among the imams (religious leaders/scholars) of the Muslims who denies that *Jinn* may enter the body of the epileptic and others. Anyone who denies this and claims that Islam denies it is lying about Islam. There is nothing in the proofs of Shari'ah (Islamic law) to show that it does not happen." As regards the causes of epilepsy, Ibn Taymiyah explained the causes. He stated that: "When the *Jinn* touch a person with epilepsy, it may be because of desire or love, just as happens between one human and another . . . or it may − as is usually the case − be because of hatred and punishment, such as when a person has harmed them or they think that he has harmed them deliberately, either by urinating on them or pouring hot water on them or killing them, even if the person did that unknowingly. There are ignorant and wrongdoing ones among the Jinn who may punish a person more than he deserves, or they may be playing with him and mistreating him, like foolish people among mankind.
>
> (Islamqa.info.(c))

Few orientalists, physicians and scientists admit that there are some kinds of epilepsy for which modern clinical medicine cannot discover the cause and the aetiology is of unknown origin. They failed to acknowledge the true cause of some kinds of epilepsy. However, there are Western-oriented physicians that acknowledge this kind of epilepsy. It is worth noting that not everyone who has epilepsy is possessed by the *Jinn*, because epilepsy may have organic or physical causes. It is also important to note that an individual should not be regarded as being *Jinn* possessed if any of the symptoms mentioned in the following section occur. There is no certainty or clear diagnosis that an individual has been possessed by *Jinn* until after the Qur'an has been recited over them, so these symptoms should not be taken as definitive evidence of *Jinn* possession. However, in many cases, the patient may be suffering from a psychotic disorder rather than *Jinn* possession. This may have a significant impact on the diagnosis and intervention strategies involving both the faith healer and the psychiatrist.

Explanation of the causes of being possessed

Many reasons have been put forward by scholars and faith healers of the causes of *Jinn* possession. Ibn Taymiyah explained that

> possession of the human by the *Jinn* can occur from desires, lusts, passions and zealousness in the same way that a human is in accord with another human....And it also occurs, and this is the majority case, due to hatred and revenge. For example, one of the humans harms a *Jinn* or the *Jinn* thinks that the human was trying to harm them by urinating on some *Jinn* or throwing hot water on them or a human might kill a *Jinn*, even though the human may not have realised that. Among the *Jinn* is ignorance and wrongdoing and, therefore, they get revenge from humans above and beyond what is just. And it could occur from the horseplay or simply evil acts of the *Jinn* in the same way the evil is done by the foolish of the humans.

(19:205)

According to Sheikh Muhammad Taahir 'Abdul-Muhsin (Philips, 2008, p. 219) the main reasons why *Jinn* possess humans include

> Walking around the house naked; being isolated and unprotected by the Prophetic morning and evening prayers; entering the toilet without the fortifying prayers because the toilets are among the dwelling places of the *Jinn*; pouring hot water on the *Jinn* without mentioning Allah's name; and going without making the fortifying prayers to areas of the *Jinn*, like mountain tops and garbage dumps, hurting them by urinating on them or stepping on them – The *Jinn* may then ignorantly hurt the person much more than he deserves.

(p. 219)

Sheikh Abdullaah Mushrif al-Amree in his unpublished manuscript, 'Iqtiraan ash-Shaytaan bi al-Insaan,' stated that the reasons why people are possessed by *Jinn* include: extreme fear, extreme anger, extreme jealousy, devotion to lust, human aggression against devils, and love of demons for humans. He mentioned that "Human aggression could be in the form of pouring hot water on the places where devils reside or urinating in holes or cracks in the ground." He reiterated that:

> The Prophet (ﷺ) prohibited us from urinating in holes and cracks in the earth because they are places where the *Jinn* reside. The love of demons for humans is very, very common. When male *Jinn* possess human females and we communicate with them, they often readily admit that they are in love with them. And when female *Jinn* possess men, they often express the same.
>
> (Philips, 2008, p. 229)

Other reasons reported include the abandonment of religion, the lack of prayer and supplications, magical spells, falling in love with a man or woman.

Jinn-related effects

Possession worldwide is found more commonly in women and marginalised groups (Dein, and Illaiee, 2013). Most of those who treat *Jinn* possession claim that the majority of those attending their services are women. According to Sheikh Abdul-Khaaliq Al-Attaar (Philips, 2008), the percentage of *Jinn* possession among women is greater than among men, and this percentage is consistent with the texts of the Qur'an and the Sunnah. The effects of *Jinn* possession include physical, psychological and spiritual effects. The *Jinn* had been reported to affect the physical health of an individual ranging from common ailments, unexplained pains and bruises, to more serious medical disorders. Diseases including infertility, heavy bleeding and menstrual irregularities, and infections are common among women. In men, the disorders include sexual problems related to impotency and premature ejaculation

Psychological disorders include intense fear, panic attacks, phobias, depression, dissociative identity disorder, personality disorders, obsession bipolar disorders, suicidal ideation, hallucinations, delusions and schizophrenia. There is also stirring up hatred between people, causing enmity and division between people such as husband and wife, business partners, friends and family. In some cases there are tampering with, and causing damage to houses and material possessions (causing fires, throwing furniture about, throwing stones at the house). The *Jinn* also affects the spiritual dimension of the individual by blocking the person from obeying Allah, turning away, in particular, from acts of worship and obedience, the remembrance of Allah (*Dhikr*) and reading the Qur'an. The ultimate goal is to get the individual involved in disbelief.

Signs and symptoms of *Jinn* possession

Some of the symptoms from which it may be known whether a person has been possessed by the *Jinn* are reported from those dealing with the spiritual interventions, as prescribed in Islam, *Ruqyah* (incantation). The signs and symptoms may vary from individual to individual depending on the nature and type of *Jinn* possession and the nature of the individual. The symptoms of possession include (Islamqa.info.(a, b)):

- Turning away and reacting strongly when hearing the call to prayer (adhan) or Qur'an.
- Episodes of losing consciousness and/or epileptic attacks, especially when Qur'an is recited for the possessed person.
- Frequent nightmares during sleep and a lot of disturbing dreams.
- Tendency to avoid people accompanied by out-of-the-norm behaviour.
- The *Jinn* who possesses him might speak when Qur'an is recited for the possessed person.
- The devil who is dwelling in him may speak when Qur'an is recited over him.

Scholars such as Dr Abul-Mundir Kaheel Ibn Ibraaheem Ameen (2005) have divided the symptoms into two categories: those which occur when one is awake, and those which occur when one is asleep (see Table 11.2).

Table 11.2 Symptoms of *Jinn* possession

Symptoms when one is awake:	Symptoms when one is asleep:
Turning away, in particular, from acts of worship and obedience, the remembrance of Allah.	Frightening nightmares, which includes seeing various kinds of creatures such as ghosts or apparitions.
Erratic behaviour in one's words, deeds and movements.	Insomnia, anxiety and fear upon waking.
Being quick to get angry or weep with no apparent cause.	Talking loudly in one's sleep, or moaning and groaning.
Paralysis of a limb (with no medical cause).	
Seizures (with no medical cause).	
Sitting in the toilet for a long time, and talking to oneself.	
Constant headache with no medical cause, which is not eased by painkillers.	
Irregular menstruation in women.	
Not producing children although both husband and wife are medically sound and able to reproduce.	
Depression.	

Source: Adapted from Ameen, A. (2005). *The Jinn and Human Sickness: Remedies in the Light of the Qur'aan and Sunnah* (N. Khattab, trans.), Riyadh: Darussalam.

Ameen (2005) lists the various types of illnesses a *Jinn* may inflict upon an individual: intense fear, psychological disorders (for example, depression, anxiety etc.), physical sickness, hallucinations, creating animosity between individuals, sexual problems and causing damage to material possessions (with fire, for example). According to Ashqar (2003), any signs or symptoms where there is no substantial evidence or organic or psychological problems may also be *Jinn*-related.

The following excerpts are from a collection of interviews of Muslim exorcists from Philips (2008) 'Exorcist Tradition in Islam.' According to Sheikh Abdullaah Mushrif al-'Amree, Riyadh, the symptoms of *Jinn* possession include "depression, headaches, continual movements in the bodies or disturbing dreams" (p. 255). Sheikh Muhammad Taahir 'Abdul-Muhsin, Cairo, stated that "some of the signs are that a person mentions that he is uneasy, he finds himself getting up and sitting down frequently, he speaks unintelligibly, etc. This is called demonic possession (*Sara' al-jinn*)." Sheikh Abdul-Khaaliq al-'Attaar, Cairo, stated that the symptoms are expressed "during sleep include nightmares, sleeplessness, broken sleep, uneasiness, the grinding of teeth, and dreams of *Satan* in the form of carnivorous animals." The symptoms while awake, include "feelings of anxiety, forgetfulness, hopelessness, lethargy and immobility. Included among the signs are being easily angered, crying, and staring aimlessly or avoiding eyes of others" (p. 227).

Sheikh Alee Mushrif al-'Amree, Madinah, Saudi Arabia, stated that

> a man may come to me complaining that he feels as though chains are tied to his body between his stomach and his neck and at times something seems to suffocate him. One possessed by a *jinnee* exhibits some strange movements and speaks without realising it, experiences nightmares or a state of immobility at the time of going to sleep or between the state of wakefulness and sleep, these are among the beginning signs of possession.
>
> (Philips, 2008, p. 260)

According to Sheikh Muhammad al-Funaytil al-'Unayzee, Riyadh, Saudi Arabia, those possessed will

> act unnaturally, always looking at the ground, or gets up suddenly and walks around. The possessed are generally unable to sit still in one place for any length of time. He frequently goes to the toilet and seems to be generally uneasy. Sometimes he displays a strange, eerie smile. He may laugh in an abnormal way without any reason, as if he is seeing things we cannot. I have noticed this among the twenty or so cases which I have treated.
>
> (Philips, 2008, p. 267)

Sheikh Sa'd Muhammad, Cairo, Egypt, stated that in relation to a *Jinn*-possessed woman,

> The first sign of possession in a woman is that her menses becomes irregular. She also feels a kind of suffocation which is quite different from

psychological depression or medical asphyxia. It comes to her at night in the form of a nightmare, even if she is regular in her formal prayers and uses the prescribed daily supplications. Other signs are continuous movements and pains which seem to travel around the body.

(Philips, 2008, p. 243)

It is worth noting that in some cases, the *Jinn* will manifest itself during the recitation of Qur'anic verses and at other times it will hide. Sometimes they listen to a great deal of religious admonition, yet do not respond. In many cases the *Jinn* speak in other languages or other dialects common to the region of the country. If it is a female *Jinn*, it speaks with a female voice, and a male *Jinn* with a male voice. In many cases, the *Jinn* communicate with the possessed person's voice. A summary of symptoms of *Jinn* possession from Islamic scholars and healers is presented in Table 11.3.

Conclusion

It is acknowledged by Islamic psychologists, Islamic counsellors, physicians and psychiatrists that both *Jinn* possession and dissociative identity disorder exist in reality and have different aetiology and presenting symptoms. However, what complicates things is that some of the classifications of symptoms overlap and this is where the boundaries get blurry between mental health problems and *Jinn*-related possessions. Thus, this can be perceived as one and the same thing in certain cases. The lack of clarity about the relationship between *Jinn* possession and mental health problems has significant clinical implications. Mental health professionals should be aware of the narrative of their patients. Lim et al. (2015) suggested that in order to have more effective engagement with the patient, it would seem advisable to "to tailor interviewing techniques to obtain more specific information about symptomatology, coping mechanisms, and the sociocultural context of patients' complaints" (p. 11). Multi-professional agencies need to be involved where a dual diagnosis of *Jinn* possession and mental health problems are identified; this mean involving the local Imam or faith leaders for consultation and advice.

References

Al-Ashqar, Umar S. (2003) *The World of the Jinn and Devils in the Light of the Qur'an and Sunnah*. (Islamic Creed Series, Volume 3). Riyadh, Saudi Arabia: International Islamic Publishing House

Al-Habeeb, T. A. (2003) A pilot study of faith healers' views on evil eye, Jinn possession, and magic in the Kingdom of Saudi Arabia, *Saudi Society of Community and Family Medicine Journal*, 10, 3.

Ameen, A. (2005) *The Jinn and Human Sickness: Remedies in the Light of the Qur'aan and Sunnah* (N. Khattab, trans.). Darussalam, Riyadh.

Table 11.3 Summary of symptoms of *Jinn* possession from Islamic scholars and healers

Scholars	Signs and symptoms of Jinn possession
Dr. Abu'l-Mundhir Khaleel ibn Ibraaheem Ameen	Intense fear, depression, anxiety, hallucinations, creating animosity between individuals, physical sickness, sexual problems and causing damage to material possessions.
Sheikh Abdullaah Mushrif al-'Amree	Depression, headaches, continual movements in the bodies or disturbing dreams. Strange movements and speaks without realising it. State of immobility at the time of going to sleep or between the state of wakefulness and sleep.
Sheikh Muhammad Taahir 'Abdul-Muhsin	Uneasy, getting up and sitting down frequently, he speaks unintelligibly.
Sheikh Abdul-Khaaliq al-'Attaar	Nightmares, sleeplessness, broken sleep, uneasiness, the grinding of teeth and dreams of *Satan* in the form of carnivorous animals. Anxiety, forgetfulness, hopelessness, lethargy, immobility, easily angered, crying and staring aimlessly or avoiding eye contact. Supernatural strength.
Sheikh Muhammad al-Funaytil al-'Unayzee	Restlessness, always looking at the ground, or gets up suddenly and walks around. Frequent use of toilets. Uncomfortable, displays a strange, eerie smile. Laugh in an abnormal way without any reason, as if he is seeing things.
Sheikh Sa'd Muhammad	Women: menses becomes irregular. Suffocation which is quite different from psychological depression or medical asphyxia. Nightmare, movements and pains which seem to travel around the body.
Sheikh 'Alee Mushrif al-'Amree	Chains are tied to his body between his stomach and his neck, suffocation, exhibits some strange movements and speaks without realising it, nightmare.
Sheikh Muhammad ibn Sa'iyyid ad-Dawsaree	Way that the possessed walks, epilepsy (*sara'*), which is not caused by the *jinn*. At other times they are affected by the evil eye. Heart beat faster or becomes irregular without medical explanation. Speak in the voice of the possessed.
Sheikh Assim Alhakeem	Strong repulsion when hearing Qur'an or Aathan (call for prayers), nightmares, avoidance of people, out-of-the-norm behaviour. Episodes of losing consciousness and/or epileptic attacks, especially when Qur'an is recited.

Source: Adapted from Abu Ameenah Bilal Philips (2008) *The Exorcist Tradition in Islam*. Birmingham: Al-Hidaayah Publishing & Distribution.

American Psychiatric Association (2000) *Diagnostic and Statistical Manual of Mental Disorders, Fourth Edition, Text Revision (DSM-IV-TR).* Arlington, VA: American Psychiatric Press.

American Psychiatric Association (2013) Diagnostic and Statistical Manual of *Mental* Disorders (Fifth Edition) (DSM-5). Arlington, VA: American Psychiatric Press.

Aziz S. (2001) Do souls of the dead return back to the World? *As-Sunnah Newsletter*, 13.

Begum, M. (2016) Can jinn possession and mental illness be the same thing? http://inspir itedminds.org.uk/2016/10/21/can-jinn-possession-and-mental-illness-be-the-same-thing/ (accessed 14 September 2017).

Bourguignon, E. (2004) *Possession and trance*, in C. R. Ember, and M. Ember (Eds.), *Encyclopaedia of Medical Anthropology: Health and Illness in the World's Cultures.* New York: Springer Science, Vol. 1, pp. 137–145. http://dx.doi.org/10.1007/0-387-29905-X_15.

Bressert, S. (2018). Dissociative Disorder: Not Otherwise Specified (NOS). *Psych Central*. https://psychcentral.com/disorders/dissociative-disorder-not-otherwise-specified-nos/ (accessed 1 June 2018).

Cohen, E. (2008) What is spirit possession? Defining, comparing, and explaining two possession forms, *Ethnos*, 73, 1, 1–25.

Craffert, P. F. (2015) What does it mean to be possessed by a spirit or demon? Some phenomenological insights from neuro-anthropological research, *HTS Theologise Studies/Theological Studies*, 71, 1 Art. #2891, 9. http://dx.doi.org/10.4102/hts.v71i1.2891.

Dein, S., and Illaiee, A. S. (2013) Jinn and mental health: Looking at jinn possession in modern psychiatric practice, *The Psychiatrist*, 37, 9, 290–293. Doi: 10.1192/pb.bp.113.042721.

Delmonte, R., Giancarlo Lucchetti, G., Moreira-Almeida, A., and Farias, M. (2016) Can the DSM-5 differentiate between nonpathological possession and dissociative identity disorder? A case study from an Afro-Brazilian religion, *Journal of Trauma & Dissociation*, 17, 3, 322–337. Doi:10.1080/15299732.2015.110335.

El-Islam, F. (1995) Cultural aspects of illness behaviour, *The Arab Journal of Psychiatry*, 6, 13–18.

Hussein, F. (n.d.) *Dissociative Identity Disorder.* Islam Online Archive https://archive.islamon line.net/?p=6485 (accessed 19 March 2018).

Ibn Taymiyah, Shaykh al-Islam. *Majmu' al-Fatawa.* Editors: Amir al-Jazzar & Anwar al-Baz. Egypt: Dar al Wafa & Dar Ibn HazmIrmak, M.K.J (2014) Schizophrenia or possession? *Journal of Religion and Health*, 53, 3, 773–777. https://doi.org/10.1007/s10943-012-9673-y

Islamqa info (a) 125543: *Determining if One is Afflicted by Evil Eye or Possessed.* https://islamqa. info/en/125543 (accessed 19 March 2018).

Islamqa info (b) 240: *Black Magic and Satanic Possession.* https://islamqa.info/en/240 (accessed 19 March 2018).

Islamqa info (c) 1819: *Jinn Entering Human Bodies.* https://islamqa.info/en/1819 (accessed 19 March 2018).

Khalifa, N., and Hardie, T. (2005) Possession and jinn, *Journal of the Royal Society of Medicine*, 98, 351–353.

Lewis, I. M. (2003) *Ecstatic Religion: A Study of Shamanism and Spirit Possession.* 3rd ed. Abington: Oxon: Routledge.

Lim, A., Hoek, H. W., and Blom, J. D. (2015) The attribution of psychotic symptoms to Jinn in Islamic patients. *Transcultural Psychiatry*, 52, 1, 18–32. Doi.org/10.1177/1363461514543146.

Littlewood, R. (2016) *Possession States*, Chapter 3. In Jean Sybil La Fontaine, The Devil's Children: From Spirit Possession to Witchcraft: New Allegations that Affect Children, Abingdon, Oxon: Routledge.

Neyaz, H. A., Aboauf, H. A., Alhejaili, M. E., and Alrehaili, M. N. (2017) Knowledge and attitudes towards epilepsy in Saudi families, *Journal of Taibah University Medical Sciences*, 12, 1, 89–95.

Neuner, F., Pfeiffer A., Schauer-Kaiser, E., Odenwald, M., Elbert, T., and Ert, V. (2012) Haunted by ghosts: Prevalence, predictors and outcomes of spirit possession experiences among former child soldiers and war-affected civilians in Northern Uganda, *Social Science & Medicine,* 75, 3, 548–554.

Obeid, T., Abu Laban, A., Al-Ghatani, F., Al-Malki, A. R., and Al- Ghamdi, A. (2012) Possession by 'Jinn' as a cause of epilepsy (Saraa): A study from Saudi Arabia, *Seizure* 21, 245e249.

Philips, A. A. B. (2008) *The Exorcist Tradition in Islam*. Birmingham: Al-Hidaayah Publishing & Distribution.

Sheikh, A. (2005) Jinn and cross-cultural care, *Journal of the Royal Society of Medicine*, 98, 8, 339–340.

Sidran Institute (2016) *Dissociation*. Sidran Traumatic Stress Institute. www.sidran.org/resources/for-survivors-and-loved-ones/what-is-a-dissociative-disorder/ (accessed 19 March 2018).

Whitwell, F. D., and Barker, M. G. (1980) Possession states in psychiatric patients in Britain, *British Journal of Medical Psychology*, 53, 4, 287–295.

Chapter 12

Obsessive-compulsive disorder
Islamic manifestations

Introduction

Obsessive-compulsive disorder (OCD) is a common mental health condition in which a person has uncontrollable obsessive thoughts and compulsive behaviours. OCD is a chronic and long-lasting disorder and the unwanted thoughts, ideas or sensations (obsessions) urge them to repeat the rituals (behaviours) over and over. OCD can occur in different forms. There are a variety of different types of obsessions and compulsions. The obsessions (repeated thoughts, urges or mental images) include the fear of germs or contamination, aggressive thoughts towards self and others, and unwanted forbidden or taboo thoughts involving sex, religion and harm. The compulsions (repetitive behaviours) include excessive cleaning and/or handwashing, arranging things in a symmetrical or in a perfect order, repeatedly checking on things and compulsive counting. Both obsessional thoughts and compulsion behaviours make an individual dysfunctional and significantly interfere with a person's daily activities and social interactions. The nature of intensity of these obsessions and compulsions may vary among those presenting with OCD and some individual may present with multiple obsessions of aggressive, sexual and religious obsessions.

Religion or religious beliefs have often been thought to play a part in the genesis of some cases of obsessive-compulsive disorder (OCD). Obsessive-compulsive disorders related to religiosity and are referred in the literature as Scrupulosity. It has been suggested that individuals with Scrupulosity OCD tend to focus excessively on a few specific rules and rituals while neglecting other aspects of the religion (Tahir, 2011). From an Islamic perspective, obsessive-compulsive disorders related to religiosity differ from devout faith and practice. In a Hadith narrated by Abu Huraira (May God be pleased with him), it is reported that the Prophet (ﷺ) said,

> The religion of Islam is easy, and whoever makes the religion a rigour, it will overpower him. So, follow a middle course (in worship); if you can't do this, do something near to it and give glad tidings and seek help (of Allah) in the morning and at dusk and some part of the night.
>
> (Bukhari (a))

This chapter examines the Islamic manifestations of obsessive-compulsive disorder.

Obsessive-compulsive disorder

Obsessive-compulsive disorder (OCD) is a heterogeneous group of symptoms that include intrusive thoughts, rituals, preoccupations and compulsions. Obsessive-compulsive disorder was previously explained as a form of 'melancholia.' In seventeenth-century Europe, obsessions and compulsions were often described as symptoms of religious melancholy. Modern concepts of OCD began to evolve in the nineteenth century. However, in the 9th Century, Abu Zayd Ahmad ibn Sahl al-Balki, Islamic scholar and polymath describes human psychopathology, the diagnoses of psychological disorders including stress, depression, fear and anxiety, phobia and obsessive-compulsive disorders. Al-Balhki's Sustenance for Bodies and Souls (Maṣāliḥ al-Abdān wa-al-Anfus) (Badri, 2013) decribes the diagnostic criteria, the symptomatology and treatment of OCD.

In OCD, the recurrent obsessions or compulsions incapacitate the individual's daily activities, occupational functioning, social relationships and activities. Those suffering may be presenting with an obsession or a compulsion, or both.

The DSM-V (APA, 2013) lists OCD as a distinct, separate category. In the previous version (DSM-IV), OCD was listed under anxiety disorders. The ICD-10 (WHO, 2010) lists OCD (F42) under neurotic, stress-related and somatoform disorders. The DSM-V (APA 2013) provides clinicians with the criteria for diagnosing obsessive-compulsive disorder. This is based on the presence of obsessions, compulsions or both. The obsessional behaviour must be recurrent, persistent with intrusive thoughts that may lead to anxiety or distress. In order to relieve the distress, the individual attempts to ignore or suppress such thoughts, urges or images. The compulsions are behavioural repetitive acts that are performed in response to an obsession. In fact the 9th-century Islamic scholar, Al-Balkhi' s diagnostic criteria matched the all the criteria for OCD diagnosis in DSM-V (APA 2013)!

Al-Bakhi claimed that although OCD is a psychological disorder, its aetiology is "shared with organic bodily aspects" (Badri 2013, p. 54). This is confirmed by the findings from research studies that showed that hereditary and other organic and neurologic aetiology are the causation of OCD. Research into the biological/neurochemical causes and effects of OCD has revealed a link between OCD and neurochemical transmitters with the involvement of serotonergic, dopaminergic and glutamatergic genes (Grünblattab et al., 2014). Research studies report that parents, siblings and children of an individual with OCD have a greater chance of developing OCD than does someone with no family history of the disorder. The findings from twin studies provide evidence that the development of OCD in families is due in part to genetic factors (Tambs et al., 2009; Nestadt et al., 2010). From a psychoanalytic approach, Freud developed a conceptualisation of OCD that the patient's psyche responded in a maladaptive behaviour to conflicts between the id and the super-ego. That is the conflict between instinctual sexual or aggressive impulses and the demands of morality and reality. From a behavioural perspective, people with OCD associate certain cues, objects or situations with fear, and thus learn to avoid the anxiety or fear. Performance of rituals is the coping strategy in reducing the fear. That is classic conditioning. From a cognitive-behavioural approach, there is the implication of specific faulty or negative cognition in the development and maintenance of the disorder. This means that there is a misinterpretation of their thoughts. These cognitions include: overestimation of threat, self-overstated responsibility, intrusive thoughts, perfectionism and intolerance of uncertainty (Frost and Steketee, 2002). Individuals with OCD interpret their intrusive, obsessive thoughts as 'catastrophic,' and will continue to use the avoidance approach and/or perform ritual behaviours. Some of the examples of obsessions and compulsions are presented in Table 12.1.

Diagnostic considerations

There are clinical drawbacks in the making of a diagnosis of OCD. Several medical and psychiatric disorders which may feature symptoms similar to OCD may contribute to a misdiagnosis.

Clinicians should be consider OCD in their differential diagnosis when evaluating medical conditions including Tourette disorder and other tic disorders,; temporal lobe epilepsy, head trauma, post-encephalitic complications, trichotillomania and neuro-dermatitis. Another pitfall is the failure to identify the co-occurring disorders (dual diagnosis) frequently encountered in

Table 12.1 Examples of obsessions and compulsions

Obsessions	Compulsions
• Fear of self-harm and others. • Fear of contamination though illness, cross infection through contact with germs, actual or perceived objectionable substances, dirt or dust. • Superstitious thoughts. • Intrusive thoughts, urges. • Unwanted images. • Excessive religious or moral doubt. Repeated imagining of losing control of aggressive urges. • Checking intrusive sexual thoughts or urges. • Repeated imagining of losing control of sexual urges.	• Touching. • Rituals – house cleaning, hand and body washing. • Excessive ordering/arranging things. • Excessive checking that activities have been done. • Excessively detailed diary planning. • Hoarding certain objects or struggling to throw things away. • Repetitive request for reassurance. • Counting numbers or thinking about specific words. • Avoiding certain locations or situations that might trigger obsessions or intensify them. • Excessive praying/supplications. • Need to confess.

patients with OCD. These psychiatric disorders include: schizophrenia, personality disorder, phobias, generalised anxiety disorder, panic disorder, eating disorders, addictive behaviours and depressive disorders.

Religiosity and obsessive-compulsive disorder

The relationship between religiosity and OCD has been observed in several studies. However, there is limited research on the associations between Muslim religious beliefs and practices and OCD. The literature indicates that individuals who tend to have a variety of obsessions are more likely also to have religious obsessions (Tek and Ulug, 2001; Akbar, 2016). Tek and Ulug (2001) suggested that it is through religion that OCD expresses itself rather than religion being a determinant of the disorder. Assarian et al. (2006) support this finding that the contents of obsessions and compulsions are influenced by religiosity. The findings of Yorulmaz et al. (2009) supports, in line with previous findings, the notion of the association between religiosity and OCD. In a study of Canadian Christian and Turkish Muslim students (Inozu et al., 2012), Muslim students with high religiosity reported more compulsive symptoms than highly religious Christians. The authors suggested that in both samples of Canadian Christian and Turkish Muslim students, the relationship between religiosity and obsessional behaviours was mediated by thought control.

It is well recognised that maladaptive or faulty cognitions or thought-action fusion (TAF) is a cognitive bias presumed to underlie the development and maintenance of OCD (Amir et al., 2001; Shafran and Rachman, 2004 ; Piri and Kabakçi, 2007). The findings from Williams et al.'s (2013) study indicated that obsessional thoughts are not attributable to religion per se, but that the belief systems may mediate maladaptive or faulty cognitions in the maintenance of OCD. However, caution must be taken in generalising the findings to Muslim communities.

Some of the samples under investigation are derived from university students and cannot be deemed representative. However, most of the studies in the literature have limited samples and may not represent the Muslim communities because of its heterogeneity and diversity.

Obsessive-compulsive disorder and Scrupulosity

Obsessive-compulsive disorders related to religiosity are referred to as Scrupulosity. The concept of Scrupulosity is characterised as one in which

> the sufferer's primary anxiety is the fear of being guilty of religious, moral, or ethical failure. Those afflicted with Scrupulosity fear that their effort to live according to their spiritual values not only isn't good enough, but is in direct violation of God.
>
> (Foss, 2013)

Pollard (2010) stated that Scrupulosity is "a form of Obsessive Compulsive Disorder involving religious or moral obsessions. Scrupulous individuals are overly concerned that something they thought or did might be a sin or other violation of religious or moral doctrine" (p. 1.) This psycho-behavioural disorder involves pathological guilt about moral or religious issues or fears supplemented with mental or behavioural compulsions which affect individuals of various religions across the world. However, it has been suggested that "in cases of secular moral Scrupulosity, an individual may obsess about the moral implications of behaviours unrelated to specific culture-bound religious practice, such as being a bad person by not recycling a sheet of paper" (Siev, 2010). Scrupulous OCD is regarded as the fifth most common obsession, with 6% of participants reporting this as their primary obsession and that religious obsessions occur in 25% of individuals with OCD (Antony et al., 1998).

There are some similarities and differences between OCD and Scrupulosity. Although the symptoms presented by an individual with Scrupulosity may seem quite different from those in other forms of OCD, the fundamental processes in the development and maintenance of the disorder are quite analogous. All forms of OCD cause the individual to experience the same obsessional and compulsive cycle including obsession, anxiety, compulsion which cause the individual to be in distress and dysfunctional. The compulsive behaviours are relief efforts to counter the effects of the obsessional thoughts in order to reduce the anxiety of fear. One of the fundamental differences between Scrupulosity and OCD, is that in Scrupulosity OCD the individual is overpowered by their devotion and practice of their religion which can lead to compulsive religious practices and rituals (Deacon and Nelson, 2008). In Scrupulosity OCD, these obsessional thoughts involve intrusive religious blasphemous thoughts, compulsive prayer, hyper-morality, unwarranted concern about committing a sin and cleaning/washing rituals (Himle et al., 2011). Fear of sin and fear of God have been identified as the key dimensions of Scrupulosity OCD. According to Foss (2013), the "obsessive thoughts in Scrupulosity often take the form of 'What if. . .' questions, such as 'what if I just sinned' or 'what if I don't actually believe in God'?" Religious practice and devotion are not necessarily the cause of Scrupulosity. From an Islamic perspective, OCD is quite different from the whispers of Satan or self-talk (*Waswâs*) (Mohamed et al., 2015).

Presentations of Scrupulosity

There is great diversity in the presentation of Scrupulosity. These range from obsessional intrusive thoughts, doubts, impulses, images and behavioural rituals such as purification. According to Abramowitz et al. (2014), the idiosyncratic and heterogeneous nature of Scrupulosity OCD may make "one patient might turn to religious icons as a way of relieving obsessional fear, another might avoid such icons because they trigger unwanted blasphemous thoughts" (p. 141). Abramowitz and Jacoby (2014) identified at least four presentations of this problem based on clinical observations: ego dystonic intrusive thoughts that may or may not related in part within a religious framework; ego dystonic thoughts specific to religion; ego syntonic thoughts of a religious nature, specific to religious belief; and obsessional doubts about whether religious rules and obligatory rituals and commandments have been followed correctly. The content of obsessions amongst Muslims is focused on purity and religious themes (Okasha et al., 1994; Abramowitz and Jacoby, 2014). An overview of the presentation of Scrupulosity is presented in Table 12.2.

The role of Satan (Shaytan) in Scrupulosity OCD

In Islam, the devil is called Shaytan (Satan) and Iblees is one of the *Jinn*. Everything that happens among the believers and non-believers is the whispering of Satan, as an obsessive whisperer, to prevent people from the remembrance of God. Al-Bakhi stated that

> The origin of this obsessive disorder. . . . [is] from the devil appointed to a person (the qareen) that srives to spoil one's life in this world and the Hereafter.
>
> (Badri, 2013, p. 63)

Table 12.2 Presentations of Scrupulosity

Obsessions	Types	Framework	Examples	Compulsions
Ego dystonic intrusive thoughts.	Images/vision: sex, violence, immoral acts.	General and no specific to religion.	Obsessional thoughts about violence towards one's partner.	Repeated prayer or excessive purification.
Ego dystonic thoughts.	Images/vision.	Specific to religion.	Obsessional image about burning or desecrating a religious document such as the Bible or the Qur'an.	Purification in the form compulsive handwashing rituals.
Ego syntonic thoughts.	Images/vision.	Specific to religion.	Questioning one's own religious belief or interpretations of texts.	Repeated prayer or excessive purification.
Doubts and uncertainty.	Images/vision.	Specific to religion.	Questioning one's performance of prayer or supplications not being the standard required or near perfection.	Repeated prayer or excessive purification.

Source: Adapted from Abramowitz, J.S. and Jacoby, R.J. (2014) Scrupulosity: A cognitive – behavioural analysis and implications for treatment, *Journal of Obsessive-Compulsive and Related Disorders*, 3: 140–149.

The enmity between man and Satan originated when God, the Almighty, created Adam. Satan was from amongst the '*Jinn*' who disobeyed the command of his Lord (Qur'an 18:50); full of pride (Qur'an 2:34) and full of arrogance (Qur'an 7:12). As a result, Satan becomes an outcast and stated that (Interpretation of the meaning) "(Iblees) said,

> My Lord, because You have put me in error, I will surely make (disobedience) attractive to them [i.e. mankind] on earth, and I will mislead them all.
> Except, among them, Your chosen servants.
>
> (Sūrat Al-Hijr (The Valley of Stone) 15:39–40)

From then on, Iblees' primary goal is to mislead people by various means until the Day of Judgement. Allah told us about that in the Qur'an (Interpretation of the meaning):

> (Satan) said, "Because You have put me in error, I will surely sit in wait for them on Your straight path. Then I will come to them from before them and from behind them and on their right and on their left, and You will not find most of them grateful (to You)."
>
> (Sūrat Al-A'raf (The Elevations) 7:16–17)

Iblees thus declared his enmity to human beings and openly declared his devious strategy. The ultimate goal of Satan is to make people enjoin what is forbidden or going astray from the remembrance of God, and eventually to turn them into disbelievers. Despite Iblees' persuasive and obsessive nature, they do not have power to force people into evil or cause people to act against their own free will. However, they can affect moods and thought process and implant evil suggestions.

Understanding obsession from an Islamic perspective

The term obsession is the English equivalent of the Arabic term of '*Alwiswas*.' In Arabic dictionaries it has several meanings like "self-talk, the voice of the jewellery, which is also the name of the Satan (devil), and fisherman whispered" (Mohamed et al., 2015, p. 290). Obsession is also described as "The state of being besieged; – used specifically of a person beset by a spirit from without or the act of besieging" (hamariweb.com). Mohamed et al. (2015) suggested that if the spirit-oriented obsession "is associated with the devil, then it should be followed with the term '*Al Khanas*' as a whisperer that disappears for a period and then reappears" (p. 290). From an Islamic perspective, the obsessional thoughts are the 'whispering of Shaytan (Satan)'. Accordingly, Satan is an "obsessive whisperer but not all obsessions are [from] Satan" (Mohamed et al., 2015, p. 290).

The Islamic manifestations of obsessive-compulsive disorder are categorised into different typologies. According to Mohamed et al. (2015,

pp. 290–291), the three types of obsessives according to the Islamic understanding include:

- First: self-talk, which relates to pleasure, self-love, wishes and desires, irre-
  spective of whether it is acceptable (halal) or forbidden (haram).
- Second: the whispers of Satan, the obsessive whisperer, who is the enemy
  of man in command of his religion.
- Third: OCD is the most important characteristic that is contrary to the
  nature of the individual and it is not sufficient to seek refuge with Allah
  from Satan to get rid of those obsessions.

The sources of the Qur'an and Hadith indicate the roles of Satan in nudging or
tempting people to commit unlawful behaviour (for example, murder, enmity,
hatred, the spread of immorality and fornication, drinking alcohol, worshipping
idols). Allah says in the Qur'an (Interpretation of the meaning):

> *And We have already created man and know what his soul whispers to him, and We
> are closer to him than (his) jugular vein.*
>
> (Sūrat Qaf (Qaf) 50:16)

> *Then Satan whispered to him; he said, "O Adam, shall I direct you to the tree of
> eternity and possession that will not deteriorate?"*
>
> (Sūrat Ta Ha (Ta Ha) 20:120)

> *Who whispers (evil) into the breasts of mankind From among the jinn and mankind.*
>
> Sūrat Nas (People or Mankind) 114:5–6)

> *And if there comes to you from Satan an evil suggestion, then seek refuge in Allah.
> Indeed, He is the Hearing, the Knowing.*
>
> (Sūrat Fussilat (Presented in Detail)41:36)

Narrated Abu Huraira: The Prophet (ﷺ) said,

> Allah has accepted my invocation to forgive what whispers in the hearts of
> my followers, unless they put it to action or utter it.
>
> (Bukhari (b))

Anas ibn Malik reported: The Messenger of Allah (ﷺ), was in the company of
one of his wives when a man passed by them. The Prophet called to him and
when he came, the Prophet said,

> "She is my wife." The man said, "O Messenger of Allah, I do not doubt you
> in the least." The Prophet said, "Verily, Satan flows through the human
> being like blood."
>
> (Muslim (a))

Shaykh al-Islam Ibn Taymiyah (a) (May Allah have mercy on him) said:

> They smell a good smell or a bad smell (meaning the angels, who smell a good smell) when a person is thinking of a good deed, as was narrated from Sufyan ibn 'Uyaynah. But the devils do not need that (smell) in order to know; rather they even know what is in the heart of the son of Adam, and they see and hear what he says to himself. Moreover, the devil has full control over man's heart, then when man remembers Allah he withdraws, and when he neglects to remember Him, he whispers to him. He knows whether he is remembering Allah or is neglecting to remember Him, and he knows the whims and desires of his heart and makes them appear attractive to him.

Within the realm of *Jinn* and Satan, it is acknowledged that *Jinn* or Satan is close to the heart of the believer or a disbeliever. It is stated that "The Shaytan is aware of what a person is thinking to himself, and he knows his inclinations and his whims and desires, both good and bad, so he whispers to him accordingly" (Islamqa, 2009).

In a Fatwa (a ruling on a point of Islamic law given by a recognised authority), the eminent Shaykh Ibn Baz (May Allah have mercy on him) stated that the Prophet Muhammad (ﷺ)

> told us that the Shaytan dictates evils to man and calls him to evil, and he has some control over his heart. And he can see, by Allah's will, what a person wants and intends to do of both good and bad deeds. The angel also has some control over his heart that makes him inclined towards good and calls him to good. This control is something that Allah has enabled them to have, i.e., He has given some power to the companions from among the *jinn* and from among the angels; even the Prophet (ﷺ) had a Shaytan with him who was the companion from among the *Jinn*.
>
> (Islamqa, 2009)

Conclusion

Many Muslims suffer from OCD and Scrupulous OCD. However, when diagnosing OCD, it would be pre-requisite to understand the patient from a cultural and religious context. In Islam, an emphasis on cleanliness, purity and religio–ritualistic behaviours are the norm. In most cases, excessive prayers, supplications and other 'compulsive' behaviours should not be regarded as part of the pathology of OCD. When the behaviours are excessive and beyond the demands of religious practices, then they can be considered as OCD symptomatology. However, this must be validated by both health professionals and spiritual leaders (Imam).

References

Abramowitz, J. S., and Jacoby, R. J. (2014) Scrupulosity: A cognitive – behavioral analysis and implications for treatment, *Journal of Obsessive-Compulsive and Related Disorders*, 3, 140–149. http://dx.doi.org/10.1016/j.jocrd.2013.12.007.

Akbar, S. A. (2016) *Obsessive-Compulsive Symptoms and Scrupulosity Among Muslims Living in the United States*. University of North Carolina at Chapel Hill. https://cdr.lib.unc.edu/index ablecontent/uuid:7558ee47-3b51-4ceb-b68f-0b7a0cb02a68 (accessed 10 March 2018).

Amir, N., Freshman, M., Ramsey, B,, Neary, E., and Brigidi, B. (2001) Thought-action fusion in individuals with OCD symptoms, *Behaviour Research and Therapy*, 39, 7, 765–776.

Antony, M. M., Downie, F., and Swinson, R. P. (1998) *Diagnostic issues and epidemiology in obsessive compulsive disorder*, in R. P. Swinson, M. M. Antony, S. S. Rachman, M. A. Richter, R. P. Swinson, M. M. Antony, M. A. Richter (Eds.), Obsessive-compulsive disorder: Theory, research, and treatment. New York: The Guilford Press, pp. 3–32.

APA (2013) *Diagnostic and Statistical Manual of Mental Disorders (DSM – 5)*. Arlington, VA: American Psychiatric Association.

Assarian, F., Biqam, H., and Asqarnejad, A. (2006) An epidemiological study of obsessive compulsive disorder among high school students and its relationship with religious attitudes, *Archives of Iranian Medicine*, 9, 2, 104–107

Bukhari (a) Sahih al-Bukhari. 39. In-book reference: Book 2, Hadith 32. USC-MSA web (English) reference: Vol. 1, Book 2, Hadith 39.

Bukhari (b) Sahih al-Bukhari. Hadith Dar-us-Salam reference 2528, In-book reference: Book 49, Hadith 13. USC-MSA web (English) reference: Vol. 3, Book 46, Hadith 705.

Deacon, B., and Nelson, E. A. (2008) On the nature and treatment of Scrupulosity, *Pragmatic Case Studies in Psychotherapy*, 4, 2, 39–53.

Foss, K. (2013) *Scrupulosity: Where OCD Meets Religion, Faith, and Belief*. https://ocdla.com/ scrupulosity-ocd-religion-faith-belief-2107, (accessed 21 September 2017).

Frost, R. O., and Steketee, G. (Eds.) (2002) *Cognitive Approaches to Obsessions and Compulsions: Theory, Assessment, and Treatment*. Amsterdam, Netherlands: Pergamon/Elsevier Science Inc.

Grünblattab, E., Hauserab, T. U., and Walitzaabd, S. (2014) Imaging genetics in obsessive-compulsive disorder: Linking genetic variations to alterations in neuroimaging, *Progress in Neurobiology*, 121, 114–124 hamariweb.com. Obsession meaning in Arabic http://hamari web.com/dictionaries/obsession_arabic-meanings.aspx (accessed 10 March 2018).

Himle, J. A., Chatters, L. M., Taylor, R. J., and Nguyen, A. (2011) The relationship between obsessive-compulsive disorder and religious faith: Clinical characteristics and implications for treatment, *Psychology of Religion and Spirituality*, 3, 4, 241–258.

Inozu, M., Karanci, A. N., and Clark, D. A. (2012) Why are religious individuals more obsessional? The role of mental control beliefs and guilt in Muslims and Christians, *Journal of Behavior Therapy and Experimental Psychiatry*, 43, 3, 959–966. Doi: 10.1016/j.jbtep.2012.02.004. Epub 2012 Mar 12.

Islamqa. (2009) Islamqa.118151: *Does the Devil Know the Thoughts and Intentions of Man?* https://islamqa.info/en/118151 (accessed 22 September 2017).

Mohamed, N. R., Elsweedy, M. S., Elsayed, S. M., Rajab, A. Z., and Elzahar, S. T. (2015) Obsessive-compulsive disorder, an Islamic view, *Menoufia Medical Journal*, 28, 2, 289–94.

Muslim. Hadith on Satan: The devil runs through the minds of people just like blood. Sahih Muslim 2174. https://abuaminaelias.com/dailyhadithonline/2012/09/12/hadith-on-satan-the-devil-runs-through-the-minds-of-people-just-like-blood/ (accessed 10 March 2018).

Nestadt, G., Grados, M., and Samuels, J. F. (2010) Genetics of OCD. *The Psychiatric Clinics of North America*, 33, 1, 141–158. http://doi.org/10.1016/j.psc.2009.11.001.

Okasha, A. A., Saad, A. A., Khalil, A. H., and Dawla, A. (1994) Phenomenology of obsessive-compulsive disorder: A transcultural study, *Comprehensive Psychiatry*, 35, 3, 191–197. Doi:10.1016/0010–440X(94)90191–0.

Piri, S., and Kabakçi, E. (2007) An evaluation of some of the relationships between thought-action fusion, attributional styles, and depressive and obsessive-compulsive symptoms), *Turk Psikiyatri Derg. Turkish journal of psychiatry*, 18, 3, 197–206. (Article in Turkish)

Pollard, A. (2010) *Scrupulosity*. https://iocdf.org/wp-content/uploads/2014/10/IOCDF-Scrupulosity-Fact-Sheet.pdf (accessed10 March 2018).

Shafran, R., and Rachman, S. (2004) Thought-action fusion: A review, *Journal of Behavior Therapy and Experimental Psychiatry*, 35, 2, 87–107.

Shaykh al-Islam Ibn Taymiyah. Cited in Islamqa.118151: Does the Devil Know the Thoughts and Intentions of Man? https://islamqa.info/en/118151 (accessed10 March 2018).

Siev, J. (2010) *What is Scrupulosity?* Massachusetts General Hospital OCD and Related Disorders Program. https://mghocd.org/wp-content/uploads/2011/01/Scrupulosity.pdf (accessed10 March 2018).

Tambs, K., Czajkowsky, N., Røysamb, E., Neale, M. C., Reichborn-Kjennerud, T., Aggen, S. H., Harris, J. R., Ørstavik, R. E., and Kendler, K. S. (2009) Structure of genetic and environmental risk factors for dimensional representations of DSM-IV anxiety disorders, *British Journal of Psychiatry*, 195, 4, 301–307.

Tahir, M. A. (2011) Islamic Solution for OCD (Waswaas) – A Comprehensive Guide. http://islamandpsychology.blogspot.com/2011/08/islamic-solution-for-ocd-waswaas.html (accessed10 March 2018).

Tek, C., and Ulug, B. (2001) Religiosity and religious obsessions in obsessive-compulsive disorder, *Psychiatry Research*, 104, 2, 99–108

WHO (2010) ICD-10. International Statistical Classification of Diseases and Related Health Problems 10th Revision. http://apps.who.int/classifications/icd10/browse/2010/en (accessed10 March 2018).

Williams, A. D., Lau, G., and Grisham, J. R. (2013) Thought-action fusion as a mediator of religiosity and obsessive-compulsive symptoms, *Journal of Behavior Therapy and Experimental Psychiatry*, 44, 2, 207–212. Doi: 10.1016/j.jbtep.2012.09.004. Epub 2012 Oct 4.

Yorulmaz, O., Gencoz, T., and Woody, S. (2009) OCD cognitions and symptoms in different religious contexts, *Journal of Anxiety Disorders*, 23, 401–406.

Chapter 13

Typology of *Waswâs al-Qahri* (overwhelming whisperings)

Introduction

Waswâs is the whispering of the devil or the devil's insufflations (*Waswâs-il-Khannas*, Qur'an:114) over and over again, as *Waswâsah* by itself suggests repetition. This evil suggestion is to test the believer in having thoughts of disbelief, obsession related to purification and the fear of losing control in acts of worship. All believers are subjected to these thoughts and whispers from Satan or *Jinn* but for some, it becomes an obsession and compulsion. *Waswâs al-Qahri* is a complex psycho-spiritual problem found in Muslim populations. It is akin to pathological obsessive-compulsive disorder (OCD) but the diagnosis is not included in the Diagnostic Statistical Manual (DSM-V) (APA, 2013) or the International Statistical Classification of Diseases and Related Health Problems (ICD-10) (WHO, 2016). This chapter examines the different types and sources of *Waswâs al-Qahri*, the common obsession in Muslims, and the criteria for the diagnosis of *Waswâs al-Qahri*.

Waswâs al-Qahri (overwhelming whisperings or *Waswâs*)

Waswâs al-Qahri (In Arabic 'overwhelming whisperings') is a manifestation of some kind of obsessive-compulsive disorder commonly expressed in Muslim populations. This disorder plays a significant role in many psychological disorders that involve anxiety, phobic anxiety, cognitive distortions, personality disorders and obsessional neurosis. Muslims who suffer from *Waswâs al-Qahri* showed, beyond acceptable behaviours, extreme acts and behaviours in acts of worship and their daily activities. Awad (2017) describes *Waswâs al-Qahri* as "consisting of intrusive thoughts that cause cognitive dissonance (mental distress due to contradictory beliefs, values, or thoughts), and poses a risk to a person's spiritual and psychological homeostasis" (p. 4). This condition has been described as a

> sickness which befalls some people like any other kind of sickness. It refers to repeated thoughts, movements, ideas or notions which are of a loathsome nature that a person would ordinarily reject and strive to resist. He also realises that they are wrong and have no meaning, but there is something

that is pushing him towards them and he usually fails to resist them. The strength of these Waswâs may vary, so much so that they appear – to non-specialists – to be very strong and it seems that the sick person is doing that willingly. This kind of Waswâs may also affect a person in his worship and in his worldly affairs.

(Islamqa, 2005)

Muslims with *Waswâs al-Qahri* have anxieties or fear that their acts in the process of ablution (wudu, ritual washing before prayer) or the prayer itself are somehow inadequate and that the acts must be repeated until reaching a self-defined perfection. Other behaviours include being contaminated by germs, being unclean (due to urine incontinence), and soul searching and questioning one's faith. Accordingly, the acts of worship, "perpetuated by irrational fears and catastrophic thinking, become a source of anguish instead of spiritual nourishment" (Awad, 2017, p. 3). From an Islamic perspective, these unwanted thoughts are whispered into the minds and hearts of people by Shaytan/Satan/*Jinn*/devil.

Sources of *Waswâs*

There are three sources of *Waswâs*: the Nafs (or self, ego, soul), which is inclined to evil, the devils among the *Jinn* (demons) and the devils among mankind. The first source of *Waswâs* is from the *Nafs al-Ammara Bissu'* (The Soul which Commands). According to Utz (2011), the intrusive thoughts are from the "Nafs itself, which may be inclined to evil" (p. 253). This kind of Nafs, by its intrinsic nature nudges human beings into evil actions. Allah says (Interpretation of the meaning):

> *Indeed, the soul is a persistent enjoiner of evil . . .*
> (Sūrat Hud (Hud The Prophet) 12:53)

Allah also says (Interpretation of the meaning):

> *And We have already created man and know what his soul whispers to him, and We are closer to him than (his) jugular vein.*
> (Sūrat Qaf (Qaf) 50:16)

For the second source of *Waswâs* are the devils among the *Jinn*. This *Waswâs* entices an individual to do something against the teaching of his religious beliefs and practices. Furthermore, it instils doubt within a believer about his faith. Allah says (Interpretation of the meaning):

> *Then Satan whispered to him; he said, "O Adam, shall I direct you to the tree of eternity and possession that will not deteriorate?"*
> (Sūrat Ta Ha (Ta Ha) 20, p. 120)

And Allah says, describing the third source, which are the devils among mankind (Islamqa, 2005) (Interpretation of the meaning):

> *Say, "I seek refuge in the Lord of mankind,*
> *The Sovereign of mankind.*
> *The God of mankind,*
> *From the evil of the retreating whisperer -*
> *From among the jinn and mankind."*
>
> (Sūrat Nas (Mankind) 114–1–6)

These *Waswâs* may come from the *Jinn* or from the sons of Adam (human beings) (Islamqa, 2005). That is, the whisperings may be from among the *Jinn* or from human beings. According to Al-Hasan (Islamqa, 2011) "both are devils; the devil from among the *Jinn* whispers into people's hearts, and the devil from among mankind comes openly." In addition Qataadah (May Allah have mercy on him) (Islamqa, 2011) stated that "Among the *Jinn* are devils and among mankind are devils, so seek refuge with Allah from the devils of mankind and the *Jinn*." Ibn al-Qayyim (a) (May Allah have mercy on him) also refers to the two kinds of *Waswâs* from the *Jinn* and from human being. He stated that "The *Jinni* whispers into the hearts of man and the human also whispers into the hearts of man."

The main issue here is how to differentiate between *Waswâs* that comes from Shaytan and *Waswâs* from the Nafs. According to Shaykh al-Islam Ibn Taymiyah (a) (May Allah have mercy on him) stating from other scholars, he said:

> Abu Haazim made a comparison between the *Waswâs* caused by the Nafs and that caused by the Shaytan, and said: Whatever your Nafs hates for your Nafs is from the Shaytan, so seek refuge with Allah from it. And whatever your Nafs likes for your Nafs is from your Nafs, so forbid it from it.
>
> (Majmoo' al-Fataawa, 17/529, 530)

It has been suggested that another major difference between *Waswâs* that comes from Shaytan and *Waswâs* from the Nafs is that *Waswâs* from the Nafs

"it is what urges the person to commit a specific sin and repeatedly seeks to make him do it." Whereas, the *Waswâs* that comes from the Shaytan makes sin appear attractive until the Muslim falls into it; if the Shaytan is unable to achieve that, he moves on to another sin, and if that does not work he moves on to a third, and so on (Islamqa 2005).

One of the common *Waswâs* coming from Shaytan that happens to Muslims is the repetition of his ablution (wudu) as the individual does not know how many times he washed during ablution. If this is not managed, the *Waswâs* will become a chronic obsessive problem. This is what is called *al-Waswâs al-Qahri* (overwhelming *Waswâs* or OCD).

Typology of *Waswâs al-Qahri*

An understanding of the typology of *Waswâs al-Qahri* indicates that the disorder can manifest itself in many different ways. An approach to understanding of *Waswâs al-Qahri* holds that there are discrete subtypes of the disorder. Abdullah (2017) identified two types of *Waswâs*: Type I and Type II depending on severity of the conditions. Type I is the most common and less severe one to which everyone is susceptible and Type II is the severe *Waswâs al-Qahri*. Type I *Waswâs al-Qahri* is characterised by whispers, reoccurring negative fleeting thoughts and feelings that do not interfere in the daily normal and spiritual activities of the individual. According to Awad (2017) "*Waswâs* often begins in the form of a person being more careful and deliberate with acts of worship and progresses until the acts of worship that the individual ordinarily finds comforting or fulfilling become major hardships" (p. 10).

Type II *Waswâs al-Qahri* is more severe and debilitating with a gradual onset and is closely related to obsessive-compulsive disorder. Awad (2017) identified three categories of *Waswâs al-Qahri* in clinical settings:

- *Waswâs al-Qahri Fee Aqeedah* (belief).
- *Waswâs al-Qahri Fee Ibadah* (worship).
- *Waswâs al-Qahri Fee Taharah* (purification).

There is also another typology of *Waswâs al-Qahri* identified in clinical setting: which is related to the fear of losing control. This has been classified as *Waswâs al-Qahri Fee Kwaf Min Fuqdan al Saytara* (fear of losing control).

Waswâs al-Qahri Fee Aqeedah (belief)

One category of *Waswâs al-Qahri* is *Waswâs al-Qahri Fee Aqeedah*. That is having obsessional compulsive disorder relating to the belief system of the individual. The Arabic word '*Aqeedah* stems from the root '*Aqada*, which conveys meanings of certainty, affirmation or confirmation in the religion or creed. *Aqeedah* refers "to those matters which are believed in, with certainty and conviction, in one's heart and soul. They are not tainted with any doubt or uncertainty" (Islamqa, 1998). The principles of belief are mentioned in the following verse of the Qur'an (Interpretation of the meaning):

> *The Messenger believes in what has been sent down to him from his Lord, and (so do) the believers. Each one believes in Allah, His Angels, His Books and His Messengers. They say, 'We make no distinction between one and another of His Messengers' – and they say, 'We hear, and we obey. (We seek) Your forgiveness, our Lord, and to You is the return (of all).'*
>
> (Sūrat Al-Baqarah (The Cow) 2:285)

In a famous Hadith (Hadith Gibreel), the Messenger of Allah (ﷺ) stated that

> Faith is to believe in Allah, His angels (the) meeting with Him, His Apostles, and to believe in Resurrection.
>
> (Bukhari (a))

In *Waswâs al-Qahri Fee Aqeedah*, the faith is either questioned or there seemed some doubts about a particular aspect of the belief system. The intrusive, negative thoughts and doubts are created by the *Jinn*. Shaykh al-Islam Ibn Taymiyah (May Allah have mercy on him) said in Kitab al-Eeman: "The believer may suffer from the whispers of the Shaytan insinuating thoughts of *kufr* (disbelief), which may make him feel distressed. A Sahabah (May Allah be pleased with them) said, 'O Messenger of Allah, some of us think thoughts which we would rather fall from heaven to earth than speak of them.' He said, "That is a clear sign of faith" (Islamqa, 2002). Abu Hurayrah (May Allah be pleased with him) narrated that the Prophet (ﷺ) said:

> The Shaytan comes to one of you and says, Who created such and such? Who created such and such? Until he says: Who created your Lord?! If that happens to any of you, let him seek refuge with Allah and put a stop to these thoughts.
>
> (Bukhari (b))

However, some of these intrusive thoughts are perceived as part of the trials for the believers as these thoughts are loathed and are pushed away from the heart. This is Type I *Waswâs al-Qahri*.

It is stated that

> the seekers of knowledge and devoted worshippers experience *Waswâs* and doubts which others do not face, because they (the others) are not following the way prescribed by Allah, rather they are following their own whims and desires and neglecting to remember their Lord.
>
> (cited in Islamqa, 2009)

This is regarded as a clear sign of faith. It was narrated that Abu Hurayrah (May Allah be pleased with him) said:

> Some of the companions of the Messenger of Allah (ﷺ) came to the Prophet (ﷺ) and said to him, "We find in ourselves thoughts that are too terrible to speak of." He said, "Are you really suffering from that?" They said, "Yes." He said, "That is a clear sign of faith."
>
> (Muslim (a))

Imam Al-Nawawi said in his commentary on this Hadith:

> The Prophet's words, 'That is a clear sign of faith' mean, the fact that you think of this *Waswâs* as something terrible is a clear sign of faith, for if you dare not utter it and you are so afraid of it and of speaking of it, let alone believing it, this is the sign of one who has achieved perfect faith and who is free of doubt.
>
> (Islamqa, 2002)

In another Hadith, it was narrated from Ibn 'Abbas (May Allah be pleased with them both) that a man came to the Prophet (ﷺ) and said,

> "I think thoughts to myself, which I would rather be burnt to a cinder than speak of them." The Prophet (ﷺ) said, "Praise be to Allah, Who has reduced all his (the Shaytan's) plots to mere whispers."
>
> (Abu Dâwûd (a))

Those suffering from Type I *Waswâs al-Qahri*, it is recommended that these type of whisperings from Shaytan be resisted and refuse to be controlled by it. The Prophet (ﷺ) said,

> Allah forgives my followers those (evil deeds) their souls may whisper or suggest to them as long as they do not act (on it) or speak.
>
> (Bukhari (c))

Waswâs al-Qahri Fee Ibadah (worship)

This is *Waswâs* in matters of worship and religious rituals. *Ibadah* incorporates many definitions. The word *Ibadah*, in linguistic terms, means submission and surrender. The technical meaning of *Ibadah* refers to acts of worship. However, Shaykh al-Islam ibn Taymiyah (b) defined worship as: "It is a comprehensive term that encompasses all what Allah loves of words and deeds whether inward or outward." Ibn al-Qayyim (b) said: "Worship is the utmost degrees of love to Allah while accompanied by complete surrender." *Jinn* or Shaytan can also whisper into the believers' hearts during the compulsory acts of worship like daily prayers, fasting and giving in charity. The main problem with this kind of *Waswâs* is creating doubts and uncertainty in the believers about their performance of prayer or ablution. The individuals feel that their worship is not to the standard expected and thereby not fulfilling the tenets of their belief system. And this lack of imperfection may lead them liable to God's punishment. According to Awad (2017) "Any detail about their act of worship that might be imperfect will lead to irrational fear and catastrophizing that they have inadvertently apostatized from the religion and/or might go to Hell" (p. 10).

There are constant distractions and thought intrusions by Shaytan during the prayer that some lack the focus and concentration required. There is also a tendency to lose track of the Qur'anic recitations during the prayer and/ or loose count of the number of *rakat* (consists of the prescribed movements and words while offering prayers to God). It is stated that one of the Sahabah (companions) 'Uthman Bin Abi Al-Aas (May Allah be pleased with him), complained to the Messenger of Allah (ﷺ) about *Waswâs* during prayer, and he said: "The Shaytan comes between me and my prayers and my recitation, confusing me therein." The Messenger of Allah (ﷺ) said:

That is a devil called *Khanzab*.

(Muslim (b))

Shaykh Ibn 'Uthaymeen (a) (May Allah have mercy on him) said:

If a person experiences so many doubts that he can hardly do anything without doubting it – if he does wudoo' (Ablution) he doubts it, and if he prays he doubts it, and if he fasts he doubts it – then this also does not mean anything, because this is a kind of sickness. What we discussed above applies to the healthy person who is free of sickness; if a person is experiencing a great deal of doubt like this, then it is to be assumed that his mind is not stable, so no attention should be paid to these doubts.

Some individuals may seem to be 'excessive' in their worship, especially the daily prayers and this could be perceived as pathological if from a different religious worldview. The issue is how to differentiate between those with a pathological problem and those who are 'deeply' religious or undertaking supererogatory prayers. According to Akbar (2016), "knowledge is especially important for differentiating between religious practice and pathological behaviors" (p. 6). This is supported from the findings of Rosmarin et al. (2010) that religious (Orthodox Jews) individuals were more accurate at identifying 'normal' religious rituals from OCD (pathological) rituals compared to individuals with less religious knowledge (non-Orthodox Jews). Notwithstanding the non-Muslim sample of population of Rosmarin et al's (2010) study, one could extrapolate, tentatively, that this may be applicable to Muslims in general. That is, familiarity or having religious knowledge from the Qur'an and Sunnah increases sensitivity to distinctions between enhanced religious practices and *Waswâs al-Qahri* in worship and pathological obsessive-compulsive disorder. The role of the Imam or faith leader have an important role in this diagnosis.

Some believers get so many doubts (*Waswâs*) during the process of prayer that they start doing extra prostrations at the end of the prayer. This is known as *Sajda-e-Sahw* which is performed when an individual believes they have made some mistake (addition or omission) in any essential act of prayer or when we are in doubt. Shaykh al-Bahooti (May Allah have mercy on him) said:

The prostration of forgetfulness is prescribed when one of the reasons for it is present, namely doing something extra, omitting something, or not being sure (of how many rak'ahs one has prayed), except in the case of funeral (*Janaazah*) prayer. This does not include when one's mind wanders, because it is not possible to avoid it, so it is forgiven.

However, this type of doubt happened to most people but those suffering from *Waswâs* get many doubts about the rituals of prayers that it becomes an obsession to perform this type of procedure after every prayer.

Waswâs al-Qahri Fee Taharah (purification)

Waswâs al-Qahri Fee Taharah is obsession related to purification. The word *Taharah* linguistically means cleanliness. In Shari'ah (Islamic Jurisprudence) it is the removal of *al-Hadath al-Asghar* (minor impurity) and *al-Hadath al-Akbar* (Major impurity), and filth from clothing, body and places of Salah (prayer) (Al-Quduri). This purification is not only related to the cleanliness of body but also clothing, places and all aspects of a Muslim's life. According to the evidences in the Qur'an, Sunnah and Ijmaa' (consensus of scholars), it is considered an obligation. Allah says in the Qur'an (Interpretation of the meaning):

> *Indeed Allah loves those who are constantly repentant and He loves those who purify themselves.*
> (Sūrat Al-Baqarah (The Cow) 2:222)

> *And your clothing purify.*
> (Sūrat Al-Muddaththir (The One who covers Himself) 74:4)

Narrated by Ali ibn Abu Talib (May Allah be pleased with him), Prophet Muhammad (ﷺ) stated that

> The key to pray is purification.
> (Abu Dâwûd (b))

It was narrated that Abu Bakrah said: "The Messenger of Allah (ﷺ) said:

> Allah does not accept any Salat (prayer) without purification.
> (Ibn Majah)

In another Hadith, Abu Malik at-Ash'ari reported that the Messenger of Allah (ﷺ) said, "Purification is half of the faith" (Muslim (c)).

Purity is of three types. According to Al-Haj (2016), the types of purification include the physical, ritual and spiritual. As can be seen from the Qur'an and Hadiths, if a Muslim is not pure and clean, then he cannot perform prayer or touch the Noble Qur'an. For example, ablution (wudu) is a pre-requisite for the performance of prayer. That is going through the rituals of washing the face, arms, wipe over the head, and wash the feet (or wipe over socks).

The ablution is invalidated by flatulence, using the bathroom, sleep, loss of consciousness due to insanity, fainting, intoxication and medicines that cause loss of consciousness whether the duration is brief or long, according to scholarly consensus.

For those suffering from *Waswâs al-Qahri* in purification, there are an obsessions (thoughts) and compulsions with cleanliness. Some believers exaggerate in cleaning themselves after relieving themselves or constantly washing the traces of impurity with water. This type of excess in behaviour comes from the *Waswâs* of the Shaytan, who intends thereby to make worship difficult for the Muslims and cause him distress and grief. There is the constant presence of irrational fear of contamination from unclean things and doubts about performing the ablution in the correct way. However, research from Muslim populations suggests that washing behaviours appear to be related to concerns about purity (cleaning compulsions) rather than contamination (Okasha et al., 1994 2001; Ghassemzadeh et al., 2005; Mahintorabi et al., 2015). The findings of the study by Okasha et al. (1994) showed that most commonly occurring obsessions were religious and contamination obsessions (60%) and somatic obsessions (49%), and the most commonly occurring compulsions were repeating rituals (68%), cleaning and washing compulsions (63%) and checking compulsions (58%). Ghassemzadeh et al.'s (2005) study on Iranian patients with OCD showed that OCD washing is one of the most common ritual behaviours in the Iranian population. In a study of Muslim women in Australia, the findings of a study by Mahintorabi et al. (2017) showed that the most common compulsions reported by "participants were performing excessive washing and repeating rituals before prayer, and these behaviours were carried out to prevent being punished by God" (p. 1). The irrational fear of purification creates doubts about the validation of the ablution thus the ritualistic repetitive behaviours become apparent. Accordingly, no validated ablution means no validated prayers. In summary, this form of transgression in purification includes obsession during urinating or defecating, obsession in the purification of clothing, repetition in ablution or taking a purifying bath.

Waswâs al-Qahri Fee Kwawf min Fuqdan al Saytara (fear of losing control)

This is the fear of losing control due to obsessive-compulsive disorder. In proper Arabic transliteration, it is *Kwaf insilal al Saytara bi Sabab Waswâs Istahwadhiat*.

Some individuals have the cognitive and affective experiences of losing control of one's life. The loss of control generally refers "to lack of the ability to provide conscious limitation of impulses and behavior as a result of overwhelming emotion" (Griffin et al., 1990, p. 24:1). This lack of control is part of a pattern of behaviour that also involves other maladaptive thoughts and actions in the other dimensions of *Waswâs al-Qahri* in belief, purification and worship. Losing control may fall into two categories: autogenous with an internal locus of control and reactive with an external locus of control. The latter category is true in regards to Muslims with *Waswâs al-Qahri Fee Kwawf min Fuqdan al Saytara*. This type of loss of control issue is related, in the context of Muslims, to beliefs, values and faith. This phenomena can be fleeting, frequent, or persistent, may be most prevalent in aggression (self-harm or harming others); sexuality (thoughts about sexual obscenities/images or of engaging in unwanted sexual behaviours); and belief system (thoughts of violating religious rules or engaging in immoral behaviour). The loss of control is part of the trials and tribulations or form of punishment due to previous sins. It is also a path towards delayed gratification and self-purification of the soul (*Tazkiyah an-Nafs*). Muslims are mindful that God has control over all things. Suhaib reported that Allah's Messenger (ﷺ) said:

> Strange are the ways of a believer for there is good in every affair of his and this is not the case with anyone else except in the case of a believer for if he has an occasion to feel delight, he thanks (God), thus there is a good for him in it, and if he gets into trouble and shows resignation (and endures it patiently), there is a good for him in it.
>
> (Muslim (d))

Common obsession in Muslims

Examples of obsessions and compulsions including recurring thoughts about being impure or unclean, and questioning one's faith appear to be the most common forms amongst Muslim men and women. The fear of a lack of purity are most often found among women. Tables 13.1 and 13.2 present some examples of the obsessions and compulsions of Muslims.

Diagnosis of *Waswâs al-Qahri*

Many Muslims experienced "common" *Waswâs al-Qahri*, including doubts, uncertainty, disturbing thoughts and reflections in their normal life and in particular during the acts of worship. Although these cause a constant ordeal of irritation, stress and confusion, these are not regarded as pathological. An example of this type of common *Waswâs al-Qahri* is when strange or disturbed thoughts enter the consciousness of the individual during prayer. The individual starts losing focus and loses track of the unit of prayer (*Rakat*). Currently there is no defined, formal criteria for the diagnosis of *Waswâs al-Qahri* but experienced Imam and those who treat *Waswâs al-Qahri* with spiritual interventions are able to identify this condition. Awad (2017) suggested that the

> informal diagnosing generally happens when a person is distressed or shows impairment due to irrational fears about aspects of the religion; (ii) for a

Table 13.1 Common obsessions in Muslims

Typology	Obsessions
Waswâs al-Qahri Fee Aqeedah (Belief)	• Blasphemous thoughts. • Doubting the religion. • Questions about God's existence. • Fear of losing touch with God. • Retrospectives memories: Doubts that one had committed major sins in the past. • Excessive concern with halal (legal) and haram (forbidden) or right/wrong or morality.
Waswâs al-Qahri Fee Ibadah (Worship)	• Doubt whether I performed ablution correctly or not. • Doubt whether I performed the prayer correctly or not. • Intrusive images during prayer or reciting Qur'an. • Fear of having sinned or broken a religious ritual. • Prayers have been recited incorrectly.
Waswâs al-Qahri Fee Taharah (Purification)	• Fear of contamination with body fluids (examples: urine, faeces). • Fear of contamination with dirt or germs. • Doubt whether I performed ablution correctly or not. • Fear of impurities when doing ablution and while performing prayer. • Irrational fear and constant feeling that my clothes are unclean. • Doubts of passing wind, and nullification of ablution.
Waswâs al-Qahri Fee Kwawf min Fuqdan al Saytara (Fear of Losing Control)	• Fear of acting on an impulse to self-harm. • Fear of acting on an impulse to harm others. • Fear of violent or horrific images in one's mind. • Fear of obscenities in one's mind. • Fear of doubts and uncertainty.

significant period of time and; (iii) behaves in maladaptive ways (excessively repeating acts of worship, checking, ruminating, etc.).

(p. 9)

The suggested criteria for diagnosing *Waswâs al-Qahri* is presented in Table 13.3. The following case study is an example of someone suffering from *Waswâs al-Qahri in Purification and Worship.* This is an abridged version (Islamqa, 2001).

For some months I have been having a problem with *Waswâs* in both my prayers and when performing wudu (ablution). I keep forgetting what I have washed in my wudu and keep forgetting how many raka'ah (unit of prayer) I have prayed. It has reached a point where I am making sajdah as – sahu (prostration for forgetfulness in prayer) for every single prayer

Table 13.2 Common compulsions in Muslims

Typology	Compulsions
***Waswâs al-Qahri Fee Aqeedah* (Belief)**	• Excessive praying (not prescribed or recommended) to counter blasphemous or sacrilegious thoughts that could result in going to hell. • Compulsive behaviours in general.
***Waswâs al-Qahri Fee Ibadah* (Worship)**	• Re-performing prayer to achieve perfection. • Doing extra prostrations (*Sajda e Sahw*) in every prayer. • Excessive, repetitive utterances of God's forgiveness. • Re-reading passages from the Qur'an to attain perfection.
***Waswâs al-Qahri Fee Taharah* (Purification)**	• Washing hands excessively or in a certain method not prescribed. • Excessive showering, bathing, tooth brushing, grooming or toilet routines. • Performing ablution several times. • Taking a lot of time in doing ablution. • Spending too much time in all purification/washing activities, e.g. washing hands after meal. • Protecting religious symbols, ornaments, books, or pictures from 'contamination.' • Doing other things to prevent or remove contact with contaminants.
***Waswâs al-Qahri Fee Kwawf min Fuqdan al Saytara* (Fear of Losing Control)**	• Excessive checking that you did not/will not harm others. • Excessive checking that you did not/will not self-harm. • Excessive checking that nothing terrible happened or some arbitrary worship has not been performed. • Excessive checking that you did not make a mistake, error or commit a sin. • Excesive checking of number of sins committed.

Table 13.3 Suggested criteria for diagnosing *Waswâs al-Qahri*

i	Recurrent, intrusive and persistent thoughts that cause marked anxiety or distress;
ii	Symptoms are persistent for a significant period of time;
iii	Excessive fear of having acted counter to one's personal values and morals;
iv	Impairment due to irrational fears about aspects of the religion;
v	Inordinate focus on moral and religious perfection;
vi	Overt behavioural compulsions;
vii	Use maladaptive coping mechanisms (excessively repeating acts of worship, checking, ruminating, etc.);
viii	Ritualised 'undoing' behaviours to counteract perceived sins and transgressions;
ix	Avoidance behaviours;
x	Beyond enhanced religious practices.

because my mind always strays. The more I concentrate on my prayer, the more it occurs. Sometimes I think I must have prayed 6 or 7 raka'ahs (units of prayer) for a four raka'ah prayer because I simply cannot recall how much I have prayed and so I continue until I am certain. The more I do this, the worse the problem gets. I want to ignore the waswas. With regards to wudhu (ablution) I have a combination of problems as I feel that I have not washed properly after using the bathroom or if my clothes get wet that there is something impure on my clothes. When making wudu, I feel like I have not washed properly. I try to ignore these whisperings but I am terrified that if I ignore it and I am wrong, that my prayers will not be answered. I have reached a point where my prayers can take up to an hour or more to perform and have become merely a ritual without any khushoo' (focus) because of these problems. I finish one prayer and start fearing how I am going to manage to get through the next one. I feel I am trapped because there is no way I can miss a prayer as I know this is exactly what shaytan wants me to do.

Conclusion

Waswâs al-Qahri is a complex disorder which is clearly misunderstood by orientalist and Eurocentric health professionals. The pathological condition is the development of unwanted, intrusive obsessions and compulsions related to religious beliefs, acts of worship and acts of purification. In addition, the individual with *Waswâs al-Qahri* experiences a sense of a loss of control in the cognitive, affective and behavioural domains. Many Muslims suffering from *Waswâs al-Qahri* are concerned about the implications of the disorder in relation to accountability. From the edicts (fatwas) of many of the eminent Scholars of Islam, there is a general consensus that the individual shall not, Insha'Allah (God willing), be judged/punished by Allah. Shaykh Ibn 'Uthaymeen (b) (May Allah have mercy on him) said:

> Allah will not punish the one who suffers from compulsive Waswâs, because He, may He be exalted, says (Interpretation of the meaning): "Our Lord! Put not on us a burden greater than we have strength to bear" and "Allah burdens not a person beyond his scope" (Qur'an 2:286). But the one who is suffering from Waswâs has to frequently seek refuge with Allah from the accursed Shaytan and ignore it; if he does that, then it will depart from him by Allah's leave.

The same is applicable to someone who utters blasphemous words (disbelief) due of this compulsive *Waswâs al-Qahri* which was beyond his control. It is worth noting the statements made by Shaykh Ibn al-Qayyim. He stated that "There are thousands of things which the people afflicted with *Waswâs* take as a part of religion, cloaked in 'precaution,' whereas, precaution is to be exercised in following the Sunnah." More research is needed with Muslim communities to better understand this condition as previous research concerning religiosity and OCD has mainly focused on the Judeo-Christian tradition. This has implications for both clinical and spiritual intervention strategies.

References

Abdullah, S. (2017) *The Waswas from the Jinn possession.* https://practicalselfruqya.com/2017/01/25/the-waswaas-from-the-possessing-jinn/ (accessed 20 March 2018).

Abu Dâwûd (a) Cited in The Devil Whispers. . . www.islam21c.com/spirituality/the-devil-whispers/ (accessed 20 March 2018).

Abu Dâwûd (b) Chapter no: 1, Book of Purification (Kitab Al-Taharah). Hadith no: 61. http://ahadith.co.uk/chapter.php?cid=35&page=7&rows=10 (accessed 20 March 2018).

Akbar, S. A. (2016) *Obsessive-Compulsive Symptoms and Scrupulosity Among Muslims Living in the United States.* University of North Carolina at Chapel Hill. https://cdr.lib.unc.edu/index ablecontent/uuid:7558ee47-3b51-4ceb-b68f-0b7a0cb02a68 (accessed 20 March 2018).

Al-Haj (2016) Cited *in* Awad, N. (2017) *Clinicians, Imams, and the Whisperings of Satan.* Las Colinas, TX: Yaqeen Institute of Islamic Research, https://yaqeeninstitute.org/wp-content/uploads/2017/07/FINAL-Clinicians-Imams-and-the-Whisperings-of-Satan-1.pdf (accessed 20 March 2018).

Al-Quduri. Cited in What is the meaning of Taharah linguistically and in Shari'ah? http://islamwa sunnah.com/fatwa/index.php?option=com_content&view=article&id=47:what-is-the-meaning-of-taharah-linguistically-and-in-shariah&catid=35:introduction (accessed 5 October 2017).

American Psychiatric Association (2013) *Diagnostic and Statistical Manual of Mental Disorders.* 5th ed. Washington, DC: Author.

Awad, N. (2017) *Clinicians, Imams, and the Whisperings of Satan.* Las Colinas, TX: Yaqeen Institute of Islamic Research, https://yaqeeninstitute.org/wp-content/uploads/2017/07/FINAL-Clinicians-Imams-and-the-Whisperings-of-Satan-1.pdf (accessed 20 March 2018).

Bukhari (a) Sahih al-Bukhari 50. In-book reference: Book 2, Hadith 43. USC-MSA web (English) reference: Vol. 1, Book 2, Hadith 48.

Bukhari (b) Sahih al-Bukhari 3276: Book 59, Hadith 85. USC-MSA web (English) reference: Vol. 4, Book 54, Hadith 496.

Bukhari (c) Sahih al-Bukhari 6664. In-book reference: Book 83, Hadith 42 USC-MSA web (English) reference: Vol. 8, Book 78, Hadith 657.

Ghassemzadeh, H., Khamseh, A., and Ebrahimkhani, N. (2005) Demographic variables and clinical features of obsessive-compulsive disorder in Iran: A second report, in B. E. Ling (Ed.), *Obsessive Compulsive Disorder Research.* Hauppauge: Nova Science Publishers Inc., pp. 243–271.

Griffin, J. B Jr (1990) *Loss of Control*, in H. K. Walker, W. D. Hall, J. W. Hurst (Eds.), *Clinical Methods: The History, Physical, and Laboratory Examinations.* 3rd ed. Boston: Butterworths. Chapter 204, www.ncbi.nlm.nih.gov/books/NBK317/ (accessed 20 March 2018).

Ibn Majah. Sunan Ibn Majah. English reference: Vol. 1, Book 1, Hadith 274 Arabic reference: Book 1, Hadith 287. https://sunnah.com/urn/1252730.

Ibn al-Qayyim (a) Cited in Islamqa (2011) 59931: What is meant by "jinn and men" in Sūrat al-Naas, https://islamqa.info/en/59931 (accessed 20 March 2018).

Ibn al-Qayyim (b) al-Kafiya Ash-Shafiya fi al-Intisar by al-Najiya sect p. 32. Cited in What is worship ('Ibadah)? http://knowingallah.com/en/articles/what-is-worship-ibadah (accessed 20 March 2018).

Islamqa (1998) 951: *What is 'Aqeedah?* https://islamqa.info/en/951 (accessed 20 March 2018).

Islamqa (2001) 11449: He is suffering from serious Waswâs. https://islamqa.info/en/11449 (accessed 20 March 2018).

Islamqa (2002) 12315: *Suffering From Waswas (Insinuating Whispers) of the Shaytan About the Essence of Allah.* https://islamqa.info/en/25778 (accessed 20 March 2018).

Islamqa (2005) 39684: *Sources of Waswâs and Accountability.* https://islamqa.info/en/39684 (accessed 20 March 2018).

Islamqa (2009) 12315: *Suffering From Waswas (Insinuating Whispers) of the Shaytan About the Essence of Allah,* https://islamqa.info/en/12315 (accessed 2 June 2018)

Islamqa (2011) 59931: *What is meant by "jinn and men" in Soorat al-Naas?* https://islamqa.info/en/59931 (accessed 27 September 2017).

Mahintorabi, S., Jones, M. K., Harris, L. M., and Zahiroddin, A. (2015) Religious observance and obsessive compulsive washing among Iranian Women, *Behaviour Research and Therapy,* 7, 35–42.

Mahintorabi, S., Jones, M. K., and Harris, L. M. (2017) Exploring professional help seeking in practicing Muslim Women with obsessive compulsive disorder washing subtype in Australia, *Religions,* 8, 137. Doi: 10.3390/rel8080137.

Muslim (a) Cited in Islamqa (2009) 12315: *Suffering From Waswas (Insinuating Whispers) of the Shaytan About the Essence of Allah.* https://islamqa.info/en/12315 (accessed 20 March 2018).

Muslim (b) Cited in Islamqa 25778: *Disturbed by Waswas (Whispers From the Shaytan) and Evil Thoughts. https://islamqa.info/en/25778* (accessed 20 March 2018).

Muslim (c) *Sahih Muslim 223* Book 2, Hadith 1.USC-MSA web (English) reference: Book 2, Hadith 432.

Muslim (d) *Sahih Muslim 2999.* In-book reference: Book 55, Hadith 82. USC-MSA web (English) reference: Book 42, Hadith 7138.

Okasha, A., Saad, A., Khalil, A. H., el Dawla, A. S., and Yehia, N. (1994) Phenomenology of obsessive-compulsive disorder: A transcultural study, *Comprehensive Psychiatry,* 35, 3, 191–197.

Okasha, A., Ragheb, K., Attia, A. H., Seif el Dawla, A., Okasha, T., and Ismail, R. (2001) Prevalence of obsessive compulsive symptoms (OCS) in a sample of Egyptian adolescents, *L'Encephale,* 27, 1, 8–14.

Rosmarin, D. H., Pirutinsky, S., and Siev, J. (2010) Recognition of Scrupulosity and non-religious OCD by Orthodox and non-Orthodox Jews, *Journal of Social and Clinical Psychology,* 29, 8, 930–944.

Shaykh al-Bahooti *Kashshaaf al-Qinaa',* 2/465. Cited in Islamqa (2004) 34570: Should a person do the prostration of forgetfulness for absentmindedness? https://islamqa.info/en/34570 (accessed 20 March 2018).

Shaykh Ibn al-Qayyim. *Kitab ar-Ruh: Soul's Journey After Death.* Cited in Tahir, M. A. (2011) Islamic Solution for OCD (Waswaas) – A Comprehensive Guide. http://islamandpsychology.blogspot.com/2011/08/islamic-solution-for-ocd-waswaas.html (accessed 20 March 2018).

Shaykh al-Islam Ibn Taymiyah (a) Majmoo' al-Fataawa, 17/529, 530. Cited in Islamqa (2011) 59931: What is meant by "jinn and men" in Soorat al-Naas. https://islamqa.info/en/59931 (accessed 27 September 2017).

Shaykh al-Islam ibn Taymiyah (b) al-'Ubudiyya p. 38. Cited in *What is worship ('Ibadah)?* http://knowingallah.com/en/articles/what-is-worship-ibadah (accessed 20 March 2018).

Shaykh Ibn 'Uthaymeen (a) Cited in Islamqa (2012) 171689: *He started to pray, then he wasn't sure whether he formed the intention to pray or not; does he have to repeat it?* https://islamqa.info/en/171689 (accessed 20 March 2018).

Shaykh Ibn 'Uthaymeen (b) Fataawa Noor 'ala ad-Darb, 24/2 Cited in Islamqa (2013) 200949: *He suffers from compulsive waswaas and speaks words of kufr; does he have to do anything?* https://islamqa.info/en/200949 (accessed 20 March 2018).

Tahir, M.A. (2011) Islamic Solution for OCD (Waswaas) – A Comprehensive Guide. http://islamandpsychology.blogspot.com/2011/08/islamic-solution-for-ocd-waswaas.html (accessed 20 March 2018).

Utz, A. (2011) *Psychology from the Islamic Perspective.* Riyadh, Saudi Arabia: International Islamic Publishing House.

WHO (2016) *International Statistical Classification of Diseases and Related Health Problems* 10th Revision (ICD-10). Geneva: World Health Organization.

Chapter 14

Magic, witchcraft and demonic possession from an Islamic perspective

Introduction

Belief in witchcraft, sorcery, magic, ghosts and demons is widespread and pervasive among the global Muslim communities. This is manifested in the theological concept of magic, witchcraft and *Jinn* from the Qur'an and the Hadiths of Prophet Muhammad (☙), and from the therapeutic incantations. There were distinct stages in the historical foundation of magic, sorcery and witchcraft in Islam. According to Hamès (2008), pre-Islamic Arabia "provided the usual magical tools for protection, healing, divination which were integrated and legitimized by the Islamic institution" (p. 189) From the ninth–tenth centuries onwards, the traditions of magic, astrology and talismanic practices from the Greco-Irano-Indian orientation had a significant influence on the culture of Arabia. As a consequence "Islam gradually reacted and, as far as witchcraft was concerned, focused its efforts on the condemnation and elimination of the astrological framework and on its replacement by intrinsically Islamic elements" (Hamès, 2008, p. 189).

Conceptually, the notion of *Sihr* (magic), witchcraft and demons are still little active in the consciousness of Muslims. It is reported that substantial numbers of Muslims continue to believe in the existence of witchcraft and very few Muslims believe the use of sorcery is an acceptable practice under Islam (Pew Research Center, 2012). However, the levels of belief vary widely across the countries. In sub-Saharan Africa, the proportion of Muslims who say witchcraft or sorcery is more prominent in Tanzania about 9-in-10 (92%) as compared to about 1-in-6 in Ethiopia (15%). In the Middle East and North Africa, more than three-quarters of Muslims in Tunisia (89%) and Morocco (78%) believe in witchcraft, compared with as few as 16% in Egypt, and 14% in the Palestinian territories. Among the Southeast Asian countries surveyed, Indonesian tops the league where Muslims are the most convinced that witchcraft is real (69%). In South Asia, Pakistani Muslims (50%) are more likely than their counterparts in Afghanistan (35%) or Bangladesh (9%) to believe in the existence of sorcery. In Southern and Eastern Europe, Albanian Muslims are the most likely to believe in witchcraft (43%), compared with a third or fewer elsewhere in the region. In Turkey, about half of Muslims (49%) believe that sorcery exists, no more than 3-in-10 in any of the Central Asian nations (Azerbaijan, Kazakhstan, Kyrgyzstan, Tajikistan and Uzbekistan) surveyed believe witchcraft is real (Pew Research Center, 2012).

Throughout the Muslim world there are sorcerers, fortune tellers, and traditional healers; many are in violation of interpretations of the Shari'ah (Islamic law). All magical and witchcraft practices are denounced as un-Islamic by scholars and clerics. Several countries including Egypt, Bahrain, Afghanistan, Gaza and Saudi Arabia have stricter laws regarding these un-Islamic practices. From an orientalist narrative, this is regarded as witch hunts and is not coherent with the European scientific revolution and the Enlightenment's rationalist ideologies. Thus, the accepted, long-established, theologically sanctioned supernatural tradition is well engrained in the Islamic way of life and shapes all dimensions of the human beings: physical, social, psychological and spiritual. This chapter examines witchcraft and magic (*Sihr*) and how these affect Muslims in general.

Concept of *Sihr* and witchcraft

Magic and sorcery, resulting with the contact with the *Jinn*, are recognised as real in Islam. There is a link and interaction between black magic and witchcraft and religion. Many Muslims developed all sorts of physical or psychological disorders or both as a result of magic and witchcraft. *Jinns* are responsible for the cause of *Sihr* and you cannot have *Sihr* without *Jinn* (Qadhi, 2014). It is the power of the *Jinn* that the sorcerer or magician uses to commit devilish acts. *Sihr* is the Arabic word for magic or witchcraft. Literally, the definition of *Sihr* is : "Every effect whose cause or origin is subtle, mysterious or supernatural is Sihr" (Lisaanul Arab and Qaamoos). From a theological perspective, Qadhi (2014) defines *Sihr* as the invoking of "*Jinn* to do something that appears from our world to be supernatural." It is reported that Shumar said: Ibn 'A'ishah said: *Sihr* is so called in Arabic because it changes health to sickness (Ameen, 2005, p. 177). *Sihr* has wider meanings which include magic or black magic (in the use of *Jinn*), dowsing, exorcism, sorcery and witchcraft. An explanation of the concept of *Sihr* is defined by Valentine (2015) as "a nebulous term covering witchcraft, sorcery and magic" (p. 199). In the context of this chapter, the concept of *Sihr* will apply

> to all things and effects whose causes and origin are unknown, subtle, mysterious, supernatural and incomprehensive, irrespective of whether the causes of the effects and manifestations are tangible or intangible, visible or invisible, material or immaterial, natural or supernatural.
>
> (Mujlisul Ulama of South Africa, 2015, p. 5)

Renowned Islamic scholar of the twentieth century, Sheikh Ibn Baz, said,

> *Sihr* (sorcery) is a word referring to something hidden. It is real and there are kinds of witchcraft that may affect people psychologically and physically,

so that they become sick and die, or husbands and wives are separated. It is a devilish action, most of which is only achieved by means of associating others with God and drawing close to the minions of Satan.

(cited in Stacey, 2012)

In this definition of *Sihr*, the issue regarding the concept is not only related to witchcraft but also to *Shirk*. *Shirk* in Arabic means taking a partner. In terms of Shari'ah or Islamic terminology, *Shirk* means ascribing a partner or rival to Allah in Lordship (*ruboobiyyah*), worship or in His names and attributes. *Shirk* may takes the form of beliefs, words or actions. For a more comprehensive meaning of *Shirk* and its different types see (Islamqa, 2010a). Major and minor *Shirk* includes the association of partner with Allah, the summoning other than God, relying on others beside Allah, obeying others absolutely besides Allah, seeking help or seek refuge with others rather than Allah (living or dead), the use of amulets or talismans and the use of *Jinn*. This perspective of *Sihr* provided another dimension in the understanding of the concept. Allah says in the Qur'an (Interpretation of the meaning):

So do not attribute to Allah equals while you know (that there is nothing similar to Him).
(Sūrat Al-Baqarah (The Cow) 2:22)

In another verse, Allah says in the Qur'an (Interpretation of the meaning):

And they have attributed to Allah equals to mislead (people) from His way. Say, Enjoy yourselves, for indeed, your destination is the Fire.
(Sūrat Ibraheem (Prophet Abraham) 14:30)

In the Hadith narrated by 'Abdullah, the Prophet (ﷺ) said

Whoever dies while still invoking anything other than Allah as a rival to Allah, will enter Hell (Fire).

(Bukhari (a))

It was narrated from 'Uqbah ibn 'Aamir al-Juhani that a group came to the Messenger of Allah (ﷺ) (to swear their allegiance (bay'ah) to him). He accepted the bay'ah of nine of them but not of one of them. They said,

"O Messenger of Allah, you accepted the bay'ah of nine but not of this one." He said, "He is wearing an amulet." The man put his hand (in his shirt) and took it off, then he (the Prophet) (ﷺ) accepted his bay'ah. He said, "Whoever wears an amulet has committed shirk."

(Ahmad)

The texts of the Qur'aan and Sunnah indicate that *Shirk* and the ascribing of rivals to Allah sometimes puts a person beyond the pale of Islam or nullify

Islam. The use of a talisman or amulets takes the form of actions in *Shirk* to dispel or ward off calamity or shield their wearers but are also objects that reflect occult practices.

Witchcraft beliefs vary among the global diversity of cultures. Witchcraft refers to "harmful actions carried out by persons presumed to have access to supernatural powers" (Ashforth, 1998). Shaykh Al-Qayyim (Islamqa, 2010b) said: "The witchcraft which can cause sickness, lethargy, mental sickness, love, hatred and delusions is something that does exist and is known by the masses. Many people know it from experience." Shaykh Adel Ben Taher Al-Miqbil defines witchcraft as knots and talisman (Rogeberg, 2017). According to Rogeberg,

> the magician blows in the knots with impure saliva as a means of seeking help from the devil and disbelieve in Allah, and the magician ties knots around written words or items like hair or nails in order to get closer to the devil.
>
> (Rogeberg, 2017, pp. 108–109)

One of the precise definitions of black magic is that "it is an act which brings someone closer to the Shaytan with the latter's help" (Saleh, 2016).

Evidence for the existence of witchcraft

There is no denial that for some cultures and religions witchcraft is real in their worldview. These supernatural beliefs in witchcraft are held by a wide array of individuals with different educational and social statuses. The validity of witchcraft beliefs is not at issue here, but there is acknowledgement that in a society where people believe in supernatural forces "witchcraft is real for those who believe in it" and that "it's no use pretending (witchcraft beliefs) don't exist or seeking some ground of neutrality" (Behringer, 2004, pp. 44, 51). From an Islamic perspective, it is stated that "to deny it is to deny reality and the Shari'ah's attestation. The Shari'ah bears testimony to the real existence of *Sihr*" (Mujlisul Ulama of South Africa, 2015, p. 8). The following are some narrations of the Qur'an and Hadith which testify to the reality and validity of *Sihr* in theological Islam. Allah says in the Qur'an (Interpretation of the meaning):

> *And they followed (instead) what the devils had recited during the reign of Solomon. It was not Solomon who disbelieved, but the devils disbelieved, teaching people magic and that which was revealed to the two angels at Babylon, Harut and Marut. But the two angels do not teach anyone unless they say, "We are a trial, so do not disbelieve (by practicing magic)." And (yet) they learn from them that by which they cause separation between a man and his wife. But they do not harm anyone through it except by permission of Allah. And the people learn what harms them and does not benefit them. But the Children of Israel certainly knew that whoever purchased*

the magic would not have in the Hereafter any share. And wretched is that for which they sold themselves, if they only knew.

(Sūrat Al-Baqarah (The Cow) 2:102)

In Sūrat Yunus (Jonas), Allah says (Interpretation of the meaning):

And when they had thrown, Moses said, "What you have brought is (only) magic. Indeed, Allah will expose its worthlessness. Indeed, Allah does not amend the work of corrupters. And Allah will establish the truth by His words, even if the criminals dislike it."

(Sūrat Yunus (Jonas) 10:81–82)

In Sūrat Falaq (Daybreak), Allah says (Interpretation of the meaning):

Say, "I seek refuge in the Lord of daybreak
From the evil of that which He created
And from the evil of darkness when it settles
And from the evil of the blowers in knots
And from the evil of an envier when he envies."

(Sūrat Falaq (Daybreak) 113:1–5)

In the exegesis of the Qur'an, Ibn Kathir (a) explained that the second verse "From the evil of that which He created" means from the evil of all created things. Thabit Al-Bunani and Al-Hasan Al-Basri both said, "Hell, Iblis (Shaytan) and his progeny, from among that which He (Allah) created." Verse 4 relates to the "And from the evil of the blowers in knots," according to Mujahid, 'Ikrimah, Al-Hasan, Qatadah and Ad-Dahhak all said, "This means the witches." Mujahid said, "When they perform their spells and blow into the knots." Traditionally, one of the most popular forms of sorcery was to tie knots in a rope and then recite incantations over knots, thus bewitching or harming another person.

One of the evidences from the Sunnah comes from a Hadith narrated from 'A'ishah who said that Allah's Messenger (ﷺ) was affected by magic, so much that he used to think that he had done something which in fact, he did not do, and he invoked his Lord (for a remedy). Then (one day) he said,

"O 'Aisha! Do you know that Allah has advised me as to the problem I consulted Him about?" 'Aisha said, "O Allah's Messenger (ﷺ)! What's that?" He said, "Two men came to me and one of them sat at my head and the other at my feet, and one of them asked his companion, 'What is wrong with this man?' The latter replied, 'He is under the effect of magic.' The former asked, 'Who has worked magic on him?' The latter replied, 'Labid bin Al-A'sam' The former asked, 'With what did he work the magic?' The latter replied, 'With a comb and the hair, which are stuck to the comb, and the skin of pollen of a date-palm tree.' The former asked, 'Where is that?' The latter replied,

'It is in Dharwan.' Dharwan was a well in the dwelling place of the (tribe of) Bani Zuraiq. Allah's Messenger (ﷺ) went to that well and returned to 'Aisha, saying, 'By Allah, the water (of the well) was as red as the infusion of Hinna (1) and the date-palm trees look like the heads of devils.' 'Aisha added, Allah's Messenger (ﷺ) came to me and informed me about the well. I asked the Prophet, 'O Allah's Messenger (ﷺ), 'why didn't you take out the skin of pollen?' He said, 'As for me, Allah has cured me and I hated to draw the attention of the people to such evil (which they might learn and harm others with).'" Narrated by Hisham's father: 'Aisha said, "Allah's Messenger (ﷺ) was bewitched, so he invoked Allah repeatedly requesting Him to cure him from that magic." Hisham then narrated the above narration.

(Bukhari (b))

This Hadith shows the use of magic against the Prophet (ﷺ). It is acknowledged that this Hadith is *sahih* (the acceptability of the sayings) which was narrated by Bukhari, Muslim and other scholars of Hadith. *Ahl al-Sunnah* accept this Hadith and story and no one denies it except an innovator.

In relation to the belief of and the use of magic or sorcery, there are a number of Hadiths that indicate it is totally forbidden. Abu Huraira (May Allah be pleased with him), narrated that the Prophet (ﷺ) said:

Whoever comes to a sorcerer and believes what he says, then he has disbelieved in what was revealed to Muhammad.

(Abu Dâwûd (a))

The Prophet (ﷺ) said in the Hadith narrated on the authority of Ibn 'Abbas (May Allah be pleased with both of them):

He who acquires a branch of the knowledge of astrology, learns a branch of magic (of which he acquires more as long as) he continues to do so.

(Abu Dâwûd (b))

Abu Hurayrah (May Allah be pleased with him) narrated that the Prophet (ﷺ) said:

Whoever ties a knot and blows on it has committed sorcery and whoever commits sorcery has committed Shirk (Polytheism). Whoever wears an amulet or talisman will be subjected to its control.

(An Nasai)

'Imran ibn Hussain (May Allah be pleased with him), narrated that the Messenger of Allah (ﷺ) said:

He is not one of us whoever draws omens or omens are drawn for him, or foresees for people or people foresee for him, or performs magic or magic is performed for him, and whoever goes to a sorcerer and believes what he says has disbelieved in what was revealed to Muhammad.

(Al-Bazzar, Cited in Shaykh Abdul-Azeez Bin Baaz (a))

Classical and contemporary scholars' commentaries on magic, sorcery and witchcraft

Imam Abu 'Abdullah Muhammad ibn Ahmad ibn Abu Bakr al-Ansari al-Qurtubi was a famous classical scholar in exegesis and Hadith who commented on witchcraft. According to Al-Qurtubi,

> The Qur'an, in more than one Verse, and the Sunnah, in more than one Hadeeth, indicate that witchcraft exists and that it has an effect on the one who is bewitched. Whoever denies that is a Kaafir (denial of the Truth) who rejects what Allah and His Messenger (ﷺ) say, and denies something that is well known. It cannot be denied that witchcraft has an effect on people's hearts, creating love and hatred and instilling evil ideas, causing separation between man and wife, coming between a man and his mental faculties and causing pain and sickness. All of that is known from real life, and denying it is stubbornness.
>
> (p. 183)

Abū l-Fidā' Ismā'īl ibn 'Umar ibn Kaṯīr, known as Ibn Kathir, was a highly influential scholar expert on Qur'anic exegesis, jurisprudence as well as a historian. He stated that

> Witchcraft is real, and Allah may create whatever effect He wills when that is done. Some witchcraft is sleight of hand, like the charlatans, and some are words that can be memorized. It may be something that is learned from the devils, and it may be medicine and smoke (incense).
>
> (p. 183)

In addition, in his book on 'Witchcraft and Witches' (Ibn Kathir, 2015), he maintained that

> Sorcery is performed with the aid of the *Jinn*, whose help is attained when the sorcerer or sorceress does acts of disbelief and worships the *Jinn* and Satan. Thus they take the *Jinn* and Satan as lords besides God. Once the *Jinn* are pleased with the sorcerer or sorceress, they will do what they ask them. Sihr (sorcery) is a word referring to something hidden. It is real and there are kinds of witchcraft that may affect people psychologically and physically, so that they become sick and die, or husbands and wives are separated. It is a devilish action, most of which is only achieved by means of associating others with God and drawing close to the minions of Satan.

Imam Ibn Qudaamah al-Maqdisee known as Ibn Qudaamah was a scholar in jurisprudence and theology. He stated that,

> Magic (Sihr) is a set of 'uqad (knots), ruqa (incantations), and words uttered or written, or carried out in such a way as to affect the body of the subject (al-mashur), his heart or mind, without even coming into contact with them.

Shaykh Abdul-Azeez Bin Baz (a) stated that "Sihr (sorcery) involves associating others in worship with Allah, because sorcery cannot be learned except through worshipping the jinn and dedicating sacrificial animals and other acts of worship to them. This is Shirk." Shaykh Abdul-Azeez Bin Baz (b) also emphasised that

> It is forbidden to go to fortune-tellers, soothsayers, and sorcerers, and their likes, it is forbidden to ask or believe them, and there is also a threat against doing this. The Prophet (ﷺ) has forbidden going to them, enquiring from them or believing them, because of the great evil and the danger of serious and dire consequences that may befall people by doing this, and that they are wicked liars and evil doers.

Shaykh Muhammad bin Salih al-Uthaymeen (2012) commented that

> magic is from the greatest of unlawful things, rather it is from disbelief when the magician seeks aid through the devilish stations for his magic, or he attains it through shirk. For Allah, the Blessed and Exalted said, "They followed what the Shayaateen (devils) gave out (falsely of the magic) in the lifetime of Sulayman (Solomon). Sulayman did not disbelieve, but the Shayaateen (devils) disbelieved, teaching men magic and such things that came down at Babylon to the two angels, Harut and Marut, but neither of these two (angels) taught anyone (such things) till they had said, 'We are only for trial, so disbelieve not (by learning this magic from us)' (Qur'an 2:102).

This is evidence that learning magic is *kufr*, the magic which is taken from the devils, and upon this it is obligatory to take caution from it and to be far away from it so that a person does not fall into disbelief which expels from the religion and seeking refuge is with Allah." In another commentary, Shaykh Muhammad bin Salih al-Uthaymeen stated that

> There is no doubt that magic is a chronic disease and that it is a great crime on behalf of the magician. And the magician that seeks aid through the satanic spirits or through the devils or the Jinn is a disbeliever, and refuge is with Allah.

Conclusion

Belief in witchcraft, sorcery, magic, *Jinn* and demons is prevalent throughout the Muslim world. The wearing of amulets, consulting deviant spiritual healers and fortune tellers, shrine worship, exorcisms, animal sacrifice, astrology and numerous customs and rituals are under the umbrella of magic and witchcraft. Magic and witchcraft are forbidden in Islam whether contemporary magic (just deception or illusion), black magic (dark), sorcery and witchcraft spells (false miracles). It leads to major and minor *Shirk*.

References

Abu Dâwûd (a) Cited in Shaykh Abdul-Azeez Bin Baaz. *A Message in the Rule of Witchcraft*. http://en.islamway.net/article/12975/a-message-in-the-rule-of-witchcraft (accessed 21 March 2018).

Abu Dâwûd (b) Cited in Fatwas of Ibn Baz. Shaykh Abdul-Azeez Bin Baaz Volume 2 > *Ruling on visiting, consulting, and believing soothsayers and the like*. (Part No. 2; Page No. 120). www.alifta.net/Fatawa/FatawaChapters.aspx?languagename=en&View=Page&PageID=102&PageNo=1&BookID=14 (accessed 21 March 2018).

Ahmad 16969. Classed as Sahih by Shaykh al-Albani in *al-Silsilah al-Saheehah*, 492. Cited in Islamqa (2010) 34817: *What is the true meaning of shirk and what are its types?* https://islamqa.info/en/34817 (accessed 21 March 2018).

Al-Bazzar. Cited in Shaykh Abdul-Azeez Bin Baaz. A Message in the Rule of Witchcraft. http://en.islamway.net/article/12975/a-message-in-the-rule-of-witchcraft (accessed 21 March 2018).

Al-Qurtubi. Imam Abu 'Abdullah Muhammad ibn Ahmad ibn Abu Bakr al-Ansari al-Qurtubi. Cited in Ameen, Dr. Abu'l-Mundir Khaleel ibn Ibraheem (2005) *The Jinn and Human Sickness: Remedies in the Light of the Qur'aan and Sunnah*. Riyadh, Saudi Arabia: Darussalam Publishers.

Ameen, Dr. Abu'l-Mundir Khaleel ibn Ibraheem (2005) *The Jinn and Human Sickness: Remedies in the Light of the Qur'aan and Sunnah*. Riyadh, Saudi Arabia: Darussalam Publishers.

An Nasai. Sunan. *Book on Sanctity of Blood*, no 4079. Cited in Fatwas of Ibn Baz, Volume 6 General advice, Part No. 6 Page No. 66, www.alifta.net/Fatawa/fatawaChapters.aspx?languagename=en&View=Page&PageID=649&PageNo=1&BookID=14 (accessed 21 March 2018).

Ashforth, A. (1998) Reflections on spiritual insecurity in a modern African city (Soweto), *African Studies Review* 41, 3; 39–67

Behringer, W. (2004) *Witches and Witch-Hunts: A Global History*. Cambridge: Polity Press.

Bukhari (a) Sahih al-Bukhari. Arabic reference: Book 65, Hadith 4497. USC-MSA web (English) reference: Vol. 6, Book 60, Hadith 24.

Bukhari (b) Sahih al-Bukhari 6391. In-book reference: Book 80, Hadith 86 USC-MSA web (English) reference: Vol. 8, Book 75, Hadith 400.

Hamès, C. (2008) Problématiques de la magie-sorcellerie en islam et perspectives africaines," *Cahiers d'études africaines* 189–190 | 2008, mis en ligne le 15 avril 2011, consulté le 13 octobre 2017. http://etudesafricaines.revues.org/9842 (accessed 13 October 2017).

Ibn Kathir (a) Tafsir Ibn Kathir. www.recitequran.com/tafsir/en.ibn-kathir/113:1 (accessed 21 March 2018).

Ibn Kathir (b) Cited Ameen, Dr. Abu'l-Mundir Khaleel ibn Ibraheem (2005) *The Jinn and Human Sickness: Remedies in the Light of the Qur'aan and Sunnah*. Riyadh, Saudi Arabia: Darussalam Publishers.

Ibn Kathir (2015) Witchcraft and Witches. Brother Noah Bool Publishing. Brother Noah. Org (Back cover sypnosis).

Ibn Qudaamah. *Al Mughni /8/150 By Abu Muhammad Abdullah bin Ahmad bin Muhammad bin Qudama al-Maqdisi. Ala Mukhtasar: Abul al-Qasim Umar bin Husain bin Abdullah bin Ahmad Al-khirqi*. Riyadh, Saudi Arabia: Dar 'Alam al Kutub. Cited in Abu Hibbaan & Abu Khuzaimah Ansaari (2013) The Reality and Dangers of Black Magic, https://ahlul hadeeth.wordpress.com/2013/06/08/the-reality-and-dangers-of-black-magic/ (accessed 12 October 2017).

Islamqa (2010a) 34817: *What is the true meaning of shirk and what are its types?* https://islamqa. info/en/34817 (accessed 10 October 2017).

Islamqa (2010b) 12578:Witchcraft and Seeking Help From Practioners of it. https://islamqa. info/en/12578 (accessed 11 October 2017).

Lisaanul Arab and Qaamoos. Cited in Mujlisul Ulama of South Africa (2015) *Sihr: Magic, Witchcraft,and Sorcery*. www.themajlis.co.za/books/Sihr%20Magic%20booklet_Eread.pdf (accessed 21 March 2018).

Mujlisul Ulama of South Africa (2015) *Sihr: Magic, Witchcraft, Sorcery*. www.themajlis.co.za/ books/Sihr%20Magic%20booklet_Eread.pdf (accessed 21 March 2018).

Pew Research Center (2012) *The World's Muslims: Unity and Diversity. Chapter 4: Other Beliefs and Practices*. www.pewforum.org/2012/08/09/the-worlds-Muslims-unity-and-diversity-4-other-beliefs-and-practices/ (accessed 21 March 2018).

Rogeberg, J. (2017) *Islam in Saudi Arabia: The Homogeneous Portrayal and Heterogeneous Reality*. A Thesis Submitted to The Faculty of the School of Divinity, Liberty University Dissertation for a Master of Arts in Global Studies, http://digitalcommons.liberty.edu/cgi/ viewcontent.cgi?article=1444&context=masters (accessed 21 March 2018).

Qadhi, Y. (2014) *"The Reality of Sihr (Black Magic) Exorcisms & Jinns – Part II ~ Dr. Yasir Qadhi|* 31st October 2014." YouTube. www.youtube.com/watch?v=szMpZQL9HZo (accessed 21 March 2018).

Saleh, K. H. (Editor) (2016) *Islamic Creed- Jinn and Witchcraft- Lesson (6–7): Kinds of Black Magic*. www.nabulsi.com/en/art.php?art=12970 (accessed 21 March 2018).

Shaykh Abdul-Azeez Bin Baaz (a) Volume 2 > Ruling on visiting, consulting, and believing soothsayers and the like. (Part No. 2; Page No. 120). www.alifta.net/Fatawa/FatawaChap ters.aspx?languagename=en&View=Page&PageID=102&PageNo=1&BookID=14 (accessed 21 March 2018).

Shaykh Abdul-Azeez Bin Baaz (b) Cited in Shaykh Abdul-Azeez Bin Baaz. A Message in the Rule of Witchcraft. http://en.islamway.net/article/12975/a-message-in-the-rule-of-witchcraft (accessed 21 March 2018).

Shaykh Muhammad bin Salih al-Uthaymeen: Clarification on Issues Pertaining to Magic (Sihr) and Explanation of the Intent Behind the Prescribed Punishment. Sikhr Takhyeeliyy (Illusionary Magic) is True and Real and Has an Actual Effect. www.dajjaal.com/ liar/articles/czuhb-shaykh-muhammad-bin-salih-al-uthaymeen-clarification-on-issues-pertaining-to-magic-sihr.cfm (accessed 21 March 2018).

Stacey, A. (2012) *Sorcery in Islam (part 1 of 2): Serious sins that endanger a person's hereafter*. www. islamreligion.com/articles/5246/ (accessed 21 March 2018).

Valentine, S. R. (2015) *Force and Fanaticism: Wahhabism History, Belief, and Practice*. New York: C. Hurst & Co. Ltd.

Chapter 15

Categories and idiosyncrasies of magic and witchcraft

Introduction

The use of magic or witchcraft is to make predictions, gain knowledge or obtain assistance for any task. Sorcery or witchcraft is performed with the aid of the *Jinn* to cast spells and incantations intended to bring harm to others. Those who deal with sorcery or witchcraft often invoke the names of others besides God and undertake acts of disbelief and worships to exorcise the *Jinn*. Shaykh al-Islam Ibn Taymiyah provides the task undertaken by magicians and sorcerers. He explains that

> As for the people of (doing the seemingly) impossible amongst them, then they prepare certain potions (or materials) such as talc powder, the oil (fat) of a frog, citrus peel and what is like that. They (put this on their bodies) and walk through the fire with it, and they keep a type of snake which they take as meat and they proceed to eat it in all sinfulness. And (likewise) what they do with sugar, and laadhin (a type of fragrance), rose water, saffron water and blood. All of that is trickery (hiyal) and swindling (sha'wadhah) which is known to the one who is well-informed in these matters. And amongst them is one to whom the devils come, and they are people doing seemingly impossible things through the aid of the devils.

Among these methods employed or considered as magic and witchcraft are astrology, hypnotherapy, mesmerism, incantations, formulae, transformation, dissociative states and 'speaking in tongues' etc. Astrology is considered in the category of magic from an Islamic perspective. Ibn 'Abbas reported that the Prophet (ﷺ) said:

> A person, who has acquired knowledge of one of the sciences of Astrology, has acquired knowledge of one of the branches of *Sihr*, and the more his knowledge of Astrology is enriched, the more expansive his knowledge of *Sihr* becomes.

> (Abu Dâwûd and Ibn Majah)

Categories and types of magic and witchcraft

There are many types and levels of magic (illusion) sorcery or witchcraft. Scholars listed different kinds of witchcraft and magic. Al-Razi describes eight categories of *Sihr*. These categories include: the magic related to the worship of the seven planets who controlled the world and were behind the forces of good and evil. The magic associated with fantasies and hallucinations. The use of *Jinn* in putting a spell on an individual. The use of magic (illusion) and trickery. The use of specific medication in food and ointments. The slandering people are one of the softer forms of *Sihr*. Ar-Raghib also categorised *Sihr* in the form of "something light and subtle" (p. 36), ranging from simple trickery to using the assistance of demons, with the intention of getting close to them. Shaykh Ibn Uthaymeen (2012) explains two types of magic

> the magic through which a magician becomes a disbeliever and that is magic through the route of seeking aid from the devils. And magic through which a magician does not become a disbeliever, and this is what occurs through potions (used to harm others).

The categorisation of *Sihr* by scholars appears to include some types that include the sleight of hand, illusionary acts, the slandering of people are not considered as 'Black of Dark Magic.'

One of the most popular forms of sorcery was to tie knots in a rope and then recite incantations over knots, thus bewitching or harming another person. Any form of knot can be used to cast a spell. This is cited in Chapter 113 of the Qur'an:

> *And from the evil of those who practise witchcraft when they blow on knots.*
>
> (Sūrat Falaq (Daybreak) 113:4)

This form of sorcery was done to Prophet Muhammad (ﷺ) using a hair that was caught in a comb along with a few fibres of a date palm. After the spell was cast, the Prophet (ﷺ) began to imagine that he had sexual relations with one of his wives when he had in fact not done so. However, God did not allow it to cause him any harm. Prophet Muhammad (ﷺ) warns his followers about the dangers of sorcery or witchcraft when he states that,

> Whoever tied a knot and blew on it has committed sorcery, and whoever committed sorcery has committed *Shirk* (Polytheism). Whoever wears an amulet or talisman will be left to it.
>
> (An Nasai)

According to Wahid Ibn Abdessalam Bali (2004), there are several types of *Sihr* with different aims. These include:

- *Sihr* of Separation (*Sihr at Tafriq*);
- *Sihr* of Love (*Sihr Al-Mahabba/At-Tiwala*);

- *Sihr* of False Appearance of Objects (*Sihr At-Takhyli*);
- *Sihr* of Lunacy (*Sihr Al-Junun*);
- *Sihr* of Lethargy (*Sihr Ahkhumui*);
- *Sihr* of Bad Dreams and HearingVoices (*Sihr Af-Hawatif/ Hemr*);
- *Sihr* of Being Ill (*Sihr Al-Maradh*);
- *Sihr* of Bleeding Following Menses (*Sihr An-Nazif*);
- *Sihr* of Impending of Marriage;
- *Sihr* of Sexual Dysfunction (*Sihr Rabt Ar-Rabt*);
- *Sihr* of Fertility.

The kinds of magic or witchcraft are related to love, marriage, sexual dysfunction, fertility, excess bleeding, separation, health and sickness, lethargy etc. The psychological signs and symptoms include suspicion, distortion of perception, hallucination, obsession, compulsion, confused speech, restlessness, seclusion, anxiety, depression, dreams and nightmares, fear, anger and lack of sexual feeling. The physical symptoms include: frequent headaches, lethargy, constant pain in one part of the body, epilepsy or seizure, paralysis of one area of the patient's body, disability in one of the sense organs, bleeding (women) after regular menstruation, severe tightness in the chest, stomach aches, pain in the lower part of the spine, physical obstruction of the vagina and lack of lubrication in the vagina. The types, aims and symptoms of *Sihr* or witchcraft are presented in Table 15.1.

Imam Qurtubee said,

> The reality is some forms of magic affect the heart, for example, hatred, love, facing something good or overcoming badness. Sometimes the sorcery affects the body for example feeling bodily pain or having an illness. The concept that is denied with regards to magic is the ability to interchange objects into animals and vice versa.

Magic, witchcraft and psychosomatic disease

Psychosomatic disorders are a group of psychiatric disorders in which psychological factors play an important role in creating and exacerbating of medical/ physical conditions. Gregory (1987) notes that

> Diseases are designated as psychosomatic if two conditions are fulfilled: if (i) the symptoms are accompanied by demonstrable physiological disturbances of function and (ii) the illness as a whole can be interpreted as a manifestation or function of the patient's personality, conflicts, life history, etc. The first condition distinguishes psychosomatic illness from psychoneurosis, particularly conversion hysteria, in which, by definition, the physical symptoms are not accompanied by demonstrable physiological disturbances.

In psychosomatic disorder, there is the relationship between body, mind and spirit. Psychosomatic disorders are those whose roots lie not in organic causes but in psychological distress.

Table 15.1 The types, aims and symptoms of *Sihr*

Types	Aim/explanation	Symptoms
Sihr of Separation (*Sihr at Tafriq*)	To separate spouses, or stir up hatred between friends or partners.	▪ A sudden change in attitude from love to hate. ▪ Suspicion. ▪ Exaggerating the causes. ▪ Distorted perception of the person in dispute. ▪ Poor image of the person in dispute.
Sihr of Love (*Sihr Al-Mahabba/At-Tiwala*)	To force (by the use of *Jinn*) a man loves his wife (seen as an act of polytheism).	▪ Excessive love and passion. ▪ Extreme desire to have sexual intercourse. ▪ Impatience of remaining without having sexual intercourse. ▪ Extreme lust at the sight of one's wife. ▪ Blind obedience to one's wife.
Sihr of False Appearance of Objects (*Sihr At-Takhyli*)	Use of magic for obtaining money or showing skills of changing things.	▪ A fixed object would appear to be mobile and vice versa. ▪ A small object would appear large, while a large object would appear small. ▪ The false appearance of objects.
Sihr of Lunacy (*Sihr Al-Junun*)	To induce madness and change in behaviour.	▪ Severe absentmindedness and forgetfulness. ▪ Confused speech. ▪ Bulging eyes and deviation of sight. ▪ Restlessness. ▪ Inability to do a task regularly. ▪ Disinterest in one's appearance. ▪ May have epileptic fit.
Sihr of Lethargy (*Sihr Ahkhumui*)		▪ Love of seclusion. ▪ Absolute introversion. ▪ Constant silence. ▪ Anti-social. ▪ Absentmindedness. ▪ Frequent headaches. ▪ Quietness and constant lethargy.

Sihr of Bad Dreams and Hearing Voices (*Sihr Af-Hawatif/Hemr*)	▪ Nightmares. ▪ Being called in dreams. ▪ Falling from high places (in dreams). ▪ Being chased by animals (in dreams). ▪ Auditory hallucination. ▪ Whispering (*Waswas*). ▪ Suspicious of his/her friends and relatives.
Sihr of Being Ill (*Sihr Al-Maradh*)	▪ Constant pain in one part of the body. ▪ Epilepsy. ▪ Paralysis of one area of the patient's body. ▪ Total paralysis of the body. ▪ Disability in of one of the sense organs.
Sihr of Bleeding Following Menses (*Sihr An-Nazif*)	According to scholars of jurisprudence, *An-Nazif* refers to *al-istihadha* (continuous menstruation), and according to doctors, it refers to bleeding. ▪ This type of *Sihr* affects women only. ▪ This bleeding may last for months. ▪ The amount of blood could be little or large. ▪ Different from normal menses.
Sihr of Impending of Marriage	Feel uncomfortable with any prospective suitor. Poor image of the suitor. ▪ Extreme fear. ▪ Extreme anger. ▪ Extreme unawareness. ▪ Indulgence in pleasure. ▪ Occasional headaches, which persist despite medication. ▪ Severe tightness in the chest, especially between the mid-afternoon prayer and midnight. ▪ The patient sees the suitor in an ugly image. ▪ Absentminded. ▪ Anxiety during sleep. ▪ Occasional constant stomach aches. ▪ Pain in the lower part of the back.

(Continued)

Table 15.1 (Continued)

Types	Aim/explanation	Symptoms
Sihr of Sexual Dysfunction (*Sihr Rabt Ar-Rabt*)	The inability of a healthy man to have sexual intercourse with his wife. Frigidity in women.	Women: • Obstruction: It occurs when a woman prevents her husband from having sexual intercourse with her by tightly joining her legs together and obstructing his penis from entering into her vagina. (Automatic and beyond control.) • Lack of sexual feeling. • Numbness. • Lack of lubrication in vagina. • Bleeding at the time of sexual intercourse. • Blockage in the vagina. • Loss of virginity (reversible).
Sihr of Fertility	Natural and *Sihr* fertility.	• A tightness in the chest, which begins at mid-afternoon prayer and may last until midnight. • Absentmindedness. • Pain in the lower part of the spine. • Anxiety during sleep. • Nightmares.

Source: Adapted from Wahid Ibn Abdessalam Bali (2004) *Sword Against Black Magic And Evil Magicians*. Translated by Chafik Abdelghani. London: Al-Firdous Ltd.

In the modern era, the diagnosis of hysteria has been replaced with psycho-somatic disorder (Hansen, 1969).

According to Bever (2000), "Historians, anthropologists, and psychologists have tended to discount the role of 'psychosomatic' disease in witchcraft beliefs because they have misunderstood, and therefore underestimated, the connection between interpersonal relations, psychological well-being, and physical health" (p. 573).

There are many biological and medical explanations of the effects of magic and witchcraft. These range from encephalitis lethargica, Lyme disease, post-traumatic stress disorder, hysteria and psychosomatic disorders. Hysteria and epilepsy were the disorders that were most frequently associated with witch-craft or demonic possession, especially if the presenting symptoms included shaking, tremors, convulsions or loss of consciousness (North, 2015). In cases of witchcraft and magic, the individual may present with a number of disorders including psoriasis, eczema, stomach ulcers, high blood pressure and heart dis-ease, stress, anxiety and depression. In the case of psychosomatic illness, there is an actual and medically measurable physical/psychological illness with no organic cause.

Somatoform disorders

Somatoform disorders are a group of psychological disorders where the indi-viduals express subjective feelings of the conditions. There are five types of somatoform disorders: conversion disorder, somatisation disorder, pain disorder, hypochondriasis and body dysmorphic disorder. The term functional disorder or functional neurological disorder (Stone et al., 2011) is preferred when no known physical cause can be found for a physical symptom. Physical symp-toms or painful complaints of unknown aetiology are fairly common in those presenting with witchcraft and possession. The somatoform disorders represent the severe end of a continuum of somatic symptoms and many physical symp-toms appear in different parts of the body. The symptoms include unexplained extreme headaches, weight loss or gain, tiredness, nightmares, changes in voices, abdominal pain, seizures, episodes of miscarriage, amenorrhoea, infertility, impotence, persecutory feelings and hallucinations (auditory and tactile). One of the phenomena of a type of somatoform disorder is the 'open wound or sore.' This disease, which does not heal, is usually caused by vascular diseases, diabetes, infective organisms, leprosy, pyoderma gangrenosum (the body's immune sys-tem mistakenly turns upon itself, destroying its own flesh as if it were a foreign invader) and skin cancer. However, some open wound sores appear spontane-ously and defy clinical evaluation. These kinds of sores or open wounds may be the result of *Jinn* possession or witchcraft.

It is reported that the *Jinn* or evil spirits need a breach to enter the human body like an open wound (in other cases they can also enter in a moment of weakness: anger, sorrow, fear). From Islamic theology, the idea that *Jinn* can enter human bodies is evidenced in the Qur'an and Sunnah, and by the consensus of *Ahl al-Sunnah wal-Jama'ah* and by real-life events (Islamqa, 2000). In a Hadith, the Prophet Muhammad (ﷺ) stated that

> Satan runs in the body of Adam's son (i.e. man) as his blood circulates in it, and I was afraid that he (Satan) might insert an evil thought in your hearts.
> (Bukhari)

The appearance of keloid, a scar that rises above the skin, has also been reported. In some cases, individuals who have not caused injury to their skin developed 'spontaneous keloids.'

Conversion disorder (Functional Neurological Symptom Disorder) is categorised under the new category of Somatic Symptom and Related Disorders in the DSM-V (APA, 2013). Thid condition is characterised by the transformation of psychological or unconscious conflict in a physical form. It "involves symptoms or deficits affecting voluntary motor or sensory function that suggest a neurologic or other general medical condition" (Medscape.com).

This type of disorder, like those from black magic or witchcraft, often develops abruptly. The individual shows signs of deficits in sensory and behavioural functions including blindness, shaking movements, impaired coordination or balance, paralysis, seizures or other neurologic symptoms that cannot be explained by clinical evaluation.

Pain disorder, similar to somatisation disorder, is chronic pain experienced by an individual as bodily symptoms. The characteristics of this disorder refer to individuals who have bodily or somatic symptoms associated with stress, misery and impairment. The introduction to this new disorder includes the description of the diagnosis that is to be made "on the basis of positive symptoms and signs (distressing somatic symptoms plus abnormal thoughts, feelings, and behaviors in response to these symptoms) rather than the absence of a medical explanation for somatic complaints" (APA, 2013, p. 309). It is assumed that psychological factors have a major role in the onset of the disorder. Many individuals affected by witchcraft expressed muscle aches and stiffness, pain in shoulders, lower back, chest and abdominal area.

Auto-suggestion, possession and witchcraft

The concept of suggestion, from a psychological construct, has been described as "the impression upon the mind by the agency of other objects, such as gesture, signs, words, speech, physical sensations, environment, etc." (Atkinson, 2010, p. 6). Sometimes, it is the fear of witchcraft and not witchcraft itself which creates the bio-psychosocial health problems. That is a kind of self-fulling prophecy. The individual believes that she is possessed by witchcraft or *Jinn*. The development of fear or other psychological stressors are the result of having some knowledge (sometimes not the right kind of knowledge) which may trigger a 'possession' reaction. According to Bever (2008), "The knowledge that a reputed sorcerer is casting a harmful spell has been shown to be sufficient to cause some people to become ill" (p. 29). Bever (2008) also indicates the belief of being subjected to witchcraft may also cause ill health. Ameen (2005) suggested that

> some people may imagine that they have been bewitched or that so-and-so has put a spell on them because of some problem between them, so their thinking becomes confused and their lives become chaotic, and they tell themselves that they have been bewitched. If the delusion of having being possessed by the *Jinn* or having been bewitched takes hold of a person, then his thinking becomes confused and his life becomes chaotic; his glands start to malfunction and the signs of possession or bewitchment appear in him. He may suffer convulsions or lose consciousness as the result of what modern psychology calls autosuggestion.
>
> (p. 282)

A form of hypochondriasis coined as 'Imaginary disease and Possession' (*Marad Khayali Wahiaza*) also forms part of the effect of witchcraft or *Jinn*-related possession. The individual claimed to have imaginary possession. Imaginary possession is the worst type of disorder. Imaginary possession, a form of psychosomatic hypochondria, starts when the soul or mind becomes 'infected,' resulting in a false belief or negative thought process leading to behavioural action. Another understanding of this condition is that it may start with having the symptoms of 'Possession or witchcraft,' leading to specific fear or anxiety leading to health problems. The delusion of having been subjected to witchcraft or *Jinn* possession may make an individual suffer from loss of consciousness and convulsions. Imaginary epilepsy has been explained "as the result of mixing with those who are possessed, then starting to imagine oneself is afflicted with the same symptoms, or the healer suggests to the patient that he/she is afflicted" (Alruqya Healing Centre).

Many Muslim patients attending healing centres for the treatment of witchcraft or *Jinn* possession may be suffering from the psychological problem of delusion rather than actual possession. In clinical practice, very few individuals are actually possessed by *Jinn* or have been bewitched even though they may show or express symptoms of witchcraft or *Jinn* possession. Psychological interventions may be more appropriate in these cases of auto-suggestion disorders.

Conclusion

Current medical knowledge about the relationship between psychological distress, psychosomatic and somatoform disorders provide us with a better understanding of the aetiology (in some conditions), pathology and symptomatology of these conditions. Witchcraft and magic may cause many physical and psychological health problems. These supernatural phenomena, with metaphysical origin, do not work according to the rules known to orthodox Western-oriented medical culture. The conditions of witchcraft or magic may present diagnosable symptoms, but the aetiology is of unknown origin or the trigger is abnormal. The outcomes of medical and psychological interventions in these conditions are poor and limited. However, due to the religio-cultural manifestations of health and illness, considerations need to be given to the worldview of 'spiritual health' problems. Bever (2009) maintained that

> In the long run, both the intellectual and the institutional implications of the medicalisation of witchcraft beliefs contributed significantly to the decline of magical beliefs in general, but in the short run, accommodation to, rather than rejection of, religious beliefs.
>
> (p. 275)

Ultimately, Bever (2008) stated that there is "a substantial body of evidence suggesting that there are natural processes which are not adequately explained by current scientific understanding" (p. 36). Thus, it is a matter of clinical judgement that provides the labelling of psychiatric disorders. O'Hagan (1999) argued that "It is easy to see that having unusual beliefs or hearing voices that others cannot hear are factual occurrences. But attaching the label of mental illness or disability to these facts is purely a judgement." Perhaps a better understanding of the nature and process of atypical manifestations of magic and witchcraft may provide better clinical decisions.

References

Abu Dâwûd and Ibn Majah. Cited in Islamqa (2014) 152097: Is there any report to suggest that the astrologers knew about the birth of Ibraaheem (peace be upon him) and warned Nimrood about him? https://islamqa.info/en/152097 (accessed 21 March 2018).

Alruqya Healing Centre (Abu Nadeer) *Jinn and Devils (MASS)*. http://ruqyainlondon.com/article/jinn-and-devils (accessed 21 March 2018).

Ameen, A. M. (2005) *Dr. Abu'l Mundhir Khaleel ibn Ibraaheem Ameen. The Jinn and Human Sickness Remedies in the Light of the Qur'aan and Sunnah*. Riyadh, Saudi Arabia: Darussalam Publications.

American Psychiatric Association (APA) (2013) *Diagnostic and Statistical Manual of Mental Disorders. DSM-5.* 5th ed. Washington, DC: Author.

Ar-Raghib. Cited in Wahid Ibn Abdessalam Bali (2004) *Sword Against Black Magic And Evil Magicians.* Translated by Chafik Abdelghani. London: AI-Firdous Ltd.

Al-Razi. Tafsir Al-Razi (2/244) Cited in Wahid Ibn Abdessalam Bali (2004) *Sword Against Black Magic And Evil Magicians.* Translated by Chafik Abdelghani. London: AI-Firdous Ltd.

Atkinson, W. W. (2010) *Suggestion and Auto-Suggestion.* New York: Cosimo Classics.

Bever, E. (2000) Witchcraft fears and psychosocial factors in disease. *Journal of Interdisciplinary History,* 30, 4, 573–590.

Bever, E. (2008) *The Realities of Witchcraft and Popular Magic in Early Modern Europe: Culture, Cognition, and Everyday Life*. Houndsmill: Palgrave Macmillan.

Bever, E. (2009) Witchcraft prosecutions and the decline of magic, *Journal of Interdisciplinary History*, xl, 2, 263–293.

Bukhari. Sahih al-Bukhari 6219.In-book reference: Book 78, Hadith 243.USC-MSA web(English) reference:Vol. 8, Book 73, Hadith 238.

Gregory (1987) cited in Crabtree, V (2008) *Psychosomosis – the placebo and nocebo effectscuring and causing disease with the mind*. http://www.humantruth.info/psychosomosis.html (accessed 2 June 2018) from Gregory, R. L.(1987) *The Oxford Companion to the Mind*. Oxford: Oxford University Press.

Hansen, C. (1969) *Witchcraft at Salem*. New York: George Braziller, p. 10.

Imam Qurtubee. Summarised from Fath ul-Baaree 10/222–223. Cited in Hibbaan, A. and Ansaari, A. K. (2013) The Reality and Dangers of Black Magic, https://ahlulhadeeth. wordpress.com/2013/06/08/the-reality-and-dangers-of-black-magic/ (accessed 21 March 2018).

Islamqa (2000)1819: *Jinn Entering Human Bodies*. https://islamqa.info/en/1819 (accessed 21 March 2018).

Medscape.com. Conversion Disorders. https://img.medscape.com/pi/iphone/medscape app/html/A287464-business.html (accessed 2 June 2018)

North, C. S. (2015) The classification of hysteria and related disorders: Historical and phenomenological considerations, *Behavioral Sciences*, 5, 4, 496–517. http://doi.org/10.3390/bs5040496.

O'Hagan, M. (1999) *A call to open the door: A psychiatric disability perspective on 'rethinking care'*. World Network of Users and Survivors of Psychiatry(WNUSP). www.dinf.ne.jp/doc/english/resource/acallto_eng.html (accessed 21 March 2018).

Shaykh al-Islam Ibn Taymiyah. *Magic and the Occult*. Shaykh al-Islam Ibn Taymiyah: Distinction Between Illusionary Tricks Involving Deception And Those Involving the Devils – Part 2. www.dajjaal.com/liar/articles/oykkt-shaykh-al-islam-ibn-taymiyyah-distinction-between-illusionary-tricks-involving-deception-and-those-involving-the-devils – part-2.cfm (accessed 21 March 2018).

Shaykh Muhammad bin Salih al-Uthaymeen (2012) *Clarification on Issues Pertaining to Magic (Sihr) and Explanation of the Intent Behind the Prescribed Punishment*. www.dajjaal.com/liar/articles/czuhb-shaykh-muhammad-bin-salih-al-uthaymeen-clarification-on-issues-pertaining-to-magic-sihr.cfm (accessed 21 March 2018).

Stone, J., Lafrance, W. C., Jr., Brown, R., Spiegel, D., Levenson, J. L., and Sharpe, M. (2011). Conversion disorder: Current problems and potential solutions for DSM-5, *Journal of Psychosomatic Research*, 71, 369–376. Doi:10.1016/j.jpsychores.2011.07.005.

Wahid Ibn Abdessalam Bali (2004) *Sword Against Black Magic And Evil Magicians*. Translated by Chafik Abdelghani. London: Al-Firdous Ltd.

Part III

Prevention, therapeutic and spiritual interventions

Chapter 16

Understanding the Muslim patient

A framework for assessment and diagnosis

Introduction

In Islam, there is no separation between psychological and spiritual health as they are both intertwined in the worldview of Muslims toward health. It is increasingly clear that specific attributions or causal explanations of health and illness can be fully understood only by taking into account the wider belief and value system of the individual (Rassool and Sange, 2014). A spiritual approach emphasises that the belief system shapes its understanding of health and illness and this has a significant influence on the directions for interventions. For some individuals, the impact of experiencing psycho-spiritual problems can be stressful and distressing, for others it may be a process of emancipation, purification and transformation. Muslims, by virtue of their religious belief, attribute the ultimate cause of illness to God. According to Rassool (2000), Muslims believe an illness is not something viewed in the negative sense, but rather as a positive event that purifies the body. As narrated by Abu Sa'id Al-Khudri and Abu Huraira, it is reported that the Prophet Muhammad (ﷺ) said that:

> No fatigue, nor disease, nor sorrow, nor sadness, nor hurt, nor distress befalls a Muslim, even if it were the prick he receives from a thorn, but that Allah expiates some of his sins for that.
>
> (Bukhari)

The seeking of treatment for ill health does not conflict with seeking help from Allah. In relation to mental health, many Muslims failed to seek treatment from mainstream psychiatric health services because of their convictions of suffering from *Jinn* possession or witchcraft. In addition, Muslims are hesitant to seek help from mental health professionals because of their assumed lacked of understanding of Islamic beliefs and practice and that treatment interventions may not be congruent with Islamic values. It has been suggested that understanding Islamic values and beliefs can be beneficial in treatment interventions through the incorporation of such beliefs that help in drug adherence and modification of different psychotherapeutic techniques (Sabry and Vohra,

2013). The aims of the chapter are to provide a framework for assessment and screening of Muslim patients in the therapeutic process and to examine the diagnosis of evil eye, and *Jinn* possession.

Understanding the Muslim patient

Muslim patients accord a great deal of authority to healthcare professionals. During the past few decades, the relationship between doctors and patients has evolved from a largely paternalistic model to a more collaborative approach based on respect for autonomy, nonmaleficence, beneficence and justice. Westra et al. (2009) pointed out that "The four principles approach has been popularly accepted as a set of universal guidelines to fulfil the need of a 'culturally neutral approach to thinking about ethical issues in health care'" (p. 1383). However, these 'universal principles' may have an impact on the patient-practitioner relationship process.

Muslims are a heterogeneous group made of diverse cultural entities despite having core commonalities in terms of religious beliefs and practices. Thus, there are variations in the degree to which one identifies with being Muslim in faith, function or culture (Ali et al., 2009). Healthcare practitioners should be aware not to develop stereotypical assumptions about beliefs and practices, but should be cognisant of individual health beliefs and behaviours. There are a number of Islamic religious beliefs that will affect the attitudes and behaviours of Muslim patients seeking psychological help. Health beliefs are especially important in the area of mental health in which there is often an aversion to seeking help, especially outside the lay referral system and the family. Some of the significant religio-cultural issues faced by mental health practitioners and counsellors include greeting, modesty, eye contact, self-disclosure, family involvement and communication (see Rassool, 2016).

Research studies both in the UK and the US have provided valuable insight into the health beliefs and Islamic values regarding the utilisation of healthcare. In the UK, the findings of a study showed that respect of the individual's dignity and privacy, community roles and importance, genuineness of provider, gender preference of the healthcare provider, modesty issues for men and women, language barriers, therapeutic touch and the use of prayer and visitation of the sick for healing purposes were indicated as important (Cortis, 2000). In the US study (Walton et al., 2014), the specific health beliefs important to Muslim women to participation in medical or psychological care include: making autonomous healthcare decisions without the assistance of a male family member; preference for a female healthcare provider; access to medical and rehabilitation services if provided by a female, but not when provided by a male healthcare provider; believe in the use of prayer, recitation of Qur'an, fasting, charity to be beneficial to their physical health; and are comfortable with the use of physical touch in medicine and rehabilitation evaluation and treatment, if the provider is female. Many Muslims failed to take up healthcare services due to knowledge and familiarity with formal services, perceived social stigma, and the use of informal-indigenous resources which often hinder use of professional services (Aloud, 2004). Having basic knowledge of these factors can enable health-care professionals to provide more culturally appropriate or congruent inter-ventions. This would also enable decision-making about relationship building, assessment, communication and management strategies. In the context of using psychosocial interventions as part of the intervention strategies, it has been sug-gested that cultural sensitivity remains as one of the important characteristics of effective counselling (Sumari and Jalal, 2008). Although Muslims patients may come to a psychiatrist or counsellor for help with their mental health problem, they may still be influenced to look to their religious and cultural heritage to address their psycho-spiritual needs.

Assessment in practice

Delivering high-quality care to Muslim patients means having an appropriate framework for the assessment of complex needs. The great diversity of cultural, ethnic and linguistic groups within Muslim communities, each of which has its own cultural characteristics and worldview of health and illness presents con-stant challenges to healthcare providers. In the initial assessment of the Muslim patient, the focus is to assess the patient's preferred language in case the patient does not share the same language as the healthcare professional. The use of a professional translator may be valuable in case of necessity. Sometimes the family may act as part of the collateral assessment. Religio-cultural factors also have a significant influence on the presentation of illness behaviours so the importance of enquiring about a patient's individual customs and preferred practices are important. The therapeutic alliance developed during the process of engagement would enable the health professional to better understand the presenting and expressed symptoms of the patient. Expressions of symptoms may differ among the diverse communities of Muslims. Mental disorders are sometimes expressed according to social and cultural groups' understanding of the body's functioning (Hofmann and Hinton, 2014). It has been suggested that if there is a lack of diagnostic consistency within the same culture, an even greater challenge is achieving diagnostic consistency in a different cultural group (Canino and Algeria, 2008). These disparities may hamper the option of identifying a mental health problem. Other barriers in the assessment process may include: the patient's beliefs about psychological problems; the patient's attitudes toward accepting the Western method of treatment interventions; or the healthcare services offered may be culturally inappropriate. The issues of suicide, sexual behaviours and alcohol and drug (substance misuse) may provide some uneasiness for both the healthcare professionals and the patient. These are taboo subjects in the Muslim community. It is important that sensitivity is applied when assessment concerning suicidal thoughts, and may require special phrasing (for example, 'Have you been wishing that God would allow you to die somehow?') (Ali et al., 2009). It is important to examine the family dynamics and the psychosocial stressors emanating from the family.

The assessment of cultural identity, worldview, acculturation and spirituality-religiosity of the client ensures that the healthcare professional conducts good practices in the provision of culturally sensitive intervention. According to Ibrahim and Dykeman (2011), cultural assessment requires an "exploration with the client in relation to his or her presenting problem, his or her culture, religion/spirituality and acculturation" (p. 389). The principles of assessment and of Muslim patients with mental health problems are presented in Table 16.1.

For some Muslim patients, the primary presenting mental health problems issue may be psycho-spiritual in nature so that a full spiritual assessment is warranted. This assessment would enable the healthcare professional to understand "the patient's belief system, values, and religious practice" in order to "engage the client in a way that is ethno-religiously congruent and that does not potentially violate their religious tradition and practices" (Eck, 2002, p. 269). The rationale for the inclusion of spiritual assessment of Muslim clients is important for a number of reasons. These include a more objective understanding of the patient's worldview; the perception of the causation of health and illness; to identify the relationship between the presenting problems and the spiritual dimension; and to enable decision-making on spiritual or religious

Table 16.1 Principles of assessment of Muslim patients with mental health problems

- A holistic assessment of a patient includes culture and religious beliefs, presenting problems and collateral information from significant others.
- Inquire about patients' cultural identity to determine their ethnic or racial background.
- Identify language ability and the patient's preferred method of communication. Make necessary arrangements if translators are needed.
- Identify the cultural or religious beliefs the patient holds about health and illness (What do you think has caused your current problem?).
- Identify the personal and social meaning the patient attaches to his psychological state (What do you think your illness does to you?).
- Examine the expectations of the patient about his problem.
- Examine the patient's (and significant others') therapeutic goals or what are their expectations of the healthcare interventions.
- Identify the treatment interventions received by the patient in their own culture.
- Assess the need for spiritual interventions that may be required (in consultant with an Iman or faith healer) to complement psychological interventions.
- Consider cultural factors related to the psychosocial environment and levels of functioning.
- Identify patient's major support and family configurations and include the family in the assessment process and treatment interventions.

Source: Adapted from Rassool, G. Hussein (2014) *Cultural Competence in Caring for Muslim Patients*. Basingstoke, Hampshire: Palgrave Macmillan.

Table 16.2 Sample questions on spirituality-religiosity

- Whether you consider yourself a religious person?
- What religion you practice?
- How did you come to incorporate spirituality or religion into your life?
- How do your religious beliefs affect your day-to-day life?
- Do you find comfort in religious practices such as prayer, making supplications and/or fasting?
- Do you have family and/or social network who practice your religion?
- Are you attached in any religious groups in your community? Do you find this to be a source of support?
- Do you find that your religious connection is helpful to you in dealing with stress?

Source: Adapted from Rahiem, F.T. and Hamid, H. (2012) 'Mental Health Interview and Cultural Formulation,' in S. Ahmed and M. Amer (Eds.), *Counselling Muslims: Handbook of Mental Health Issues and Interventions*, New York: Routledge, p. 52–66.

interventions. According to Koenig et al. (1996), the spiritual assessment undertaken "validates religion as an important part of the patient's life and identifies a potential coping resource. It also provides vital information that is necessary in designing any future interventions that may include the patient's religious faith" (p. 169). In Table 16.2, a sample of questions has been adapted from Rahiem and Hamid (2012).

Risk assessment and management are core elements of good practice in mental health intervention. The aim of risk assessment is to identify risk factors which can be used to determine the likelihood of 'harm' to self and others. The element of risk assessment that requires attention from healthcare professionals includes the assessment of a risk of violence to others, the individuals' vulnerability to dangers or exploitations such as sexual, financial, occupational and familial – particularly when their judgement or cognitive functioning is seriously impaired (Rassool and Winnington, 2006).

The assessment process is the first phase of the treatment journey and it is important to ensure ensuring that comprehensive data is collected in a systematic manner. This would enable healthcare professionals not only to identify future outcomes, but also to evaluate the appropriateness and relative success of different intervention strategies. Lukoff et al. (1992) pointed out that assessments help counsellors (healthcare professionals) to differentiate between problems that are entirely religious or spiritual, those that are a mental disorder with religious or spiritual content, and those that are psycho-religious or psycho-spiritual problems but are not considered a mental disorder.

Diagnosis of evil eye and *Jinn* possession

Evil eye and *Jinn* possession can be recognised in several ways: self-diagnosis, observation of symptoms, screening tool and through diagnostic *Ruqyah* (incantations for spiritual healing).

Observing symptoms

The symptoms of evil eye, *Jinn* possession and witchcraft vary for different people when touched by these supernatural phenomena. According to Al Habeeb (2003), "the triad of somatic symptoms such as apparent paralysis, dyspnoea and tremors may indicate *Jinn* psychopathology, while anorexia and abortions may anchor the diagnosis of evil eye and magic" (p. 35). In addition, other symptoms that include "abnormal movements, seizure-like state, transient psychotic disturbance, and reversible altered consciousness was partly compatible with the diagnostic criteria of possession state as laid down in major classifications" (p. 35). Those who deal with *Ruqyah* have mentioned some of the symptoms which may be used for the diagnosis of evil eye or *Jinn* possession. However, these symptoms, as presented in Table 16.3, are not definitive symptoms and may vary in some cases, and may be more or less in other cases.

Ruqyah diagnosis

The most effective method for the diagnosis of *Jinn* possession is *Ruqyah* (incantation). This will be examined comprehensively in Chapter 19 on spiritual interventions. *Ruqyah* can be divided into two categories: *Ruqyah* which is compliant with the Islamic jurisprudence (*Ruqyah Ash Shari'ah*) and the deviant *Ruqyah* which contains polytheistic practices (*Ruqyah Ash Shirkiyyah*). The *Ruqyah* mentioned in this book is *Ruqyah Ash Shari'ah*. There are many websites providing *Ruqyah* online and the attendance of a particular therapy centre.

Table 16.3 Symptoms for diagnosis of evil eye and Jinn possession

Symptoms of evil eye	Symptoms of Jinn possession
• Headaches that move from one part of the head to another. • Yellow pallor in the face. • Sweating and urinating a great deal. • Weak appetite; tingling, heat or cold in the limbs. • Palpitations in the heart. • Pain in the lower back and shoulders. • Sadness and anxiety. • Sleeplessness at night. • Strong reactions due to abnormal fears. • A lot of burping, yawning and sighing. • Withdrawal and love of solitude. • Apathy and laziness. • A tendency to sleep; health problems with no known medical cause.	• Turning away and reacting strongly when hearing the adhan (call to prayer) or Qur'an. • Fainting, seizures and falling when Qur'an is read over him. • A lot of disturbing dreams. • Being alone, keeping away from people and behaving strangely. • The devil who is dwelling in him may speak when Qur'an is recited over him.

Source: Islamqa (2009)125543: Determining if One is Afflicted by Evil Eye or Possessed, *https://islamqa.info/en/125543* (accessed 21 March 2018).

Individuals with *Jinn* possession or witchcraft may not tolerate the recitation of the Qur'an during *Ruqyah*. The effects differ from individual to individual and may include spontaneous changes in involuntary actions (for example, vomiting, involuntary muscular movements) or emotions (for example, screaming, crying, sinister laughing) or showing total resistance to the therapy.

Self-diagnosis

There are different types of self-diagnosis of *Jinn* possession, including the listening of Qur'anic recitations (audio) and self-diagnosis questionnaire. Different *Ruqyah* or healing centres would use different methods, procedures or approaches and the type of questions used in self-diagnosis questionnaire. For the audio approach, there is the request to listen to some recitations for about five times continuously or in some cases seven times or any odd amount. The individual would then self-reflect on the following questions:

- What is the general feeling or emotional reaction after listening to the audio recording?
- Is the emotional reaction normal or unexplained?
- Was there a feeling of something moving inside you?
- Did you notice behavioural changes as restless, irritation, inability to listen to the recitation, wanted to move away or shut off the recitation immediately?

If you have certain reactions, then you should consult a *Ruqyah* centre immediately.

Some of the websites on *Ruqyah* healing list a number of symptoms under various categories for evil eye, *Jinn* possession and witchcraft. If you identify as suffering some of the conditions listed, you are deemed to be a victim of evil eye, *Jinn* possession or witchcraft. In which case, you are requested to have *Ruqyah* performed. Other sites provide a combination of some supplications from the Sunnah and supplications derived from Qur'anic verses made into a brief *Ruqyah*. You are required to recite the *Ruqyah* repeatedly for self-diagnosis, for example, the evil eye. It is also acceptable to recite this *Ruqyah* near a person suspected of being touched by the evil eye. It is advised to discontinue the *Ruqyah* if symptoms appear after reciting once, twice or thrice and seek professional help. Some of the websites provide the treatment for evil eye, *Jinn* possession and witchcraft.

Possession scale screening tool

The Pisang *Jinn* Possession Scale, developed by Rahman (2014), is a scale measuring the likelihood or severity of *Jinn* possession. The author of this tool reported that the scale was developed using both psychological and somatic symptoms and collected from over 1000 clients. The author reported that the psychometric assessment of the scale has shown good validity and reliability. It can be use both for diagnostic of *Jinn* possession and evaluation of effectiveness of therapeutic interventions. It is claimed that the use of the Pisang *Jinn* Possession Scale performs "a better diagnosis of *Jinn* possession compared to diagnosis using *Ruqyah*" (Rahman, 2014, p. 9). However, Rahman (2014) has identified the limitations of the instrument is when the patient failed to disclose all their symptoms. He suggested that *Ruqyah* diagnosis can possibly detect *Jinn* possession in some of these cases.

Conclusion

Complaints or concerns regarding *Jinn* possession or being victim of witchcraft may be a challenge to healthcare professionals because of interactions between cultural and religious beliefs and conventional medicine. The method of assessment depends on whether the complaints constitute a mental health emergency. Evidently, in any case of alleged *Jinn* possession or witchcraft, underlying organic disorders should be excluded by physical examination and investigations. Any underlying mental health problems should be treated by the usual psychiatric methods, but the clinician should respect the religious and cultural issues and avoid directly contradicting statements from the patient or relatives about the reality of possession or victims of evil eye or witchcraft. Khalifa and Hardie (2005) suggested that when medicine invites conflict with culture and religion, the therapeutic alliance suffers. Healthcare professionals need to be clear about the purpose of any assessments they are undertaking and be sensitive to the possible cultural and religious issues affecting illness. Above all, there is a need to develop cultural competence in order to enhance the assessment process.

References

Ali, O., Abu-Ras, W., and Hamid, H. (2009) *Muslim Americans. NKI Center of Excellence in Culturally Competent Mental Health.* http://ssrdqst.rfmh.org/cecc/index.php?q=node/25 (accessed 21 March 2018).

Al-Habeeb, T. A. (2003) A pilot study of faith healers' views on evil eye, Jinn possession, and magic in the kingdom of Saudi Arabia, *Journal of Family & Community Medicine*, 10, 3, 31–38.

Aloud, N. (2004) Factors affecting attitudes toward seeking and using formal mental health and psychological services among Arab-Muslim population. *Doctoral Dissertation*, School of The Ohio State University, Ohio, USA.

Bukhari. Sahih al-Bukhari 5641, 5642. In-book reference: Book 75, Hadith 2. USC-MSA web (English) reference: Vol. 7, Book 70, Hadith 545.

Canino, G., and Algeria M. (2008) Psychiatric diagnosis – is it universal or relative to culture? *Journal of Child Psychology and Psychiatry*, 49, 3, 237–250.

Cortis, J. D. (2000) Perceptions and experiences with nursing care: A study of Pakistani (Urdu) communities in the United Kingdom, *Journal of Transcultural Nursing*, 11, 2, 111–118.

Eck, B. E. (2002) An exploration of the therapeutic use of spiritual disciplines in clinical practice, *Journal of Psychology and Christianity*, 21, 3, 266–280.

Hofmann, S. G., and Hinton, D. E. (2014) Cross-cultural aspects of anxiety disorders, *Current Psychiatry Reports*, 16, 6: 450. http://doi.org/10.1007/s11920-014-0450-3.

Ibrahim, F. A., and Dykeman, C. (2011) Counseling Muslim Americans: Cultural and spiritual assessments, *Journal of Counseling and Development*, 89, 4, 387–386.

Islamqa (2009) 125543: *Determining if One is Afflicted by Evil Eye or Possessed*. https://islamqa.info/en/125543 (accessed 21 March 2018).

Khalifa, N., and Hardie, T. (2005) Possession and Jinn, *Journal of the Royal Society of Medicine*, 98, 8, 351–353.

Koenig, H. G., Larson, D. B., and Matthews, D. A. (1996) Religion and psychotherapy with older adults, *Journal of Geriatric Psychiatry*, 29, 2, 155–174.

Lukoff, D., Lu, F., and Turner, R. (1992) Toward a more culturally sensitive DSM-IV: Psychoreligious and psychospiritual problems, *Journal of Nervous and Mental Disease*, 180, 11, 673–682.

Rahiem, F. T., and Hamid, H. (2012) *Mental Health Interview and Cultural Formulation*, in S. Ahmed and M. Amer (Eds.), *Counselling Muslims: Handbook of Mental Health Issues and Interventions*. New York: Routledge, pp. 52–66.

Rahman, A. H. (2014) *Jinn Possession in Mental Health Disorder*. www.pisang.uk/images/files/jinn%20possession%20in%20mental%20health%20disorder.pdf (accessed 21 March 2018).

Rassool, G. H. (2000) The crescent and Islam: Healing, nursing and spiritual dimensions. Some considerations towards an understanding of the Islamic perspectives on caring, *Journal of Advanced Nursing*, 32, 2, 1476–1484.

Rassool, G. H., and Winnington, J. (2006) Framework for Multidimensional Assessment, in G. Hussein Rassool (Ed.), *Dual Diagnosis Nursing*. Oxford: Blackwell Publications.

Rassool, G. H., and Sange, C. (2014) Chapter 6: Islamic Belief Affecting Healthcare, in G. Hussein Rassool (Ed.), *Cultural Competence in Caring for Muslim Patients*. Basingstoke, Hampshire: Palgrave Macmillan.

Rassool, G. H. (2016) Understanding the Muslim Client, in G. Hussein Rassool (Ed.), *Islamic Counselling; An Introduction to Theory and Practice*. Hove, East Sussex: Routledge.

Sabry, W. M., and Vohra, A. (2013) Role of Islam in the management of psychiatric disorders. *Indian Journal of Psychiatry*, 55, Suppl. 2, S205–S214. http://doi.org/10.4103/0019-5545.105534.

Sumari, M., and Jalal, F. H. (2008) Cultural Issues in Counseling: An International Perspective, *Counselling, Psychotherapy, and Health*, 4, 1, Counseling in the Asia Pacific Rim: A Coming Together of Neighbors Special Issue, 24–34.

Walton, L. M. Akram, F., and Hossain, F. (2014) *Health Beliefs of Muslim Women and Implications for Health Care Providers*. http://aquila.usm.edu/cgi/viewcontent.cgi?article=1132&context=ojhe (accessed 21 March 2018).

Westra, A. E., Willems, D. L., and Smit, B. J. (2009) Communicating with Muslim parents: "The four principles" are not as culturally neutral as suggested, *European Journal of Pediatrics*, 168, 11, 1383–1387. http://doi.org/10.1007/s00431-009-0970-8.

Chapter 17

Therapeutic interventions
Spiritual dimensions

Introduction

There is generally reluctance among many Muslims, depending upon education and socioeconomic background, acculturation and religious devoutness, to seek mental health services. This is due to the connection of religious beliefs to therapeutic intervention as God is perceived as the ultimate helper (Barise, 2005). The findings from a study by Meer and Mir (2014) indicate that religious beliefs are considered protective and encourage seeking social support. In addition, the adherence and acting on religious beliefs encourages resilience, hope and promotes 'positive religious coping' (Pargament et al., 2001). Research indicates that interventions drawing on faith (Islamic counselling) can be effective in addressing and preventing mental health problem and speeds recovery from anxiety and depression in Muslims (Townsend et al., 2002). Generally and universally, Muslims would rather admit that they have a '*Jinn*' or possession problem rather than a mental health problem. In their study of beliefs about *Jinn*, black magic and evil eye among Muslims in the UK, Khalifa et al. (2011) found that almost 80% of the participants believed in *Jinn* and almost half of them believed that *Jinn* could cause physical and mental health problems in humans. However, a significant majority of Muslims with mental health problems are more likely to consult a faith healer or an Imam rather than the mainstream non–Muslim secular counsellor or psychiatrist.

Islam teaches Muslims to seek protection and refuge in Allah from the evils of envy, jealousy and *Jinn* possession through the recitation of prayers, verses from the Qur'an and supplications. This chapter examines the use of spiritual interventions such as *Dhikr* (Remembrance of God) and *Ruqyah* (Incantations).

Dhikr

Dhikr, also spelled *Zikr* (Arabic: 'reminding oneself,' or 'mention') is the remembrance of God in which short supplications are repeatedly recited silently. The purpose is the remembrance and the glorification of Allah. *Dhikr* is enacted in the heart, uttered with the tongue and embedded in good deeds. According to Sheik Sayyed As Sabeeq (1986) *Dhikr* refers to

> All words of praise and glory to Allah, extolling His Perfect Attributes of Power and Majesty, Beauty and Sublimeness, whether one utters them by tongue or says them silently in one's heart, are known as zhikr or remembrance of Allah. He has commanded us to remember Him always and ever.

Ibn Al-Qayyim refers to *Dhikr* as "any and every particular moment when you are thinking, saying or doing things which Allah likes." Ibn Al-Qayyim (2004) also stated that once a person forsakes the recitation of the Qur'an, he or she has abandoned all means of healing the sick.

It is stated in *al-Mawsoo'ah al-Fiqhiyyah al-Kuwaitiyyah* (21/222), that

> The evidence for it being encouraged (mustahabb) is the fact that Allah has enjoined it in many verses, and He has forbidden its opposite, namely heedlessness and forgetfulness. He has connected success to constantly remembering Him a great deal. He has praised those who do that and described them as being those who benefit from His signs, and stated that they are people of understanding. He has told us of the loss of those who are distracted from *dhikr* by other things. He has told us that the reward of those who remember Him is that He Himself remembers them and mentions them. He has told us that remembrance of Him is greater than everything, and He has described *dhikr* as being the twin of righteous deeds. He has made dhikr the beginning and end of righteous deeds in many verses.

In a Hadith, The Prophet (ﷺ) said,

> Allah says: 'I am just as My slave thinks I am (i.e. I am able to do for him what he thinks I can do for him) and I am with him if He remembers Me. If he remembers Me in himself, I too, remember him in Myself; and if he remembers Me in a group of people, I remember him in a group that is better than they; and if he comes one span nearer to Me, I go one cubit nearer to him; and if he comes one cubit nearer to Me, I go a distance of two outstretched arms nearer to him; and if he comes to Me walking, I go to him running.'
>
> (Bukhari (a))

It is acknowledged that the Qur'an is ultimately the best *Dhikr* and get rewarded 10 rewards for every letter read. Other remembrance of God includes the following:

- All praise is for Allah. (*Alhamdulillah.*)
- "I praise Allah (or All praise if to Allah) above all attributes that do not suit His Majesty." (*SubhanAllah, SubhanAllah wa bihamdihi.*)

- I praise Allah (or All Praise if to Allah) above all attributes that do not suit His Majesty. All praise is for Allah. There is no deity worthy of worship besides Allah. Allah is Great. (*SubhanAllah wal hamdulillah, wa la ilahaillAllah wa Allahu Akbar.*)
- There is no power or might except (by) Allah. (*La hawla wa la quwwata illa billah.*)
- I seek Allah's forgiveness. (*Astaghfirullah.*)
- Reciting verses of *Ayatul al-Kursiy* (Sūrat Qur'an (Verse of the Throne) 2:255).

Both the remembrance of Allah (*Dhikr*) and the reciting the Qur'an would protect people with regard to dealing with the evil eye and *Hasad* (destructive envy), and other kinds of harm from the devils of mankind and the *Jinn*. It is stated that "Remembrance of Allah is one of the greatest acts that will save the person from Satan" (Al Ashqar, 1998, p. 182). The Messenger of Allah (ﷺ) used to seek refuge with Allah for himself. The most effective means of seeking refuge that is available to the Muslim is reciting the Qur'an, above all reciting the *Mi'wadhatayn* (the last two chapters of the Qur'an, *al-Falaq* (Qur'an:113) and *al-Naas* (Qur'an:114), *Al-Fatihah* (Qur'an:1) and *Ayatul al-Kursiy* (Qur'an 2, p. 255).

The Messenger of Allah (ﷺ) stated that

> In the name of Allah, I place my trust on Allah. O Allah! Indeed, I seek refuge in you for that I misguide anyone or that I become misguided or that I force others to err or that I be forced to do so, or that I oppress or become oppressed or I act ignorantly or any act of ignorance be carried out on me.
> (Abu Dâwûd and Tirmidhi)

In another saying, the Prophet Muhammad (ﷺ) said,

> If one says one-hundred times in one day: "None has the right to be worshipped but Allah, the Alone Who has no partners, to Him belongs Dominion and to Him belong all the Praises, and He has power over all things (i.e. Omnipotent)," one will get the reward of manumitting ten slaves, and one-hundred good deeds will be written in his account, and one-hundred bad deeds will be wiped off or erased from his account, and on that day he will be protected from the morning till evening from Satan, and nobody will be superior to him except one who has done more than that which he has done.
> (Bukhari (b))

In the context of the preceding discussion, in order to ward of all evils influencing our heart and soul, the remembrance of Allah, the Almighty, becomes a priority in our lives. According to the Islamic creed, the reliance of Allah only is the solution. Imam An-Nawawi (a) (May Allah have mercy on him) said that "When the Shaytan hears dhikr (remembrance of Allah) he slinks away, and *Laa ilaaha ill-Allah* is the best of dhikr, and the most effective remedy for warding off 'waswasah' is to remember Allah a great deal." Abu Hurairah (May Allah be pleased with him) reported: The Messenger of Allah (ﷺ) said:

> Allah the Exalted says: 'I am as my slave expects me to be, and I am with him when he remembers Me. If he remembers Me inwardly, I will remember him inwardly, and if he remembers Me in an assembly, I will remember him in a better assembly (i.e., in the assembly of angels).'
>
> (Bukhari and Muslim (a))

The remembrance of Allah brings many other benefits such as spiritual well-being, tranquillity and softening of the heart. Allah says in the Qur'an (Interpretation of the meaning):

> *Those who believe (in the Oneness of Allah – Islamic Monotheism), and whose hearts find rest in the remembrance of Allah, Verily, in the remembrance of Allah do hearts find rest.*
>
> (Sūrat Ar-Ra'd (Thunder) 13:28)

> *Is he whose heart Allah has opened to Islam, so that he is in light from His Lord (as he who is non-Muslim)? So, woe to those whose hearts are hardened against remembrance of Allah! They are in plain error!*
>
> (Sūrat Az-Zumar (The Groups) 39:22)

According to Imam an-Nawawi (b) (May Allah have mercy on him), there are many virtues of *Dhikr* and encouragement to remember Allah in the following verses: Qur'an 29:45; 2:152; 7:205; 62:10; 33:35; and 33:41–42. There are similar and other verses that extoll the virtues of remembrance of Allah.

Ruqyah

Ruqyah is referred in English as 'incantation,' consisting of reciting or writing in the form of *Dhikr* for the purpose of protection or treatment. However, the reference of *Ruqyah* as incantations implies the use of spells, charms, magic and witchcraft which is totally against the practice of Islamic beliefs and practices. *Ruqyah* from an Islamic perspective is the recitation of Qur'an, seeking of refuge, remembrance and supplications that are used as a means of treating ill health and harms. It is stated that

> There is a lot of good in *Ruqyah*, and a great deal of benefit. *Al-Fatihah, Aayat al-Kursiy, 'Qul Huwa Allaahu Ahad', al-Mi'wadhatayn* and other ayahs (verses) may be recited over the person who has been affected by *Sihr*, as well as good du'ah (supplications) narrated in the Hadiths.
>
> (Islamqa, 2000)

Ruqyah are of two types: *Ruqyah Ash Shari'ah* and *Ruqyah Ash Shirkiyah*. The *Ruqyah* that is acceptable and permissible is the *Ruqyah Ash Shari'ah* (according to Islamic jurisprudence).

Ruqyah Ash Shirkiyah and Ruqyah Ash Shari'ah

The approach of *Ruqyah Ash Shirkiyah* failed to make the stipulations of *Ruqyah Ash Shari'ah* and is not in accordance with the beliefs of *Ahlus-Sunnah Wal-Jama^ah*. This approach is embedded in associating partners with Allah, which is *Shirk*. This type of *Ruqyah* is prohibited and includes: magic, fortune telling, horoscopes, superstitious belief, charms and amulets. The Prophet Muhammad (ﷺ) said,

> (Illegal) *Ruqyah*, amulets and love-potions are (acts of) *Shirk*.
> (Imam Ahmad (a), Ibn Majah and Abu Dâwûd)

Furthermore, the Prophet (ﷺ) stated that:

> If someone ties an amulet, Allah will not accomplish his affairs for him and if someone ties a cowrie shell, Allah will not protect him.
> (Imam Ahmad (b), Ibn Hibban and Al-Hakim)

> Anyone who wears an amulet commits an act of Shirk.
> (Imam Ahmad (c))

Ruqyah Ash Shari'ah, according to Ibn Hajar, can be undertaken if three conditions are met:

- It must be with the speech of Allah (Qur'an) and his names and attributes.
- It must be in the Arabic language, or what is known to be its meaning in other languages.
- To believe that *Ruqyah* has no benefit by itself, but the benefits are from Allah.

A do-it-yourself instruction for *Ruqyah* is presented in Table 17.1.

Characteristics of a Raki (a person who treats with *Ruqyah*)

It is essential that those who practice *Ruqyah* possess certain characteristics in order to undertake such work. Ameen (2005) provides a set of requirements Muslim practitioners should respect. The individual must have strong faith (Iman) and understand the importance of spiritual healing through the Qur'an and Hadith. His obedience to Allah is unflinching and sincere in

Table 17.1 Do-it-yourself *Ruqyah*

- Make sure that you are clean of impurities. Make ablution.
- Humble yourself before Allah.
- Make du'aa at the times when your du'aa is accepted (between the *adhan* and the *iqaamah*, the last third of the night, between 'Asr and Maghrib on a Friday).
- You need to have the following things ready: water (3–5 litres per person or *Zamzam* water or rainwater); olive oil (one whole bottle per person, be greenish in colour); honey (raw and organic, Sidr honey, also Manuka honey); and black seeds (*Nigella sativa*).
- At the beginning of the week, you need to do the following: sit down with the water and olive oil open in front of you. Do the following:
- Read Surah *Al-Fatihah* three times or seven times is best.
- Read Surah *Al-Baqarah*.
- Read Surah *Ikhlas* (Qur'an: 112) *Al-Mi'wadhatayn* [last two chapters of the Qur'an -*Al-Falaq* and *Al-Naas*] three times each.
- Read *Ayatul Kursi* (Qur'an 2: 255) three times but seven times is best.
- Blow (as though you are spitting but without spittle), either at the end of each Sūrah, or after each verse, or whenever it is easy for you, into the water and the olive oil. When you have completed all of the reading, you are now prepared to begin the programme.
- Take two tablespoons of honey and dissolve them in a cup of the water that you have read upon. Add seven seeds of black seed and drink. Do this three times per day.
- Before sleep, anoint the entire body from head to foot with the olive oil that has been read upon.
- Upon waking, wash the entire body with water and soap.
- Then, take half a cup of the water that has been read upon and add it to a bucket or other container. Fill up the bucket with water from the tap and wash the entire body.
- Continue this for three whole days.

On days 4–7:

- Use olive oil that has been read upon to anoint any areas where pain is found, if any.
- Take two tablespoons of honey and dissolve them in a cup of the water that you have read upon. Add seven seeds of black seed and drink. Do this three times per day.

What to expect:

- On the first day, you will most likely not feel anything.
- On the second and third day, you may feel very ill. You may feel excessive tiredness, pain all over the body, or in certain places, or aches and pains as though you carried out strenuous exercise.
- By the fourth day, you may feel completely refreshed, as though you have a lot of energy – with the permission of Allah.
- The aches and pains will gradually go away, inshaa' Allah, over the course of the seven days.
- [If the patient does not feel better, or the seven-day programme has resulted in a worsening of symptoms, then we advise to move on to the *full Ruqyah programme*, of which the seven-day programme is repeated 1–2 times a month, in addition to other *Ruqyah*.]

Source: Adapted from 7 Day Ruqyah Detox Programme – Shaykh 'Adil ibn Ṭahir al-Muqbil. https://muhammadtim.com/ruqyah/7-day-detox (accessed 25 March 2018).

worshipping Allah, avoiding *Shirk*. His intention is sincere and ensures the maintenance of confidentiality about the affairs of the patient. Ameen (2005) suggested that the Raki should avoid abusing his status as a practitioner for wealth or fame. He should have the right kind of knowledge of the Qur'an and Sunnah, but understand the limits of his Islamic knowledge. He should also have a basic knowledge of mental health problems so that he is able to refer a patient to an Islamic counsellor or psychiatrist. The ability to refer a patient, where appropriate, is a key skills of the Raki. His role is that of being a facilitator and guidance and giving advice (when appropriate), educating the client in the creed (*Aqeedah*) and Islamic jurisprudence (*Fiqh*) and working with people to facilitate their psychological and spiritual growth and development (Rassool, 2016).

However, there are traditional healers that fail to base or deviate from the acceptable practices based on the Qur'an and Sunnah. These violations in performing *Ruqyah* by traditional healers are presented in Table 17.2.

Table 17.2 Violations in performing *Ruqyah*

- Reading on water containing saffron, and then dipping papers in it, then drying it, and after that putting (dissolving) it in water, then drinking it.
- The person who is receiving *Ruqyah* imagines the envier (evil eye) from the reading, or through ordering the *Jinn* to incarnate to the patient his envier. This is considered to be diabolism and is not permissible.
- The person who treats with *Ruqyah* is not allowed to touch the woman's body at all (who is receiving *Ruqyah*); instead he should read on her without touching. *Ruqyah* does not depend on touching.
- The person who is treating by *Ruqyah* is not allowed to write verses and Islamic supplications in stamps dipped in water containing saffron, then these stamps are put on papers instead of writing, then these papers are washed and drank by the patient.
- Reading Qur'an during *Ruqyah* by using a microphone, through the phone in a long distance, and reading on many people in the same time. *Ruqyah* must be on the patient directly.
- The usage of *Jinn* [in order] to know the envy or magic, also believing [that] the *Jinn* incarnated in the patient claiming that the envy and magic.
- Using the *Jinn* in determining the envy or magic kind, place of infection and its cure is not allowed, because having aid from *Jinn* is disbelief.
- Playing some verses of the Qur'an and supplications on a voice recorder is not a substitute for *Ruqyah*; because *Ruqyah* is a work that needs faith and intention while doing it, and interaction with the individual.
- Writing Qur'an and supplication on papers, and affixing it on a part of the body or putting it under the bed, are not allowed, as it is from the prohibited hanging of the charms.

Source: Adapted from *Standing Committee for Scientific Research and Issuing Fatwas* (ShaykhaAbdulaziz bin Abdullah bin Baz; Shaykh Abdulaziz bin Abdullah bin Mohammed Al-Sheikh; Shaykh; Bakr bin Abdullah Abu-Zaid; and Shaikh Saleh Bin Fawzaan) (2008). 27 Jumada al-thani 1429 (7/1/08) http://en.islamway.net/article/8773/10-violations-in-performing-ruqyah (accessed 25 March 2018).

Prophetic medicine

In Islam there has always been an approach to treat the sickness with regular medical treatments and Islamic treatments together. That is using both Prophetic medicine and conventional medicine. The Prophetic medicine *Tibb an Nabawi* – The Medicine of the Holy Prophet (ﷺ). A famous book is the 'The Prophetic Medicine' (Ibn Qayyim al-Jawziyya): English translation of at Tibb al Nabawi, Islamic Book Service, 2009). There are many Hadiths which encourage the Muslims to seek medical treatment.

Narrated Abu Huraira: The Prophet (ﷺ) said:

> There is no disease that Allah has created, except that He also has created its treatment.
>
> (Bukhari (c))

Usamah ibn Shuraik narrated: "I came to the Prophet (ﷺ) and found him with his companions. They were calm and serene as if there were birds over their heads. I greeted them and sat down. Then some Bedouins came from various places.

> They asked him: 'O Allah's Messenger! Should we seek medical treatment for our illnesses?'
>
> He replied: 'Yes, you should seek medical treatment, because Allah, the Exalted, has let no disease exist without providing for its cure, except for one ailment, namely, old age.'
>
> (Ahmad and Tirmidhi)

Anas ibn Mas'ud reported that the Prophet said:

> Verily, Allah has not let any malady occur without providing its remedy. Therefore seek medical treatment for your illnesses.
>
> (Nasa'i, Ibn Majah, and al-Hakim)

Jabir narrated that the Messenger of Allah (ﷺ) said:

> There is a cure for every disease. Whenever an illness is treated with its right remedy, it will, by Allah's permission, be cured.
>
> (Muslim)

Prophetic medicine is only suitable for those who have Imam (faith) and also trust in Allah. For a more comprehensive account of Prophetic medicine, see Prophetic Medicine and Herbalism (Onislam.net, 2014). This section will focus on the use of honey, olive oil and black seeds. It is stated that the Prophet's (ﷺ)

favourite condiments were honey, olive oil, salt and vinegar. In relation to honey, Allah says (Interpretation of the meaning):

> *Then eat from all the fruits and follow the ways of your Lord laid down (for you).*
> *There emerges from their bellies a drink, varying in colors, in which there is healing*
> *for people. Indeed in that is a sign for a people who give thought.*
>
> (Sūrat Nahl (The Bee) 16:69)

Narrated by Ibn 'Abbas: The Prophet (ﷺ) said,

> Healing is in three things: A gulp of honey, cupping, and branding with fire (cauterizing). But I forbid my followers to use (cauterization) branding with fire.
>
> (Bukhari (d))

Narrated Abu Sa'id Al-Khudri: A man came to the Prophet (ﷺ) and said,

> My brother has some Abdominal trouble.
> The Prophet (ﷺ) said to him "Let him drink honey."
> The man came for the second time and the Prophet (ﷺ) said to him, "Let him drink honey."
> He came for the third time and the Prophet (ﷺ) said, "Let him drink honey."
> He returned again and said, I have done that.
> The Prophet (ﷺ) then said,
> "Allah has said the truth, but your brother's Abdomen has told a lie. Let him drink honey." So he made him drink honey and he was cured.
>
> (Bukhari (e))

Honey is made using the nectar of flowering plants. Honey is a complex combination of sugars (fructose, glucose and sucrose); most of the minerals (potassium, chlorine, sulphur, calcium, sodium, phosphorus, magnesium, silicon, iron, manganese and copper); proteins (amino acids); organic acids (apple and lemon acid); Vitamins C and some B complex vitamins (riboflavin, pantothenic acid, pyridoxine, biotin, nicotinic acid), essential oils; enzymes, esters, antibiotic agents, and yet unidentified components.

Olive oil is also used in Prophetic medicine. Olive oil contains palmitic acid, oleic acid, linoleic acid, stearic acid, meristic acid and glycerides. It dissolves in alcohol, ether, chloroform and liquid paraffin. As regards to the olive tree, Allah says (Interpretation of the meaning):

> *And (We brought forth) a tree issuing from Mount Sinai which produces oil and*
> *food for those who eat.*
>
> (Sūrat Al-Mu'minun (Believers) 23, p. 20)

(the oil of) a blessed olive tree, neither of the east nor of the west.
(Sūrat An Nur (Light) 24:35)

The importance of olive is emphasised in the Qur'an in several verses (Qur'an 6:99; 6:14; 16:11; and 95:1–8).

It was narrated from 'Umar that the Messenger of Allah (ﷺ) said:

Season (your food) with olive oil and anoint yourselves with it, for it comes from a blessed tree.

(Ibn Majah)

Narrated by 'Umar ibn al-Khattaab (May Allah be pleased with him) that the Messenger of Allah (ﷺ) said:

Eat olive oil and anoint yourselves with it, for it comes from a blessed tree.
(Tirmidhi, 1851)

Olive oil is extracted from the ripened fruits. According to Ibn Al-Qayyim (2009), the red coloured oil is better than the blackish one.

Olive oil also contains vitamins E and K, and polyphenols, which provide a defence mechanism that delays aging and prevents carcinogenesis, athero-sclerosis, liver disorders, and inflammations. Oleates in the oil also promote bone formation in children, protect the bones of the elderly and offers strong protection in the fight against breast cancer.

(Onislam.net, 2014, p. 31)

Black cumin (*Nigella sativa*)

The black cumin is referred to as black caraway, black sesame, onion seed or Roman coriander. Ahmad et al. (2013) in a review on the therapeutic potential of *Nigella sativa* indicated that:

Extensive studies on Nigella Sativa have been carried out by various researchers and a wide spectrum of its pharmacological actions have been explored which may include antidiabetic, anticancer, immunomodula-tor, analgesic, antimicrobial, anti-inflammatory, spasmolytic, bronchodi-lator, hepato-protective, renal protective, gastro-protective, antioxidant properties.

(p. 337)

The findings of the review showed that the

pharmacological potential of *N. Sativa* seeds, its oil and extracts and some of its active principles, particularly TQ and alpha-hederin, possess remarkable *in vitro* and *in vivo* pharmacological activities against a large variety of diseases and found to be relatively safe.

(p. 349)

From an Islamic perspective, the black cumin seeds have been widely used in the treatment of different diseases and ailments and have been considered as one of the greatest forms of healing medicine. Narrated by Khalid bin Sa'd:

> We went out and Ghalib bin Abjar was accompanying us. He fell ill on the way and when we arrived at Medina he was still sick. Ibn Abi 'Atiq came to visit him and said to us, "Treat him with black cumin. Take five or seven seeds and crush them (mix the powder with oil) and drop the resulting mixture into both nostrils, for 'Aisha has narrated to me that she heard the Prophet (🕌) said:
> This black cumin is healing for all diseases except 'As-Sam.'
> Aisha said, 'What is As-Sam?' He said, 'Death.'"

(Bukhari (f))

Narrated Abu Huraira:

> I heard Allah's Messenger (🕌) said:
> There is healing in black cumin for all diseases except death.

(Bukhari (g))

All the three substances are used as a complementary medicine with *Ruqyah*. The recitation of Qur'anic verses (*Ruqyah*) and ingestion of olive oil are typical treatments for possession by *Jinn* spirits (Dein and Illaiee, 2013).

References

Abu Dâwûd. *Sunan Abu Dâwûd* hadith 5053; Tirmidhi, Hadith: 3427. Cited in Al-Ashqar, U. S. (1998) *The World of the Jinn and Devils*. Translated by Jamaal-al-Din M. Zarabozo. Boulder CO: Al-Basheer Company for Publications and Translations, p. 186.

Al-Ashqar, U. S. (2003) *The World of the Jinn and Devils in the Light of the Qur'an and Sunnah*. Riyadh: International Islamic Publishing House.

Ahmad, A., Husain, A., Mujeeb, M., Khan, S. A., Najmi, A. K., Siddique, N. A., Zoheir A. Damanhouri, and Anwar, F. (2013) A review on therapeutic potential of Nigella Sativa: A miracle herb, *Asian Pacific Journal of Tropical Biomedicine*, 3, 5, 337–352. http://doi.org/10.1016/S2221-1691(13)60075-1.

Ahmad and Tirmidhi. Cited in Fiqh-us-Sunnah Volume 004, Funerals and Dhikr, Fiqh 4.005C. http://hadithcollection.com/fiqh-ussunnah/382-Fiqh-us%20Sunnah%20Section%2059.%20Sickness,%20Expiation%20Of%20Sins/21371-fiqh-us-sunnah-volume-004-funerals-and-dhikr-fiqh-4005c.html (accessed 22 March 2018).

Ameen, Abu'l-Mundhir Khaleel ibn Ibraaheem (2005) *The Jinn & Human Sickness: Remedies in the Light of the Qur'aan & Sunnah*. Riyadh, Saudi Arabia: Darussalam.

An Nasa'i, Ibn Majah, and al-Hakim. Cited in Fiqh-us-Sunnah Volume 004, Funerals and Dhikr, Fiqh 4.005C. http://hadithcollection.com/fiqh-ussunnah/382-Fiqh-us%20 Sunnah%20Section%2059.%20Sickness,%20Expiation%20Of%20Sins/21371-fiqh-us-sunnah-volume-004-funerals-and-dhikr-fiqh-4005c.html (accessed 22 March 2018).

Barise, A. (2005) Social work with Muslims: Insights from the teachings of Islam, *Critical Social Work*, 6, 114–132.

Bukhari (a) Sahih al-Bukhari 7405. In-book reference: Book 97, Hadith 34USC-MSA web (English) reference:Vol. 9, Book 93, Hadith 502.

Bukhari (b) Sahih al-Bukhari 3275 . In-book reference: Book 59, Hadith 84. USC-MSA web (English) reference:Vol. 4, Book 54, Hadith 495.

Bukhari (c) Sahih al-Bukhari 5678. In-book reference: Book 76, Hadith 1. USC-MSA web (English) reference:Vol. 7, Book 71, Hadith 582.

Bukhari (d) Sahih al-Bukhari 5680. In-book reference: Book 76, Hadith 3. USC-MSA web (English) reference:Vol. 7, Book 71, Hadith 584.

Bukhari (e) Sahih al-Bukhari 5684. In-book reference: Book 76, Hadith 7. USC-MSA web (English) reference:Vol. 7, Book 71, Hadith 588.

Bukhari (f) Sahih al-Bukhari. In-book reference: Book 76, Hadith 10. USC-MSA web (English) reference:Vol. 7, Book 71, Hadith 591.

Bukhari (g) Sahih al-Bukhari 5688. In-book reference: Book 76, Hadith 11. USC-MSA web (English) reference:Vol. 7, Book 71, Hadith 592.

Bukhari and Muslim (a) Sunnah.com reference: Book 16, Hadith 28Arabic/English book reference: Book 16, Hadith 1435.

Dein, S., and Illaiee, A. S. (2013) Jinn and mental health: Looking at jinn possession in modern psychiatric practice, *The Psychiatrist*, 37, 9, 290–293.

Ibn Hajar. Cited in Ruqyah – Spiritual Healing. www.missionislam.com/health/ruqiyah recitation.html (accessed 22 March 2018).

Ibn Majah. Sunan Ibn Majah Vol. 4, Book 29, Hadith 3319. Arabic reference: Book 29, Hadith 3444.

Ibn al-Qayyim (2004) Al-Fawa'id: A collection of wise sayings. (Umm Al-Qura, trans.). Al-Mansura, Egypt: Umm Al-Qura.

Ibn Al-Qayyim (2009) The Prophetic Medicine, in *A translation of Imam Ibn al-Qayyim's At-Tibb an-Nabawi*. India: Islamic Book Service.

Imam Ahmad (a) *Musnad* 1:381; Ibn Majah, Sunan, Book of Medicine 3530; Abu Dâwûd, Sunan, Book of Medicine 3883, Verified to be authentic by Al-Albani in as-Sahihah no. 331.

Imam Ahmad (b) *Musnad*, 4:154. Ibn Hibban in Mawarid Al-Zam'an, and Al-Hakim in Al-Mustadrak.

Imam Ahmad (c) Musnad, 4:156. No. 17458. https://archive.org/details/MusnadAhmed BinHanbalVolume4ByRmp (accessed 22 March 2018).

Imam An-Nawawi (a) Cited in IqraSense.com. The Story of Satan (Shaitaan), his tactics, and methods to ward off his influences and whispers. www.iqrasense.com/satan-and-evil/ satan-story-shaitaan-tactics-methods-to-ward-off-influences-whispers.html (accessed 22 March 2018).

Imam An-Nawawi (b) Al-Imam Abu Zakariya Yahya bin Sharaf An-Nawawi Ad-Dimashqi. Riyad as-Salihin : The Meadows of the Righteous, https://web.archive. org/web/20110714123930/www.sunnipath.com/library/Hadith/H0004P0000.aspx (accessed 22 March 2018).

Islamqa (2000) 11290: How to deal with sihr (magic/witchcraft). https://islamqa.info/en/11290 (accessed 22 March 2018).

Khalifa, N., Hardie, T., Latif, S., Jamil, I., and Walker D. M. (2011) Beliefs about Jinn, black magic and evil eye among Muslims: Age, gender and first language influences, *International Journal of Culture and Mental Health*, 4, 1, 68–77.

Meer, S., and Mir, G. (2014) Muslims and depression: The role of religious beliefs in therapy. *Journal of Integrative Psychology and Therapeutics*. Doi: http://dx.doi.org/10.7243/2054-4723-2-2.

Mawsoo'ah al-Fiqhiyyah al-Kuwaitiyyah (21/222) Cited in Islamqa (2017) 253005: The virtue of remembering Allah (dhikr), may He be exalted; is everyone who remembers Allah little a hypocrite? https://islamqa.info/en/253005 (accessed 22 March 2018).

Muslim. Cited in Fiqh-us-Sunnah Volume 004, Funerals and Dhikr, Fiqh 4.005C. http://hadithcollection.com/fiqh-ussunnah/382-Fiqh-us%20Sunnah%20Section%2059.%20Sickness,%20Expiation%20Of%20Sins/21371-fiqh-us-sunnah-volume-004-funerals-and-dhikr-fiqh-4005c.html, (accessed 22 March 2018).

Onislam.net (2014) *Prophetic Medicine& Herbalism*. www.muslim-library.com/dl/books/English-Prophetic-Medicine-Herbalism.pdf onIslam.net website 1435AH / 2014AC (accessed 22 March 2018).

Pargament, K. I., Tarakeshwar, N., Ellison, C. G., and Wulff, K. M. (2001) Religious coping among the religious: The relationship between religious coping and well-being in a national sample of Presbyterian clergy, elders, and members, *Journal of Scientific Study of Religion*, 40, 497–513.

Rassool, G. H. (2016) *Islamic Counselling. An Introduction to Theory and Practice*. Hove, East Sussex: Routledge.

Sheik Sayyed As Sabeeq (1986) *Fiqh-Us-Sunnah* Volume 004, Funerals and Dhikr, Fiqh 4.099. http://hadithcollection.com/fiqh-ussunnah/386-Fiqh-us%20Sunnah%20Section%2063.%20Burial/21457-fiqh-us-sunnah-volume-004-funerals-and-dhikr-fiqh-4099.html, (accessed 22 March 2018).

Tirmidhi (1851) Classed as Sahih by Al-Albani in Sahih at-Tirmidhi. Cited in Islamqa (2015), https://islamqa.info/en/196796 (accessed 22 March 2018).

Townsend, M., Kladder, V., Ayele, H., and Mulligan T. (2002) Systematic review of clinical trials examining the effects of religion on health, *Southern Medical Journal*, 95, 1429–34.

Chapter 18

Prevention and protection from evil eye, *Jinn* possession and witchcraft

Introduction

The Qur'an and the Prophetic traditions or the Sunnah are the central sources of references for the prevention and protection of Muslims in relation to the evils of humans and *Jinn*. The scholars have prescribed many invocations and supplications, derived from the Qur'an and Sunnah, as a protection of evil eyes, *Jinn* possession and witchcraft. The Islamic paradigm in the prevention and the treatment of the harmful influences of the evil eye, *Jinn* possession, witchcraft and obsessional disorders (*Waswâs al-Qahri*) is based on the concept of monotheism, oneness of God (*Tawheed*), and trust in God only (*Tawakkul*). This chapter examines the prevention and protection of Muslims in relation to the evil eye and *Jinns*. The literature will be drawn from the Qur'an, Sunnah, scholars and the clinical experiences of faith healers (Raki) and Imams.

Preventing the evil of envy, eye-casting and sorcery

Shaykh Ibn al-Qayyim al-Jawziyya (a) (May Allah have mercy on him) suggests preventing the evil of envy, eye-casting and sorcery. In Table 18.1 is a summary of these preventive measures.

General interventions: seeking refuge with Allah

Seeking refuge with Allah is the most important aspect of Islamic interventions to fight against all human and *Jinn* evils. The Prophets and Messengers incessantly seek refuge with Allah as indicated in several verses of the Qur'an including (11:47; 12:23; and 2:67). Seeking refuge in Allah is both an action of the heart and the tongue. The term *Isti'adha* is an abbreviation for saying 'I seeking refuge in Allah' (*Aoothubillah*).

The most common way of seeking refuge with Allah is to say:

أعوذ بالله من الشيطان الرجيم

- I seek refuge with Allah, from the accursed shaytan.

Table 18.1 Ibn Qayyim: ten things for combatting evil eye and envy

- One should seek Allah's protection from the evil of the envious, eye-casters and sorcerers.
- One is to observe Taqwa [God consciousness] of Allah, by following His commands, and avoiding His prohibitions. Allah looks after whoever does that.
- One should exercise patience towards the envious. Patience is the key to safety, for evil turns unto whoever starts it.
- One is to put one's trust in Allah. Allah suffices whoever puts his trust in Him. This is a powerful means to overcoming and enduring harm that would be otherwise unbearable.
- One is not to occupy oneself with the envious, for example, one is to ignore or dismiss them from one's thoughts, and not to be afraid of them.
- One is to get nearer to Allah and be faithful to Him. Nearness and sincerity to Allah provide one with great protection. Whoever does that is never lost.
- One is to repent of one's sins, seeking Allah's forgiveness, resolving not to return to them. Nothing is as harmful as sins, known or not.
- One is to give charity as much as possible. This is a great means of protection from affliction, envy and the evil eye. As is wisely said, "Cure your illnesses with charity."
- One is to treat others well, for good treatment, particularly of such people as the envious, the unjust and the harm doers, breeds amicability on the one hand, and alleviates or eliminates hatred and enmity on the other. Allah says, *"The good deed and the evil deed are not alike. Repel the evil deed with one which is better than lo! He, between whom and you there was enmity (will become) as though he was a bosom friend"* [(Sūrat Fuṣṣilat (Explained in Detail) 41:34)].
- One has to observe pure *Tawheed* [Unicity of God]. *Tawheed* is the securest refuge for believers. One has to believe without the slightest doubt that Allah is the only originator of all causes, and that no benefit or harm can occur without His permission.

Source: Translated from *Bada'i' al-Fawa'id*, by Ibn al-Qayyim, 2, 764–776.

According to Ibn Kathir, *Isti'adha* means:

> I seek refuge with Allah from the cursed Satan so that he is prevented from affecting my religious or worldly affairs, or hindering me from adhering to what I was commanded, or luring me into what I was prohibited from.
>
> (Ibn Kathir)

We are required to seek of refuge from Allah. Allah says (Interpretation of the meaning):

> *Say, I seek refuge in the Lord of mankind,*
> *The Sovereign of mankind.*
> *The God of mankind, From the evil of the retreating whisperer*
> *– Who whispers [evil] into the breasts of mankind –*
> *From among the jinn and mankind*
>
> (Sūrat Nas (Mankind) 114:1–6)

Narrated by Anas bin Malik, The Prophet (ﷺ) used to say:

> O Allah! I seek refuge with You from worry and grief, from incapacity and laziness, from cowardice and miserliness, from being heavily in debt and from being overpowered by (other) men.

> (Bukhari (a))

> *Allaahumma inni a'oodhu bika min al-hammi wa'l-hazani, wa a'oodhi bika min al-'ajzi wa'l-kasali, wa a'oodhu bika min al-jubni wa'l-bukhli, wa a'oodhi bika min ghalabat il-dayn wa qahri al-rijaal.*

The Prophet (ﷺ) used to seek refuge with Allah for Al-Hasan and Al-Husain (His grandchildren) and say:

> Your forefather (i.e. Abraham) used to seek Refuge with Allah for Ishmael and Isaac by reciting the following: 'O Allah! I seek Refuge with Your Perfect Words from every devil and from poisonous pests and from every evil, harmful, envious eye.'

> (Bukhari (b)

> *U'eethukumaa bikalimaatil-laahit-taam-mati min kulli shaitaanin wa haam-matin, wa min kulli 'ainin laammatin.*

Narrated by 'Aisha (the wife of Allah's Apostle) said: When Allah's Messenger (ﷺ) fell ill. Gabriel used to recite these verses:

> In the name of Allah. He may cure you from all kinds of illness and safeguard you from the evil of a jealous one when he feels jealous and from the evil influence of eye.

> (Muslim (a))

Qamar (2013) suggested that "Seeking refuge with Allah gives a powerful feeling of security that acts like a psychological shield" (p. 48). However, for this shield to be effective, the two fundamental dimensions of the belief system – namely the belief in oneness of Allah and the trust in Allah – must be adhered to.

Prevention before evil eye occurs

In terms of prevention, this is done by seeking Allah's blessings. The seeking of blessings from Allah would cancel out the evil eye that someone has put on another person. It is narrated in *Al-Saheehayn* that 'Aishah (May Allah be pleased with her) said: The Messenger of Allah (ﷺ) used to tell me to recite *Ruqyah* (incantation) for protection against the evil eye. (Islamqa, 2003). In another Hadith, the Messenger of Allah (ﷺ) commanded us to pray for blessing for everything that we like. He said:

> If one of you sees something that his brother has, let him pray for blessing for Him [*Baarik Allaahu fih*].
>
> (Cited in Ameen, 2005, p. 268)

It was narrated that Sahl ibn Haneef said: The Messenger of Allah (ﷺ) said:

> If one of you sees something that he likes in himself or his wealth, let him pray for blessing for it, for the evil eye is real.
>
> (Ibn Al-Sunni, Imam Ahmad and Al-Haakim)

From an explanation given Al-Qurtubi, these sayings indicate that the evil eye cannot do any harm if the person who is doing it prays for blessing; rather it can only do harm if he does not pray for blessing. He stated that "Every Muslim who likes something must pray for blessing, for if he prays for blessing, that will ward off any potential harm, beyond a doubt." The approach to seek blessings is from making supplications. The Messenger of Allah (ﷺ)

> "*Baarik Allaahu fih (May Allaah bless it)*" or "*Allaahumma baarik 'alayhi (O Allah, bless it)*."

And one may say

> *MaSha' Allah (that which Allah wills (will come to pass)).*

According to The Permanent Committee for Scholarly Research and Ifta' (a), "anyone who sees anything he admires, be it a person, vehicle, home or anything else, should say '*Ma sha'a Allah la quwwata illa bi-Allah* (Whatever Allah wills [will come to pass], there is no power except with Allah);'" for Allah, the Exalted, said, "*It was better for you to say, when you entered your garden: 'That which Allâh wills (will come to pass)! There is no power but with Allâh!' If you see me less than you in wealth, and children.*" The protection from the evil eye, according to the same Fataawa, can be achieved by:

> the remembrance of Allah through reciting Ayat-ul-Kursiy (Qur'an 2:255) after observing Prayer (Salah) and when going to sleep. Reciting *Surah Al-Ikhlas and Al-Mu'awwidhatayn* (Surahs Al-Falaq and Al-Nas) three times every morning and every evening and when going to sleep is also recommended. You should also put your trust in Allah, depend on Him and believe that all good and evil are controlled by Allah, Glorified and Exalted be He. Whatever He wills is destined to happen and whatever He does not will is not destined to happen. Thus Allah protects His Servants from the evil eye and whatever may harm them.

There are several supplications that can be used for protection of evil eye and these include:

I seek refuge in the perfect words of Allah from the evil of that which He has created.
A'oodhu bi kalimat-illah il-tammati min sharri ma khalaqa.
I seek refuge in the perfect words of Allah from His wrath and punishment, from the evil of His slaves and from the evil promptings of the devils and from their presence.
A'oodhu bi kalimat-illah il-tammati min ghadabihi wa 'iqabihi, wa min sharri 'ibadihi wa min hamazat al-shayateeni wa an yahduroon.

And one may recite the words of Allah:

None has the right to be worshipped but He and in Him I put my trust and He is the Lord of the Mighty Throne.
(Qur'an 9, p. 129 – Interpretation of the meaning)

Hasbi Allahu la ilaha illa huwa, 'alayhi tawakkaltu wa huwa Rabb ul-'arsh il-'azeem.

And there are other similar supplications that are prescribed in Shari'ah.

Protection against *Jinn* possession

The fortress against the devils, *Jinn* and witchcraft is to adhere to the teachings of the Sunnah. That is to recite the 'Throne verse' (Ayat al-Kurisy), and it is stated that "if a person recites *Ayat al-Kursiy* at night, he will continue to have protection from Allah, and no *shaytan* will come near him until morning. And Allah is the Protector" (Shaykh Ibn 'Uthaymeen). The Permanent Committee for Scholarly Research and Ifta' (b) stated

Muslims must fortify themselves against the devils from among *Jinn* (creatures created from fire) and mankind by having strong faith in Allah and by putting their trust in Him and seeking refuge with Him and beseeching Him. They should recite the Du'a's (supplications) prescribed by the Prophet (ﷺ) for refuge and protection. They should often recite *Al-Mu'awwidhatayn* (*Surahs Al-Falaq and Al-Nas*), *Surah Al-Ikhlas, Surah Al-Fatihah, and Ayat-ul-Kursiy* (the Qur'anic Verse of the Throne, *Surah Al-Baqarah*, 2:255). One of the Prophetic Du'a's for refuge and protection is to say:

I seek refuge with the Perfect Words of Allah from the evil of what He has created.

And:

I seek refuge with the Perfect Words of Allah from His Anger and Punishment, and from the evil of His creatures, and the incitements of devils and their presence.

And the Saying of Allah (Exalted be He): Allâh is sufficient for me. *Lâ ilâha illa Huwa* (none has the right to be worshipped but He) in Him I put my trust and He is the Lord of the Mighty Throne. This is in addition to other supplications prescribed by Shari'ah (Islamic law).

In addition to the above shields, it is important for protection against evils to strengthen one's faith, and remember Allah often (*Dhikr*); it was narrated from al-Harith al-Ash'ari that the Prophet (ﷺ) said:

> Allah commanded Yahya ibn Zakariya (peace be upon him) five things to follow and to enjoin upon the Children of Israel . . . and he commanded them to remember Allah, and the likeness of that is a man who was being pursued by the enemy, until he reached a strong fortress in which he found protection; similarly a man cannot find protection from the shaytan except by remembering Allah.
>
> (Tirmidhi (a))

The call of prayer (the adhan) is also a fortress against evils. It was narrated that Suhayl ibn Abi Salih said:

> My father sent me to Bani Harithah, and there was with me a slave of ours, or a companion of ours. Someone called out his name from a garden, and the one who was with me looked into the garden and did not see anything. I mentioned that to my father, and he said, 'If I had known that this was going to happen to you, I would not have sent you. But if you hear a voice then make the call for prayer, for I heard Abu Hurairah (May Allah be pleased with him) narrating that the Messenger of Allah (ﷺ) said:'
> When the shaytan hears the call to prayer, he runs away fast.
>
> (Muslim (b))

Reciting Qur'an offers protection against the devil. Allah says (Interpretation of the meaning):

> *And when you (Muhammad) recite the Quran, We put between you and those who believe not in the Hereafter, an invisible veil (or screen their hearts, so they hear or understand it not).*
> (Sūrat Al-Isra (The Night Journey) 17:45)

There is also the recommendation to eat a special kind of date '*Ajwah*' (grown in the City of Madinah, Saudi Arabia, costing around 70 Saudi Riyals per kilogramme). There are many Hadiths relating to the use of *Ajwah* dates for protection. It is narrated that the Messenger (ﷺ) said,

> If somebody takes seven *Ajwah* dates in the morning, neither magic nor poison will hurt him that day.
>
> (Bukhari (c))

Ajwah dates are from paradise.

(Tirmidhi (b))

[Referring to eating seven *Ajwah* dates] He will not be harmed by anything until he reaches the evening.

(Muslim (c))

Some scholars are of the view that all types of dates are efficacious against poison and witchcraft. Islamic scholars including Shaykh 'Abd ar-Rahmaan as-Sa'di, Shaykh 'Abd al-'Azeez ibn Baaz, and Shaykh Muhammad ibn 'Uthaymeen (May Allah have mercy on them) are of the view that the Hadith applies specifically to the people of Madinah and those in the vicinity, because of their physical makeup which is accustomed to that environment (Islamqa, 2016). Shaykh Ibn al-Qayyim (c) (May Allah have mercy on him) said: "This hadith is addressed to a specific audience, such as the people of Madinah and those in the vicinity." A summary of the protective measures against evils and *Jinns* is presented in Table 18.2.

References

Al-Qurtubi. Tafseer Al-Qurtubi, 9/27. *Tafseer e Qurtubi Arabic (Al Jam'e Al Ahkam Al Quran)* 24 Vols – Ar-Risala. http://hasbunallah.com.au/tafseer-e-qurtubi-arabic-al-jame-al-ahkam-al-quran/ (accessed 22 March 2018).

Ameen A. M. I. (2005) *Dr. Abu'l-Mundhir Khaleel ibn Ibraaheem Ameen. The Jinn and Human Sickness: Remedies in the Light of the Qur'aan and Sunnah*. Riyadh, Saudi Arabia: Darusalaam.

Bukhari (a) Sahih al-Bukhari 6369. In-book reference: Book 80, Hadith 66. USC-MSA web (English) reference: Vol. 8, Book 75, Hadith 380.

Bukhari (b) Sahih al-Bukhari 3371. In-book reference: Book 60, Hadith 50. USC-MSA web (English) reference: Vol. 4, Book 55, Hadith 590.

Bukhari (c) Sahih Bukhari, Book 71, Hadith 664 (also 663, 672). Ibn Kathir. Tafsir Ibn Kathir. What does Isti'adhah mean. www.qtafsir.com/index.php?option=com_content&task=view&id=93 (accessed 22 March 2018).

Ibn Al-Sunni, Imam Ahmad and Al-Haakim. Ibn Al-Sunni in *'Aml al-Yawm wa'l-Laylah*, p. 168; and by al-Haakim, 4/216. Classed as Sahih by al-Albani in *al-Kalim al-Tayyib*, 243. Cited in Islamqa (2000) 7190: Can a man harm his beautiful wife with the "evil eye"? https://islamqa.info/en/7190 (accessed 22 March 2018).

Islamqa (2003) 20954: The Evil Eye and Protection Against it. https://islamqa.info/en/20954 (accessed 22 March 2018).

Islamqa (2016) 254034: Eating seven dates in the morning and the impact of believing in that on the healing effect. https://islamqa.info/en/254034 (accessed 22 March 2018).

Muslim (a) Muslim 2/188. in *Kitaab AuSalaam, Baab Al-Tibb Wwa'l- Marad Wa'l-Ruqa*, 5/32.

Muslim (b) Sahih Muslim | Book 26 | Chapter 15. Hadith Number 5424.

Muslim (c) Sahih Muslim 2047. Cited in Ajwa the king of dates. http://saudiarabiadates.com/benefits.htm (accessed 22 March 2018).

Qamar, A. H. (2013) The concept of the 'Evil' and the 'Evil Eye' in Islam and Islamic faith-healing traditions, *Journal of Islamic Thought and Civilization*, 3, 2, 44–53.

Table 18.2 Protective measures against devils and *Jinn*

• I seek refuge with Allah from the accursed shaytan.	A'oodhu Billahi min al-Shaytan il-rajeem
▪ Qur'an 113: 1–5. Say, "I seek refuge in the Lord of daybreak And from the evil of darkness when it settles From the evil of that which He created And from the evil of the blowers in knots And from the evil of an envier when he envies.	Qul aAAoothu birabbi alfalaq Min sharri ma khalaq Wamin sharri ghasiqin ithawaqab Wamin sharri annaffathatifee alAAuqad Wamin sharri hasidin itha *Hasad*
▪ Qur'an 114: 1–6. Say, I seek refuge in the Lord of mankind, The Sovereign of mankind. The God of mankind, From the evil of the retreating whisperer Who whispers [evil] into the breasts of mankind – From among the *Jinn* and mankind.	Qul aAAoothu birabbi annas Maliki annas Ilahi annas Min sharri alwaswasi alkhannas Allathee yuwaswisu fee sudoori annas Mina aljinnati wannas
▪ Qur'an 2: 255. None has the right to be worshipped but He...	Allah! La ilaha illa Huwa
▪ Qur'an 2: 1–286.	The whole Chapter 2 Sūrat Al-Baqarah
▪ Qur'an 2: 285–286. Last two verses of Surat al-Baqarah at night.	Amana arrasoolu bimaonzila ilayhi min rabbihi walmu/minoona kullun amanabillahi wamala-ikatihi wakutubihiwarusulihi la nufarriqu bayna ahadin min rusulihiwaqaloo samiAAna waataAAna ghufranakarabbana wa-ilayka almaseer. La yukallifu Allahu nafsanilla wusAAaha laha ma kasabatwaAAalayha ma iktasabat rabbana latu-akhithna in naseena aw akhta/narabbana wala tahmil AAalayna isrankama hamaltahu AAala allatheena minqablina rabbana wala tuhammilnama la taqata lana bihi waAAfuAAanna waghfir lana warhamnaanta mawlana fansurna AAalaalqawmi alkafireen
▪ There is no god except Allah Alone with no partner or associate; His is the Sovereignty and His is the praise, and He is able to do all things [100 Times].	La ilaha ill-Allah wahdahu la shareeka lah, lahu'l-mulk wa lahu'l-hamd wa huwa 'ala kulli shayin qadeer.
▪ Remembering Allah often.	*Dhikr*
▪ Call to prayer.	The *adhan*
▪ Reciting Qur'an offers protection against the Shaytan.	Allah says (Interpretation of the meaning): *And when you (Muhammad) recite the Qur'an, We put between you and those who believe not in the Hereafter, an invisible veil (or screen their hearts, so they hear or understand it not)* [Qur'an17:45].
▪ Eat seven dates daily – morning.	*Ajwa* (or other dates).

Shaykh Ibn al-Qayyim al-Jawziyya (a) Cited in Usmani, Z. (2012) Evil Eye, Sorcery and Jinn possession: Remedies in the light of the Qur'an and Sunnah. Believer's Path Institute. www.facebook.com/believerspathinstitute (accessed 22 March 2018).

Shaykh Ibn al-Qayyim al-Jawziyya (b) Cited in Islamqa (2016) 254034: Eating seven dates in the morning and the impact of believing in that on the healing effect. https://islamqa.info/en/254034 (accessed 22 March 2018).

Shaykh Ibn 'Uthaymeen. Majmoo' Fatawa. Cited in Islamqa (2008) 10513: Protection From the Jinn. https://islamqa.info/en/10513 (accessed 22 March 2018).

The Permanent Committee for Scholarly Research and Ifta' (a) The sixth question of Fatwa no. 18649. (Part No. 1; Page No. 110). www.alifta.net/Fatawa/FatawaChapters.aspx?languagename=en&View=Page&PageID=10533&PageNo=1&BookID=7 (accessed 22 March 2018).

The Permanent Committee for Scholarly Research and Ifta' (b) Fatwa no. 6387. (Part No. 1; Page No. 274). www.alifta.net/Fatawa/FatawaChapters.aspx?languagename=en&View=Page&PageID=139&PageNo=1&BookID=7 (accessed 22 March 2018).

Tirmidhi (a) Jami' at-Tirmidhi: Vol. 5, Book 42, Hadith 2863. Arabic reference: Book 44, Hadith 3102.

Tirmidhi (b) Jami' at-Tirmidhi 2068. Sahih and it was authenticated by Shaikh al-Albani.

Chapter 19

Spiritual interventions with evil eye, *Jinn* possession and witchcraft

Introduction

The spiritual interventions in the treatment of the harmful influences of the evil eye, *Jinn* possession and witchcraft include seeking refuge in Allah, prayers, supplications, *Ruqyah* and charity (*Sadaqa*). There is also the use of Cupping (*Hijama*) and the use of Senna as part of the complementary therapy derived from the Prophetic Islamic medicine. In a study of faith healers' views on evil eye, *Jinn* possession and magic, the findings from Al-Habeeb's (2003) study showed that the modes of therapeutic interventions most frequently prescribed by the faith healers include *Ruqyah*, Hadiths, regular performance of prayers, physical punishment, temporary strangulation, cautery, *Saaout* (snuff – inhalation of a herb powder), local application of a paste made of different types of herbs, drinking water mixed with herbs, water mixed with paper with written Qur'anic verses, and local application of oil and drinking some oils. What is interesting is that more than three-quarters (77.3%) of the faith healers studied (N = 35) advise their clients to consult psychiatrists for further treatment. In terms of health outcome, the majority of the faith healers (96%) stated that their patients showed marked improvement as a result of the treatment interventions. It is important for readers to note that the use of physical punishment and strangulation during exorcism of a *Jinn* is not an acceptable practice. This abominable practice has led to some notorious cases since it is associated with complications such as severe suffocation and even death (Vendura and Geserick, 1997; Younis, 2000).

This chapter examines spiritual interventions in cases of afflictions with evil eye, *Jinn* possession and witchcraft The literature will be drawn from sources of the Qur'an, Sunnah, scholars and the clinical experiences of faith healers (Raki) and Imams.

Provisos and procedures for spiritual interventions

There are certain provisos and procedures that faith healers and those receiving the spiritual interventions should adhere to for an effective outcome of the therapeutic, spiritual intervention. Shaykh Ibn Qayyim al-Jawziyya (a) stated that

> Treatment of fits due to spirit-possession requires two factors on the part of the possessed and on the part of the healer.
>
> 1) On the part of the possessed it requires
>   (a) personal strength and turning to the Creator of these spirits truthfully, and
>   (b) the correct method of seeking refuge wherein the heart and tongue will be in harmony. Indeed this type of treatment is, in fact, warfare, and the warrior will not be able to defeat his enemy unless he possesses two qualities: that his weapon itself be good and sharp and that his arm be strong. If either of these two conditions are not met, a long sword will be of no value And if both are missing? The heart which is in a state of desolation and ruin with respect to *Tawheed* [belief in the unity of Allah], trust in Allah, fear of Allah and turning to Him, will have no weapon.
>
> 2) The requirement on the part of the exorcist is that he also possess both [of the above-mentioned] factors.
>
> (p. 69)

For magic and witchcraft, it is important to identify and find the charm used in the bewitchment. It is only by dismantling the charm that the spell will be broken and the '*Jinn* possession' will be extinct. Shaykh Ibn al-Qayyim al-Jawziyya (a) stated, " Removing the charm and neutralising it is the most profound treatment" (p. 124). This approach was used by Prophet Muhammad on the occasion of his own bewitchment. Zayd ibn Arqam reported that a Jew, by the name of Labeeb ibn A'sam [from the Zuraaq clan], cast a spell on the Prophet (ﷺ). When he began to suffer from it, *Jibreel* came to him and revealed the two chapters for seeking refuge (Mu'awwidhataan) and then said to him,

> "Surely, it was a Jew who cast this spell on you, and the magical charm is in a certain well." The Prophet (ﷺ) sent 'Alee ibn Alee Talib to go and fetch the charm. When he returned with it, the Prophet (ﷺ) told him to untie the knots, one by one, and to recite a verse from the two chapters with the undoing of each knot. When he did so, the Prophet (ﷺ) got up as if he had been released from being tied up.
>
> (Ahmad and An Nasa'i)

According to Philips (2008), "Although destroying the charm is the best method of breaking the spell, it is the most difficult, unless someone confesses or the charm is discovered accidentally. The Prophet (ﷺ) only found out the location of the charm by revelation" (p. 135). Part of the procedure, the practice of the Prophet (ﷺ) is to address the possessing spirit and command it, through advice and admonishment, to leave the body of the individual. This procedure was proposed by Ibn Taymiyah (2007), who said that

> the *Jinn* should be addressed and informed that their acts are either abominable and prohibited or vile and tyrannical. They are informed [of this] so that evidence may he brought against them on the Day of Judgment and that they are made aware that they have broken the laws of Allah and His Prophet, whom He sent to both worlds – that of men and *Jinn*. [In summary], if the *Jinn* attack a human, they should be informed of Allah and His Messenger's ruling on the matter, and proof of their error should be pointed out. They should be instructed to be righteous and to abstain from evil, just as is done with humans.
>
> (pp. 32–33)

Another approach is undertaken if the *Jinn* refuses or is reluctant to leave the individual possessed. In these circumstances, the faith healers would use harsh language and shower the *Jinn* with Allah's curse. According to Ibn Taymiyah (2007),

> The commanding of a *Jinnee* [*Jinn*] to righteousness and its prohibition from evil should be carried out in the same way that humans are admonished. Whatever is allowable in the case of humans is also allowable in the case of *Jinn*. For example, the repelling of *Jinn* might require scolding, threatening and even evoking Allah's curse.
>
> (pp. 64–65)

The following Hadith provides ample evidence for the foundation in the practice of seeking refuge in Allah from the *Jinn* and cursing them by Allah's curse.

Abu Darda' reported: Allah's Messenger (ﷺ) stood up (to pray) and we heard him say:

> I seek refuge in Allah from thee.

Then said:

> "Curse thee with Allah's curse" three times, then he stretched out his hand as though he was taking hold of something.

When he finished the prayer, we said: Messenger of Allah, we heard you say something during the prayer which we have not heard you say before, and we saw you stretch out your hand. He replied:

> Allah's enemy Iblis came with a flame of fire to put it in my face, so I said three times: "I Seek refuge in Allah from thee." Then I said three times:

"I curse thee with Allah's full curse." But he did not retreat (on any one of these) three occasions. Thereafter I meant to seize him. I swear by Allah that had it not been for the supplication of my brother Sulaiman he would have been bound, and made an object of sport for the children of Medina.

(Muslim (a))

The final step in the whole process of *Ruqyah* is the recitation of chapters and verses of the Qur'an as a cure for possession as well as other health conditions.

Spiritual interventions in evil eye remedy

There are several therapeutic interventions in the remedy of evil eye. The Prophet (ﷺ) said:

The evil eye is real and if anything were to overtake the divine decree, it would be the evil eye. When you are asked to take a bath (to provide a cure) from the influence of the evil eye, you should take a bath.

(Muslim Ahmad and al-Tirmidhi)

'A'ishah (May Allah be pleased with her) stated that:

The one who had put the evil eye on another would be ordered to do Wudu' [ablution], then the one who had been struck by the evil eye would wash with it (that water).

(Sunan Al-Bayhaqi)

Ahmad, Malik, al-Nasai and Ibn Hibban narrated from Sahl ibn Haneef that the Prophet (ﷺ) came out and travelled with him towards Makkah, until they were in the mountain pass of al-Kharar in al-Jahfah. There Sahl ibn Haneef did ghusl (bathed), and he was a handsome white-skinned man with beautiful skin. 'Amir ibn Rabee'ah, one of Banu 'Adiyy ibn K'ab looked at him whilst he was doing ghusl and said: "I have never seen such beautiful skin as this, not even the skin of a virgin," and Sahl fell to the ground. They went to the Messenger of Allah (ﷺ) and said,

"O Messenger of Allah, can you do anything for Sahl, because by Allah he cannot raise his head." He said, "Do you accuse anyone with regard to him?" They said, "'Amir ibn Rabee'ah looked at him." So the Messenger of Allah (ﷺ) called 'Amir and rebuked him strongly. He said, "Why would one of you kill his brother? If you see something that you like, then pray for blessing for him." Then he said to him, "Wash yourself for him." So he washed his face, hands, forearms, knees and the sides of his feet, and inside his *izaar* (lower garment) in the vessel. Then that water was poured over him, and a man poured it over his head and back from behind. He did that to him, then Sahl got up and joined the people and there was nothing wrong with him.

For a comprehensive account of how this washing is done, see Ameen (2005). That is,

> If it is known or suspected that a person has been afflicted by the evil eye, then the one who put the evil eye on him should be ordered to wash himself for his brother. So a vessel of water should be brought, and he should put his hand in it and rinse out his mouth into the vessel. Then he should wash his face in the vessel, then put his left hand into the vessel and wash his right knee, then put his right hand in the vessel and wash his left knee. Then he should wash inside his garment. Then the water should be poured over the head of the one on whom he put the evil eye, pouring it from behind in one go. Then he will be healed, by Allah's leave.
>
> (Islamqa, 2003)

In the event that an individual is afflicted by the evil eye but is unaware who put the evil eye on him/her, the recommended spiritual interventions as prescribed by the Shari'ah (Islamic Jurisprudence) is reciting *Ruqyah* and *Dhikr*. The sick person should hold his hands up together and recite into them *Al-Fatihah, Aayat Al-Kursiy and al-Mi'wadhatayn* then blow into his hands and wipe them all over his body. The sick person may also recite these verses over olive oil and smear it on the site of pain, and he may wash and drink from that water. According to a Fataawa from Shaykh Ibn 'Uthaymeen

> If a person blows with saliva after reciting Qur'an, such as *al-Fatihah* – which is a kind of *Ruqyah* and is the greatest kind of *Ruqyah* that may be recited over a sick person – so he recites *al-Fatihah* then blows into the water – there is nothing wrong with this. Some of the Salaf did this, and it is effective and beneficial by Allah's leave. The Prophet (ﷺ) used to blow into his hands when going to sleep, after reciting *Qul Huwa Allaahu Ahad*, and *Qul A'oodhu bi Rabbi'l-Falaq* and *Qul 'A'oodhu bi Rabbi'l-Naas*, then he would wipe his hands over his face and whatever he could of his body. And Allah is the Source of strength.

The Prophet (ﷺ) said,

> There is no *Ruqyah* except in the case of the evil eye or fever.
>
> (Tirmidhi, Abu Dawud)

The angel Gabriel (Jibreel) (Peace be upon him) used to do *Ruqyah* for the Prophet (ﷺ) and say,

> In the name of Allah I perform *Ruqyah* for you, from everything that is harming you, from the evil of every soul or envious eye may Allah heal you, in the name of Allah I perform *Ruqyah* for you.

- *Bismillahi arqeeka min kulli shayin yudheeka, min sharri kulli nafsin aw 'aynin hasid Allaahu yashfeek, bismillahi arqeek.*

The use of truffle has also been recommended as part of the Prophetic medicine and the Sunnah in the treatment of evil eye. Truffle (which is very expensive) is an underground plant that grows without being cultivated by man and the Arabs used to call it *Banat Ar-Ra'd*, or the 'Daughter of Thunder.' It was narrated from Abu Sa'eed and Jabir that the Messenger of Allah (ﷺ) said:

> Truffles are a type of manna, and their water is a healing for eye (diseases). And the 'Ajwah [Dates from Madinah] are from Paradise, and they are healing for possession.
>
> (Ibn Majah (a))

Shaykh Ibn Al-Qayyim al-Jawziyya (b) (May Allah have mercy on him) provided three alternative explanations about the previous Hadith.

- Truffle water is not used alone to cure eye diseases, but is mixed with other eye medicines.
- After exposing truffle to fire, its water is used as a medicine once it has been distilled, because fire purges it from waste and humidity.
- The water referred to here is rainwater, which is the first to fall on the earth, according to Ibn Al-Jawzi (May Allah have mercy on him) and this is the weakest opinion. It was also said that its water is a medicine when it is used on its own to alleviate eye pain. For other purposes, it is to be mixed with other compositions.

It is reported in a Fatwa (Islamweb.net, 2010) that Imam An-Nawawi (May Allah be pleased with him) said that the right opinion is that its water is an absolute medicine. According to him, the truffle should be squeezed and its water dropped into the eyes. He also said that he and other men saw completely blind persons who applied truffle water to their eyes recover their eyesight. In the same Fatawa, it was mentioned that Imam Qataadah narrated that Abu Hurayrah squeezed a truffle, put its water in a flask, and then applied it to a girl's eyes and they recovered. Humble (2015) recommended "Take a very small piece [of truffle], boil in 1 litre of water for 10 minutes. Drink one mint-tea-sized cup (the cups that are just a bit bigger than Arab coffee cups), once or twice per day."

In a study of the use and ethnomycological practices of desert truffles among the native people of the Algerian Northern Sahara, Bradai et al.'s (2015) findings showed that Native Saharan people use truffles for food, promoting tourism, increasing fertility and treatment of eye diseases and fatigue. In a review of the use of truffles, El Enshasy et al. (2013) concluded that truffles produce a wide variety of interesting bioactive compounds of high medical value and were used for millennia in the treatment of different diseases. For a more comprehensive account on how to treat the evil eye with *Ruqyah* and *Dhikr*, see Chapter 3 (Ameen, 2005).

Treatment intervention with *Jinn* possession and witchcraft

The treatment of *Jinn* possession and witchcraft needs to be compliant within the paradigm of the Shari'ah. This caution is emphasised because "Whoever is affected by *sihr* should not treat it with *sihr*, because evil cannot be removed by evil, and *kufr* [denial of the Truth] cannot be removed by *kufr*. Evil is removed by good" (Islamqa, 2000). The treatment of witchcraft and magic by the use of *Jinns* or the devils involved in witchcraft and magic is called *An-Nushrah*. Shaykh Ibn al-Qayyim al-Jawziyya (c) stated that '*An-Nushrah*' is a practice mainly intended to break spells and it consists of two types.

- The first type consists in breaking spells by reciting over spells, which is the work of the devils, and this type is what Al-Hasan means by his words. Thus, in order to break a spell, both the sorcerer and the one magically possessed are to offer some practices dedicated and mostly endeared to the devils. [That is counteracting magic with its like and this is the work of the devil].
- The second type of *An-Nushrah* breaks spells by reciting *Ruqyah* (legal incantations), seeking refuge in Allah, taking permissible (halal) medicine and making supplications to Allah – these are all permitted forms of *An-Nushrah*.

(p. 221)

Consequently, when the Prophet (ﷺ) was asked about *An-Nushrah* (treating magic with magic), he said:

> This is the work of the Shaytan.

(Abu Dawud)

Al-Maghribee (2013) suggested that *An-Nushrah* was prevalent during one of the actions of the Jahiliyyah period (period of time and state of affairs in Arabia before the advent of Islam and referred to as the 'Age of Ignorance'), and it is well known that Satan enticed the believers to deviate from what is acceptable and permissible. Shaykh 'Abd al-'Azeez ibn Baaz (a) said:

> Given that there are so many charlatans lately, who claim to be doctors and to treat people by means of magic and witchcraft, and they have become widespread in some countries and they exploit the naïveté of the ignorant, I thought that in the spirit of sincerity towards Allah and His slaves, that I should explain the grave danger that this poses to Islam and the Muslims, because it involves dependence on something other than Allah and going against His command and the command of His Messenger (ﷺ) so I say, seeking the help of Allah.

The therapeutic interventions prescribed in Shari'ah for *Jinn* possession and witchcraft are presented in Table 19.1.

Table 19.1 Therapeutic interventions with *Jinn* possession and witchcraft

Recitation of the Qur'an	
Recite Surah Al-Fatihah [7 times]	Qur'an 1:1–7.
Recite Surah Al-Ikhlas	Qur'an 112:1–4.
Recite Surah Al-Falaq	Qur'an 113:1–5.
Recite Surah Al-Nas	Qur'an 114:1–6.
Make Supplication [3 times or more]: O Allah, Lord of mankind, remove the harm and heal him, for You are the Healer and there is no healing except Your healing, with a healing which does not leave any disease behind.	*Allaahumma Rabb al-naas, adhhib il-ba's, washfi anta al-Shaafi laa shifaa'a illa shifaa'uka shifaa'an laa yughaadir saqaman*
Make Supplication [3 times]: In the name of Allah I perform *Ruqyah* for you, from every thing that is harming you, from the evil of every soul or envious eye may Allah heal you, in the name of Allah. I perform *Ruqyah* for you.	*Bismillaah arqeeka min kulli shay'in yu'dheeka, wa min sharri kulli nafsin aw 'aynin haasid Allaah yashfeek, bismillaah arqeek*
Verses which speak of *Sihr*, which may be recited into water:	
Recite Surah Al-A'raf	Qur'an 7:117–119.
Recite Surah Yunus	Qur'an 10:79–82.
Recite Surah Ta Ha	Qur'an 20:65–69.

However, according to Shaykh 'Abd al-'Azeez ibn Baaz (b) (May Allah have mercy on him), if the verses of the Qur'an (*Surahs al-Fatihah, Aayat al-Kursiy,* "*Qul Huwa Allaahu Ahad,*" and *al-Mi'wadhatayn*) mentioned in Table 19.1 are recited into water, then the water is poured over the person who has been affected by *Sihr* or is being prevented by magic from having intercourse with his wife, then he will be healed by Allah's Leave. Another method is the use of seven Lotus leaves which are grounded and added to the water, according to Shaykh 'Abd al-Rahmaan ibn Hasan (May Allah have mercy on him). It has also been suggested that an "individual may be treated with *al-Fatihah* alone and be healed, or with *Qul Huwa Allaahu Ahad* and *al-Mi'wadhatayn* on their own, and be healed" (Islamqa, 2000). The proviso, for both the practitioner and the one being treated, is putting one's trust in Allah with sincere belief that He is the only cure for everything.

The use of Cupping (*Hijamah*)

The practice of Cupping (*Hijamah*) forms an integral part of Islamic Prophetic medicine. The use of Cupping as complementary interventions has also been suggested by Shaykh Muhammed Salih Al-Munajjid (1997). It is regarded as a safe, non-invasive and economical way of curing and preventing many diseases. Minute incisions are introduced on the skin, at selected points, and the blood is allowed to accumulate on the surface of the skin and then sucked out by using a little vacuum system. The practice of Cupping is strongly recommended and emphasised in a number of narrations from the Messenger of Allah (ﷺ). Ibn 'Abbas (May Allah be pleased with them both) reported that the Prophet (ﷺ) said:

> Healing is to be found in three things: drinking honey, the knife of the cupper, and cauterization of fire.
>
> (Bukhari)

Abu Hurayrah (May Allah be pleased with him) reported that the Prophet (ﷺ) said:

> Whoever is treated with cupping on the seventeenth, nineteenth or twenty first, will be healed from all diseases.
>
> (Abu Dawud and al-Bayhaqi)

Shaykh Ibn al-Qayyim al-Jawziyya (b) (May Allah have mercy on him) mentioned in his work *Zaad al Ma'aad* that the Messenger of Allah (ﷺ) was cupped on the top of his head [*Hijama*] when he was afflicted with *Sihr* (witchcraft) and that it is of the best of cures for this ailment if it is performed correctly (pp. 125–126). It must be pointed out that *Hijama* alone is not the Sunnah way of treating *Jinn* possession and witchcraft. *Hijama* complements the *Ruqyah* process.

Use of Senna

Senna is an herb, the leaves of which are used to treat a number of physical conditions including constipation, irritable bowel syndrome (IBS), haemorrhoids and weight loss. In the context of magic and witchcraft, it is used to remove *Sihr* which sticks in the stomach.

It was narrated that ibn 'Abbas said: The Messenger of Allah (ﷺ) said:

> The best medicines which you use are those which are administered through the side of the mouth, nose drops, cupping and laxatives.
>
> (Tirmidhi)

Ibrahim bin Abu 'Ablah said: I heard Abu Ubayy bin Umm Haram, who had prayed with the Messenger of Allah (ﷺ) facing both the Qibla, saying: I heard the Messenger of Allah (ﷺ) say:

> You should use *Senna* and the *Sannut* [cumin], for in them there is healing for every disease, except the Sam.
> It was said: "O Messenger of Allah, what is the Sam?"
> He said: "Death."
>
> (Ibn Majah (b))

The indication for the use of Senna is when the substances used for witchcraft are still inside the body. According to Abderraouf (2015),

> Sorcery in the stomach is perceived as a foreign body and the stomach attacks it through its natural defenses. However our body cannot remove it naturally and it keep irritating the stomach and intestine causing internal wounds, cramps, ulcers, bleeding and vomiting.

Induced vomiting is the initial method of getting rid of the 'ingested' substances. If this fails, the patient is given a drink of Senna. How to prepare the drink is provided in Ameen (2005, p. 221).

The use of Sana Makki (Senna leaves from Mecca), with Qur'anic verses-blown water, as an infusion is another method of getting rid of the black magic or witchcraft. Abderraouf (2015) suggested that

> When sorcery and/or *Jinn* present in the body, the patient can feel various discomforts during treatment, because all that is being removed. The number of times the infusion has to be taken varies with the kind of sorcery that was consumed, and how many times the patient had eaten it. The criteria are: as long as there are stomach pains/cramps present during treatment, and other discomforts in the body, sorcery is still there. If there is no more sorcery, the only infusion's effect will be diarrhoea.

It is worth pointing out that Senna is contra-indicated in case of pregnancy (unless prescribed by a physician) and conditions including nausea, vomiting, stomach pain, diarrhoea, inflammatory bowel disease, intestinal ulcers and heart disease.

Practices not permissible (haram)

There are many traditional-cultural practices amongst the Muslim communities in the use of charms, beads, amulets, bracelets and necklaces adorned with blue beads, *Ta'weez* [amulet] in the protection and treatment of *Jinn* possession, magic or witchcraft. Unfortunately, most kinds of *Ta'weez* that are to be found in the Muslim world today contain blasphemous, obnoxious and objectionable things and are therefore forbidden. For example, it is common for some Muslims to tie charms or amulets onto their children to protect them against the evil eye. The Messenger of Allah (ﷺ) said:

> Whoever ties on an amulet has committed Shirk.
>
> (Ahmad)

It was narrated from Zaynab the wife of 'Abd-Allaah ibn Mas'ood from 'Abd-Allaah that he said: I heard the Messenger of Allah (ﷺ) said:

> "Spells (*Ruqyah*), amulets and love-charms are *Shirk*." I said, "Why do you say this? By Allah, my eye was weeping with a discharge and I kept going to

so and so, the Jew, who did a spell for me. When he did the spell, it calmed down." 'Abd-Allaah said: "That was just the work of the Shaytan who was picking it with his hand, and when (the Jew) uttered the spell, he stopped. All you needed to do was to say as the Messenger of Allah (ﷺ) used to say: *'Adhhib il-ba's Rabb al-naas ishfi anta al-Shaafi laa shifaa'a illa shifaa'uka shifaa'an laa yughaadiru saqaman* (Remove the harm, O Lord of mankind, and heal, You are the Healer. There is no healing but Your healing, a healing which leaves no disease behind.'"

(Abu Dawud and Ibn Majah)

According to The Permanent Committee for Scholarly Research and Ifta',

It is not permissible to treat the harm caused by the cast of evil eye with what was mentioned [the incense of alum, herbs, leaves, and the like], as they are not among the usual means of treatment. The meaning behind using incense may be to pacify the devils from among the *Jinn* and to seek their help in healing. The evil eye, however, should be treated by the lawful *Ruqyah* (reciting Qur'an and saying supplications over the sick seeking healing) and other prescribed supplications that are authentically reported in the Sahih (authentic) Hadith.

In addition, the Fatwa stated that

binding amulets, bracelets and necklaces adorned with blue beads and metal pieces of the shape of a crescent, or animal teeth or bones etc. with the thought that they will keep one safe from Evil and bring good and bad fortune is without a doubt – Shirk.

There are different opinions on the whether it is forbidden (haram) to wear amulets that contain Qur'anic verses. It is beyond the scope of this chapter to undertake a critical examination of the issues. However, The Scholars of the Standing Committee (Shaykh 'Abd al-'Azeez ibn Baaz, Shaykh 'Abd-Allaah ibn Ghadyaan, Shaykh 'Abd-Allaah ibn Qa'ood) said: "The scholars are agreed that it is haram to wear amulets if they contain anything other than Qur'an, but they differed concerning those which do contain Qur'an. Some of them said that wearing these is permitted, and others said that it is not permitted. The view that it is not permitted is more likely to be correct because of the general meaning of the ahadeeth [Hadith], and in order to prevent means of *Shirk*. Furthermore Shaykh al-Albani (May Allah have mercy on him) said:

This misguidance is still widespread among the Bedouin, fellahin (peasants) and some of the city-dwellers. Examples include the pearls which some drivers put in their cars, hanging them from the rear-view mirror. Some of them hang an old shoe on the front or back of the car; some hang a horse-shoe on the front of their house or shop. All of that is to ward off the evil eye, or so they claim. And there are other things which are widespread because of ignorance of Tawheed and the things which nullify it such as actions of *shirk* and idolatry which the Messengers were only sent and the Books were only revealed to put an end to. It is to Allah that we complain of the ignorance of Muslims nowadays, and their being far away from their religion.

Conclusion

In addition to the *Ruqyah* itself, Ameen (2005) provides a list of supplements a patient should observe. The patient who is possessed or afflicted with witchcraft should fear Allah, put his trust in Him, exercise patience and continue to make supplications. Muslims are made cognisant that the true healer is Allah, and not the practitioner who recites the *Ruqyah* or those who use charms and amulets. The use of charms and amulets is forbidden as a form of protection against *Jinn* possession, magic or witchcraft. Some Muslims are ignorant regarding the unicity of Allah (*Tawheed*) and those beliefs and behaviours that nullify and corrupt the faith from the matters of *Shirk* and *kufr* (disbelief). Other reasons why Muslims use these *Ta'weez* include cultural traditions, followers of 'blind faith,' and ignorance on the reliance and trust in Allah. The main reason is that people say 'through this amulet my supplications are answered or I'm protected' – instead of relying on Allāh as source of strength and protection. Many people, when feel insecure they start looking for 'Ta'weez' (thinking it will protect or save them. This is amongst the tricks of Shaytan, because he knows a Muslim will not worship an idol but this type of *Shirk* works on them (i.e. Muslims) (Muflihun. com, 2015). Allah, the Almighty, Knows best.

References

Abderraouf, B. H. (2015) *The Treatment*. www.benhalimaabderraouf.fr/index.php/en/the-ruqyah/treatment (accessed 22 March 2018).

Abu Dawud. Cited in Islamqa (2000) 11290: *How to deal with sihr (magic/witchcraft)*. https://islamqa.info/en/11290 (accessed 22 March 2018).

Abu Dawud, 3861, and al-Bayhaqi, 9/340. Cited in Islamqa (1998) 3268: Al-hijaamah (cupping): What Islam says about it, its benefits and the times when it should be done, https://islamqa.info/en/3268 (accessed 22 March 2018).

Abu Dawud, 3883 and Ibn Majah, 3530. This hadeeth was classed as Sahih by al-Albani in al-Silsilat al-Saheehah, 331 and 2972.

Ahmad. Musnad Ahmad 16969, Classed Sahih by al-Albani. Refer, Zaad Al-Ma'aad, 4/170. Or al-Silsilah as-Sahihah (492).[Zaad Al-Ma'aad 4:170].

Ahmad, and An Nasai, Cited in Philips, A. A. B. (2008) *The Exorcist Tradition in Islam*. Birmingham: Al-Hidaayah Publishing & Distribution. Authenticated by al-Albani in Sahih Sunan an-Nasa'i Vol. 3, pp. 855–856, no. 3802, but neither version mentions the recital of the mu'awwadhataan. Mention of the mu'awwadhataan in relation to this incident comes in versions reported by al-Bayhaqee in Dalaa'il an-Nubuwwah, Vol. 7, p. 92, and by 'Abd ibn Humayd in his Musnad.

Ahmad, Malik, al-Nasai and Ibn Hibban. Classed as Sahih (authentic) by Al-Albani in al-Mishkat. Cited in Islamqa (2003) 20954: The Evil Eye and Protection Against it. https://islamqa.info/en/20954 (accessed 22 March 2018).

Al-Habeeb, T. A. (2003) A pilot study of faith healers' views on evil eye, jinn possession, and magic in the kingdom of Saudi Arabia, *Journal of Family & Community Medicine*, 10, 3, 31–38.

Al-Maghribee, A. M. (2013 An-Nushrah during Jahiliyyah (Counteracting Magic with its Like) – Sharh Kitaabit-Tawheed by Sheikh Saaleh al-Fawzaan – Abu Muhammad al-Maghribee (2013). https://abdurrahman.org/2013/07/06/an-nushrah-during-jahiliyyah-counteracting-magic-with-its-like-sharh-kitaabit-tawheed-by-sheikh-saaleh-al-fawzaan-abu-muhammad-al-maghribee-audioeng/ (accessed 22 March 2018).

Ameen A. M. I. (2005) *Dr. Abu'l-Mundhir Khaleel ibn Ibraaheem Ameen. The Jinn and Human Sickness: Remedies in the Light of the Qur'aan and Sunnah.* Riyadh, Saudi Arabia: Darussalam.

Bradai, L., Neffar, S., Amrani, K., Bissati, S., and Chenchouni, H. (2015) Ethnomycological survey of traditional usage and indigenous knowledge on desert truffles among the native Sahara Desert people of Algeria, *Journal of Ethnopharmacology*, 162, 31–38. Doi: 10.1016/j.jep.2014.12.031. Epub 2014 Dec 29.

Bukhari. 10/136. *Sahih Al Bukhari* Volume 7, Book 71, Number 603. Cited in Islamqa (1998) 3268: Al-hijaamah (cupping): What Islam says about it, its benefits and the times when it should be done. https://islamqa.info/en/3268 (accessed 22 March 2018).

El Enshasy, H., Elsayed, E. A., Aziz, R., and Wadaan, M. A. (2013) Mushrooms and truffles: Historical biofactories for complementary medicine in Africa and in the Middle East. *Evidence-Based Complementary and Alternative Medicine* : eCAM, 2013, 620451. http://doi.org/10.1155/2013/620451.

Humble, T. M. (2015) *Using Truffle Water.* https://muhammadtim.com/posts/using-truffle-water (accessed 22 March 2018).

Ibn Majah (a) Sunan Ibn Majah English reference: Vol. 4, Book 31, Hadith 3453. Arabic reference: Book 31, Hadith 3579.

Ibn Majah (b) Sunan Ibn Majah Vol. 4, Book 31, Book of Chapters on Medicine, Hadith 3457.

Ibn Taymiyah. Taqi ud Deen Ahmad Ibn Taymiyah (2007) *Essay on the Jinn (Demons). Abu Ameenah Bilal Philips (Translator).* Riyadh, Saudi Arabia: International Islamic Publishing House (IIPH).

Islamweb.net (2010) A Prophetic medicine for eye diseases Fatwa No : 6810. Fatwa Date: Shawwaal 19, 1431/29-9-2010. http://islamweb.net/emainpage/index.php?page=showfatwa&Option=FatwaId&Id=6810 (accessed 3 June 2018).

Islamqa (2000) 11290: *How to deal with sihr* (magic/witchcraft). https://islamqa.info/en/11290 (accessed 22 March 2018).

Islamqa (2003) 20954: *The Evil Eye and Protection Against it.* https://islamqa.info/en/20954 (accessed 22 March 2018).

Muflihun.com (2015) Danger of Wearing Ta'weez. https://muflihun.com/articles/taweez (accessed 22 March 2018).

Muslim (a) Sahih Muslim Vol. 1, Book 4, Book of Prayers, Hadith 1106.

Muslim Ahmad and al-Tirmidhi. Cited in Islamqa (2003) 20954: The Evil Eye and Protection Against it. https://islamqa.info/en/20954 (accessed 22 March 2018).

Philips, A. A. B. (2008) *The Exorcist Tradition in Islam.* Birmingham: Al-Hidaayah Publishing & Distribution.

Shaykh 'Abd al-'Azeez ibn Baaz (a) Majmoo' Fataawa al-Shaykh Ibn Baaz, 3/274–281. Cited in How to deal with sihr (magic/witchcraft). https://special.worldofislam.info/index.php?page=Sihr/how_to_deal_with_sihr (accessed 22 March 2018).

Shaykh 'Abd al-'Azeez ibn Baaz (b) Majmoo' Fataawa wa Maqaalaat Mutanawwi'ah li Samaahat (p. 70). Cited in Islamqa (2000) 11290: How to deal with sihr (magic/witchcraft). https://islamqa.info/en/11290 (accessed 22 March 2018).

Shaykh 'Abd al-'Azeez ibn Baaz, Shaykh 'Abd-Allaah ibn Ghadyaan, Shaykh 'Abd-Allaah ibn Qa'ood. The Scholars of the Standing Committee. Fataawa al-Lajnah al-Daa'imah, 1/212. Cited in Islamqa (2001) 10543: Ruling on amulets and hanging them up; do amulets ward off the evil eye and hasad (envy)? https://islamqa.info/en/10543 (accessed 22 March 2018).

Shaykh 'Abd al-Rahmaan ibn Hasan. Fath al-Majeed, 11290: How to deal with sihr (magic/witchcraft). https://islamqa.info/en/11290 (accessed 21 November 2017).

Shaykh Muhammed Salih Al-Munajjid (1997) Cited in Islamqa (1998) 240: Black Magic and Satanic Possession. https://islamqa.info/en/240 (accessed 22 March 2018).

Shaykh al-Albani. In Silsilat al-Ahaadeeth al-Saheehah, 1/890, 492. Cited in Islamqa (2001) 10543: Ruling on amulets and hanging them up; do amulets ward off the evil eye and hasad (envy)?. https://islamqa.info/en/10543 (accessed 24 November 2017).

Shaykh Muhammed Salih Al-Munajjid (1997)240: Black Magic and Satanic Possession. https://islamqa.info/en/240 (accessed 22 March 2018).

Shaykh Ibn Qayyim al-Jawziyya (a) Zad al-Ma'ad (Provisions Of The Afterlife). Beirut, Lebanon: Dar-al-Kotob Al Ilmiyah. Translation Ismail Abdus Salam.

Shaykh Ibn Al-Qayyim al-Jawziyya (b) Cited in Islamicweb (2010) Fatwa No: 6810A Prophetic medicine for eye diseases. Fatwa Date : Shawwaal 21, 1431 / 29–9–2010. www.islamweb.net/emainpage/index.php?page=showfatwa&Option=FatwaId&Id=6810 (accessed 22 March 2018).

Shaykh Ibn al-Qayyim al-Jawziyya (c) Cited on page 221 in Shaykh Salih Al-Fawzan (2005) Concise Commentary on Book of Tawheed. Riyadh, Saudi Arabia: Al-Maiman Publications House.

Shaykh Ibn 'Uthaymeen. Fataawa al-Shaykh Ibn 'Uthaymeen (a) 1/107.Cited in Islamqa (2003) 21581: Ruling on reciting Qur'an and blowing into water. https://islamqa.info/en/21581 (accessed 22 March 2018).

Sunan Al-Bayhaqi, 9/252. Cited in Ameen A.M.I (2005) Dr. Abu'l-Mundhir Khaleel ibn Ibraaheem Ameen. The Jinn and Human Sickness: Remedies in the Light of the Qur'aan and Sunnah. Riyadh, Saudi Arabia: Darusalaam.

The Permanent Committee for Scholarly Research and Ifta' (Part No. 1; Page No. 275). Fatwa no. 4393. www.alifta.net/Fatawa/FatawaChapters.aspx?languagename=en&View=Page&PageID=140&PageNo=1&BookID=7 (accessed 22 March 2018).

Tirmidhi, 2057 and Abu Dawood, 3884. Cited in Islamqa (2000) 7190: Can a man harm his beautiful wife with the "evil eye"? https://islamqa.info/en/7190 (accessed 22 March 2018).

Tirmidhi Narrated and classed as Hasan by Al-Tirmidhi; narrated and classed as Sahih by Al-Haakim and by Abu Na'eem in Tibb Al-Nabawi. Cited in Ameen (2005) The Jinn and Human Sickness: Remedies in the Light of the Qur'aan and Sunnah. Riyadh, Saudi Arabia: Darussalam, p. 220.

Vendura, K., and Geserick, G. (1997) Fatal exorcism. A case report, Archiv für Kriminologie, 200, 73–78.

Younis, Y. O. (2000) Possession and exorcism: an illustrative case, The Arab Journal of Psychiatry, 11, 56–59.

Chapter 20

Islamic-based cognitive behavioural therapies and spiritual interventions with *Waswâs al-Qahri* (obsessive-compulsive disorder)

Introduction

Chapters 12 and 13 focus on obsessive-compulsive disorder (OCD) and its Islamic pathological equivalence of *Waswâs al-Qahri*. The treatment interventions for OCD include cognitive behavioural therapy (CBT) and pharmacological management. Low-intensity cognitive behaviour therapy interventions for obsessive-compulsive disorder have also been suggested (Lovell et al., 2017). There is evidence to suggest that cognitive behavioural therapy is an effective treatment for OCD (Greist et al., 2003; NICE, 2006). There is also evidence that brief strategic therapy (BST) is highly efficacious in treating OCD (Pietrabissa et al., 2016).

The protocol of good practice and interventions needs to be directed for those Muslims who are experiencing *Waswâs al-Qahri* but do fit in the paradigm of psychiatric psychopathology.

NICE (2005) suggested that

> Obsessive-compulsive symptoms may sometimes involve a person's religion, such as religious obsessions and Scrupulosity, or cultural practices. When the boundary between religious or cultural practice and obsessive-compulsive symptoms is unclear, healthcare professionals should, with the patient's consent, consider seeking the advice and support of an appropriate religious or community leader to support the therapeutic process.

This chapter will examine the use of a modified cognitive behavioural therapy and spiritual interventions in the management of Scrupulosity-based *Waswâs al-Qahri*.

Cognitive behavioural therapy

It is generally assumed, from a historical viewpoint, that cognitive behavioural therapy (CBT) in its present form was developed and promoted by individuals such as Albert Ellis (1962) and Aaron Beck (1976). However, from an Islamic narrative, Abu Zayd Ahmed ibn Sahl Balkhi, known as Al-Balkhi, was "the first known cognitive psychologist, the first to consider that faulty thinking leads to psychological problems of anxiety, anger and sadness and suggesting cognitive therapies for anxiety and mood disorders" (Badri, 2013, p. 17). The Islamic scholar Al-Balkhi also focused on how to eliminate emotional disorders by simply concentrating on changing one's inner thinking and irrational beliefs and introduced the concept of reciprocal inhibition (*al-ilaj bi al-did*), and his therapy could be termed today as 'Rational Cognitive Therapy' (Haque, 2004; Badri, 2013, p. 17). Al-Balkhi used four therapeutic techniques: relaxation technique, reciprocal inhibition (same graded technique used in systematic desensitization); rational cognitive therapy to change cognitions and beliefs; and use of psycho-spiritual religious cognitive approach (Badri, 2013, pp. 32–33).

Cognitive behavioural therapy is a form of psychotherapeutic interventions that emphasises that our cognitions (thoughts) drive our feelings and behaviours. Cognitive behavioural theory is based on the principles that an organism's activity has three modalities: behaviour, emotion and cognition. The cognitive model, according to Beck (1976), describes how people's perceptions of, or the way they interpret information about, situations influence their emotional, behavioural (and often physiological) reactions. That is, the development of patterns of negative or irrational thoughts is dependent on the perception of information.

An elaborated definition of CBT theory has been proposed by Dobson and Dozois (2010) in the form of three essential propositions:

- Thinking and cognitions affect behaviour;
- Cognitive activity is accessible and is amenable to change;
- Desired behavioural change may follow from changes in thinking.

These propositions suggest that individual interpretation of events can affect the response to those episodes and the modification of these cognitions into acceptable pattern of positive behavioural changes. However, in general, cognitive theories maintain that maladaptive or irrational thinking (cognitions) contribute to the maintenance of emotional and psychological problems (Ellis, 1962; Beck, 1976).

Modern CBT refers to a family of therapies including meta-cognitive therapy, mindfulness-based therapy, mindfulness-based cognitive therapy, dialectical behaviour therapy, acceptance and commitment therapy, Internet-based CBT and the utilisation of mobile devices as an augmentation to CBT (Bee et al., 2008; Hofmann and Asmundson, 2008; Linehan, 2000; Hofmann, 2011; Sauer-Zavala et al., 2012; Hofmann et al., 2013; Segal et al., 2013; Khoury et al., 2013; Swain et al., 2013; Beck and Haig, 2014; Mundy and Hofmann, 2014). There are different techniques and approaches, with a similar underlying philosophy, and these combine a variety of cognitive, problem-solving, behavioural and emotion-focused techniques. The focus involves changing or modifying these maladaptive cognitions, and replacing them with more constructive thoughts in order to positively affect belief (core and intermediate) emotion and behaviour. One of the key features of CBT is "its action-oriented and problem-solving approaches to managing thoughts, emotions and behaviours more effectively" (Rassool, 2016, p. 137). The therapist (or counsellor) uses a number of cognitive and behavioural techniques as part of the therapeutic process. The techniques to modify beliefs include the use of 'Socratic' questioning, Guided discovery, Behavioural experiments, Cognitive continuum, Intellectual–emotional role plays, Using others as a reference point, Acting 'as if' and Self-disclosure.

Other activities include: the use of homework and outside-of-session techniques. The commonly in-use behavioural therapies for OCD include Exposure and Response Therapy (ERP); Paradoxical Intention; Habituation (Satiation) Training; and Thought Stopping. Veale (2007) has suggested the following 'Good practice' points in cognitive behavioural therapy for OCD. These include:

- Patients should have clearly defined problems and goals for therapy.
- There should be a shared formulation of the problem that provides a neutral explanation of the symptoms and of how trying to avoid and control intrusive thoughts and urges maintains the patient's distress and disability.
- Do not become engaged in the content of obsessions and requests for reassurance, and do not argue about the likelihood of a bad event happening – help patients to use their formulation and the cognitive-behavioural model of OCD, and use a Socratic dialogue to focus on the process and consequences of their actions.
- Do not give up using exposure and response prevention: integrate it with the cognitive approach in the form of behavioural experiments to make predictions.
- Ensure that patients do not incorporate new appraisals or self-reassurance as another compulsion or way of neutralizing.

Religious-based cognitive behavioural therapy

There is a growing trend in the emergence of literature and research on the efficacy of religious-based therapy, in general, and Islamic-based cognitive behavioural therapies. The application of the cultural or religious compatibility hypothesis is that if Islamic values and practices are believed to be incompatible with therapeutic interventions, this makes Muslims reluctant to use Western-oriented psychotherapeutic interventions. The cultural compatibility hypothesis asserts that similarities between the client's culture and therapy and culturally enhanced behavioural health interventions provide culturally adapted interventions or lead to desired therapeutic outcomes and provide benefit to intervention outcomes (O'Sullivan and Lasso, 1992; Fraser et al., 2009; Sue et al., 2009; Barrera et al., 2013). Thus, it is an assumption that an Islamic-based cognitive behavioural therapy would be more beneficial for Muslim patients.

The findings from Koenig's study (2012) showed that religious CBT mirrors conventional CBT treatments while adding religious content and motivation to the process (Koenig, 2012).

The literature indicates that certain psychotherapeutic interventions that explicitly integrate clients' spiritual and religious beliefs in therapy are effective (Pearce et al., 2015). The findings from Loewenthal et al.'s study (2001) indicated that Muslims believed in the efficacy of religious coping methods, in the case for depression and were most likely to use religious coping behaviour. Azhar et al.'s study (1994) indicated that those receiving religious psychotherapy showed significantly more rapid improvement in anxiety symptoms than those who received supportive psychotherapy and drugs only. In a meta-analytic review of 46 spiritual intervention studies, Worthington et al. (2011) concluded that patients with spiritual beliefs in spiritually integrated psychotherapies showed greater improvement than patients treated with other psychotherapies.

However, the effectiveness of CBT among Muslim populations still raises some concerns as most of the studies that have examined the efficacy of CBT have been conducted with individuals of a Western, Judeo-Christian background (Hamdan, 2008). Although these research efforts point to the efficacy of cognitive interventions based on Islamic principles for Muslim clients, there are concerns regarding various methodological issues (Hamdan, 2008). More research is necessary to study modified cognitive behavioural therapy with Islamic spiritual interventions to make definitive statements about the empirical soundness and robustness of such approaches. A critical review of the research literature on religious and Muslim-based cognitive therapies is provided by Beshai et al. (2013) and Lim et. al. (2014).

Islamic-based cognitive behavioural therapy for Muslim clients to overcome OCD

The philosophical and theoretical bases of cognitive behavioural therapy from an Islamic perspective are examined in Beshai et al. (2013) and Rassool (2016). There has been some adaptation of cognitive behaviour therapy (CBT) in the treatment of Muslim patients suffering from psycho-spiritual problems. The modified approach of cognitive behaviour therapy is also referred to as 'Islamically Modified Cognitive Behavioural Therapy' (Husain and Hodge, 2016), 'Muslim-Based Cognitive Behavioural Therapy' (Waqar, 2016) or Islamic-Based Cognitive Behaviour Therapy (Rassool, 2016). It is reported that OCD, in Arab and Islamic populations, is viewed and managed mostly on the basis of religion (Okasha et al., 2001). However, it has been suggested by Badri (2000) that the Islamic-based cognitive therapy approach is more appropriate for patients who are cognitively able to think properly because of the integration between action and thinking in this approach (Badri, 2000).

The eminent and distinguished Professor Malik Badri, who is the father of modern Islamic Psychology and Islamic-based cognitive therapy, developed

"A new technique for the systematic desensitization of pervasive anxiety and phobic reactions" (Badri, 1967). It was named by Meyer and Chesser (1970) as "behavioural psychotherapy" but Badri preferred to call it, 'Cognitive Systematic Desensitization' (Badri, 2014). A more comprehensive account of the technique is found in Badri (1967, 2014) and Khan (2015). The Islamic-based model approach is based on the influence of religion on the misinterpretation of unacceptable intrusive thoughts caused by *Jinn* possession and witchcraft. There is evidence to suggest that religious cognitive behaviour therapy can be effective to reduce OCD severity symptoms and enhance Quality of Life in religion-oriented OCD patients in Islamic culture (Akuchekian et al., 2011 2015; Mohamed et al., 2015).

Islamic-based cognitive therapy approach: the therapeutic process

There are unique facets and several techniques in the Islamic cognitive therapy approach that have been developed by Muslim scholars. According to Rassool (2016), there are "significant cognitions from the Islamic faith that can be incorporated into the counselling process with Muslim clients" (p. 145). Al-Bakhi, the pioneer of cognitive behavioural therapy, suggested emphasising the importance in the development of positive thoughts:

> like Allah the Almighty had built the universe and determined the survival of its people thus the Allah created a safety reasons more than destruction reasons consequently healing is the origin of all diseases. Therefore Allah created therapy for each illness.
>
> (p. 292)

The classical Islamic scholar Al Ghazali Abu Hamid bin Muhammad (1998) proposed the use of 'Opposite therapy' a technique which focuses on the use of imagination ('use of imagination in pursuing the opposite'). The patient has to imagine the act in the opposite way and then integrate this opposite act into his or her behaviour.

Contemplation or deep thought is another technique in Islamic cognitive therapy. According to Ibn Qayyim, "Deep thought (contemplation) . . . is the beginning of and key to all good . . . it is the best function of the heart and the most useful to it." Rosila and Yaacob (2013) suggested that in contemplating,

> the patient is advised to be relaxed and free their mind from any worldly affairs, but imagine in depth on the Oneness of God who create, sustain and cherish all the creations. The focus of contemplation also goes to the life in hereafter which is the ultimate aim of every mankind.
>
> (p. 185)

In a model of spiritually modified cognitive interventions Hodge and Nadir (2008) focus on self-control and change; self-worth (Worth in Allah); high frustration tolerance; acceptance of others; achievement; needing approval and love; accepting responsibility; accepting self-direction; and self-acceptance. They maintained that "the self-statements used in Western cognitive therapy are replaced with statements drawn from Islamic teaching" (p. 36). These generalised statements need to be evaluated for congruence with Islamic values and placed within the Islamic narrative or worldview. Some examples of Islamic-based self-statements that replace unhealthy or irrational thought patterns and foster enhanced positive functioning are presented in Table 20.1.

Table 20.1 Cognitive statements modified with Islamic tenets

Statements	Sources	Examples
Self-control and change	Qur'an 2:183 Qur'an 24:31 Qur'an 79:40	Fast in the month of Ramadan and extra fasting (Monday and Thursday) in order to learn self-restraint and self-control. We "lower our gaze" to resist temptation. Controlling the soul (Nafs).
Worth in Allah	Qur'an 3: 28	We have worth because we are created by Allah. We are created with strengths and weaknesses.
High frustration tolerance	Qur'an 29:2–3 Qur'an 3:179 Qur'an 2:155–157 Qur'an 3:142 Qur'an 21:35	Trials and tribulations. Testing is according to one's faith; the most severely tested among mankind are the Prophets, then the next best and the next best. The Prophet (peace and blessings of Allah be upon him) said: "When I fall ill, my pain is equivalent to the pain of two men among you" (Bukhari, 5648). Allah tests His slaves with different kinds of trials.
Acceptance of others	Qur'an 2:178 Qur'an 16:91 Qur'an 29:70 Qur'an 4:2 Qur'an [about 200 verses]	Because people are created with weaknesses, people will make mistakes. Islam tells us not to judge others for their shortcomings, but to accept people with their strengths and weaknesses.
Achievement	Qur'an 4:70–71 Qur'an 65:3	Although human approval and accomplishment is beneficial, they are not necessary for a productive life. As it says in the Qur'an, he who relies on Allah, Allah is enough for him.

(Continued)

Table 20.1 (Continued)

Statements	Sources	Examples
Needing approval and love	Qur'an 13:28	True satisfaction and solace is found in our relationship with Allah. Our regular remembrance of Allah helps us to know that He loves us.
Accepting responsibility	Qur'an 2:24 Qur'an 2:195	Islam teaches us to take responsibility for our actions and our situation without blaming others. The Prophet (peace and blessings of Allah be upon him) said: "O my servants, it is only your deeds that I record for you and then recompense for you, so let him who finds good praise Allah and let him who finds other than that blame no one but himself" (Muslim 2577).
Reliance in Allah	Qur'an 5:23 Qur'an 3:159 Qur'an 65:3 Qur'an:11:123	Relying on Allah is one of the greatest forms of worship. Reliance on Allah means entrusting one's affairs to Allah and relying on Him in all matters. Entrusting one's affairs to Allah entails not turning to something or someone else for support.
Self-awareness	Qur'an 41:53	Knowledge of self is the key to the knowledge of God, according to the saying: "He who knows himself knows God" [Hadith].

Source: Adapted from Hodge, D. R. and Nadir, A. (2008) Moving toward culturally competent practice with Muslims: Modifying cognitive therapy with Islamic tenets, *Social Work*, 53, 31–41.

According to Hodge and Nadir (2008), the statements in Table 20.1 highlighted

> a balance among personal agency, personal accountability, and God's role in the transformation process. It focuses on the importance of relying on God as part of successfully gaining self-discipline and making change in one's life. In addition to referencing God, the statement also includes activities that may help Muslims practice self-restraint . . . develop and maintain self-control.
>
> (pp. 37–38)

In order to facilitate the change of cognitions, Qur'anic verses and Hadiths can be used in this process. According to Badri (2011), the "Qur'anic verses and Hadith serve as analogies to facilitate a deeper understanding of the problems of the patients and consequently impact upon treatment effectiveness" (p. 13).

The use of the 'Analogy technique' (Hussain, 2011) can be used in the process of Islamic-based cognitive therapy in congruence with the patient's spiritual narratives. Hussain (2011) suggested that

> as therapists use analogy to facilitate understanding of their situation, the ayaaat/ahadith [verses of the Qur'an and Hadith] and their surrounding circumstances are used, since the words of the Creator will most aptly summarise the experience of creation. . . . The ayaaat/ahadith present analogies where both the patient and psychologist may use the information, to explain, empathise, sympathise and understand the patient experience.
>
> (pp. 17–18)

In Hamdan's cognitive restructuring model (2008), it is important first to teach the patients to identify and evaluate automatic thoughts and dysfunctional core beliefs and assumptions that lead to problem behaviours. Hamdan (2008) also proposed that cognitions from the Islamic faith can be used as alternative explanations to dysfunctional thoughts and the specific ones chosen would depend upon the presenting problem and the needs of each particular client.

Hamdan (2008) suggested that some of the beneficial cognitions from the Islamic perspective include focusing on: understanding the temporal reality of this world; understanding the nature of this life and the Hereafter; recalling the purpose and effects of distress and afflictions; trusting and relying on Allah (*Tawakkul*); understanding that after hardship there will be ease; focusing on the blessings of Allah; remembering Allah and reading [the] Qur'an; supplication (*Du'aa*).

Other techniques that can be accommodated within Islamic-based cognitive behavioural therapies include the use of supplications, prayers, the power of suggestion (Rosila and Yaacob, 2013) or remembered wellness (Benson, 1996). CBT's emphasis on homework, practical and outside-of-session assignments mesh particularly well with the Islamic traditions and may be particularly appealing to Muslim clients (Abudabbeh and Hays, 2006; Hodge and Nadir, 2008).

Mindfulness-based cognitive therapy (MBCT)

Mindfulness meditation has become a trendy 'third wave' therapy in dealing with the triggers, emotions and thoughts that create and feed negative thought processes. Mindfulness-based cognitive therapy (MBCT) (Segal et al. (2013) combines mindfulness exercises (meditative practices, breathing exercises) with elements of cognitive therapy and has originally been designed to prevent relapse in depression. In this therapy, patients are taught how to break away from negative thought patterns that can cause psychological problems like depression or OCD. MBCT is recommended by the National Institute for Health and Care Excellence (NICE, 2016) as an effective treatment for people who suffer from recurrent episodes of depression. The use of mindfulness-based cognitive therapy might be a complementary treatment strategy and an adjunct to CBT

(Fairfax, 2008). The findings of a study from Hertenstein et al. (2012) showed that patients with OCD find aspects of the current MBCT protocol acceptable and beneficial. Key et al. (2017) suggest that the use of MBCT for OCD as an augmentation therapy is acceptable to patients and provides some additional relief from residual symptoms.

However, the approach of Mindfulness therapy may not be compatible with Islamic beliefs and practices. Mindfulness meditation is rooted in the ontological assumptions of Buddhism. According to Saloojee (2016),

> Mindfulness does not demand fealty to such core principles of Buddhism such as reincarnation, or some of its ethical prohibitions like abstaining from luxury in food and material possessions; alcoholic drinks; instrumental music; singing and dancing; jewellery, perfumes and cosmetics; and all sensual overindulgences. Many Westerners, especially those who are not tied to institutional faith, do not appear to have reservations in accepting the Buddhist belief of no God and the unity of all being (which is a mainstay belief in many new Western modalities of spirituality).

Some 'Cultural Muslim' therapists support the use of mindfulness meditation because it is trimmed of its Buddhist ontological doctrine. In addition, there are claims that mindfulness is embedded in the very foundation of Islam. According to the proponent of this approach, "the five daily prayers is mindful movement, a meditation of gratitude and humility in front of our creator. Mindfulness goes hand in hand with the pillars of faith and examples from the Prophets life" (Mindful Muslims). If this is the case, why not encourage patients to delve in reflections, supplications, remembrance of Allah (*Dhikr*) and other spiritual practices. However, the claim that 'mindfulness' meditation is an integral part of Islamic spirituality is not refuted. But there is a profound difference between the Islamic-based contemplation and mindfulness from the orientalists. According to Saloojee (2016), the philosophical or theological difference is that "Islam prescribes Divine-mindfulness. Allah is *al-Raqib*, the Ever-Watchful and the Ever-Vigilant. Divine-mindfulness in Islam translates as *muraqabah*, which is to be experientially aware of Allah watching you." In addition, the theological underpinning of mindfulness therapy is not congruent with the creed of '*Ahlus-Sunnah Wal-Jama^ah*'(the majority of the Muslim nation). They are the people who rightfully followed the methodology of Prophet Muhammad (ﷺ). Saloojee (2016) argued that

> Muslims should not be uncritical in accepting mindfulness meditation.... The *'aqidah* [religious belief system], or creed, at the heart of mindfulness should be of even graver concern. Its oneness of everything, akin or similar to Monism, is categorically rejected by Islam, which teaches that there exists a Creator and created.

The author went on to say that

> As it wouldn't be fair for Muslims to immediately deny some of the apparent therapeutic benefits of modern mindfulness meditation, it is equally unfair to be wilfully blind or ignorant to its great probable harms. And, for argument's sake, even if the benefits were many, the harms negligible and the practice of mindfulness was purely therapeutic, our embracing of mindfulness to find peace and serenity represents a mindlessness of our own faith.

In other words, the harms outweighed the benefits and the approach is in dissonance with Islamic beliefs and practices. But 'mindfulness' or contemplation is permissible (halal) if practised within the boundaries of *Shari'ah* (Islamic law).

Dhikr-based cognitive therapy (DBCT)

It is proposed that *Dhikr* (remembrance of Allah) is prescribed for Muslims instead of mindfulness therapy as there is no greater approach to Allah's nearness than constant remembrance. *Dhikr* of Allah is stressed over a hundred times in the Qur'an. There are no rules or restrictions to adhere to in relation modality, frequency or timing of *Dhikr*. Allah says (Interpretation of the meaning):

> *O you who have believed, remember Allah with much remembrance.*
> (Sūrat Ahzab (The Companions of the Combined Forces) 33:41)

> *Who remember Allah while standing or sitting or [lying] on their sides.*
> (Sūrat Ali 'Imran (The Family of 'Imran) 3:191)

In a Hadith, the Messenger of Allah (ﷺ) said:

> If your hearts were always in the state that they are in during *dhikr*, the angels would come to see you to the point that they would greet you in the middle of the road.
>
> (Muslim)

Imam Nawawi in his *Sharh Sahih Muslim* commented on this Hadith saying: "This kind of sight is shown to someone who persists in meditation (*muraqaba*), reflection (*fikr*), and anticipation (*iqbal*) of the next world." Mu'adh ibn Jabal said that the Prophet (ﷺ) also said:

> The People of Paradise will not regret except one thing alone: the hour that passed them by and in which they made no remembrance of Allah.
>
> (Bayhaqi and Tabarani)

Dhikr is certainly genuine mindfulness meditation and this could be combined with cognitive behavioural therapy to form the *Dhikr*-based cognitive therapy (DBCT). This combination should be subjected to clinical and research evidence to evaluate its effectiveness with *Waswâs al-Qahri*.

Conclusion

There is wide consensus among Islamic scholars and practitioners that the underlying principles on which cognitive therapy rests are congruent with Islamic values (Rassool, 2016). In order to increase the level of congruence with Islamic beliefs and practices, the Islamic-based cognitive behavioural therapy should be implemented in clinical practice with Muslim patients. Some of the current approaches and models used require greater development and refinement backed by evidence-based research. In fact, the more religious-oriented Muslim clients would derive substantial benefits from cognitive therapy modified with Islamic tenets.

References

Abudabbeh, N., and Hays, P. A. (2006) Cognitive-Behavioral Therapy with People of Arab Heritage, in P. A. Hays, and G. Y. Iwamasa (Eds.), *Culturally responsive cognitive-behavioral therapy: Assessment, practice, and supervision.* Washington, DC: American Psychological Association, pp. 141–159.

Akuchekian, S. H, Almasi, A., Meracy, M. R, Jamshidian, Z. (2011) Effect of religious cognitive-behavior therapy on religious content obsessive compulsive disorder and marital satisfaction, *Journal of European Psychiatric Association*, 26, 1742.

Akuchekian, S. H., Nabi, L. N., Najafi, M., and Almasi, A. (2015) The affect of religious cognitive-behavior therapy on quality of life obsessive – compulsive disorder, *International Journal of Behavioral* Research & *Psychology*, 3, 1, 71–74. Doi: dx.doi.org/10.19070/2332–3000-1500013.

Al-Balkhi. Cited in Mohamed, N. R., Sh Elsweedy, M., Elsayed, S, M. Rajab, A. Z. Elzahar, S. T. (2015) Obsessive-compulsive disorder, an Islamic view, *Menoufia Medical Journal*, 28, 2, 289–294.

Al-Ghazali, Abu Hamid bin Muhammad (1998) *Ilya' Ulum al-Din.* Vol. 2, Beirut: Dar alKutub al-'Ilmiah.

Azhar, M. Z., Varma, S. L., and Dharap, A. S. (1994) Religious psychotherapy in anxiety disorder patients, *Acta Psychiatrica Scandinavia*, 90, 1, 1–3.

Badri, M. B. (1967) A new technique for the systematic desensitization of pervasive anxiety and phobic reactions, *The Journal of Psychology*, 65, 201–208. Published online: 15 Nov 2012. www.tandfonline.com/doi/abs/10.1080/00223980.1967.10544865

Badri, M. (2011) Foreword. Hussain, F. A (2011) *Therapy from the Quran and Ahadith: A Reference Guide for Character Development.* Riyadh, Saudi Arabia: Maktaba Dar-us-Salaam.

Badri, M. (2000) *Contemplation: An Islamic Ppsychospiritual Study.* Kuala Lumpur: Shelbourne Enterprise Sdn, Bhd

Badri, M. (2013) *Translation and Annotation: Sustenance of the Soul the Cognitive Behavior Therapy of a Ninth Century Physician by Abu Zayd al-Balkhi.* Richmond, Surrey: International Institute of Islamic Thought.

Badri, M. (2014) Cognitive systematic desensitization: An Innovative therapeutic technique with special reference to Muslim patients, *American Journal of Islamic Social Sciences*, 31, 4, 1–12.

Barrera, M., Castro, F. G., Strycker, L. A., and Toobert, D. J. (2013) Cultural adaptations of behavioral health interventions: A progress report. *Journal of Consulting and Clinical Psychology*, 81, 2, 196–205. http://doi.org/10.1037/a0027085.

Bayhaqi in *Shu'ab al-iman* (1:392 #512–513) and by Tabarani. Haythami in *Majma' al-zawa'id* (10:74) said that its narrators are all trustworthy *(thiqat)*, while Suyuti declared it *hasan* in his *Jami' al-saghir* (#7701).

Bee, P. E., Bower, P., Lovell, K., Gilbody, S., Richards, D. Gask, L., and Roach, P. (2008) Psychotherapy mediated by remote communication technologies: A meta-analytic review, *BMC Psychiatry*, 8, 60.

Beck, A. T. (1976) Cognitive therapy and the emotional disorders. New York: International Universities Press.

Beck, A.T., and Haigh, E. A. (2014) Advances in cognitive theory and therapy: The generic cognitive model, *Annual Review of Clinical Psychology*, 10, 1–24.

Benson, H. (1996) *Timeless Hhealing: The Power and Biology of Belief*. London: Simon & Schuster Ltd.

Beshai, S., Clark, C. M., and Dobson, K. S. (2013) Conceptual and pragmatic considerations in the use of cognitive-behavioral therapy with Muslim clients, *Cognitive Therapy and Research*, 37, 1, 197–206. Doi: 10.1007/s10608–012–9450-y.

Dobson, K. S., and Dozois, D. J. (2010) Philosophical and Theoretical Bases for the Cognitive-Behavioral Therapies, in K. S. Dobson (Ed.), *Handbook of Cognitive-Behavioral Therapies*. 3rd ed. New York: The Guilford Press, pp. 3–38.

Ellis, A. (1962) *Reason and Emotion in Psychotherapy*. Secaucus, NJ: Lyle Stuart.

Fairfax, H. (2008) The use of mindfulness in obsessive compulsive disorder: Suggestions for its application and integration in existing treatment, *Clinical Psychology & Psychotherapy*, 15, 53–59. Doi: 10.1002/cpp.557.

Fraser, M. W., Richman, J. M., Galinsky, M. J., and Day, S. H. (2009) *Step 5: Dissemination of Findings and Program Materials: The Challenge of Evidence-Based Practice*, in T. Tripodi (Ed.), *Intervention Research: Developing Social Programs*. New York: Oxford University Press, pp. 105–132.

Greist, J. H., Bandelow, B., Hollander, E., Marazziti, D., Montgomery, S. A., Nutt, D. J., Okasha, A., Swinson, R. P., and Zohar, J. (2003) WCA [World Council of Anxiety] recommendations for the long-term treatment of obsessive-compulsive disorder in adults, *CNS Spectrum*, 8, 8 Suppl 1, 7–16.

Hamdan, A. (2008) Cognitive restructuring: An Islamic perspective, *Journal of Muslim Mental Health*, 3, 1, 99–116.

Haque, A. (2004) Psychology from Islamic perspective: Contributions of early Muslim scholars and challenges to contemporary Muslim psychologists, *Journal of Religion and Health* 43, 4, 357–377.

Hertenstein, E., Rose, N., Voderholzer, U., Heidenreich, T., Nissen, C., Thiel, N., Herbst, N., and Külz, A. K. (2012) Mindfulness-based cognitive therapy in obsessive-compulsive disorder – A qualitative study on patients' experiences, *BMCPsychiatry*, 12, 185. https://doi.org/10.1186/1471-244X-12-185.

Hofmann S. G, and Asmundson, G. J. (2008) Acceptance and mindfulness-based therapy: New wave or old hat? *Clinical Psychological Review*, 28, 1–16.

Hofmann, S. G. (2011) *An Introduction to Modern CBT: Psychological Solutions to Mental Health Problems*. Oxford: Wiley-Blackwell.

Hofmann, S. G., Asmundson, G. J., and Beck, A. T. (2013) The science of cognitive therapy, *Behavior Therapy*, 44, 199–212.

Hodge, D. R., and Nadir, A. (2008) Moving toward culturally competent practice with Muslims: Modifying cognitive therapy with Islamic tenets, *Social Work*, 53, 31–41.

Hussain, F. A. (2011) *Therapy from the Quran and Ahadith: A Reference Guide for Character Development*. Riyadh, Saudi Arabia: Maktaba Dar-us-Salaam.

Husain, A., and Hodge, D. R. (2016) Islamically modified cognitive behavioral therapy: Enhancing outcomes by increasing the cultural congruence of cognitive behavioral therapy self-statements, *International Social Work*, 59, 3, 393–405. https://doi.org/10.1177/0020872816629193.

Ibn Qayyim al-Jawziyyah (n.d.) *The Key to the House of Bliss (Miftah Dar al-Sa'adah)*. Riyadh, Saudi Arabia: Ri'asat al-Ifta.

Imam Nawawi. Sahih Muslim Bi sharh Li Imam An Nawawi (18 Volumes in 10 books) https://nmusba.wordpress.com/2013/03/18/sahih-muslim-bi-sharh-li-imam-an-nawawi-18-volumes-in-10-books/ (accessed 30 November 2017).

Key, B. L., Rowa, K., Bieling, P., McCabe, R., and Pawluk, E. J. (2017) Mindfulness-based cognitive therapy as an augmentation treatment for obsessive-compulsive disorder. *Clinical Psychology & Psychotherapy*, 2, 5, 1109–1120. Doi: 10.1002/cpp.2076. Epub 2017 Feb 13.

Khan, R. K. (2015) An interview with Professor Malik Badri about his contributions to the Islamisation of psychology, *Intellectual Discourse*, 23, 1, 159–172.

Khoury, B., Lecomte, T., Fortin, G., Masse, M., Therien, P., Bouchard, V., Chapleau, M. A., Paquin, K., and Hofmann, S. G. (2013) Mindfulness-based therapy: A comprehensive meta-analysis, *Clinical Psychology Review*, 33, 763–771.

Koenig, H. G. (2012) Religious versus conventional psychotherapy for major depression in patients with chronic medical illness: Rationale, methods, and preliminary results, *Depression Research and Treatment*, 2012, 460419. Doi: 10.1155/2012/460419. Epub 2012 Jun 13.

Lim, C., Sim, K., Renjan, V., Sam, H. F., and Quah, S. L. (2014) Adapted cognitive-behavioral therapy for religious individuals with mental disorder: A systematic review, *Asian Journal of Psychiatry*, 9, 3–12. Doi: 10.1016/j.ajp.2013.12.011.

Linehan, M. M. (2000) The empirical basis of dialectical behavior therapy: Development of new treatments versus evaluation of existing treatments, *Clinical Psychology Science Practice*, 7, 113–119.

Lovell, K., Bower, P., Gellatly, J., Byford, S., Bee, P., McMillan, D., et al. (2017) Low-intensity cognitive-behaviour therapy interventions for obsessive-compulsive disorder compared to waiting list for therapist-led cognitive-behaviour therapy: 3-arm randomised controlled trial of clinical effectiveness, *PLOS Medicine*, 14, 6, e1002337. https://doi.org/10.1371/journal.pmed.1002337.

Loewenthal, K. M., Cinnirella, M., Evdoka, G., and Murphy, P. (2001) Faith conquers all? Beliefs about the role of religious factors in coping with depression among different cultural-religious groups in the UK, *British Journal of Medical Psychology*, 74, 3, 293–303.

Meyer, V., and Chesser, E. S. (1970) *Behaviour Therapy in Clinical Psychiatry (Modern Psychology)*. Harmondsworth: Penguin Books Ltd.

Mindful Muslims. *Embracing and honoring the human condition through Awareness and compassion*. http://mindfulmuslims.org/faq/ (accessed 2 June 2018)

Mohamed, N. R., Sh Elsweedy, M., Elsayed, S. M., Rajab, A. Z., Elzahar, S. T. (2015) Obsessive-compulsive disorder, an Islamic view, *Menoufia Medical Journal*, 28, 2, 289–294.

Mundy, E. A., and Hofmann, S. G. (2014) Cognitive-behavioral therapy: Next generation of treatments. *Focus*, 12, 3, 267–274. Doi:10.1176/appi.focus.12.3.267.

Muslim. Cited in Dhikr is the greatest obligation and a perpetual divine order. http://sunnah.org/ibadaat/dhikr.htm (accessed 22 March 2018).

NICE (2005) *Obsessive-Compulsive Disorder and Body Dysmorphic Disorder: Treatment* Clinical Guideline [CG31]. London: National Institute for Health and Care Excellence (NICE).

NICE (2006) *Obsessive-Compulsive Disorder: Core Interventions in the Treatment of Obsessive-Compulsive Disorder and Body Dysmorphic Disorder*. London: National Institute for Health and Clinical Excellence (NICE), The British Psychological Society & The Royal College of Psychiatrists.

NICE (2016) National Institute for Health and Care Excellence. *Depression in Adults: Recognition and Management*. www.nice.org.uk/guidance/cg90 (accessed 22 March 2018).

Okasha, A., Ragheb, K., Attia, A. H., Seif El Dawla, A., Okasha, T., and Ismail, R. (2001) Prevalence of obsessive compulsive symptoms (OCS) in a sample of Egyptian adolescents, *Encephale*, 27, 8–14.

O'Sullivan, M. J., and Lasso, B. (1992) Community mental health services for hispanics: A test of the culture compatibility hypothesis, *Hispanic Journal of Behavioral Sciences*, 14, 4, 455–468. Doi: 10.1177/07399863920144004.

Pearce, M. J., Koenig, H. G., Robins, C. J., Nelson, B., Shaw, S. F., Cohen, H. J., and King, M. B. (2015) Religiously integrated cognitive behavioral therapy: A new method of treatment for major depression in patients with chronic medical illness, *Psychotherapy (Chicago, Ill.)*, 52, 1, 56–66. http://doi.org/10.1037/a0036448.

Pietrabissa, G., Manzoni, G. M., Gibson, P., Boardman, D., Gori, A., and Castelnuovo, G. (2016) Brief strategic therapy for obsessive – compulsive disorder: A clinical and research protocol of a one-group observational study, *BMJ Open*, 6, 3, e009118. http://doi.org/10.1136/bmjopen-2015-009118.

Rassool, G. H. (2016) *Islamic Counselling: An Introduction to Theory and Practice*. Hove, East Sussex: Routledge.

Rosila, N., and Yaacob, N. (2013) Cognitive therapy approach from Islamic psycho-spiritual conception, *Procedia – Social and Behavioral Sciences*, 97, 182–187.

Saloojee, R. (2016) *Modernity, Mindfulness & Divine-Mindfulness*. http://almadinainstitute.org/blog/modernity-mindfulness-divine-mindfulness/ (accessed 22 March 2018).

Sauer-Zavala, S., Boswell, J. F., Gallagher, M. W., Bentley, K. H., Ametaj, A., and Barlow, D. H. (2012) The role of negative affectivity and negative reactivity to emotions in predicting outcomes in the unified protocol for the transdiagnostic treatment of emotional disorders, *Behaviour Research Therapy*, 50, 551–557.

Segal, Z. V., Williams, J. M. G., and Teasdale, J. D. (2013) *Mindfulness-Based Cognitive Therapy for Depression*. 2nd ed. New York: Guilford Press.

Sue, S., Zane, N., Nagayama Hall, G. C., and Berger, L. K. (2009) The case for cultural competency in psychotherapeutic interventions, *Annual Review of Psychology*, 60, 525–548. http://doi.org/10.1146/annurev.psych.60.110707.163651.

Swain, J., Hancock, K., Hainsworth, C., and Bowman, J. (2013) Acceptance and commitment therapy in the treatment of anxiety: A systematic review, *Clinical Psychology Review*, 33, 965–978.

Veale, D. (2007) Cognitive – behavioural therapy for obsessive – compulsive disorder, *Advances in Psychiatric Treatment*, 13, 6, 438–446. Doi: 10.1192/apt.bp.107.003699.

Waqar, H. (2016) *The Efficacy of Religious and Muslim Based Cognitive Behavioural Therapy*. www.14publications.com/articles/the-efficacy-of-religious-and-muslim-based-cognitive-behavioural-therapy/ (accessed 22 March 2018).

Worthington, E. L., Jr, Hook, J. N., Davis, D. E., McDaniel, M. A. (2011) Religion and spirituality, *Journal of Clinical Psychology: In Session*, 67, 204–214. Doi: 10.1002/jclp.20760.

Chapter 21

Spiritual interventions with *Waswâs al-Qahri*

Introduction

Waswâs al-Qahri is a unique disorder from other types of obsessive–compulsive disorder (OCD needs more specialised spiritual interventions in combination with Islamic-based CBT. The spiritual interventions with *Waswâs al-Qahri* are based on the teaching of the Qur'an and Sunnah. It could in the form of self-treatment or treatment by a therapist or an Imam. The spiritual interventions range from seeking refuge in Allah, supplications, *Dhikr* and *Ruqyah*. Ibn Hajar al-Haythami, when asked about a remedy for *Waswâs al-Qahri*, suggested that it is important

> to ignore them completely, no matter how frequently they may come to mind. When these whispers are ignored, they do not become established; rather they go away after a short time, as many people have experienced. But for those who pay attention to them and act upon them, they increase until they make him like one who is insane or even worse, as we see among many of those who have suffered from them and paid attention to them and to the devil whose task it is to insinuate these whispers, whom the Prophet (🕌) warned us against. . . , as was explained in Sharh Mishkaat al-Anwaar.

In general, the advice for those suffering from *Waswâs al-Qahri* should "should seek refuge with Allah and turn away from the *Waswâs*" (Islamqa, 2002a). Scholars including Al-'Izz ibn 'Abd al-Salam stated that

> the treatment for *Waswâs* is to believe that this is an idea from the *Shaytan* and that *Iblees* is the one who is bringing these thoughts to his mind, and he should strive to fight him. Then he will have the reward of the mujahid (warrior), because he is fighting the enemy of Allah. If he does that, then the *Shaytan* will flee from him. This is what mankind has been tested with from the beginning of time, and Allah has given him (*Iblees*) some power over man as a test for him, so that Allah may show the truth to be true and falsehood to be false, even though the disbelievers may hate that.

This chapter examines the different spiritual interventions that can be used to help prevent or reduce the consequences of *Waswâs al-Qahri*.

Self-treatment

There are a number of solutions in the therapeutic process to be implemented if affected by *Waswâs al-Qahri*. Allah says in the Qur'an (Interpretation of the meaning):

> *And if an evil suggestion comes to you from Satan, then seek refuge in Allah. Indeed, He is Hearing and Knowing.*
>
> (Sūrat Al-A'raf (The Elevations) 7:200)

The individual needs to say,

> *Aamantu Billaahi wa Rasoolihi* (I believe in Allah and His Messenger).

Abu Hurayrah narrated that the Prophet (ﷺ) said:

> Satan comes to one of you and says, 'Who created such and such? Who created such and such?' until he says, 'Who created your Lord?' When he reaches this far (i.e., when such a question is provoked within him), let him seek refuge with Allah and refrain from such thoughts.
>
> (Bukhari, Muslim and Abu Dâwûd)

The recommended activities in the treatment package include the above and the sufferer is encouraged to

> Try to stop thinking about that as much as possible, and keep busy with things that will distract you from it. Finally we advise you to keep on turning to Allah in all situations, and to ask Him for help, and to beseech Him, and to ask Him to make you steadfast until death, and to cause you to die doing righteous deeds.
>
> (Islamqa, 2002b)

Uthman b. Abu al-'As reported that he came to Allah's Messenger (ﷺ) and said: Allah's Messenger, the Satan intervenes between me and my prayer and my reciting of the Qur'an and he confounds me. Thereupon Allah's Messenger (ﷺ) said:

> That is (the doing of a) Satan (devil) who is known as *Khinzab*, and when you perceive its effect, seek refuge with Allah from it and spit three times to your left. I did that and Allah dispelled that from me.
>
> (Muslim)

The one who is subjected to the 'whispering devil' may also be dispelled by strengthening the connection between himself/herself and his Lord by doing acts of worship and obedience and by refraining from evil things.

Another approach is:

> to seek refuge from the Shaytan and spit drily to his left three times if the *Waswâs* of the Shaytan comes to him whilst he is praying. He is commanded to keep company with good people and avoid bad people. Whoever is negligent with regard to any of these matters will fall into the traps of his *nafs* which is inclined to evil, or will respond.
>
> (Iqrasense)

In addition, the individual must:

> strengthen his faith by doing acts of worship including reading the Qur'an and recite the *dhikrs* (words of remembrance) prescribed in Shari'ah (Islamic law), morning and evening. He must occupy himself in seeking knowledge, for although the Shaytan may gain power over a worshipper, he cannot gain power over one who has knowledge.
>
> (Iqrasense)

According to Sekandari (2017), the reduction of anxiety about the obsession (thought) would lead to a significant reduction in the obsessions and compulsions. She stated that

> When *Shaytan* is thoroughly convinced that he can no longer use such things as unwanted thoughts to annoy you, or undermine your faith, he will eventually begin to tire of that approach and only try it now and again, just to check that you have not reverted to being concerned by such attacks.

General treatment of *Waswâs al-Qahri*

Shaykh Ibn Taymiyah stated that

> Many of the scholars said [referring to *Waswâs al-Qahri*]: hating that, disliking it and shunning it is clear faith. Praise be to Allah that the most the Shaytan can do is whisper, for when the devil from the *Jinn* is defeated, it whispers (*Waswâs*) and when the human devil is defeated, he lies. *Waswâs* affects everyone who tries to focus on Allah in his worship and *dhikr* (remembrance of Allah) etc. So one has to be steadfast and patient and persist in *dhikr* or prayer; he should not feel distressed because if he persists, that will divert the plot of the Shaytan away from him, for the plot of the Shaytan is weak.

In another publication, Shaykh Ibn Taymiyah said:

> This *Waswâs* may be gotten rid of by seeking refuge with Allah and ignoring it, so that if [the Shaytan] says, 'you did not wash your face,' you should say, 'Yes, I did wash my face;' if he thinks that he did not form the intention (for prayer) or say *Allahu Akbar*, he should say in his heart, 'Yes I did form the intention and say *Allahu Akbar*.' He should cling steadfastly to the truth and ward off the *Waswâs* that goes against it, so that the Shaytan will see how strong and steadfast he is in adhering to the truth, and will leave him alone. Otherwise when he (the Shaytan) sees that he is influenced by doubts and responsive to *Waswâs*, he will send him more *Waswâs* until he will be unable to resist and his heart will become receptive to the seductive whispers of the devils of the *Jinn* and of mankind, and he will move from one thing to another until the Shaytan drives him to his doom.

The general instructions include the following:

- Remind yourself is part of trials and tribulations.
- Have complete trust (*Tawakkul*) in Allah because He is the only one who can cure you.
- Gain the right kind of knowledge. Ignorance causes misconception and knowledge removes such misconceptions.
- Seeking Allah help and beseeching Him, for He answers the one who is in distress if he calls upon Him, and grants him relief. Allah said (Interpretation of the meaning):

> *Call upon Me; I will respond to you.*
>
> (Sūrat Ghafir (The Forgiver) 40:60)

> *And [mention] Job, when he called to his Lord, "Indeed, adversity has touched me, and you are the Most Merciful of the Merciful."*
>
> (Sūrat Al-Anbiya (The Prophets) 21:83)

Narrated Abu Huraira, the Prophet (ﷺ) said:

> There is no disease that Allah has created, except that He also has created its treatment.
>
> (Bukhari)

When experiencing the recurring negative thought, the best option is not to be overwhelmed by Shaytan, turning away from *Waswâs* and get distracted from those thoughts or compulsions by keeping busy with worship and seeking refuge in Allah. Hence the Prophet (ﷺ) told the one who was affected by *Waswâs*:

> Let him seek refuge with Allah and stop (such thoughts).
>
> (Bukhari and Muslim (a))

It is stated that

> let him seek refuge with Allah and stop (such thoughts), mean that: if these whispers come to his mind, let him turn to Allah, may He be exalted, to ward off the evil thereof from him, and let him turn away from thinking about that, and let him understand that this thought is one of the whispers of the Shaytan, who is only trying to corrupt and tempt him. So let him turn away from listening to his whispers, and let him hasten to cut them off by focusing on something else. And Allah knows best.
>
> (Islamqa, 2015)

- Constantly remembering Allah and reciting Qur'an, especially *Sūrat al-Fatihah, Al-Baqarah, Al-Mu'awwidhataan*, and *Ayat al-Kursiy*.
- Specific remembrance of the morning and evening and other supplications which can be found in the Fortress of the Muslim (Al-Qahtaani, 1996).

The Prophet (ﷺ) said:

> There is no one who says in the morning of every day and the evening of every night '*Bismillah illadhi la yadurru ma'a ismihi shay'un fi'l-ard wa la fi'l-sama' wa huwa al-samee' ul-'aleem* (In the name of Allah with Whose name nothing can harm on earth or in heaven, and He is the All-Hearing, All-Knowing),' three times but nothing will harm him.
>
> (Tirmidhi and Abu Dâwûd)

As a form of protection, with regard to this *Dhikr*, it is Sunnah to say it three times every morning and evening, as the Prophet (ﷺ) taught. It is explained that the words "with Whose name nothing can harm on earth or in heaven" mean: whoever seeks refuge in the name of Allah, no calamity can harm him from the direction of the earth or from the direction of heaven. And the words "and He is the All-Hearing, All-Knowing" mean: "He hears all that people say and knows all their deeds, none of which are hidden from Him on earth or in heaven" (Islamqa, 2016). It is only by increasing performing both the mandatory and optional acts of worship that the faith will be strengthened and prevent the cursed Satan from reaching the heart. The seeker is striving to purify his heart.

- Adhere to the Sunnah of Allah and the Messenger of Allah (ﷺ).
- *Ruqyah* (see Chapter 19).
- Seek an Islamic counsellor/psychiatrist if one has implemented these for some time and is still affected.

The Prophet (ﷺ) said:

> Seek medical treatment, for Allah has not created any disease but He has also created a cure for it, except for one disease: old age.
>
> (Ibn Majah)

Conclusion

Waswâs al-Qahri is a complex psycho-spiritual disorder that requires spiritual interventions and sometimes a combination of spiritual and Islamic-based CBT. *Waswâs al-Qahri* in its severe forms may include conditions such as disturbing/blasphemous thoughts; purity/contamination related phobias (always feeling impure, countless baths); extreme guilt and uncertainty about your inner spiritual state; extreme doubts about purity or state of faith; sexual disorientation; and obscene sexual thoughts about sacred relations and personalities. Muslims suffering from *Waswâs al-Qahri* or the severe form of obsessive-compulsive disorder should be aware that they are not committing a sin. That is because the Prophet (ﷺ) said:

> Allah has forgiven for my *ummah* (followers) that which is whispered to them and which crosses their minds, so long as they do not act upon it or speak of it.
>
> (Bukhari and Muslim (b))

However, the best treatment of all the forms of *Waswâs al-Qahri* is prevention. Muslims should be fully cognisant of the preventative measures from being a victim of *Waswâs*. Ideally, the spiritual and psychological interventions for *Waswâs al-Qahri* will require an Islamic counsellor/psychotherapist and not a Muslim who happens to be a counsellor/psychotherapist/behaviourist who practices a Western-oriented model of therapy.

References

Al-'Izz ibn 'Abd al-Salam. Cited in Islamqa (2002a) 62839: Remedy for Whispers from Shaytan. https://islamqa.info/en/62839 (accessed 22 March 2018).

Al-Qahtaani, S. (1996) *Fortification of the Muslim Through Remembrance and Supplication from the Qur'an and the Sunnah*. Riyadh, Saudi Arabia: Safir Press.

Bukhari. *Sahih al-Bukhari* 5678. In-book reference: Book 76, Hadith 1. USC-MSA web (English) reference: Vol. 7, Book 71, Hadith 582.

Bukhari and Muslim (a) Cited in Islamqa (2015) 224718: Treating waswasah by seeking refuge with Allah from the Shaytan and ignoring it. https://islamqa.info/en/224718 (accessed 22 March 2018).

Bukhari and Muslim (b) Bukhari, 6664; Muslim, 127Cited Islamqa (2002) 62839: Remedy for Whispers from Shaytan. https://islamqa.info/en/62839 (accessed 22 March 2018).

Bukhari, Muslim, Abu Dâwûd. Sahih Bukhari. Book of the beginning of creation, no 3276; Muslim, Sahih, Book of Faith, no 134; Abu Dâwûd, Sunan, Al – Sunnah, no 4727.

Ibn Hajar al-Haythami Fataawa al-Fiqhiyyah al-Kubra (1/149) Cited in Islamqa (2002a) 62839: Remedy for Whispers from Shaytan, https://islamqa.info/en/62839 (accessed 22 March 2018).

Ibn Majah. English reference: Vol. 4, Book 31, Hadith 3436. Arabic reference: Book 31, Hadith 3562.

Iqrasense. *The Story of Satan (Shaitaan), his tactics, and methods to ward off his influences and whispers*. www.iqrasense.com/satan-and-evil/satan-story-shaitaan-tactics-methods-to-ward-off-influences-whispers.html (accessed 22 March 2018).

Islamqa (2002a) 62839: Remedy for Whispers from Shaytan. https://islamqa.info/en/62839 ((accessed 22 March 2018).

Islamqa (2002b) 25778: Disturbed by Waswâs (Whispers From the Shaytan) and Evil Thoughts. https://islamqa.info/en/25778 (accessed 22 March 2018).

Islamqa (2015) 224718: Treating waswasah by seeking refuge with Allah from the Shaytan and ignoring it (accessed 22 March 2018).

Islamqa (2016) 126587: *Adhkaar for morning and evening that protect against harm.* https://islamqa.info/en/126587 (accessed 22 March 2018).

Muslim. Sahih Muslim 2203.In-book reference: Book 39, Hadith 92. USC-MSA web (English) reference: Book 26, Hadith 5463.

Sekandari, N. (2017) OCD: Obsessive Compulsive Disorder and Scrupolosity in Islam. http://mentalhealth4muslims.com/ocd-obsessive-compulsive-disorder-and-scrupolosity-in-islam/ (accessed 22 March 2018).

Shaykh Ibn Taymiyah (a) Majmoo' al-Fatawa, 22/608. Cited in Islamqa (2001) 20159: Does one suffering from waswas get rewarded, and what should they do? (accessed 22 March 2018).

Shaykh Ibn Taymiyah (b) Dar al-Ta'arud, 3/318. Cited in Islamqa (2001) 20159: Does one suffering from waswas get rewarded, and what should they do? (accessed 22 March 2018).

Tirmidhi and Abu Dâwûd. Tirmidhi in *Sunan in Tirmidhi* (no. 3388), Abu Dâwûd (5088). Tirmidhi said: It is Hasan Sahih ghareeb. It was classed as *Sahih by Ibn al-Qayyim* in *Zaad al-Ma'aad* (2/338) and by al-Albani in *Sahih Abu Dâwûd.*

Chapter 22

Islamic counselling
The Dodo Bird revival

Introduction

> and he who relieved a Muslim from hardship Allah would relieve him from the
> hardships to which he would be put on the Day of Resurrection . . .
>
> (Muslim (a))

Counselling from an Islamic perspective is not a new theoretical construct and
clinical application but is alluded to in the psycho-spiritual practices of Islam.
This is a revival of Islamic counselling rather than a new development in the
sphere of the helping process. Counselling psychology has traditionally been
Eurocentric based on Judeo-Christian tradition, and this has neglected the cultural and religious context of Muslim psychological needs. In addition, there
is a lack of a spiritually oriented approach in mainstream counselling psychology. Rassool (2016) suggested that "This mono-cultural perspective often operates from the assumption that counselling and psychotherapy, conceptualised
in Western, individualistic terms, are applied to meet the needs of the Muslim
clients" (p. 14). In addition, the author argued that "Besides, individuals' perceptions and beliefs regarding health and sickness, especially mental health, are
deeply rooted in the spiritual traditions of Muslims communities" (p. 14). It is
stated that the "lack of knowledge about the beliefs and values of a religious
group that is under continuous scrutiny can be problematic within a clinical
setting, especially in light of the potential importance spirituality may have for
a client" (Haque and Kamil, 2012, p. 3).

The cultural reality of many developed countries has changed drastically in
the last five decades due to the clustering of visible minorities and newborn
Muslims. The emergence of Muslim communities are a reality and the social
and economic marginalisation and health disparity may compound the burden
of mental health problems. Muslims afflicted with evil eye, *Jinn* possession and
witchcraft may also be suffering from psychological problems, and '*Jinn*-related
illnesses' (Maarouf, 2007). There are reported cases of Muslim patients with
both *Jinn* possession and a psychiatrically diagnosed problem including anxiety

states, depression, obsessive–compulsive disorder and schizophrenia. Dein and Illaiee (2013) maintained that

> it is important to distinguish spirit possession as an altered state with the replacement of identity from psychopathological conditions that include the individual's belief that the disorder is caused by a spirit or in which beliefs about spirits are part of a larger condition.
>
> (p. 293)

Regardless whether the problem is evil eye, *Jinn* possession or witchcraft or when medical and psychiatric services become involved, an inclusive, holistic approach is good practice involving both *Ruqyah* and Islamic counselling.

It is worth pointing out that Muslim counsellors should have a proper understanding of Islamic beliefs and practices so that their approaches are free from Western-oriented and cultural conditioning in their professional training. As Badri (2015) pointed out, "the blind reception of Muslim psychologists to its theories and practices" (p. 166). This means that Muslim psychologists are following blindly the theories and practice of Western or Judeo-Christain psychology. However, there are "distinct and quantifiable differences between an Islamic counsellor/psychotherapist and the therapy he or she may practice and a Muslim who happens to be a counsellor and who practices a conventional therapy model" (Imam Hassan, 2017). The 'Lizard Hole' analogy is applicable here. Badri (2015), while presenting his paper "Muslim psychologists in the lizard's hole," at an international conference, stated that

> The way the lecture was received by Muslim psychologists astonished me. The 'lizard's hole' title comes from the famous Hadith of the Prophet (ﷺ) that prophesised that in the future, Muslims are going to blindly emulate the ways of life of the Jews and Christians. He said [the Prophet] that they will follow them even if they get themselves into a lizard's hole.
>
> (p. 167)

Counsellors should be guarded in the application of counselling models and therapeutic techniques which reflect the religio-cultural heritage that shaped Western society and do not always reflect the religious, sociocultural traditions of Muslim communities.

What is Islamic counselling?

The formal and informal literature encompassed a number of tentative explanations and definitions of Islamic counselling. In reality, many authors discussed Islamic psychology rather than Islamic counselling. Even though classified as a new phenomenon, Islamic counselling is actually as old as the beginning of spirituality in Islam. The term Islamic counselling, according to Stephen Maynard and associates (2017), "is understood to mean a way of understanding and working with human nature that is founded on profound teachings from the revelation of The Quran and Prophetic models of practice (Sunnah)." Rassool (2016) provides a comprehensive definition of Islamic counselling. It is

> a form of counselling which incorporates spirituality into the therapeutic process. Islamic counselling is a contemporary response that has much in common with other therapeutic modalities, but is based on an Islamic understanding of the nature of human beings. The goal of this type of integrative counselling is to address a variety of underlying psychological needs from a faith-based perspective.
>
> (p. 18)

Islamic counselling addresses a variety of underlying psychological and spiritual needs from a faith-based perspective and emphasises spiritual solutions in the purification of the body, soul and spirit (*Tazkiyah" an Nafs*).

When studying its historical location, Islamic counselling is in total contrast with Western-oriented counselling because it is derived from the Qur'an and Sunnah, and Islamic psychology. Allah says in the Qur'an (Interpretation of the meaning):

> *Help you one another in virtue, righteousness and piety; but do not help one another in sin and transgression.*
>
> (Sūrat Al Ma'idah (The Table) 5:2)

In the preceding verse of the Qur'an, Allah commands His believing servants to help one another perform righteous, good deeds and to avoid sins. That is, one should consult his fellows, advise them and cooperate with them. In addition, there is a need to help and support one another, whether he was unjust or the victim of injustice. So, helping and doing good to others is part of the process. The Messenger of Allah (ﷺ) said to provide general counselling and marital counselling on a regular basis to couples. According to Khan, Prophet Muhammad (ﷺ) used the 'Therapeutic Triad' of empathy, positive regard and genuineness dealing with others. This approach in dealing with people was way ahead of Rogers and others in the advocacy in the use of empathy in effective counselling.

On the authority of Abu Ruqayyah Tameem ibn Aus (May Allah be pleased with him) the Prophet (ﷺ) said,

> The religion is *Naseehah*. (Sincere advice) The people said, 'To whom?' The Prophet replied, 'To Allah and His Book and to His Messenger and to the Leaders of the Muslims and to the common folk of the Muslims.'
>
> (Muslim (b))

Giving *Naseehah* involves facilitating Muslims in the counselling relationship in protecting them from harm, helping them in times of need, providing what is beneficial for them, encouraging them to do good and forbidding them from evil with kindness and sincerity, and showing mercy towards them.

In this context, Islamic counselling is fundamentally a religious and moral undertaking. Even the mainstream counselling has a moral responsibility implicitly or explicitly but this may not be deeply rooted in the conscious of the counsellor or psychotherapists (Bergin, 1980; Grant, 1992; Jafari, 1998). The differences between counselling and Islamic counselling are presented in Table 22.1. The contrast is made on the basis of focus, purpose, process and intervention strategies; religious relationship; the sources of knowledge; what causes illness and maintains sound mental health and responses to illness; and the values, growth and development of both types of counselling.

Table 22.1 Differences between counselling and Islamic counselling

	Counselling (mainstream)	Islamic counselling
Orientation	Judeo-Christian	Islamic
Religious relationship	Oppositional. Secular	Integrated
Sources of knowledge	Man-made theories: Empirical. Androgenic. Eurocentric.	Divine revelation (Qur'an) and Sunnah
What causes illness?	Bio-psychosocial factors	Bio-psychosocial + spiritual factors
Sound mental health	No divine intervention	Submission to God Integration of material and spiritual life
Values	Materialistic Socio-moral value structure Value laden and dependent	God consciousness Spiritual-Divine Will Islamic values and morality
Growth and development	Psychosocial development and spiritual (not religious)	Religious, spiritual and psychosocial development
Focus	Limited focus on the physical world	Disregard for spiritual aspects of human beings. Seen and Unseen world
Purpose	Promotes personal growth/self-understanding/self-actualisation	Promotes the clear purpose and meaning of life
Process	Individual-based and individual-focused	Mutual responsibility Collectivistic Social obligation Healthy altruism
Responses to illness	Psychological reactions	Spiritual reactions: patience and prayers

	Counselling (mainstream)	Islamic counselling
Relationship between mind and body	Mind-body interaction	Mind-body-soul interaction
Personal development	Unlimited freedom	Bonded freedom
Intervention strategies	Based on Humanistic, cognitive behavioural and psychoanalytical interventions	Based on Humanistic, cognitive behavioural and spiritual interventions
Dream technique	Dream work – Freudian's analysis	Use of dreams – dream analysis according to Prophetic tradition
Undesired (negative) behaviour	Rationalisation	Therapy of repentance (Taubah)

Source: Adapted from Rassool, G. Hussein (2016) *Islamic Counselling: An Introduction to Theory and Practice*, Hove, East Sussex: Routledge.

From a Western androcentric and Eurocentric approach, Islamic counselling would not 'constitute' formal counselling but holds the same therapeutic value as mainstream counselling approaches. Rassool (2016) maintained that "the application of theories, concepts and intervention strategies from mainstream counselling outside the *Tawheed* paradigm is therefore rejected" (p. 18). However, this may be regarded as the '*Dodo Bird Conjecture*' (Rosenzweig, 1936), which refers to the claim that all counselling or psychotherapies, regardless of their specific components, produce corresponding and equal outcomes. The aims of Islamic counselling include:

> addressing a variety of underlying psychosocial and spiritual needs from a faith-based perspective; changing or reframing the negative behaviours of the individual for his own benefits and the community; to instil Islamic values; to enable the client to reflect on the relationships the Creator.
>
> (Rassool, 2016, p. 18)

Islamic counselling practice model

Rassool's Islamic counselling practice model (2016) is a tool for the counselling process rather than a rigid template for counselling practice. The Islamic counselling practice model is presented in Figure 22.1. This 10-stage model has been conceptualised for a variety of problem behaviours and intervention strategies.

The proposed model consists of selected concepts (Al-Jawziyyah, n.d.) and is based on Stage of awakening (*Qawmah*) and intention (*Niyyat*); Stage of consultation (*Istisharah*); Stage of contemplation (*Tafakkur*); Stage of guidance-seeking (*Istikhaarah*); Stage of wilful decision ('*Azm*); Stage of goal-and-route vision (*Basirah*); Stage of absolute trust in God (*Al-Tawakkul -Allah*); Stage of action ('*Amal*); Stage of help-seeking (*Isti'aanah*); Stage of self-monitoring

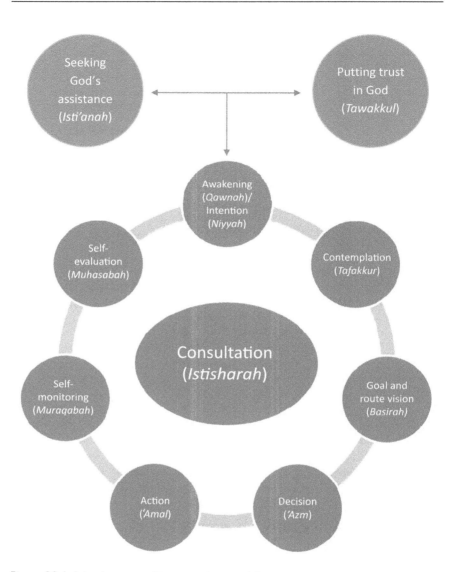

Figure 22.1 Islamic counselling practice model

Source: Rassool, G.Hussein (2016) *Islamic Counselling: An Introduction to Theory and Practice.*
Hove, East Sussex: Routledge, p. 216 [Reproduced with kind permission from Routledge].

(*Muraqabah*); and Stage of evaluation (*Muhasabah*). The Islamic counselling
practice model is a circular (or spiral) rather than a linear model. Generally, it
is assumed that when one stage was completed, a client would move into the
next stage. While that is a possibility, it is more likely that client may go through

several cycles of awakening (*Qawnah*) contemplation (*Tafakkur*), goal and route vision (*Basirah*) before either reaching the action (*'Amal*) or exiting the system without the attainment of the desired and permissible goals The stages are not clearly delineated, and many stages must be re-experienced, or readjusted partly or completely and the client passes through the counselling process and enters and exits at any stage and often recycles several times.

One of the Islamic counselling practice model's major benefits is that it is flexible enough to enable counsellors to meet the diversity of Muslim cultures. However, the practice model is based on the assumption that the client is a Muslim as this model is slanted toward an Islamic theological perspective and practice model orientation. Barise (2005) maintained that counsellors must be aware of, and respect the different levels of religiosity within the Muslim community and the clients must be allowed to choose the extent to which they want to adhere to this model. In this context, counsellors could help their clients who are working on religious issues feel as though their religious values are an accepted part of the counselling process and therefore an important part of the solution to the problems as well (Podikunju-Hussain, 2006). The proposed practice model is also appropriate for those clients who are not motivated to change because it is adaptable to the client's set of psychosocial and spiritual needs. The proposed model allows the involvement of family members as it also critically important for counsellors to become familiar with the cultural expectations of the broader family (Springer et al., 2009). The involvement of the family in the counselling process would enable the family member(s) to understand what the client is experiencing, resulting in better psychosocial and spiritual support for the client.

A concept selected for inclusion in the Islamic counselling practice model is: Contract (*Musharata*) (Al-Ghazali, 1853/1986). This contract, in the context of the proposed model, is twofold. A personal contract made towards the meeting of identified goals. The identified goals, the target of therapy, are negotiated between the counsellor and the client during the stage of contemplation (*Tafakku*r), of the counselling process (see below). In addition, a professional contract or mutual agreement is also negotiated between the counsellor and the client. The professional contract articulates the responsibilities of the counsellor and client in the context of the therapeutic relationship and counselling process. The contract may include issues of code of ethics, confidentiality, boundaries, duration of counselling sessions, fees (if appropriate), cancellation of sessions, freely given consent to this contract, records and termination of contract. This contract is endorsed by both the client and the counsellor.

Counselling the Muslim patient

In contrast to Western counselling psychotherapy, Islamic counselling use a more direct approach as most Muslims come to clinicians seeking advice or an offering of an approach to deal with their issues (Abdullah, 2007). In this counselling paradigm, the counsellor has multiple roles including counsellor and spiritual facilitator. An Islamic counsellor

> must also deal with gender-preference, different worldview from the patient, self-disclosure about sensitive issues, expressing negative thoughts or emotions towards one's family, the agreement on protection of information from the family, and inappropriate therapy or psychotherapeutic practices not congruent with Islamic practices.
>
> (Rassool, 2015, p. 323)

Spirituality in counselling is a pivotal component of the therapeutic process in Islamic counselling. Spiritual or religious-based counselling, meditation and forgiveness protocols may improve spirituality-based beliefs, practices and coping strategies in positive ways (Johnstone, 2012).

From a counsellor's standpoint, understanding clients' spirituality is quite significant as it is integral to the client bio-psychosocial, emotional and spiritual needs. Counselling Muslim patients must incorporate the statement of Islamic beliefs and practices including the concept of monotheism (*Tawheed*); the principles of faith; dignity and morality; remembrance of Allah, supplications, understanding that the world is unavoidably a temporal world; focusing on the next life and the dangers of attaching yourself to the temporary world; the roles of trials and tribulations in a Muslim journey in life; trusting; and focusing on the blessings of Allah. The worldview of Muslim patients towards health and illness incorporates the notion that health and illness become part of the continuum of being, and religious beliefs remain the salvation in both health and in sickness. This spiritual guidance may lead to positive coping strategies as Muslims typically find comfort in their religious or spiritual beliefs and practices whether there is the presence or absence of crisis. It is part of the role of the Islamic counsellor to facilitate this process by creating a setting of openness, trust and respect for client spiritual expression.

There are many approaches to counselling including the psychodynamic, client-centred, cognitive behavioural therapy, solution-focused therapy, premarital and marital counselling. A brief summary of the limitations of their use in Islamic counselling is presented here. In relation to the psychodynamic approach, Rassool (2016) stated that the psychodynamic approach to therapy and counselling is not congruent with Islamic principles. The opposition to this mode of therapy is based on incongruence of the conceptual framework on the secular notion on human nature and modalities of the psychoanalytical school with Islamic values and practices. A few of the techniques of Freud's psychodynamic approach are relevant in the Islamic context without subscribing to the secular views of the approach. This includes dream interpretation and analysis, which is valid in Islam but based on different principles. From an Islamic perspective, dreams may be interpreted in the light of the Qur'an or the Sunnah.

Client-centred therapy is more inclined to fit in the Islamic paradigm than the psychodynamic approach. However, the framework of client-centred counselling in its purest form is not fully congruent with Islamic principles and practice. From an Islamic perspective, the main concern about using the person-centred approach is the lack of direction in its egalitarian counsellor-client relationship style, and its dependence on the counsellor's personal qualities of genuineness, unconditional positive regard and empathy in facilitating the client's process of personal growth (Mohamad et al., 2011). A modified client-centred counselling approach is needed to accommodate the worldview of Muslim clients. A summary of the adapted client-centred counselling that conforms to Islamic principles to help Muslims with life and psychosocial problems is provided by Rassool (2016). For example, the counsellor needs to have a deep understanding of the religious (and cultural) background of the Muslim client, but to be aware that different clients have different levels of religious understanding. Having trust in Allah (*Tawakkul*) is one of the Islamic 'core conditions'; showing gratitude to Allah when there is improvement in the client's state or circumstances (core condition, if appropriate); understanding the worldview of the Muslim client; encourages the Muslim client to follow the Qur'an and the teachings of Prophet Mohammad (ﷺ). The use of directive and non-directive approach (psychological and spiritual direction; guiding and advising; making suggestions, disclosing thoughts and feelings); and the use of spiritual interventions; and religious support should also be applied when working with Muslim clients (p. 133).

The underlying principles on which cognitive therapy rests are congruent with Islamic values. Rassool (2016) stated that "It is the nature and the methodology in which cognitive therapy is operationalised in the Western counselling paradigm that creates the dissonance" (p. 146). Islamic counsellors need to use a spiritually modified cognitive therapy model. This has been examined in Chapter 20. However, some of the current Islamically assisted cognitive therapy models used require further refinement backed by evidence-based research. The solution-focused brief therapy model of counselling is permeated with values and indicators that are mostly congruent with Islamic beliefs. This approach mirrors the optimistic, action-oriented and practical Islamic beliefs. Rassool (2016) suggested that solution-focused brief therapy "is different from traditional modes of counselling and psychotherapy due to its emphasis on minimal self-disclosure, focusing on competencies, rather than pathology or problems and that each individual can solve their own problems" (p. 158). With some basic modifications and the integration of religious or spiritual interventions, solution-focused brief therapy model would be an appropriate psychological intervention for Muslim clients. In Islamic-oriented marital counselling, counsellors would utilise the mainstream approaches and techniques of the congruent therapies with Islamic beliefs and practices (see Rassool, 2016). The stages of Rassool's Islamic counselling practice model, the process and counselling intervention strategies are presented in Table 22.2.

Table 22.2 Stages of Rassool's Islamic counselling practice model

Stages	Process	Intervention strategies
Awakening (*Qawmah*) Intention (*Niyyat*)	*Qawmah* is often what brings the client to seek professional help. Assessment of the patient's readiness to change. Pre-contemplation. Behavioural intention: "Surely, all actions are but driven by intentions."[1]	Support, counselling, motivational interviewing and cognitive behavioural therapies.
Consultation (*Istisharah*)	*Istisharah* (consultation) is the process of collecting relevant information about the client's past and presenting problems. The counsellor consults all appropriate sources of information, starting with the client, the family or significant others.	Assessment process.
Contemplation (*Tafakkur*)	Analysing the 'issues or problems,' set realistic goals, and tentatively identify appropriate intervention strategies.	Contemplation or reflection. Engagement of client in the process.
Guidance-seeking (*Istikhaarah*)	Seeking guidance from Allah, the Almighty before decision-making.	Perform a specific prayer for guidance (*Salat-I-Istikhaarah*).
Goal-and-routevision (*Basirah*)	Compliant with the goals and action strategies.	Clarification of the goals and actions of the road map.
Willful decision ('*Azm*)	Preparation stage. Readiness to change period.	Counsellor facilitates or enables the client to make a decision for action. Enhance self-esteem and self-efficacy.
Absolute trust in God (*Al-Tawakkul -Allah*)	*Tawakkul* is a fundamental part of the Islamic creed and is translated as either a trust or being dependent. Putting our trust in God is a matter of belief and contributes to our view regarding this life.	Contemplation or reflection. Continuously used throughout the different stages of the counselling process.

Stages	Process	Intervention strategies
Action ('*Amal*)	Process involves intention and execution of the action plan.	Reinforcement and support.
Help-seeking (*Isti'aanah*)	And seek help through patience and prayer, and indeed, it is difficult except for the humbly submissive [to Allah].[2] O you who have believed, seek help through patience and prayer. Indeed, Allah is with the patient.[3]	Prayers and supplications.
Self-monitoring (*Muraqabah*)	Self-monitoring has been used in the counselling process both as an intervention strategy and as a way to collect data to evaluate the effectiveness of the intervention.	Observing and recording one's behaviours, thoughts and feelings may lead to behaviour change.
Evaluation (*Muhasabah*)	*Muhasabah* or evaluation is the last process in the Islamic counselling practice work model. Evaluation in counselling is essential in order to assess whether the counselling was helpful, there was a decrease of symptoms in clients, whether clients have improved or gained coping skills and the realisation of the desired changes.	Evaluation.

[1]   An important saying of the Prophet Muhammad (PBUH) is that: "Surely, all actions are but driven by intentions" (Bukhari and Muslim).
[2]   Al-Baqarah (The Cow) 2:45).
[3]   Al-Baqarah (The Cow) 2:153).

Conclusion

Islamic counselling should actually be seen from a broader perspective so that it covers the provision of health information, advice, therapy, guidance and counselling, advocacy and spiritual interventions. In Islamic counselling, the spiritual dimension cannot be detached from the therapeutic process. It has been suggested that if a psychologist starts with a model of psychology based on secular presuppositions, it is impossible to subsequently view religious belief or practice in a healthy light (Priester et al., 2008). Some of the techniques of the different approaches of counselling and psychotherapy which seemed to be valuable and effective with Muslim clients need further investigations for evidenced-based clinical practice.

References

Abdullah, S. (2007) Islam and counseling: Models of practice in Muslim communal life, *Journal of Pastoral Counseling*, 42, 42–55.

Al-Ghazali, Abu Hamid bin Muhammad (1853/1986) *Revival of Religious Learning* (trans. F. Karim). New Delhi: Kitab Bhavan (Original work published 1853).

Badri, M. (2015) Cited in Khan, R. K. A. W. (2015) An interview with Professor Malik Badri about his contributions to the Islamisation of psychology, *Intellectual Discourse*, 23, 1, 159–172.

Barise, A. (2005) *Social Work with Muslims: Insights from the Teachings of Islam*. http://www1. uwindsor.ca/criticalsocialwork/social-work-with-muslims-insights-from-the-teachings-of-islam (accessed 3 June 2018).

Bergin, A. E. (1980) Psychotherapy and religious values, *Journal of Consulting and Clinical Psychology*, 48, 1, 95–105. http://dx.doi.org/10.1037/0022-006X.48.1.95.

Dein, S., and Illaiee, A. S. (2013) Jinn and mental health: looking at jinn possession in modern psychiatric practice, *The Psychiatrist*, 37, 290–293. Doi: 10.1192/pb.bp.113.042721.

Grant, B. (1992) *The Moral Nature of Psychotherapy and Spiritual Values in Counseling*, in Burke Thomas and 1. G. Miranti (Eds.), *Ethical and Spiritual Values in Counseling*. Alexandria, VA: ASERVIC, pp. 34–41. https://files.eric.ed.gov/fulltext/ED340989.pdf.

Haque, A., and Kamil, N. (2012) Islam, Muslims, and Mental Health, in S Ahmed, and M Amer (Eds), *Counseling Muslims: Handbook of Mental Health Issues and Interventions*. New York: Routledge.

Hassan, A. (2017) Personal communication.

Jafari, M. F. (1998) Moral and spiritual aspects of counseling: Recent developments in the west, *Intellectual Discourse*, 6, 2, 137–157.

Johnstone, B., Yoon, D. P., Cohen, D., Schopp, L. H., McCormack, G., Campbell, J., and Smith, M. (2012) Relationships among spirituality, religious practices, personality factors, and health for five different faith traditions, *Journal of Religious Health*, 51, 4, 1017–1041. Doi: 10.1007/s10943-012-9615-8.

Maarouf, M. (2007) *Jinn Eviction as a Discourse of Power a Multidisciplinary Approach to Moroccan Magical Beliefs and Practices*. Leiden: Brill.

Mohamad, M., Mokhtar, H. H., and Abu Sama, A. (2011) Person-centered counseling with Malay clients: Spirituality as an indicator of personal growth. *Procedia – Social and Behavioral Sciences*, 30, 2117–2123. doi:10.1016/j.sbspro.2011.10.411

Muslim (a) English reference: Book 16, Hadith 1508, Arabic reference: Book 16, Hadith 1465.

Muslim (b) *An-Nawawi Forty Hadith*. Hadith 7. http://ahadith.co.uk/downloads/Commentary_of_Forty_Hadiths_of_An-Nawawi.pdf (accessed 23 March 2018).

Podikunju-Hussain, S. (2006) Working with Muslims: Perspectives and suggestions for counseling, in G. R. Walz, J. Bleuer and R. K. Yep (Eds.) *VISTAS Multicultural Issues in Counseling*. Alexandria, VA: American Counselling Association, pp. 103–106.

Priester, P. E., Khalili, S., and Eluvathingal, E. L. (2008) Putting the Soul Back into Psychology: Integrating Religion in Psychotherapy, in S. Eshun, and R. Gurung (Eds.), *Sociocultural Influences on Mental Health*. Boston: Blackwell, pp. 91–114.

Rassool, G. H. (2015) Cultural competence in counseling the Muslim Patient: Implications for mental health, *Archives of Psychiatric Nursing*, 29, 5, 321–325. Doi: 10.1016/j. apnu.2015.05.009. Epub 2015 Jun 11.

Rassool, G. H. (2016) *Islamic Counselling: An Introduction to Theory and Practice*. Hove, East Sussex: Routledge.

Rosenzweig, S. (1936) Some implicit common factors in diverse methods of psychotherapy, *American Journal of Orthopsychiatry*, 6, 3, 412–415.

Stephen Maynard & Associates (2017) *Therapeutic Islamic Counselling*. https://s3-eu-west-1.amazonaws.com/logs.omnibuilder/6a58d712-583c-445b-b925-ea1c6e3415ba/9868293f-c28b-48af-9f5f-72c46206c67f.pdf (accessed 23 March 2018).

Springer, P., Abott, D. A., and Reisbig, A.M.J. (2009). Therapy with Muslim Couples and Families: Basic Guidelines for Effective Practice, Faculty Publications from CYFS, Paper 7. http://digitalcommons.unl.edu/cgi/viewcontent.cgi?article=1006&context=cyfsfacpub (accessed 3 June 2018).

Chapter 23

Case reports of evil eye, *Jinn* possession and witchcraft

Introduction

This chapter presents a number of case reports from the diverse Muslim communities in the world. This collection of case reports includes categories according to the presentation of symptoms of evil eye, *Jinn* possession, magic/witchcraft and obsessive-compulsive disorder (OCD) and satanic whisperings (*Waswâs al-Qahri*). Some of the cases included are from clinical experiences and others are compiled from other sources. The sources of the case reports are indicated as appropriate. In the case reports where there are clear diagnosis of evil eye, *Jinn* possession and witchcraft, there is evidence of no medical or environmental cause identified, not responding to medical or psychiatric treatment and the symptoms are persistent and/or increasing in intensity. In most of the cases reported, the individuals are treated with spiritual interventions. Some cases are fundamentally psychological in nature and are treated effectively by both pharmacological and psychosocial interventions.

Case reports [CR]: evil eye

For cases of evil eye, individuals seldom use the mental health and counselling services and it is rare to see these cases in clinical practice. However, it has been established that physical problems, mental and emotional distress can be caused by the evil eye. The misfortune of the victim may manifest as sickness, loss of wealth or family, or a streak of problems in relationships and work. The person inflicting the evil eye may do so with or without intention. However, there is a danger for Muslims to blame every trivial thing that goes 'wrong' in their lives to the evil eye. Having obsessive thoughts or becoming paranoid about the evil eye in itself can become pathological (*Waswâs al-Qahri*). Some of the indications of evil eye that have no evidence of organic or medical origin include constant headache, constant yawning, itching;

burping; hot and cold flashes; constantly sneezing; the appearance of spots and boils on the body; bruising in the body is another sign for no reason; darkness underneath the eyes; despair and fear; and tightness of the chest.

[CR1] If a person looks at something he has with admiration and he does not pray for barakah (blessing) for it, by saying "*Baarik Allaahu fihi* (May Allaah bless it)" and the like, and this thing is then affected in some way, then it is possible to know that he has inflicted *Hasad* on himself (Islamqa (2010).

Case reports [CR]: *Jinn* possession

[CR1] This is a case of a 23-year-old man who presented with a history of episodes of panic attacks and displayed bizarre behaviour. He reported having a lot of disturbing dreams and kept away from people and social interaction. Once or twice a week, he would binge drink alcohol and was amnesic about the whole episodes. During his period of intoxication, he would be aggressive and at times violent towards his family. There is no physical or psychological explanation of his behaviour. He would 'speak in tongues' or having fainting or seizures when the Qur'an is read over him. The family members took him to a faith healer who performed *Ruqyah* and subsequently he showed no signs of panic attacks.

Comments

The pharmacological interventions include the prescription of anti-anxiety medication on a short-term basis complemented with *Ruqyah* and Islamic counselling.

[CR2] Mrs Amin, 36-year-old married teacher, was admitted to a local hospital following episodes of severe neglect, apathy and abnormal, disinhibited behaviour, low mood and delusional ideas. She has previously been given a diagnosis of schizophrenia but had not taken any of her regular neuroleptic medications for a few months. During her brief admission, she repeatedly expressed the belief that she was possessed by *Jinn*, having thought insertion and claimed to have supernatural power to heal. Her extended family, however, thought that she was possessed by *Jinn* and discharged her from the psychiatric unit, against medical advice. She was taken to a local faith healer, who reinforced their views and treated her in the traditional African way. However, her condition deteriorated over the next few weeks and she was readmitted to hospital.

Comments

It is debatable whether this lady did in fact have *Jinn* possession or whether she was a highly suggestible person with a possible dissociative state. However, it is clear that her lapse and relapse are due to her not adhering to her course of psychotropic medications. The complaining of hearing voices or thought insertion did not disappear after having traditional healing treatment from the faith healer. In fact, her conditions became unmanageable after seeing the traditional faith healer.

[CR3] Khalifa and Hardie (2005) reported the case of a 28-year-old woman with no previous psychiatric history who gradually became uncommunicative, withdrew from other people, and stopped eating and drinking. No underlying organic disorders were established and she was diagnosed with severe depressive illness. She underwent electro-convulsive therapy without much improvement. Her family, believing her to be possessed by *Jinn*, took her to a local faith healer.

Comments

She was treated with *Ruqyah* and after a few sessions of spiritual treatments her condition improved and she returned to her baseline behaviour. She reported being in total "amnesic" of the episode and had no explanation for what had happened to hear.

[CR5] Bragazzi and Del Puente (2012) presented a case of a 19-year-old suffering from anxiety disorder and panic attacks. Her fears were being possessed by the *Jinn* and she reported seeing *Jinn* on several occasions and had the avoidance behaviour of dark and lonely places. She reported that her mother and grandfather have suffered from demonic possession.

Comments

The pharmacological interventions include the prescription of SSRI (fluoxetine), complemented with Islamic counselling. The Imam involved in the Islamic counselling helped in reframing and restructuring her beliefs and thoughts. After a year of follow-up, she reported no episodes of panic disorder.

[CR5] Hanwella et al. (2012) reported of a 21-year-old single unemployed female who had contact with psychiatric services when she started developing possession states. At the beginning these occurred about once a day but increased in frequency to 4–5 times a day during the last month. Her symptoms, while being possessed, included eyes opened wide, stretching out her hands, and screaming loudly in anger. This episode lasted for about 10 minutes. Both the patient and the family believe that she was possessed by *Jinn*. She was given a differential diagnosis of epilepsy because of the episodic nature of the disorder. She dropped out from psychiatric services after the initial contact and sought treatment from a traditional healer.

Comments

The patient was treated by a traditional healer. She returned for a follow-up visit and had not experienced possession states for three months.

Jinn possession and witchcraft

[CR1] This 30-year-old man married with two young children presented with symptoms of depression, withdrawal and poor sleep patterns. His wife reported that he is hostile and suspicious and expressed extreme reaction to criticism. Small irrelevant matters started to make him react angrily and significantly affected the marital relationship. In addition, he burst into inappropriate laughter or crying. He is forgetful, has the inability to concentrate on basic activities. He has deterioration of personal hygiene. His speech is disorganised and incoherent at times and suffers from hallucinations. He suffered a lot of disturbing dreams and nightmares. He seemed to turn away and react strongly when hearing the adhan (call to prayer) or Qur'an. He was seen by a medical practitioner who prescribed anti-psychotic medications. His condition deteriorated.

Comments

Subsequently he was taken to see a faith healer who confirmed a diagnosis of *Jinn* possession and witchcraft. He was treated with *Ruqyah*.

Epilepsy-*Jinn* possession

[CR1] This adapted case report from Shaykh Abdullaah Mushrif al-'Amree (cited in Philips, 2008). A 28-year-old woman complained of having epileptic seizures from time to time over a period of two years and sometimes she would lose consciousness. She was prescribed anti-convulsant medications (by injections). She still had very intense seizures and her family brought her to a faith healer. The family reported that the hospital informed them that she suffered psychological problems.

Comments

When *Ruqyah* was performed, it was obvious that she was possessed, and the cause was from magic. The *Jinn* in her was a Buddhist. She did not respond immediately after recitation, but subsequently, the *Jinn* presented himself and informed us about the magician who put the spell on her and the charm's location.

[CR2] This 14-year-old boy presented with no psychiatric symptoms or any other supernatural symptoms. However, his parents reported bouts of seizures on a regular basis. After the epileptic episodes, he became hyperactive, irritable, aggressive and potentially violent. At times, he started to self-harm with cuts on his forearms. During his normal/ baseline behaviour he is an outgoing, optimistic young man with good composure. There is not a hint of aggression in his tone of voice and behaviour. He has seen many doctors and has been prescribed anti-epileptic medications. He had a MRI brain scan and there is no evidence of cranial abnormality.

Comments

I only had one session with this young man who was accompanied by his parents. I recommended that the parents take him to an Imam or faith healer for *Ruqyah* (despite no clear signs of *Jinn* possession). Since the session, I have not had any communication from his parents. This case is not clear cut as his behaviour may be due to the epileptiform discharges that may have affected his behaviour or induced aggression.

Jinn possession and Sihr (magic of separation)

This case report is taken from Sheikh Wahid Ibn Abdussalam Bali (2004) 'Sword Against Black Magic & Evil Magicians' where there are other case reports on the magic of separation examples of cases.

[CR1] A man brought his wife for treatment and said that his wife hated him very much and felt relaxed at home, during his absence. When I asked a few questions, it appeared to me, from the symptoms that she suffered from Sihr of Separation. After reciting the Ruqyah, a Jinn spoke in her person.

Comments

This is a case where the Jinn is trying to cause enmity between husband and wife and breaking a marriage. This is regarded as 'Sihr of Separation.' The woman was treated with spiritual interventions, including Ruqyah.

Case reports [CR]: black magic or witchcraft

[CR1] This young lady of 20 years old, attending university, complained of the following symptoms: anxiety, sensitive, feeling of suspiciousness, suicidal thoughts, gastro-intestinal problems, antagonism with peers and extended family, loneliness, academic performance deteriorated, changes in personality, bodily pains. There were drastic changes from baseline behaviour and there no insight into the present 'illness.' No organic or medical causes could explain her physical and psychological problems. However, there was a behavioural reactions when attempting to recite the Qur'an.

Comments

The young girl was treated with spiritual interventions (Ruqyah).

Case reports [CR]: evil eye, Jinn possession, black magic or witchcraft

Here we present a case report which exemplifies the relation between Jinn possession and black magic or witchcraft. Details have been changed to preserve anonymity. I have included a summary of her story verbatim to illustrate the complexities of the case.

My problem started when I was 22 years of age. We moved house to a more remote part of the city. When I first moved in that house I used to feel like I was being watched. As a Muslim, I thought we were protected just by reciting the Qur'an and praying regularly. Both my mother and sister reported about feeling some air push them around in the kitchen and my mother used to feel depressed and always fight with my brother. My shoes were also being hidden but when I searched for it in a place I already searched it was in plain sight. Obviously the *Jinn* were hiding it and playing trick on my mind.

I used to isolate myself, never go out with my family outside and sleep alone in the dark. I did not know that the room was haunted at all. One night, my brother came to me and telling that my sister in law was acting uncharacteristically and laughing a lot. He felt that this behaviour was not really her and that it was someone else entirely. As Muslims we know about the reality of the unseen so I wondered about that. Still I slept alone and was often woken up at midnight. I did not know what woke me up so I slept again. But one night I just could feel something touching me (tactile hallucination). I never encountered such a thing in my whole life so I was scared and started sleeping with my mother. I was not reciting daily *adhkar* (remembrance of Allah). In addition, I was not leading a highly religious lifestyle. Then my brother told me about an online university offering Islamic studies course, I decided to become more religious with the right kind of knowledge.

For my case we went to many raaqis (*Ruqyah* practitioners). But when one raaqi recited [the Qur'an] on me, the *Jinn* in my cousin spoke up and she does not remember anything now. She was just not herself and it was something else entirely, a female mischief *Jinni*. The raaqi recited and she left. She has not had any such problems anymore. For me however, it just took more recitations and use of honey, olive oil and *Ruqyah* etc. for the *Jinn* to finally speak up. One *molvi* [title given to an a learned Muslim person in India]. The *molvi* gave us Qur'anic amulet (only Qur'an was there) but even then my brother told me to take it off so I repented from it.

My dad found out that there was a crippled person from Lucknow [India] who claimed he used good *Jinn* (and we didn't know about it being out of Sunnah). We were desperate and payed a huge sum. The

Jinn spoke and I was in mixed consciousness state. I knew what was going around me but I was aware it was not me doing the talk. He said [the *Jinn*] he was in love with me etc. He tortured it but by this point, my condition was worsening and my brother was concerned about the *Aqeedah* [In Islam, *Aqeedah* is the matter of knowledge. The Muslim must believe in his heart and have faith and conviction, with no doubts or misgivings, because Allah has told him about *Aqeedah* in His Book and via His Revelations to His Messenger]. So a scholar from Madinah (City of Madinah, Saudi Arabia) claimed he would expel it in the name of *Tawheed* [principle of the unicity of God] without relying on *Jinn* and (perhaps sacrifice). I think the guy may have been a magician because he told us to not say anything to the government because the Saudi government would execute him. He had a family so we remained silent and did not ask for refund, just cut off the communication and never went back. This new raaqi now did things I can't mention here. He exploited me in the typical ways what some women have also undergone by fake raaqis who take advantage of those under the trance. He convinced my father not to accompany me etc. Alhumdulillah I was in part my senses and complained my parents and I was able to cut off ties with him too. There was a government Saudi Sheikh who gave me those Arabic stuff like Prophetic *adhkar*, honey, olive oil, holy water (*nushrah*). However, many Saudi women are afflicted by situation worse than mine so he did not have enough time to do complete day to day recitation. A Bangladeshi guy said it is too late for me now, the *Jinn* is already stubborn and the ways which they use to torture the *Jinn* is bannable when done by foreigners.

Again I went to another Saudi sheikh and this guy is pretty famous. He told me I am able to recite *Ruqyah* on myself and I am stronger than I think. He told me if I act under the influence then my parents would be worried about me. He threatened to beat me with a stick if I say it's a *Jinn* because we can't see it. Perhaps he thought I wasn't possessed because many raaqis had already recited on me and the *Jinn* was hiding outside only to return again once I returned home. He told me to consult a psychiatrist and get medicated. I did. The EEG [Electro encephalograph] scan showing I was not epileptic. I gained a lot of weight by the anti-psychotics [medications]. I didn't get better. I didn't know that I was a *Jinn* case or not and kept taking them. Then someone advised me to wean off them and become mentally stronger. By not relying on medicine I should fight the *Jinn* myself, become more spiritual instead of becoming lazy etc. When I was medicated I had a lot of side effects called EPS (Tardive dyskinesia-Parkinson like symptoms). I was placed in emergency twice because of harsh drugs like Risperidone and Haldol. Zyprexa suited me along with Venlafaxine.

I was diagnosed with depression and anxiety and mixed depression at two separate hospitals.

I believe I wasn't depressed but the hallucinations caused me to lose hope in ever getting married because of the stigma that possessed people shouldn't get married and even their kids turn out like that. In arranged marriage cultures this is seen as something worth avoiding, but with the university education I was growing stronger Islamically as my iman (faith) increased and I got less scared.

I changed all old habits and lost many friends along the way. People were scared of me. So I began speaking less and alienated myself from old friends. I had social support from my university's friends however. They never abandoned me and kept encouraging me. They said they have never heard of such cases but one senior tutor told me that Shaytan is fighting back even more because I am acquiring more religious knowledge instead of the devious things it was teaching me to do, hanging out in heedless company like before. Around this time I was diagnosed with PCOS a hormonal problem [polycystic ovary syndrome is a problem in which a woman's hormones are out of balance].

I can't see the *Jinn* in reality but I can definitely encounter it in my dreams. I know the hallucination is very real and my family believes in it too. My extended family back home [In India] were also possessed but they got better with time. I think it runs in my family as in Bengal is where I come from and there are a lot of such cases there.

Around [the year] 2015, I was diagnosed as bipolar because of an incident that happened at India that made me rethink about getting back to medication [Psychotropic]. This time I was given Kemadrin which removed the EPs side effects [Extra pyramidal] so I could take Risperidone again along with Zyprexa and Solian (Amisulpride). For months I was doing fine emotionally but the *Jinn* was still there. I gained a lot of weight and that hampered my self -esteem. I realised I was getting too old to get married around last year and decided to stop medicine for good this time,

I was given CBT [cognitive behavioural therapy] sessions online and [with] a local counsellor. This psychologist told me he wouldn't accept insurance and not help me until I took my meds [medications].

So I stopped going to him because medicine [the medications] is not the answer to a genuine *Jinn* case. My classmate told me he was possessed to and guided me to someone who imprisoned the *Jinn*. This guy is famous in US and has branches in every part of the world. He trained someone in South India and he gave me skype sessions. What they did was put me into a trance using Qur'anic recitation and then when the *Jinn* spoke they claim my third eye is open and I can give them some information long distance. I think most of this information was false however. So when the *Jinn* refused to leave me they burned him through a third person. Again I found out concerns about how this is a Sufi tradition and decided to leave it. I also heard that they convince nearly every one they have a magic case just to exploit them for more money so the whole family gets treated. They asked me to intake Senna leaves for 2 weeks. I didn't get any stomach aches because I don't think it's a magic case but they told my mother even she has various *Jinn* being sent. My mother already believes it's my uncle who did sorcery on me because he is jealous of my wealth and doesn't want me to get married out of revenge. But this has no evidence whatsoever. He advised me to get *hijama* [Cupping] regularly done and I did head *hijama* thrice and full body *hijama* four times. This only cured my migraine but the *Jinn* situation got worse. I was tempted to commit suicide once but Alhumdulillah I was guided back by Allah to keep living and not lose hope. Things will get better and I am just being tested. I sought forgiveness for wrong methods and decided to just be patient with it regardless of if I have a normal future or not.

Now I am 28 and unmedicated. I lost a lot of weight now and don't want to regain them at the expense of some medicine that doesn't even cure me because the *Jinn* get weak and strong on and off. It depends on the level of our iman state. I don't think there is a permanent cure for this yet and shifaa [cure] is in the hand of Allah alone. Maybe there is some wisdom behind it and it's actually good for me as it changed my life and way of thinking for the better. Alhumdulillah ala kulli haal. Some people even lack insight and act on the voices as I've observed and get paranoid and delusional so I am much better off because we know how to protect ourselves from the traps of the Shaytan. My graduation was postponed because of this condition. It's still not sure if its evil eye or magic or just random possession. I try not to seek answers to this because there are so many different tricksters in this field that it does me more harm than good to be curious.

I am recently going to a raaqi here. He uses *Ruqyah* and Prophetic medicine and alhumdulillah its working, I am getting epileptic and shaking showing that the *Jinn* is weak and its effecting him. Thought I am losing consciousness a lot especially when I'm in prayer I just lose myself and enter into a hypnotic trance. Then I break free of it after a while and resume the prayer so I know Allah won't hold me responsible for what I can't control. Inshaallah [If Allah will]. I feel lighter Alhumdulillah but I need to be consistent because repossession happens often. But I will stick with my *Ruqyah* regime and continue *tahajjud* [(Night Prayer], and have trust in Allah that he will cure me Inshaallah. I have understanding support system and patient family members. I will never lose my hope Inshaallah because that is exactly what they want. To get us depressed is a sign of hypocrisy and being ungrateful for being tested. I used prophetic prayers of Ayyub and Yoonus as and cry a lot and pray for mercy and then I feel like my sins are being washed and Allah provides relief for those who sincerely ask him and rely upon him in great trial.

Comments

This is a case of a young lady being possessed by *Jinn* and who has been subjected to magic or witchcraft. Her symptoms include "auditory hallucinations; tactile hallucinations (delusional parasitosis), something like an insect scratches over my skin; air runs all over my body; something talks to me telepathically; negativity about life, anger, withdrawal, solitary; communicating to friends online occasionally; dysfunctional relationships; irritated mood; no sexual desire; hate all my suitors; used to get blasphemous thoughts (ever since I became religious I can dispel it easier); when Qur'an is recited, the reaction is immediate nowadays; something cries and screams and speaks in Spanish (or maybe another language I just don't know); shaking violently; limbs twitching; talk and write too much so my thought is very disorganised; low attention span; memory loss; dissociative trances especially when praying; a train of thought consciousness assails and I am sucked into a black void; I am in another dimension entirely for a while (time passes very slowly there, I can't believe only 5 minutes passed when I regain consciousness. It's like I forced to go there against my will); bad dreams, especially at 3 am I am woken up; hormonal misbalance (polycystic ovary causes hair fall and hair growth under chin); anxiety and panic attacks; and seasonal depression."

From a medical/psychiatric perspective, she had a number of diagnoses including polycystic ovary syndrome, depression, anxiety, schizophrenia, paranoid schizophrenia, and bipolar disorders and was prescribed anti-psychotic, anxiolytics, anti-depressants and mood stabilisers etc. In addition she had counselling sessions and cognitive behavioural therapy for her mood disorders.

This is a case of misdiagnosis, inappropriate pharmacological interventions, failure of the psychiatrist/ counsellor to work with a faith healer. She suffered at the hands of 'fake' *Ruqyah* practitioners who used innovated means of *Ruqyah*. Some of them even using *Shirk* and making pacts with the Shaytan, who are taking advantage of other people's vulnerability. In addition they charged extortionate rates per session. The case is ongoing.

Case reports [CR]: obsessive-compulsive disorder (OCD) and satanic whisperings (*Waswâs al-Qahri*)

[CR1] This young lady suffers from *Waswâs al-Qahri* from past 5 years. She is afflicted with *Waswâs al-Qahri Fee Taharah* (purification) in ablution (wudu), bath (ghusl) and prayer (Salah). She spends a huge amount of time to purify herself with clean water, but she always has doubts about her cleanliness and purity. She usually takes 3 or 4 baths in a day. Her thoughts are also influenced by the *Jinn* and she would have evil thoughts about Allah and the Prophet (ﷺ). This disorder affected her eating habits, study and interpersonal relationship. She was referred to a psychiatrist who prescribed medications. She still prays regularly, reads Qur'an and lives in the Islamic way. Whenever *Waswâs* occurs, she usually seeks refuge in Allah and recites Ayatul Qursi, Surahs Falaq, Nas and Ikhlas. Despite these supplications, she is still overwhelmed by the *Waswâs* and the evil thoughts.

Comments

Allah says in the Qur'an (Interpretation of the meaning): "And if an evil whisper from Shaytan (Satan) tries to turn you away (O Muhammad) (from doing good), then seek refuge in Allah. Verily, He is the All Hearer, the All Knower" (Qur'an 41: 36). Thus, always seek refuge in Allah, the

Almighty. The advice given to this young lady is to see refuge in Allah, ignore the thoughts completely. Accordingly, "If the individual does not pay any attention to it, it will not persist; rather it will go away after a short while, as is the experience of those who are guided. But if he pays attention to it and lets this *Waswâs* control him, then it will continue to increase until it makes him like one who is insane, or even worse, as we have seen in the case of many of those who have been faced with this problem and who listened to confusing ideas and the devils who promote them" (Islamqa, 2015).

References

Bali, W. A. (2004) *Sword Against Black Magic & Evil Magicians*. London: Al-Firdous.

Bragazzi, N. L., and Del Puente, G. (2012) An Ethnopsychiatric Case Report. www.research gate.net/profile/Nicola_Bragazzi/publication/263542110_An_Ethnopsychiatric_Case_ Report/links/0deec53b2f71481b6a000000/An-Ethnopsychiatric-Case-Report.pdf (accessed 23 March 2018).

Bukhari in *Fath Al-Baari*, 6/338, and Muslim in An-Nawawi 17/17.

Hanwella, R., de Silva, V., Yoosuf, A., Karunaratne, S., and de Silva, P. (2012) Religious beliefs, possession states, and spirits: Three case studies from Sri Lanka, *Case Reports in Psychiatry*, 2012, 232740, 1–3, Doi:10.1155/2012/232740.

Islamqa (2010) 45659: *How can a person know who has envied him, and how should the one who has been envied be treated?* https://islamqa.info/en/45659 (accessed 23 March 2018).

Islamqa (2015) 224718: *Treating waswasah by seeking refuge with Allah from the Shaytan and ignoring it.* https://islamqa.info/en/224718 (accessed 23 March 2018).

Khalifa, N., and Hardie, T. (2005) Possession and jinn, *Journal of the Royal Society of Medicine*, 98, 8, 351–353.

Philips, A. A. B. (2008) *Dr. Abu Ameenah Bilal Philips The Exorcist Tradition in Islaam*. Birmingham, England: Al-Hidaayah Publishing & Distribution.

Chapter 24

Collaboration with traditional healers, faith leaders and mental health workers

Introduction

Evil eye, *Jinn* possession and witchcraft are real and part of the fabric of beliefs of Muslims. The case reports in the previous chapter illustrate the difficult interactions between cultural beliefs, psychological problems and conventional medicine. Many Muslims can mistake mental illness for evil eye, *Jinn* possession and witchcraft. Mental health problems are primarily psychological or physical in origin, whereas evil eye, *Jinn* possession and witchcraft are primarily psycho-spiritual. Bufford (1988) suggested that

> two major views conclude that these conditions are indistinguishable; both involve reductionism. They suggest that people have spiritual problems, or that they have psychological problems, but never both. We need to remember that men and women are multidimensional beings. Thus, it seems likely that problems can occur in any dimension-spiritual, psychological, or physical. Often a given problem may involve more than a single dimension.
>
> (p. 123)

In clinical practice, some of the cases presented are clear cut mental health problems or psychiatric disorders, others are patients afflicted with evil eye, *Jinn* possession and witchcraft alone. However, there is also a combination of the Possession Syndrome and mental health problems. Evil eye, *Jinn* possession and witchcraft and mental health problems are conceptually distinct phenomena and it may be problematic in a given instance, in view of the extensive overlap among symptoms, to make a differential diagnosis which phenomenon is present. In this context, there is a strong case for the collaboration between the mental health multidisciplinary team and faith leader or Imam when there is a combination of possession and underlying mental disorder. Dein and Illaiee (2013) suggested that there is

> a need for these professionals to collaborate with Imams in the provision of holistic mental healthcare which incorporates biological, psychological and

spiritual factors. Whereas mental health professionals can teach imams to recognise mental illness, Islamic religious professionals can in turn educate health professionals about the importance of religious factors in psychiatric disorders.

(p. 293)

Utilisation of services

Muslims in general make limited use of counsellors and mental health services. Studies on utilisation of hospital services by South Asian patients in the UK have consistently demonstrated levels of dissatisfaction with care in relation to meeting religious and cultural needs, although there are few studies on minority ethnic patients' utilisation of acute hospital services (Vydelingum, 2000). The potential barriers inhibiting Muslims' access to mental health services include cultural and traditional beliefs about mental health problems, stigma, lack of knowledge and familiarity of mental health services and the use 'informal-indigenous resources' (Aloud, 2004). The somatisation of mental health problems also acts as a barrier to access services as the patients may perceive their problems as a physical or spiritual problem rather than psychological problems.

However, for most Muslims, counselling is taboo. Generally most Muslims are reluctant to seek professional counselling because for some Muslims, self-disclosure of personal problems with a stranger is degrading or inappropriate. Other barriers include: professionals being insensitive to cultural and special needs (Moshtagh and Dezhkam, 2004); failure to focus on their spiritual dimension (Abdullah, 2007; Podikunju-Hussain, 2006); a lack of trust, fearing that their Islamic values may not be respected (Hedayat Diba, 2000; Hodge, 2005; Dwairy, 2006); lack of socialisation or experience with Western counselling approaches (Al-Krenawi et al., 2000; Erickson and Al-Timimi, 2002; Al-Krenawi, 2002); and lack of understanding of the conceptualisations about mental health problems (Kuittinen et al., 2017). The findings of Soorkia et al. (2011) showed that those seeking professional psychological help among South Asian students in Britain was influenced by ethnic identity, cultural mistrust, and adherence to Asian values. Other barriers for the reluctance to attend counselling include modesty, gender preference, level of acculturation and the counsellor's lack of understanding of the religious and cultural needs and cultural competence. According to Al-Issa (2000), Arab-Muslims, for example, "tend to utilize informal methods of treatment that are more closely tied to cultural values and Islamic beliefs." (p. 20). Some of the barriers in the utilisation of psychological services are presented in Table 24.1.

Lay referral system and traditional healers

Health seeking behaviour and the choice whether or not to consult an allopathic or traditional healer is a complex process. The attribution of causation of ill health that affects help-seeking behaviour may include culture, religion, age, gender, social class, advent of unusual symptoms, disability, serious illness,

Table 24.1 A summary of barriers in utilisation of psychological services

Relationship	• Lack of trust.
	• Gender preference
Language barriers	• Differences in language between counsellors and users.
	• Interpretation a different set of health beliefs.
	• Use of psychological jargon.
Cultural/religious barriers	• Self-disclosure to strangers.
	• Lack of cultural competence.
	• Lack of focus on spiritual dimension.
	• Lack of understanding of religious beliefs.
	• Fearing that their Islamic values may not be respected.
	• Religious and cultural restrictions on discussing personal issues.
	• Experience or perceive racism or stereotyping.
	• Cultural mistrust.
Approach of therapy	• Lack of preference for non-directive approach.
	• Lack of socialisation or experience with Western counselling approach.
	• Absence of spiritual dimension.
	• Lack of guidance.

health-belief system, interpersonal crisis and validation of sick role. Friedson (1961) defines a 'lay referral system' as the sequence of events – during the symptom experience and sick-role stages requiring the sick person to make a series of decisions about what to do about his symptoms. In the decision-making process, he is influenced by others family and friends who, like the sick person, are laymen. This concept may be contrasted to the "professional referral system," which is a hierarchy of diagnostic authority in which decisions are based more or less objectively on the professional needs of a case" (pp. 146–147). This means that the 'lay referral system' is utilised when a patient seeks advice from others before consulting a healer of folk medicine or a doctor. This lay referral system constitutes an informal network of immediate family or significant others who the patients rely on to help cope with illness behaviours.

There is evidence to suggest that Muslims in general tend to use the lay referral system rather than seeking professional help. In a study of British Bangladeshis by McClelland et al. (2014), the findings showed that the Bangladeshis "place greater importance on the role of religion, family and friends, and have less faith in the effectiveness of counselling and therapy than British Whites" (p. 236). Besides getting help, support and informal treatment from the lay-referral system, Muslims also make use of *Hakims* (herbal practitioners) and traditional healers. Sometimes, these patients are coerced by their families into seeking treatment from *Hakims* and traditional healers (Ismail et al., 2005). For example, Ismail et al. (2005) suggested that "This network provides a parallel system of health care that is 'invisible' to the mainstream NHS (National Health Service)" (p. 30).

There are different kinds of healers or folk healers among the diversity of Muslim communities. The traditional healers used by Arab and Muslim populations may include *Al-Fataha*, female fortune tellers; the *Khatib* or *Hajjab*, male healers providing amulets worn on the body for protection from negative energy; the Dervish, male or female healers using religious rituals and cultural traditions to treat mental illness; and *Moalj Belkoran*, male Koranic healers who use Islamic scripture as a basis of warding off evil spirits (Al-Issa, 1990; Al-Krenawi and Graham, 1996a, 1996b; Alrawi et al., 2012).

In the Indian subcontinent, these folk healers are known as *Pirs*. These *Pirs* may be consulted for a variety of illnesses and psychosocial problems perceived to have spiritual or supernatural dimensions. These disorders may include epilepsy and mental health problems (Rhodes et al., 2008). There have been concerns over the danger and malpractice of fake *Pirs* in the treatment of innocent, illiterate men and women in the name of spiritual healing. Some of the healers in this category and those practising *Ruqyah* have limited knowledge of the *Shari'ah* laws (Islamic), and based their 'treatment interventions' outside the paradigm of the Qur'an and Sunnah. The interventions by Rakis (those who practice *Ruqyah*) have been discussed in Chapter 17. There has been a proliferation of websites for the treatment of *Jinn* possession and witchcraft. Some of the websites involve rogue traditional healers or *fake sheikhs* who are charging an exorbitant amount of money for innovated practices of *Ruqyah*. There is an urgent need to educate and socialise vulnerable Muslims on the evils of these malpractices.

The lay and medical approach can give rise to serious conflicting intervention strategies which may not be beneficial for the patients and place them under serious health consequences and social crimes. There is the health concern regarding self-medication of 'healing medicines' provided by traditional healers and over-the counter medications. It has been reported that some of the over-the counter herbal medications may provide severe adverse effects, and in some cases are fatal (Chan, 2003; Izzo and Ernst, 2009; Kennedy and Seely, 2010). However, the World Health Organization (WHO) has acknowledged the contributions of traditional healers to a broad spectrum of healthcare needs that include disease prevention, management and treatment of non-communicable diseases, and psychological health problems (WHO, 2001). It has been suggested that traditional healers are "particularly skilled in identifying and using the dominant figure in the client's family, enlisting that person's help in bringing about change in the client and in mobilizing the family and community to this end" (Al-Krenawi, Graham and Kandah, 2000 p. 18). Health systems and service deliveries need to see traditional healing as a complementary system used to enhance health provision to those who are culturally and linguistically different.

Imams, faith leaders and Islamic counselling

The word Imam can also be used in a broader sense, referring to any person who leads prayer; or the local, national, or international Muslim scholars. It has been suggested that the term Muslim faith leaders are substantially more inclusive"

(Communities and Local Government, 2010, p. 10). However, the faith leaders or Imams may have a multitude of roles (advisory, theological and counselling) and their services are sought for professional, personal or religious issues. There is evidence to suggest that integrating religious elements in counselling can act as a primer in instilling and facilitating positive coping, psychological well-being (Faigin and Pargament, 2011; Brewer-Smyth and Koenig, 2014). The is a need for faith leaders or Imams to address counselling issues in their communities that reach beyond religious and spiritual concerns and include family problems, social needs and psychiatric symptoms (Ali et al., 2005). In a study of the recognition of mental health problems among Imams in the US by Ali and Milstein (2012), the findings suggest that Imams have the skills in the recognition of mental health problems and showed an inclination to refer to specialists while continuing to provide individual counselling. However, Imams are undertaking this counselling role despite having limited formal training in counselling (Ali et al., 2005) and played a major role in the promotion of Muslims' health (Isgandarova, 2011). The role of the Iman in counselling and the counselling process is examined elsewhere (Rassool, 2016). The spiritual interventions that can be incorporated in the counselling process by Imams include Iman Restoration Therapy (Abdul Razak et al., 2011), *Ruqyah* (if appropriate), supplications, prayers, *Zikr* therapy, and the use of Qur'anic verses as sources of healing.

The question of Imams referring patients to other professionals is an interesting one. It is reported that

> one of the reasons why Muslims go to imams and other Muslim leaders is that they do not want to engage in anything that violates core Islamic principles. This has implications for an imam's willingness to refer to a non-Muslim provider and on how the Imam may be an important ally for non-Muslim providers. It also has implications on which services Muslims are willing to accept.
>
> (Ali, 2016, p. 70)

This has implications for the provision of Islamic counselling and culturally competent counselling for Muslim patients. Cultural competence can influence health behaviours and reduces health inequalities, resulting in the delivery of more culturally sensitive care (Brach and Fraser, 2000; Padela et al., 2011). The findings of a study indicate that cultural competence efforts would lead "to a greater understanding of Islam and Islamic culture, thereby improving client-provider relationship and improve Muslim experiences within the health care system results in challenges and increased accommodations" (Padela et al., 2011, p. 14). The multi-faceted roles of the Imams or faith leaders may raise issues of ethical concerns. The dilemmas arising may be due to conflicting multiple roles and power elements that may have a significant influence on the nature and process of the therapeutic relationship. A framework on the ethical principles has been developed for Imams to follow when counselling community members (Siddiqui, 2014).

Collaboration of traditional healers, Imams, faith leaders and mental health professionals

Imams, faith leaders and traditional healers are usually the first point of contact for many Muslims who are seeking support with depression, anxiety, obsessional compulsive disorder, and psychosis, *Jinn* and witchcraft possession. The primary healthcare also encounters patients with mental health problems and other spiritual problems. It is "critical for the psychologist or counsellor to be able to give the client the option of integrating religious and traditional healing practices into the therapeutic process" (Amri and Bemak, 2013, p. 53). In relation to mental health, Imams or faith leaders should be part of the multiprofessional team in dealing with specific cases of evil eye, *Jinn* and witchcraft possession. Imams would have the skills to identify cases of the evil eye, *Jinn* and witchcraft possession. In cases of obsessive-compulsive disorder or *Waswâs al-Qahri*, Imams can determine which rituals or religious practices are appropriate and which are extreme, so that the appropriate psychosocial or spiritual interventions or a combination of both are offered. By having a combination of both psychosocial treatment and complementary spiritual interventions, Imams would collaborate with the mental health professionals to persuade the patients to be comply with psychotropic medications regime.

However, for this to happen, there must be basic understanding of the roles of traditional healers, Imams or faith leaders in the lives of Muslim patients by mental health professionals and vice versa. There is evidence to suggest that religious individuals often consult their faith leaders rather than clinicians for help (Miller and Hedges, 2008). There is a need for the establishment of a 'dialogue system' with all stakeholders in the provision of mental health services in the local community context. Institutional and community barriers and expectations from all sides need to be identified at the initial stage so as to guide the collaboration process in order to enhance sustainability. Where there is the involvement of faith leaders or Imams in the process of allopathic and traditional treatment, Awad (2017) suggested that "as a religious authority, the client will be more likely to comply with therapy knowing that an imam supports it, especially in communities where there is still a lot of stigma and/or myths associated with treatment" (p. 20). Psychoeducation and preventive health education should also be part of the role of the Iman or faith leaders in collaboration with mental health practitioners in raising awareness, educating the community about mental health problems and challenging the stigma about seeking mental health treatment.

With regular communication and better rapport, mental health practitioners and Imams can further their collaborative role in the provision of a holistic mental health services.

In summary, Imams, faith leaders and traditional healers are de facto health educators and mental healthcare providers. Rassool (2016) suggested that collaboration and communication should be strengthened between mental healthcare professionals and Imams or faith leaders to facilitate proper referrals and improve access to culturally appropriate mental health services. Despite having limited preparation as counsellors, traditional healers and Imams usually relied on common sense in working with clients with psychological problems (Isgandarova, 2011; Isgandarova and O'Connor, 2012). It is necessary for traditional healers, Imams and clinicians to continuously engage in constructive dialogue to move forward with combined psychosocial and spiritual interventions and thus increase mental health outcomes in Muslim patients. Above all, there is an urgent need to prepare Imams and faith leaders in the field of mental health.

References

Abdullah, S. (2007) Islam and counseling: Models of practice in Muslim communal life, *Journal of Pastoral Counseling*, 42, 42–55.

Abdul Razak, A. L., Mohamed, M., Alias, A., Adam, K. W., Kasim, N. M., and Muti, S. (2011) Iman Restoration Therapy (IRT): A new counseling approach and its usefulness in developing personal growth of Malay adolescent clients, *Revelation and Science*, 1, 3 (1433H/2011), 97–107.

Ali, O. M. (2016) The Imam and the mental health of Muslims: Learning from research with other clergy, *Journal of Muslim Mental Health*, 10, 1, 65–73. http://dx.doi.org/10.3998/jmmh.10381607.0010.106.

Ali, O. M., Milstein, G., and Marzuk, P. M. (2005) The Imam's role in meeting the counseling needs of Muslim communities in the United States, *Psychiatric Services*, 56, 2, 202–205.

Ali, O. M,. and Milstein, G. (2012) Mental illness recognition and referral practices among imams in the United States, *Journal of Muslim Mental Health*, 6, 2, http://dx.doi.org/10.3998/jmmh.10381607.0006.202.

Al-Issa (1990) Culture and mental illness in Algeria. *International Journal of Social Psychiatry*, 36, 3, 230–240.

Al-Issa, I. (2000) *Al-Jun ūn: Mental Illness in the Islamic World*. Madison, CT: International Universities Press.

Al-Krenawi, A., and Graham, J. R. (1996a) Social work practice and traditional healing rituals among the Bedouin of the Negev, *International Social Work*, 39, 177–188.

Al-Krenawi, A., and Graham, J. R. (1996b) Tackling mental illness: Roles for old and new Disciplines, *World Health Forum*, 17, 246–248.

Al-Krenawi, A., Graham, J. R., and Kandah, J. (2000) Gender utilization of mental health services in Jordan, *Community Mental Health Journal*, 36, 501–511.

Al-Krenawi, A. (2002) Mental health service utilization among the Arabs in Israel, *Social Work in Health Care*, 35, 577–590.

Aloud, N. (2004) Factors affecting attitudes toward seeking and using formal mental health and psychological services among Arab-Muslims population. *Doctoral Dissertation*, Graduate School of The Ohio State University, https://etd.ohiolink.edu/rws_etd/document/get/osu1078935499/inline (accessed 24 March 2018).

Alrawi, S., Fetters, M. D., Killawi, A., Hammad, A., and Padela, A. (2012) Traditional healing practices among American Muslims: perceptions of community leaders in southeast Michigan, *Journal of Immigrant Minor Health*, 14, 3, 489–496. Doi: 10.1007/s10903-011-9495-0.

Amri, S., and Bemak, F. (2013) Mental health help-seeking behaviors of Muslim immigrants in the United States: Overcoming social stigma and cultural mistrust, *Journal of Muslim Mental Health*, 12, 1, 43–63.

Awad, N. (2017) *Clinicians, Imams, and the Whisperings of Satan*. https://yaqeeninstitute.org/en/najwa-awad/waswas-al-qahri-a-new-disorder-to-the-clinical-literature/ (accessed 24 March 2018).

Brach C., and Fraser, I. (2000) Can cultural competency reduces racial and ethnic health disparities? A review and conceptual model, *Medical care Research and Review*, 57 (4 suppl), 181–217.

Brewer-Smyth, K., and Koenig, H. G. (2014) Could spirituality and religion promote stress resilience in survivors of childhood trauma? *Issues In Mental Health Nursing*, 35, 4, 251–256. Doi:10.3109/01612840.2013.873101.

Bufford, R. K. (1988) *"Demonic Influence and Mental Disorders – Chapter 8 of "Counseling and the Demonic."* Paper 12. http://digitalcommons.georgefox.edu/counselingandthedemonic/12 (accessed 24 March 2018).

Chan, K. (2003) Some aspects of toxic contaminants in herbal medicines, *Chemosphere*, 52, 9, 1361–1371.

Communities and Local Government (2010) *The Training and Development of Muslim Faith Leaders: Current Practice and Future Possibilities*. London: Communities and Local Government. www.communities.gov.uk

Dein, S., and Illaiee, A. S. (2013) Jinn and mental health: Looking at jinn possession in modern psychiatric practice, *The Psychiatrist*, 37, 290–293. doi: 10.1192/pb.bp.113.042721.

Dwairy, M. (2006) *Counseling and Psychotherapy with Arabs and Muslims*. New York: Teachers College Press.

Erickson, C. D., and Al-Timimi, N. R. (2002) Providing mental health services to Arab Americans: Recommendations and considerations, *Cultural Diversity – Ethnic Minority Psychology*, 7, 4, 308–332.

Faigin, C., and Pargament, K. I. (2011) Strengthened by the spirit: Religion, spirituality, and resilience through adulthood and aging. *Resilience In Aging*, 163. Doi: 10.1007/978-1-4419-0232-0_11

Friedson, K. (1961) *Patients' views of Medical Practice*. New York: Russel Sage Foundation, pp. 146–147.

Hedayat-Diba, Z. (2000) Psychotherapy with Muslims, in P. S. Richards, and A. E. Bergin (Eds.), *Handbook of Psychotherapy and Religious Diversity*. Washington, DC: American Psychological Association, pp. 289–314.

Hodge, D. R. (2005) Social work and the house of Islam: Orienting practitioners to the beliefs and values of Muslims in the United States, *Social Work*, 50, 162–173.

Isgandarova, N (2011) The concept of effective Islamic spiritual car, *The Journal of Rotterdam Islamic and social sciences*, 2, 87–117.

Isgandarova, N., and O'Connor, T. S. (2012) A redefinition and model of Canadian Islamic spiritual care, *Journal of Pastoral Care and Counseling*, 66, 2, 7.

Ismail, H., Wright, J., Rhodes, P., and Small, N. (2005) Religious beliefs about causes and treatment of epilepsy, *British Journal of General Practice*, 26–31. http://citeseerx.ist.psu.edu/viewdoc/download?doi=10.1.1.896.4882&rep=rep1&type=pdf (accessed 24 March 2018).

Izzo, A. A., and Ernst, E. (2009) Interactions between herbal medicines and prescribed drugs: An updated systematic review, *Drugs*, 69, 1777–1798.

Kennedy, D. A., and Seely, D. (2010)Clinically based evidence of drug-herb interactions: A systematic review, *Expert Opinion on Drug Safety*, 9, 79–124.

Kuittinen S., Mölsä M, Tiilikainen, M., Punamäki, R. L., and Honkasalo, M. L. (2017) Causal attributions of mental health problems and depressive symptoms among older Somali refugees in Finland, *Transcultural Psychiatry*, 54, 2, 211–238. Doi: 10.1177/1363461 516689003. Epub 2017 Jan 1.

McClelland, A., Khanam, S., and Furnham, A. (2014) Cultural and age differences in beliefs about depression: British Bangladeshis vs. British Whites, *Mental Health, Religion & Culture*, 17, 3, 225–238. http://doi.org/10.1080/13674676.2013.785710.

Miller, C. H., and Hedges, D. W. (2008) Scrupulosity disorder: An overview and introductory analysis, *Journal of Anxiety Disorders*, 22, 6, 1042–1058.

Moshtagh, N., and Dezhkam, N. (2004) Women, Gender and Mental Health in Iran, in S. Joseph (2006) *Encyclopedia of Women & Islamic Cultures, Volume 3 Family, Body, Sexuality and Health*. Leiden, Netherlands: Brill, p. 271.

Padela, A., Gunter, K., and Killawi, A. (20111) *Meeting The Healthcare Needs of American Muslims: Challenges and Strategies for Healthcare Settings*. Washington, DC: Institute for Social Policy and Understanding. www.ispu.org/wp-content/uploads/2016/09/620_ISPU_ Report_Aasim-Padela_final.pdf (accessed 24 March 2018).

Podikunju-Hussain, S. (2006) Working With Muslims: Perspectives and Suggestions for Counseling. *VISTAS Online*, Article 22, 103–106. http://counselingoutfitters.com/vistas/ vistas06/vistas06.22.pdf (accessed 24 March 2018).

Rhodes, P. J., Small, N., Ismail, H., and Wright, J. P. (2008) The use of biomedicine, complementary and alternative medicine, and ethnomedicine for the treatment of epilepsy among people of South Asian origin in the UK, *BMC Complementary and Alternative Medicine*, 8, 1, 7. [7]. Doi: 10.1186/1472-6882-8-7

Rassool, G. H. (2016) *Islamic Counselling: An Introduction to Theory and Practice*. Hove, East Sussex: Routledge.

Siddiqui, S. (2014) *A Professional Guide for Canadian Imams. Islamic Social Services Association*, Inc-Canada: Islamic Social Services Association, www.issacanada.com/professional-guide- canadian-imams/ (accessed 24 March 2018).

Soorkia, R., Snelgar, R., and Swami, V. (2011) Factors influencing attitudes towards seeking professional psychological help among South Asian students in Britain, *Mental Health, Religion & Culture*, 14, 6, 613–623.

Vydelingum, V. (2000) South Asian patients' lived experience of acute care in an English hospital: A phenomenological study, *Journal of Advanced Nursing*, 32, 1, 100–107.

WHO (2001). *Legal Status of Traditional Medicine and Complementary/Alternative Medicine: A Worldwide Review*. Geneva: World Health Organisation

Chapter 25

Facing the challenges

Strategies and solutions

Introduction

On a global level, many countries face enormous challenges in the prevention and promotion of mental health, and in the provision of culturally appropriate mental health services to marginalised and vulnerable groups, including Muslim communities. The need to give the marginalised mental health a higher priority in health and social policy is beyond dispute. Service provision and treatment interventions need to take account of the cultural and religious factors and the worldview of Muslim patients. The labelling and diagnosis of those suffering from evil eye, *Jinn* or witchcraft possession as psychotic disorders may lead to the medicalisation of spiritual problems. The growing medicalisation of spiritual problems reflects the Western scientific paradigm and modern medicine of conceptualisation of 'spiritual disease' as psychiatric disorders. It has been suggested that the "medicalisation and psychiatrisation of various existential problems, which can be seen in subsequent editions of the DSM, encourages pathologising approach towards religious or spiritual problems" (Prusak, 2016, p. 175).

Conrad (2007) describes medicalisation as "a process by which nonmedical problems become defined and treated as medical problems, usually in terms of illness and disorders" (p. 5.) The term "psychiatricization" (Knezevic and Jovancevic, 2001), or pathologising has also been used for the medical medicalisation of psychiatry. However, according to Pridmore (2013),

> a good case can be made for the validity of psychiatric disorders such as schizophrenia, major depressive disorder, bipolar disorder and obsessive compulsive disorder. And, using 'evidence based' protocols, the psychiatrist is capable of providing the best possible management for people suffering these disorders.
>
> (p. 4)

At this juncture, the psychiatric labels are valuable in guiding appropriate treatment intervention strategies. Nevertheless, it must be acknowledged that conceptualising *Jinn* possession or *Waswâs al-Qahri* as psychiatric disorders can be

double-edged. It entails negative reactions and consequences beyond the obvious stigmatisation and acts as a barrier to seek psychological help and treatment.
It is well documented that Muslims are reluctant to be labelled as suffering from
a psychiatric disorder, but prefer to attribute their distress as spiritual problems
associated with evil eye, *Jinn* and witchcraft possession. Most Muslims would
make use of the services of faith and traditional healers before consulting specialists in mental health. Mental health services would need to bridge the gap
in the provision of culturally appropriate services and must take faith and traditional healing into account in orthodox psychiatric care.

Conflict of traditional healers and mental health professionals

There is a growing demand, in the UK, for faith-based institutions to deliver
community, educational and welfare services (Home Office Faith Communities Unit, 2004). The issue of the engagement of traditional healers in the
formal mental healthcare system alongside mental health professionals has been
debated and discussed for several decades. The literature abounds about the
need for faith healers, Imams, religious/spiritual advisors to collaborate with
specialised mental health services to improve service utilisation and to serve
as bridges between the two sectors (Friedli, 2000; Farrell and Goebert, 2008;
John and Williams, 2013; Dein and Illaiee, 2013; James et al., 2014). There has
been limited interaction and integration;, for example, Imams and faith healers
with the orthodox mental health sectors. Despite the relative of the importance of Imams and faith healers in the psycho-spiritual dimension of health,
there are potential conflicts between Imams, traditional healers and the medical
establishment.

There are inherent historic tensions and mutual suspicion between religion
and psychiatry which continue to shape the delivery of mental health services
(Bhugra, 1997; Curlin et al., 2007). Patel (2011) has argued that "the greatest
obstacle to a collaboration has been the mutual suspicion between the two sectors and the concerns of the biomedical sector and the religious establishment
regarding the 'unscientific' and unorthodox practices of traditional healers"
(p. 2). In the first instance, "psychiatrists do not generally see clergy members
as collaborators in mental health care nor are they likely to refer their religious
patients to them" (Durà-Vilà, 2015, p. 67). Furthermore, in sub-Saharan Africa,
faith healers or the clergy are perceived by some mental health workers as barriers in the delivery of effective care for the mentally ill (Adeponle et al., 2007)
and that religious beliefs may lead to psychiatric disorders and symptomatology
(Watters, 1992)

Bridging the gap between a secular worldview of mental health problems with a spiritual/supernatural worldview is a complex undertaking. The
religious belief in supernatural elements in the evil eye, *Jinn* possession and
witchcraft are a matter of contention among mental health professionals. For

some professionals accepting spiritual values is antithesis to the evidence-based Western scientific paradigm. It is the conceptualisation of mental illness by the Imams and faith healers that are incongruent with perceived causal factors of mental health problems based on a medical/psychiatric paradigm. It is argued that "traditional healing uses an intuitive approach within an existential paradigm, whereas western Medicine uses an evidence-based approach within a dualistic (mind/body) paradigm" (Robertson, 2006, p. 88). The use of a spiritual model by Imam and faith healers may also be an area of potential conflict with the secular mental health services. Leavey (2010) suggested that "an engagement of spiritual and secular paradigms of illness and treatment may require considerable suspension of disbelief on both sides of the divide." (p. 587).

A major barrier in this process of collaboration includes the fact that there is a great diversity of traditional healers (Patel, 2011). In addition to the diversity of traditional healers (Imams, Fakirs, Rakis, *Hakims*), using different methods of interventions, there is a deficit in their knowledge of psychosocial interventions, including counselling, and psychiatric problems and symptomatology. It has been suggested that Imams and faith leaders are not adequately prepared in counselling psychology to fulfil that role and have not received any kind of training in counselling (Ali et al., 2005; Morgan, 2010). In recent years, a number of European universities and institutions have developed programmes for Imams or faith leaders that lead to nationally recognised qualifications and integrate Islamic theological training courses within existing universities (Communities and Local Government, 2010). In many developed and developing countries, globalisation and Muslims' immigration have led to better education and training of Imams and faith leaders in pedagogy, Islamic sciences and secular studies. However, the integration of mental health in curricula content is restricted to a few 'Centres of Excellence.' There is an urgent need to address this deficit and adequately prepare Imam and faith leaders in mental health and Islamic counselling.

Spirituality in health and social work educational curriculum

In contrast, those working in the mental health field are reported to lack training in spirituality and the religious aspects of medical and psychiatric training (Durà-Vilà et al., 2011). Furthermore, psychiatrists differed in their views as to whether spiritual or religious matters should be addressed within routine assessment and treatment planning (Cook, 2010; Cook et al., 2011; Poole and Higgo, 2011). The increased focus on spirituality in health on a global scale stemmed from a resolution by members of the World Health Organization (WHO 1985) which made the 'spiritual dimension' part and parcel of WHO Member States' strategies for health.[1] This is an affirmation that the spiritual dimension is implicit in the concept of health. The General Medical Council of United Kingdom (GMC, 2009) guidance also recommends that medical students appreciate "the importance of clinical, psychological, spiritual, religious, social and cultural factors," and respect "patients' right to hold religious or other beliefs." These factors need to be taken into account, if appropriate, in treatment interventions. The Association of American Medical Colleges (1999) has also addressed spirituality in the curriculum and outlined outcome goals and learning objectives for spirituality. The Royal College of Psychiatrists (UK) (Cook, 2013), in a position statement, supported the notion of considering spirituality and religion as a part of good clinical practice and making the exploration of patients' spiritual experience an intrinsic and necessary part of routine psychiatric care. The Spirituality and Psychiatry Special Interest Group (SPSIG) was founded to provide a forum for psychiatrists to explore the spiritual challenges presented by psychiatric illness, and how best to respond to patients' spiritual concerns (SPSIG, 2016).

Despite the growing research base on spirituality, religiousness and health, the status of teaching on spirituality in the medical curriculum varies between countries. The findings of Koenig et al.'s study (2010) showed that most US medical schools (90%) have curricular content on spirituality and health although this varies greatly in scope. In the UK, it is estimated that between 31% and 78% currently provide some form of teaching on spirituality (Neely and Minford, 2008). There is limited coverage of spirituality in the medical curriculum content in Brazil (Lucchetti et al., 2012). The extent of spiritual contents in the nursing curriculum has also been investigated.

The International Council of Nurses (ICN 2000) Code of Ethics specifies the nurse's role in promoting "an environment in which the human rights, values, customs and spiritual beliefs of the individual, family and community are respected" (p. 5). In Canada, the findings from Olson et al.'s study (2003) examining 18 Canadian undergraduate nursing programmes showed that 26 of the 39 participants stated that the term, 'spiritual dimension,' was not included in their educational programme. In the US, Lemmer (2002) investigated 250 institutions offering baccalaureate nursing programmes to explore how spirituality was being taught. The majority of programmes (81.5%), integrated spirituality throughout the curriculum, and some programmes (15.9%) delivered an elective spiritual care programme. Lewinson et al.'s (2015) review of the literature on spirituality in pre-registration nurse education and practice confirms that spirituality is established in the curriculum content. According to Gulnar (2017), "the integration of spirituality in nursing education appeared to be treated as a matter of personal choice and convenience rather than as an essential domain of teaching and learning practice in England" (p. 149). In an online survey of Canadian social work educators (Kvarfordt et al., 2017), the findings indicated that only one-third of the participants (N = 90) reported the integration of spirituality in undergraduate and postgraduate social work curriculum. Overall, there is limited uniformity in the integration of spirituality in health and social work educational curriculum in relation to content, form and the methodology of teaching spirituality. There is also the conceptual complexity of whether addressing spiritual needs also incorporates the meeting of religious needs in Eurocentric health and social care.

Diversity and cultural competence

The significant growth of the Muslim communities globally has increased the prevalence of mental health problems as a result of immigration, Islamophobia, microagression, hostility; and multiple discrimination based on place of origin, racial and national stereotypes (Change Institute, 2009). In addition, there has been an unprecedented upsurge in the number of refugees on a global scale. The refugee crises have amplified a higher risk of mental illness amongst the refugees and asylum seekers including major depression disorder, post-traumatic stress disorder, and general anxiety disorders (Laban et al., 2004; Pumariega et al., 2005; De Almeida Vieira Monteiro and Serra, 2011; Silove et al., 2017). Due to the rise in mental health problems, there exists a corresponding increase in the need for mental health services. One of a major challenges facing mental health practitioners is the provision of culturally competent care with a diversity of ethnic and linguistic groups of Muslim patients.

Cultural competence, according to Bhui et al. (2007) "included a set of skills or processes that enable mental health professionals to provide services that are culturally appropriate for the diverse populations that they serve" (p. 2). Delivering high-quality care to Muslim patients involves having an awareness of the ramifications of the Islamic faith and Islamic beliefs. Despite the cultural diversity in Muslim communities, there is some homogeneity within Muslim communities with regard to: health beliefs and practices; access to, and use of, healthcare; health risks; family dynamics; and decision-making processes (Rassool, 2014a). Rassool (2014b) suggests that having a greater awareness of "these perspectives should inform health professionals' efforts to achieve cultural competence and deliver care that is culturally sensitive" (p. 276). However, having heightened awareness and understanding of Islam and Islamic culture does not mean dealing with overly simplified summaries of Islam, and health practices risk reinforcing stereotypes and prejudices (Rassool, 2014a). The findings of a study indicate that cultural competence efforts would not only lead to a greater awareness of Islam and Islamic culture, but would improve Muslim experiences within the healthcare system and patient-provider relationship (Padela et al., 2011).

The deficit in cultural competence among mental health professionals may be due to a combination of factors. Lopes (2001) stated that the most likely outcomes of poor cultural competence include: lack of knowledge; self-protection/denial; fear; and time. However, without adequate educational preparation, mental health professionals will fail to respond to the psychosocial and spiritual problems faced by Muslims in the Western hemispheres. If education and training in cultural competence for mental health professionals are to become a reality, it should be made mandatory to alleviate health disparities among those who are culturally and linguistically different.

Promotion of mental health

The promotion and prevention of mental health are fundamental to well-being and an integral part of public health policy. Mental health, according to the World Health Organization (2001) is "a state of well-being in which the individual realizes his or her own abilities, can cope with the normal stresses of life, can work productively and fruitfully, and is able to make a contribution to his or her community" (p. 1). Mental health includes our physical, emotional, psychological, social and spiritual well-being. According to Min et al. (2013) in order to enhance mental health, "promotion, prevention, and the treatment of disease are required. These three kinds of interventions are interrelated but independent from one another" (p. 307). Some of the recommendations in the promotion of mental health (Herrman et al., 2004) include: early childhood interventions; economic and social empowerment of women; social support to old age, programmes targeted at vulnerable groups such as minorities, indigenous people, migrants and people affected by conflicts and disasters; mental health promotion activities in schools; mental health interventions at work; housing policies; violence prevention programmes and community development programmes (p. 59).

One of the approaches in changing the health status of a community is the promotion of mental health and the prevention of mental illness. One of the problems associated with mental health in the Muslim communities is the issue of cultural mistrust and stigma. The stigma of mental health problems continues to be a major barrier for individuals and families in seeking help, disclosure of mental illness is considered 'shameful,' and families are rejected and isolated for their association with mental health problems (Pridmore and Pasha, 2004; Youssef and Deane, 2006; Aloud and Rathur, 2009; Ciftci et al., 2012). This kind of public and label avoidance is perhaps the most significant way in which stigma impedes care seeking and delays treatment interventions. In order to reduce stigma in the Muslim communities, social marketing campaigns should focus on interventions at the local level and be culture specific (Corrigan, 2011). In this context, Imams, faith leaders, stakeholders and community organisations need to raise the issue of stigma and increase Muslims' awareness of mental health and help-seeking. It has been suggested that "mental health interventions can also be co-constructed by community and religious leaders in an effort to combine traditional and cultural practices with Western clinical practice" (Amri and Bemak, 2012, p. 57).

Strategies for dealing with challenges of mental health from an Islamic perspective

From an Islamic perspective, good mental health practice comes from "the unblemished belief in Allah as the Ultimate Maker and Doer, and hence any deviation from the firm acceptance of Allah's ultimate dominance over the lives of his followers leads to disintegration and disruption of inner harmony" (Sayed, 2003, pp. 449–450). The teachings of the Qur'an are a social, psychological and spiritual guide for all mankind. The Qur'an itself is a healing for the believers.

> This includes healing the heart (mental or spiritual disease) and physical healing. Allah mentions honey in the Qur'an and says that it is a healing for mankind. And He mentions the principle of preserving good health and guarding against sickness.
>
> (Islamqa, 2008)

The following are some of the verses which state that certain virtues will beneficial for the individual or for humanity as a whole: The Qur'an is healing (Qur'an 17:82); Enjoining all that is good and forbidding all that is evil; Healing for that which is in your hearts (Qur'an 10:57); Guidance benefits his own soul (Qur'an 39:41); Establish regular prayer and remembrance of (Qur'an 3:190–191, 29:45, 73:7–9); Balance/Moderation (Qur'an 2:190, 5:87, 25:63–67, 28:77); Sincerity (Qur'an 8:53, 107:4–6); Discipline, Self-Restraint and fasting (Qur'an 2:183, 22:77–78, 38:26, 79:40–41); Hope (Qur'an 3:138–139, 16:96); Gratitude (Qur'an 2:172, 31:14, 39:7); and Righteousness (Qur'an 2:60, 3:104, 4:36,16:90,49:13). In fact, "adhering to the principles and practice of the Islamic faith would result in better psychological adjustment and mental health" (Rassool, 2016, p. 55). Both the recitation of the Qur'an and the performance of the five daily prayers can be seen as a medium for contemplation, a prophylactic against stress, and a way of promoting psychological and spiritual maturity (El Azayem and Hedayat-Diba, 1994; El-Islam, 2004).

The strategies for dealing with challenges of Muslim mental health, according to Sheikh Abdul Malik Mujahid (2012), are presented in Table 25.1.

Research

Research should be at the forefront in the developmental process in the provision of culturally congruent services for Muslims. It is important to begin with understanding what the community's needs are. A health and social needs assessment at a local level is an essential starting point for service development and the development of any intervention strategy. The identification of barriers to seeking mental health services and how those barriers can be overcome would be worth exploring. There is limited research on the incidence and prevalence of Evil eye, *Jinn* and witchcraft possession. In relation to *Waswâs al-Qahri*, Awad (2017) suggested that

> there needs to be quantitative research to determine the prevalence of *Waswâs al-Qahri* in different countries, risk factors, general demographics, and duration of illness. There also need to be trials completed to see the efficacy of different types of treatment, including management by medication.

Table 25.1 Strategies for dealing with challenges of mental health from an Islamic perspective

Key stakeholders and institutions	Actions
Muslim psychiatrists, psychologists, social service providers, Muslim Ummah	• Mental health awareness campaign via online outreach, Islamic and health websites, articles and social networking, as well as speeches, workshops, lectures, multilingual brochures.
Imams or faith healers	• Khutbahs[1] (sermons) on the topic of Muslim mental health, with a special focus on breaking down the taboo nature of this issue. • Other topics include: strengthening our relationship with Allah, particularly in times of stress and difficulty; *Sabr* (patience), *Tawakkul* (trust in God) and *Shukr* (thankfulness), as well as sharing more and consuming less by practising simple living, dealing with stress and anxiety.
Masjids (mosques)/cultural centres: use of Imam, Islamic counsellor and social worker	• Mosques – first point of contact for Muslims in times of mental health crisis. • Breaking the mental health taboo in the Muslim community through programmes like lectures and workshops on these issues. • Special emphasis should be made on seeking professional help for problems like stress and depression, for instance. • Hire Islamic counsellors. • Establish mentorship programmes for Muslim children, which will offer students a way to share their stress or concerns with qualified personnel who can help them. • If this is not possible, then Muslim psychiatrists, Islamic psychologists and counsellors in the community should step forward and volunteer their services.
Islamic schools (full time and weekend)	• Teachers should be trained in a special seminar or workshop on recognising the signs of stress, depression and other mental health challenges. • Schools should incorporate short lectures in their morning assemblies on the above suggested themes. • Administrators and teachers should work together to develop lesson plans on how to deal with anger, stress and other issues.

Source: Adapted from Mujahid, A.M. (2012) *State of Muslim mental health*. http://sumo.ly/wm8Kwww.soundvision.com/article/state-of-muslim-mental-health (accessed 25 March 2018).

[1] The khutbah, however, refers to khutbat al-Jum'a, usually meaning the address delivered in the mosque at weekly (usually Friday) and annual rituals.

Research development will help solidify whether *Waswâs al-Qahri* should be classified as a type of Obsession Compulsive Disorder and what interventions are best to treat it.

(p. 27)

The point of contention here is whether *Waswâs al-Qahri* should be taken out of its spiritual domain and become part of the pathological and medicalisation of spiritual problems. This is applicable to all supernatural and psycho-spiritual phenomenon and the provision of a label or 'orientalist' diagnosis does not constitute more effective interventions. Research should also focuses on how faith leaders or Imams can collaborate with the multi-professional mental health practitioners in both residential and community settings.

Evidenced-based *Ruqyah* has been proposed to evaluate the effectiveness of this therapeutic process. According to Rahman (2014),

Research on making *Ruqyah* therapy evidence-based will not be done by measuring jinn or religious belief. Instead, the measurement will focus on the therapeutic impact of the therapy on the person's health. This approach is consistent with the method used in the evaluation other evidence-based therapies or treatment.

(p. 12–13)

Rahman (2014) also reported that there are increasing number of cases of patients who have been treated with psychotropic medications without any positive health outcomes, but show improvement in their conditions as a result of *Ruqyah* therapy. There is some evidence on the effectiveness of Qur'anic therapy. Saged et al. (2018) examine the effect of Qur'anic therapy on psychological diseases and spiritual diseases. The findings indicate that 92.6% of the patients support the contention that the Qur'an has a significant healing influence and those who regularly attended Quranic therapy sessions have been successfully treated. However, more evidenced-based spiritual interventions would be needed in order to satisfy the 'evidence-based' practice criteria of Western-oriented psychiatry.

Conclusion

The intervention strategies in mental health should actually be seen from a broader perspective so that it covers the promotion of mental health, and the provision of psychosocial, pharmacological and spiritual interventions. Mental health services are facing a daunting challenge in the provision of culturally appropriate services to meet the holistic needs of Muslim clients. For mental health practitioners in health, psychology and social work practice, the provision of culturally competent and congruent care is both a professional and an ethical requirement. The major challenges faced by mental health practitioners in working with Muslim patients include: Islamophobia, ethical issues, therapeutic alliance and trust, recognition of clinical differences in Muslim clients and communication styles (Rassool, 2016). There is a need to alter professional boundaries in mainstream psychiatry and to make the exploration of patients' spiritual experience an intrinsic and necessary part of routine psychiatric care and interventions. This should be done in collaboration with Imams or faith leaders and traditional faith healers. Psychiatrists should reduce the Eurocentric or orientalist biases in diagnosis of Muslim patients with evil eye, *Jinn* and witchcraft possession and increase cultural and religious salience in their intervention strategies. The effectiveness of holistic interventions will only be achieved when evidence-based spiritual interventions are provided under the same roof with Western-oriented psychosocial and pharmacological interventions. There are already identified challenges facing mental health practitioners; Muslim scholars and clinicians need to focus on an effective strategy in order to meet the mental health needs of Muslim patients. In effect, those suffering from spiritual diseases should also be the focus of attention. The need should be solution-focused!

Note

1 The World Health Assembly adopted resolution WHA37.13 which made the spiritual dimension a part of WHO member states' strategies for health. But this did not change the definition of 'health' in the WHO's constitution.

References

Adeponle, A. B., Obembe, A. O., Suleiman, G. T., and Adeyemi, S. O. (2007) Missed first appointments: Prevalence and associated factors in first-time attendees at an outpatient psychiatric clinic in Nigeria, *Mental Health, Religion & Culture*, 10, 6, 609–620.

Ali, O. M., Milstein, G., and Marzuk, P. M. (2005) The Imam's role in meeting the counseling needs of Muslim communities in the United States, *Psychiatric Services*, 56, 2, 202–205.

Aloud, N., and Rathur, A. (2009) Factors affecting attitudes towards seeking and using formal mental health and psychological services among Arab Muslim populations, *Journal of Muslim Mental Health*, 4, 79–103. http://dx.doi.org/10.1080/15564900802487675.

Amri, S., and Bemak, F. (2012) Mental health help-seeking behaviors of Muslim immigrants in the United States: Overcoming social stigma and cultural mistrust, *Journal of Muslim Mental Health*, 7, 1, 43–63. Doi: http://dx.doi.org/10.3998/jmmh.10381607.0007.104.

Association of American Medical Colleges (1999) Report III: *Contemporary Issues in Medicine: Communication in Medicine, Medical School Objectives Project*. Washington, DC: Association of American Medical Colleges, p. 25–26. www.gwumc.edu/gwish/pdf/1999_MSOP_III_TF_Only.pdf (accessed 24 March 2018).

Awad, N. (2017) *Clinicians, Imams, and the Whisperings of Satan*, Irving. Texas: Yaqeen Institute for Islamic Research.

Bhugra, D. (1997) *Psychiatry and Religion: Context, Consensus and Controversies*. London: Routledge.

Bhui, K., Warfa, N., Edonya, P., McKenzie, K., and Bhugra, D. (2007) Cultural competence in mental health care: A review of model evaluations, *BMC Health Services Research*, 7, 15. http://doi.org/10.1186/1472-6963-7-15.

Change Institute (2009) *Summary Report. Understanding Muslim Ethnic Communities*. London: Communities and Local Government. http://webarchive.nationalarchives.gov.uk/201209 20001411/www.communities.gov.uk/documents/communities/pdf/1203896.pdf (accessed 24 March 2018).

Ciftci, A., Jones, N., Corrigan, P. W. (2012) Mental health stigma in the Muslim community, *Journal of Muslim Mental Health*, 2, 1, Stigma, 2012, http://hdl.handle.net/2027/spo.10381607.0007.102

Conrad, P. (2007) *The Medicalization of Society. On the Transformation of Human Conditions into Treatable Disorders*. Baltimore, Maryland: The Johns Hopkins University Press.

Cook, C. C. H. (2010) The faith of the psychiatrist, *Mental Health, Religion & Culture*, 14, 1, 9–17. Doi: 10.1080/13674671003622673.

Cook, C. C. H., Powell, A., Sims, A., and Eagger, S. (2011) Spirituality and secularity: Professional boundaries in psychiatry, *Mental Health, Religion & Culture*, 14, 1, 35–42. Doi: 10.1080/13674676.2010.484935.

Cook, C. C. H. (2013) *Recommendations for Psychiatrists on Spirituality and Religion*. Position Statement PS03/2013. London: The Spirituality and Psychiatry Special Interest Group, the Royal College of Psychiatrists.

Communities and Local Government (2010) *The Training and Development of Muslim Faith Leaders. Current Practice and Future Possibilities*. London: Communities and Local Government. www.communities.gov.uk

Corrigan, P. W. (2011) Best practices: Strategic stigma change (SSC): Five principles for social marketing campaigns to reduce stigma, *Psychiatric Services*, 62, 824–826. http://dx.doi.org/10.1176/appi.ps.62.8.824.

Curlin, F. A., Odell, S. V., Lawrence, R. E., Chin, M. H., Lantos, J. D., Meador, K. G., and Koenig, H. G. (2007) The relationship between psychiatry and religion among U.S. physicians, *Psychiatric Services (Washington, DC.)*, 58, 9, 1193–1198. http://doi.org/10.1176/appi.ps.58.9.1193.

De Almeida Vieira Monteiro, A. P., and Serra, A. V. (2011) Vulnerability to stress in migratory contexts: A study with eastern European immigrants residing in Portugal, *Journal of Immigrant and Minority Health*, 13, 4, 690–696. Doi: 10.1007/s10903–011–9451–z.

Dein, S., and Illaiee, A. S. (2013) Jinn and mental health: Looking at jinn possession in modern psychiatric practice, *The Psychiatrist*, 37, 290–293. Doi: 10.1192/pb.bp.113.042721.

Durà-Vilà, G., Hagger, M., Dein, S., and Leavey, G. (2011) Ethnicity, religion and clinical practice: A qualitative study of beliefs and attitudes of psychiatrists in the UK, *Mental Health, Religion and Culture*, 14, 1, 53–64.

Durà-Vilà, G. (2015) *Medicalisation of Sadness, Depression and Spiritual Distress*. PhD Thesis, Department of Mental Health Sciences, University College London (UCL). http://discovery.ucl.ac.uk/1461034/1/Gloria%20Dura-Vila%20Medicalisation%20of%20Sadness.%20pdf%5B1%5D.pdf (accessed 24 March 2018).

El Azayem, G. A., and Hedayat-Diba, Z. (1994) The psychological aspects of Islam: Basic principles of Islam and their psychological corollary, *International Journal for the Psychology of Religion*, 4, 41–50.

El-Islam, M. F. (2004) Culture in the clinical practice of psychiatry, *Arab Journal of Psychiatry*, 15, 8–16.

Farrell, J. L., and Goebert, D. A. (2008) Collaboration between psychiatrists and clergy in recognizing and treating serious mental illness, *Psychiatric Services*, 59, 4, 437–440.

Friedli, L. (2000) A matter of faith: religion and mental health, *International Journal of Health Promotion*, 2, 2, 7–13.

General Medical Council (2009) *Tomorrow's Doctors: Outcomes and Standards for Undergraduate Medical Education*. London: GMC.

Gulnar, A. (2017) *Multiple Case Studies Exploring Integration of Spirituality in Undergraduate Nursing Education in England*. Doctoral thesis, University of Huddersfield. http://eprints. hud.ac.uk/id/eprint/34129/ (accessed 24 March 2018).

Home Office Faith Communities Unit (2004) *Working Together: Co-operation Between Government and Faith Communities – Recommendations of the Steering Group Reviewing Patterns of Engagement Between Government and Faith Communities in England*. London: Home Office.

James, B. O., Igbinomwanhia, N. G., and Omoaregba, J. O. (2014) Clergy as collaborators in the delivery of mental health care: An exploratory survey from Benin City, Nigeria, *Transcultural Psychiatry*, 51, 4, 569–580. https://doi.org/10.1177/1363461514525219.

John, D. A., and Williams, D. R. (2013) Mental health service use from a religious or spiritual advisor among Asian Americans, *Asian Journal of Psychiatry*, 6, 599–605.

Herrman, H., Saxena, S., and Moodie, R. (2004) *Promoting Mental Health: Concepts, Emerging Evidence, Practice: Summary Report. A report from the World Health Organization, Department of Mental Health and Substance Abuse in collaboration with the Victorian Health Promotion Foundation (VicHealth) and the University of Melbourne*. Geneva: WHO.

International Council for Nurses (ICN) (2000) *Code of Ethics for Nurses*. Geneva: ICN.

Islamqa (2008) 9691: The Qur'aan and medicine. https://islamqa.info/en/9691 (accessed 24 March 2018).

Kvarfordt, C. L., Sheridan, M. J., and Taylor, O. (2017) Religion and spirituality in social work curriculum: A survey of Canadian educators, *The British Journal of Social Work*, bcx069, https://doi.org/10.1093/bjsw/bcx069.

Knezevic, M., and Jovancevic, M. (2001) Model of providing psycho-social aid to refugees and displaced persons: Records of the Croatian Psychiatric Association. *European Journal of Psychiatry*, 15, 1, 33–47.

Koenig, H. G., Hooten, E. G., Lindsay-Calkins, E., and Meador, K.G. (2010) Spirituality in medical school curricula: findings from a national survey, *The International Journal of Psychiatry in Medicine*, 40, 4, 391–398.

Laban, C. J., Gernaat, H. B., Komproe, I. H., Schreuders, B. A., and De Jong, J. T. (2004) Impact of a long asylum procedure on the prevalence of psychiatric disorders in Iraqi asylum seekers in The Netherlands, *Journal of Nervous Disease*, 192, 843–851.

Leavey, G. (2010) The appreciation of the spiritual in mental illness: A qualitative study of beliefs among clergy in the UK, *Transcultural Psychiatry*, 47, 4, 571–590.

Lemmer, C. (2002) Teaching the spiritual dimension of nursing care: A survey of U.S. baccalaureate nursing programs, *Journal of Nurse Education*, 41, 482–490.

Lewinson, L.P., McSherry, W. and Kevern, P. (2015) Spirituality in pre-registration nurse education and practice: a Review of the literature. *Semantic Scholar*, 1–20. https://pdfs. semanticscholar.org/4995/386714adfee2d21d599f4a397877a0f0d7e3.pdf (accessed 24 March 2018).

Lopes, A.S. (2001) *Student National Medical Association, Cultural competency position statement*. Prepared for: SNMA 36th House of Delegates April 12–15, 2001, Annual Medical Education Conference, Atlanta GA. www.snma.org/downloads/snma_cultural_competency.pdf (accessed 24 March 2018).

Lucchetti, G., Lucchetti, A. L. G., Espinha, D. C. M., de Oliveira, L. R., Leite, J. R. and Koenig, H. G. (2012). Spirituality and health in the curricula of medical schools in Brazil, *BMC Medical Education*, 12, 78. http://doi.org/10.1186/1472-6920-12-78.

Min, J.A., Lee, C.U. and Lee, C. (2013). Mental Health Promotion and Illness Prevention: A Challenge for Psychiatrists, *Psychiatry Investigation*, 10, 4: 307–316. http://doi.org/10.4306/pi.2013.10.4.307.

Morgan, J. (2010) *Muslim Clergy in America: Ministry as Profession in the Islamic Community.* Lima, Ohio: Wyndham Hall Press. Second edition.

Mujahid, A.M. (2012) *State of Muslim mental health.* http://sumo.ly/wm8K www.soundvision.com/article/state-of-muslim-mental-health (accessed 24 March 2018).

Neely, D. and Minford, E.J. (2008) Current status of teaching on spirituality in UK medical school, *Medical Education*, 42: 176–182. doi:10.1111/j.1365–2923.2007.02980.x

Olson, J. K., Paul, P., Douglass, l., Clark, M. B., Simington, J. and Goddard, N. (2003). Addressing the spiritual dimension in Canadian undergraduate nursing education, *Canadian Journal of Nursing Research*, 35:95–107.

Padela, A., Gunter, K. and Killawi, A. (2011) *Meeting the Healthcare Needs of American Muslims: Challenges and Strategies for Healthcare Settings*, Washington, DC: Institute for Social Policy and Understanding.

Patel, V. (2011). Traditional healers for mental health care in Africa. Global Health Action, 4, 10.3402/gha.v4i0.7956, http://doi.org/10.3402/gha.v4i0.7956 (accessed 24 March 2018).

Poole, R. and Higgo, R. (2011) Spirituality and the threat to therapeutic boundaries in psychiatric practice, *Mental Health, Religion & Culture*, 14,1: 19–29, DOI: 10.1080/1367 4671003746845.

Pridmore, S. and Pasha, M.I. (2004) Religion and spirituality: Psychiatry and Islam, *Australasian Psychiatry*, 12, 4:380–385.

Pridmore S. (2013) Chapter 32. *Medicalization/Psychiatricization of distress.* Download of Psychiatry. In Pridmore, S (2006) Download of Psychiatry. Tasmania: University of Tasmania, https://eprints.utas.edu.au/287/ (accessed 24 March 2018).

Prusak J. (2016) Differential diagnosis of "Religious or Spiritual Problem" – possibilities and limitations implied by the V-code 62.89 in DSM-5, *Psychiatria Polska* (Polish Psychiatry) 50, 1:175–186. doi: 10.12740/PP/59115.

Pumariega, A.J., Rothe, E, and Pumariega, J.B. (2005) Mental health needs of immigrants and refugees, *Community Mental Health Journal*, 41,5:581–597. doi: 10.1007/s10597-005-6363-1.

Rahman, A.R. (2014) *Jinn Possession in Mental Health Disorder.* From Jinn and Sihr in Medicine: Regional Forum organised by Research Group LRGS/TD/2012/USM-UKM/KT/03 in collaboration with GAPPIMA and PISANG, UKM Malaysia, 29 30 Nov 2014, www.pisang.uk/images/files/jinn%20possession%20in%20mental%20health%20disorder.pdf (accessed 25 March 2018).

Rassool, G. H. (2014a) *Putting cultural competence all together: some considerations in caring for Muslim patients.* In: Rassool, G. Hussein (ed) Cultural Competence in Caring for Muslim Patients, Basingstoke: Palgrave Macmillan.

Rassool, G. H. (2014b) *Cultural Competence in Caring for Muslim Patients*, Basingstoke: Palgrave Macmillan.

Rassool, G. H. (2016) *Islamic Counselling: An Introduction to Theory and Practice.* Hove, East Sussex: Routledge.

Robertson, B. A. (2006). Does the evidence support collaboration between psychiatry and traditional healers? Findings from three South African studies, *South African Psychiatry Review*, 9, 87–90

Saged, A.A.G., Mohd Yusoff, M.Y.Z., Abdul Latif, F., Hilmi, S.M., Waleed Mugahed Al-Rahmi, W.M., Al-Samman, A., Alias, N. and Zeki, A.M. (2018) Impact of Quran in Treatment of the Psychological Disorder and Spiritual Illness, *Journal of Religion and Health*, https://doi.org/10.1007/s10943-018-0572-8 (accessed 25 March 2018).

Sayed, M.A. (2003). Psychotherapy of Arab patients in the West: Uniqueness, empathy and "otherness," *American Journal of Psychotherapy*, 57, 4: 445–459.

Silove, D., Ventevogel, P. and Rees, S. (2017). The contemporary refugee crisis: an overview of mental health challenges, World *Psychiatry*, 16, 2:130–139. http://doi.org/10.1002/wps.20438

Spirituality and Psychiatry Special Interest Group (2016) *Spirituality in Psychiatry for Today's World*. London: Royal College of Psychiatrists. www.rcpsych.ac.uk/workinpsychiatry/specialinterestgroups/spirituality.aspx (accessed 24 March 2018).

Watters, W. W. (1992). *Deadly Doctrine: Health, Illness, and Christian God Talk*, Buffalo, US: Prometheus Books.

World Health Organization (1985) *Handbook of Resolutions and Decisions*, Vol. II, p. 5–6, Geneva: WHO.

World Health Organization (2001). *Strengthening mental health promotion*. Geneva, World Health Organization. (Fact sheet, No. 220).

Youssef, J. and Deane, F. P. (2006). Factors influencing mental-health help-seeking in Arabic-speaking communities in Sydney, Australia, *Mental Health, Religion & Culture*, 9: 43–66. http://dx.doi.org/10.1080/13674670512331335686

Index